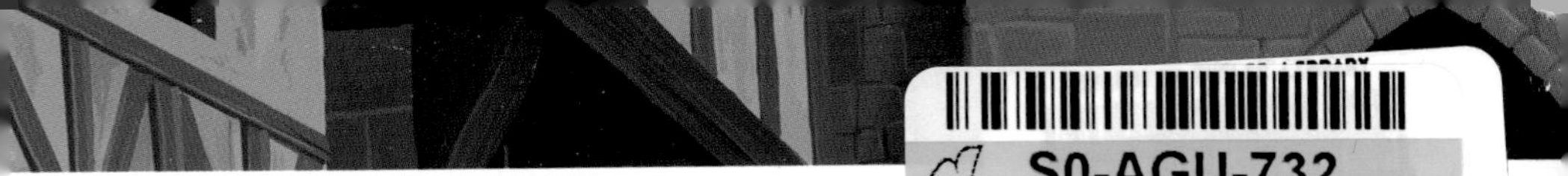

INVERLOCH

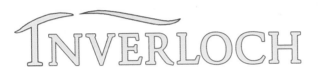

VOLUME 2

ART & STORY BY
SARAH ELLERTON

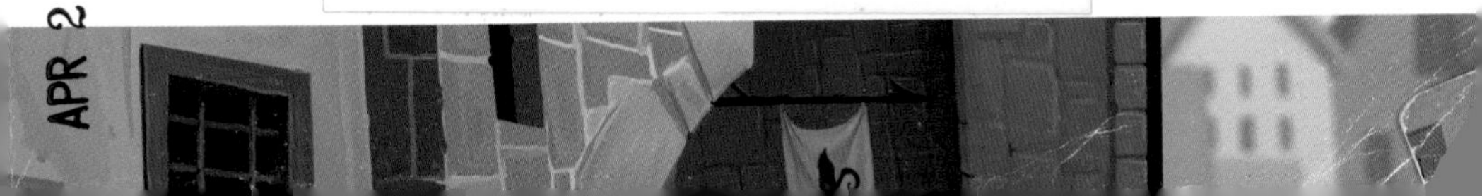

INVERLOCH
© SARAH ELLERTON 2003

First published online at www.seraph-inn.com

Publisher: Seven Seas Entertainment

Visit us online at www.gomanga.com

ISBN: 1-933164-27-1

Printed in Canada

First printing: October, 2006

10 9 8 7 6 5 4 3 2 1

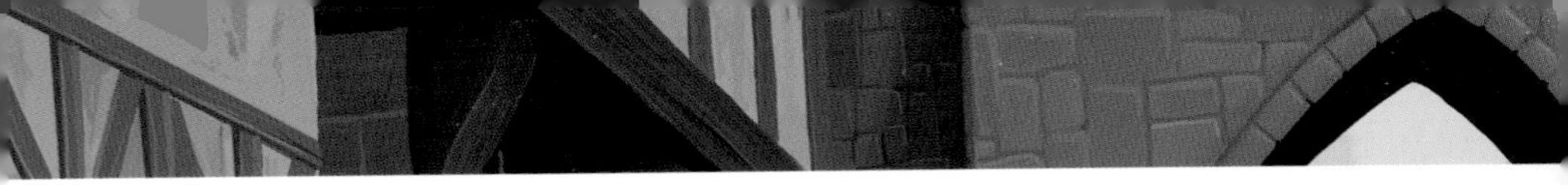

INVERLOCH
VOLUME 2

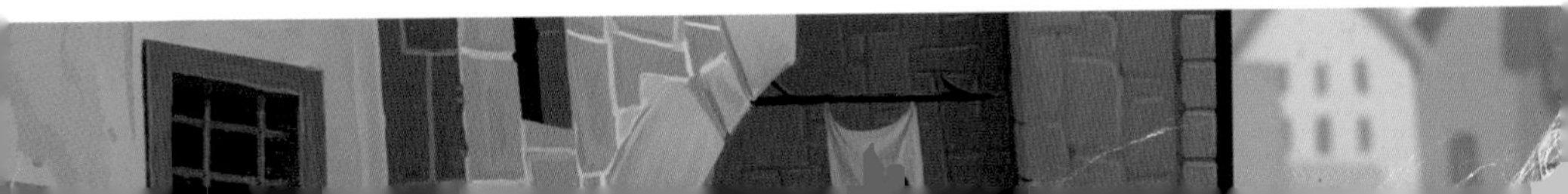

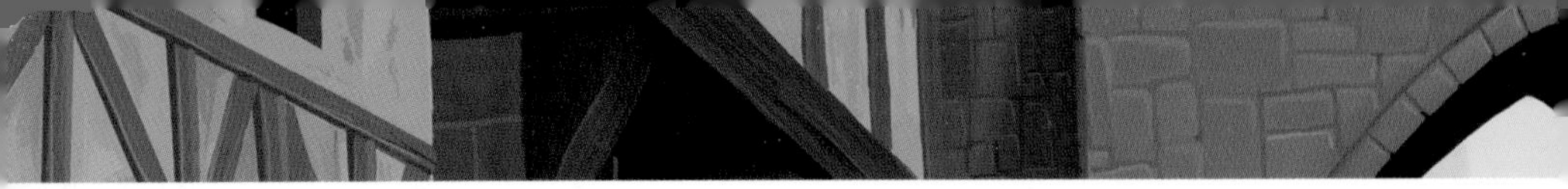

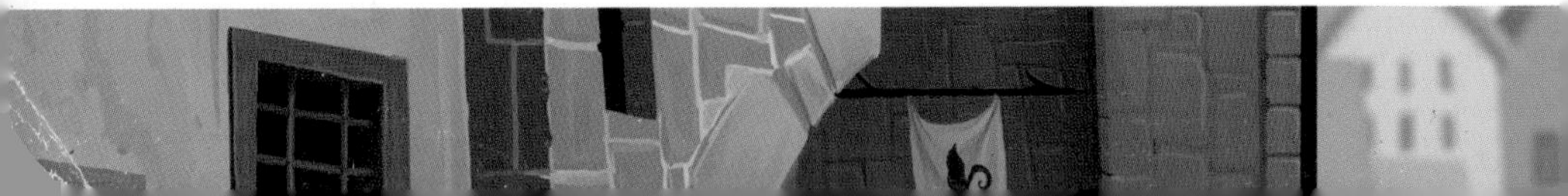

CHAPTER 6 :A TRAVELLING COMPANION

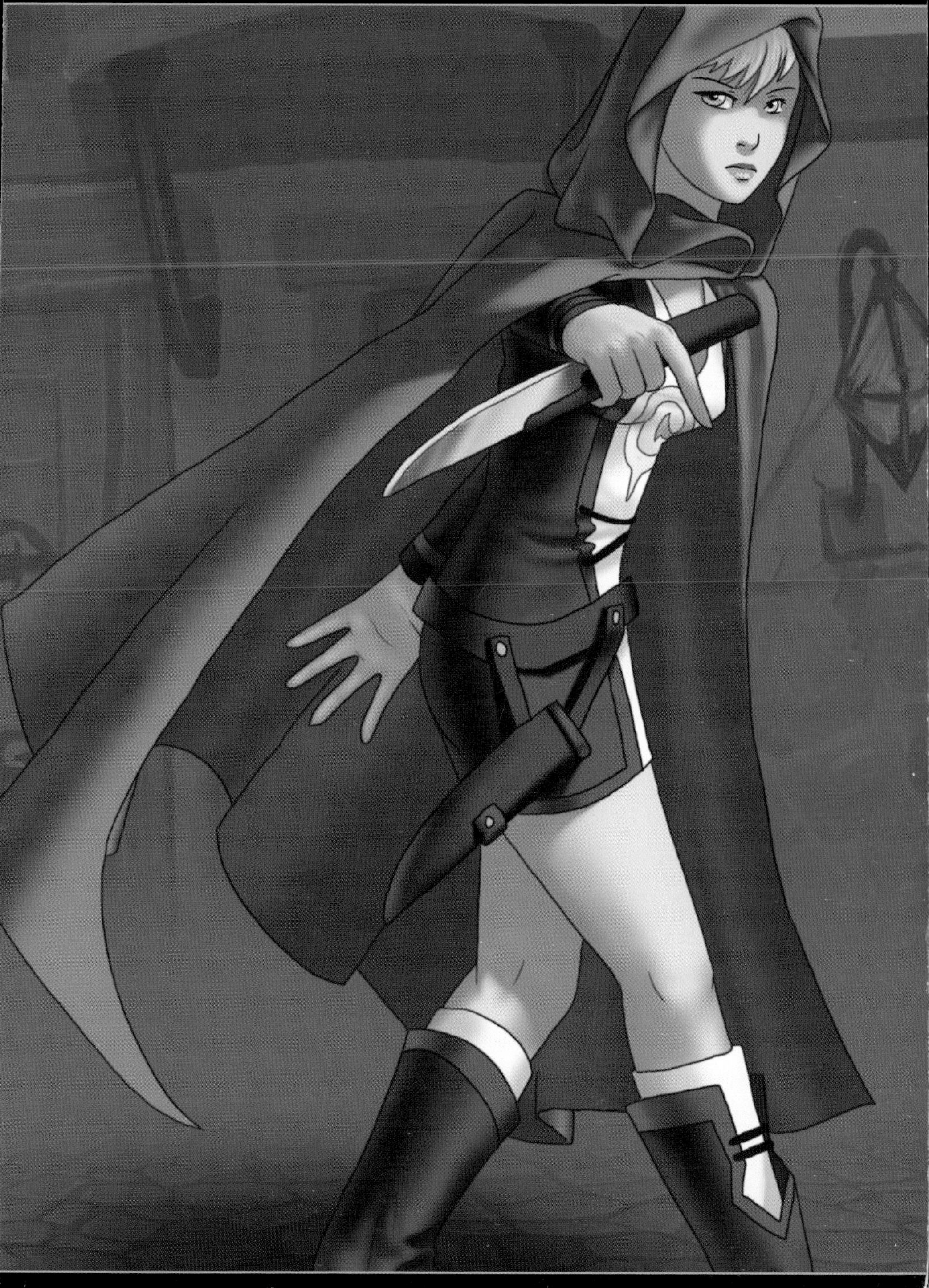

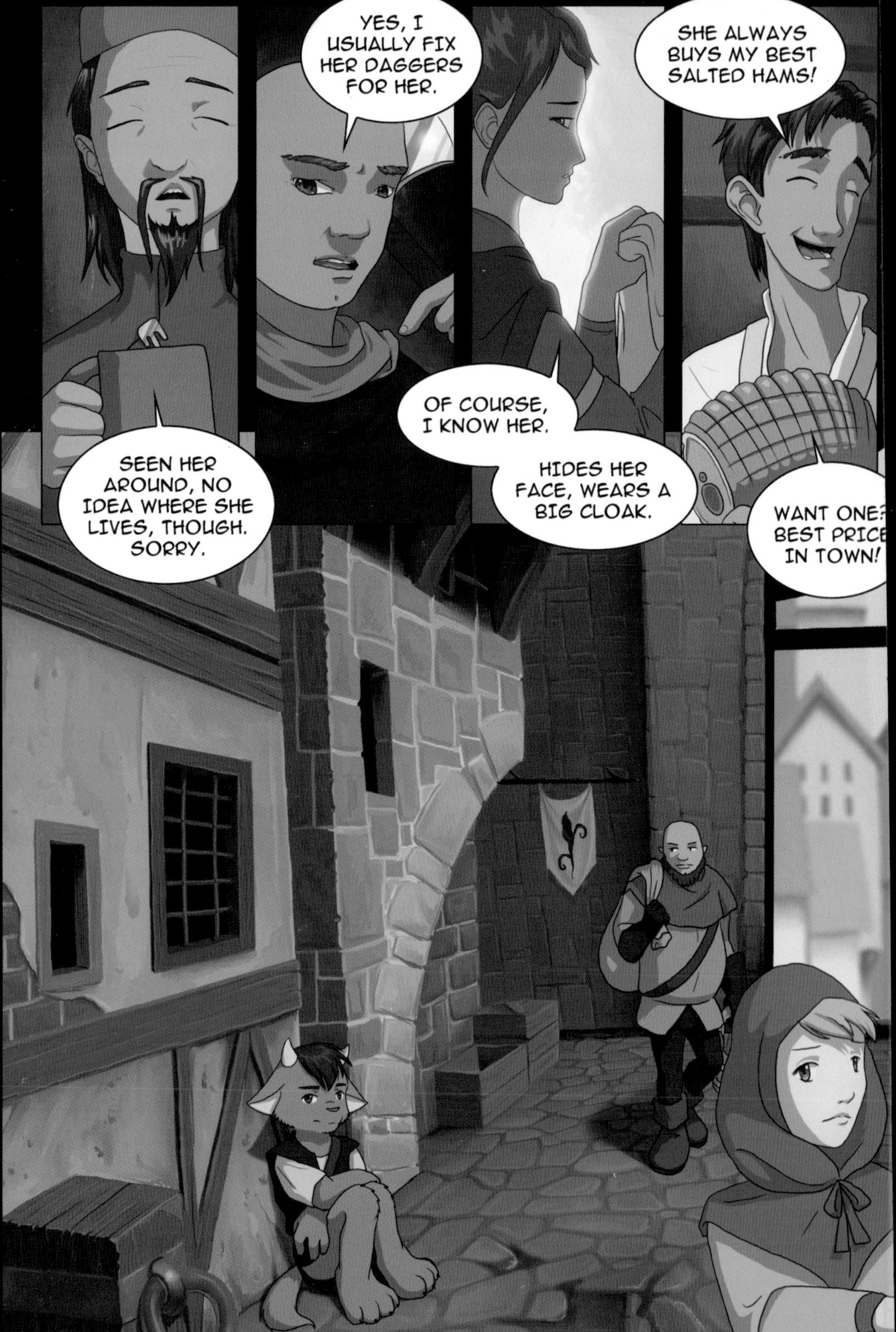
SEEN HER AROUND, NO IDEA WHERE SHE LIVES, THOUGH. SORRY.
YES, I USUALLY FIX HER DAGGERS FOR HER.
OF COURSE, I KNOW HER.
HIDES HER FACE, WEARS A BIG CLOAK.
SHE ALWAYS BUYS MY BEST SALTED HAMS!
WANT ONE? BEST PRICE IN TOWN!

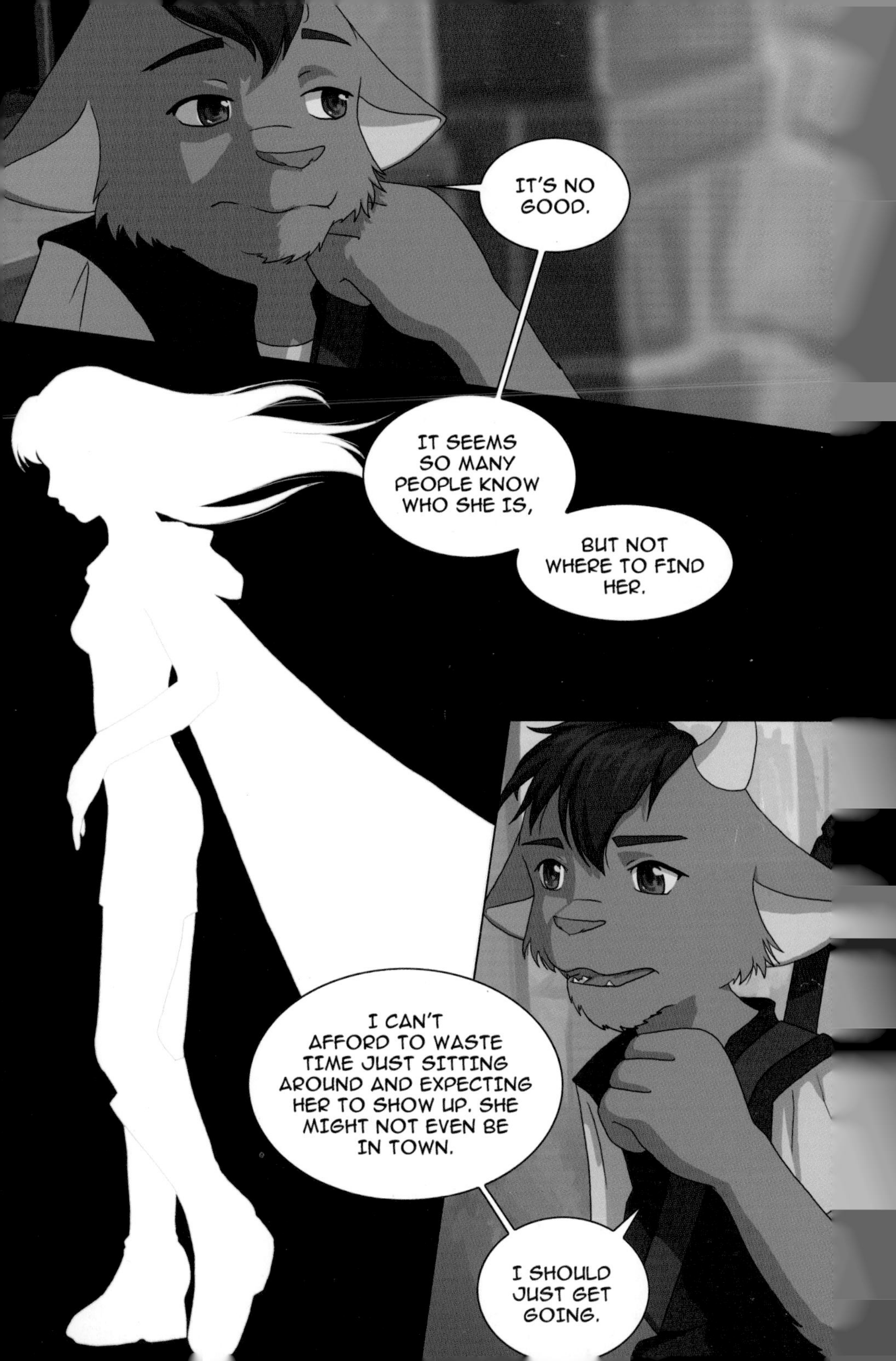
IT'S NO GOOD.
IT SEEMS SO MANY PEOPLE KNOW WHO SHE IS,
BUT NOT WHERE TO FIND HER.
I CAN'T AFFORD TO WASTE TIME JUST SITTING AROUND AND EXPECTING HER TO SHOW UP. SHE MIGHT NOT EVEN BE IN TOWN.
I SHOULD JUST GET GOING.

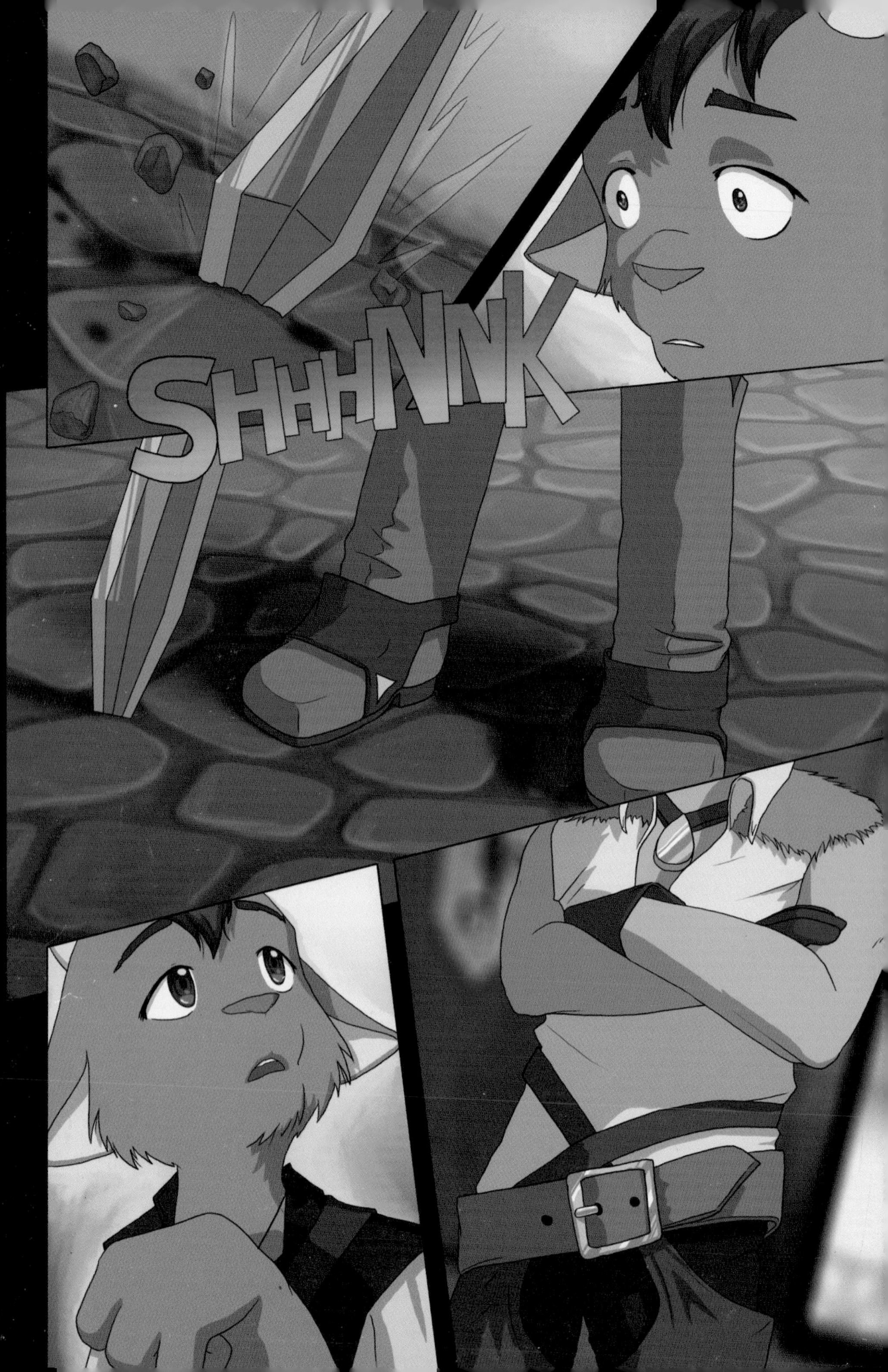
SHHHNNK

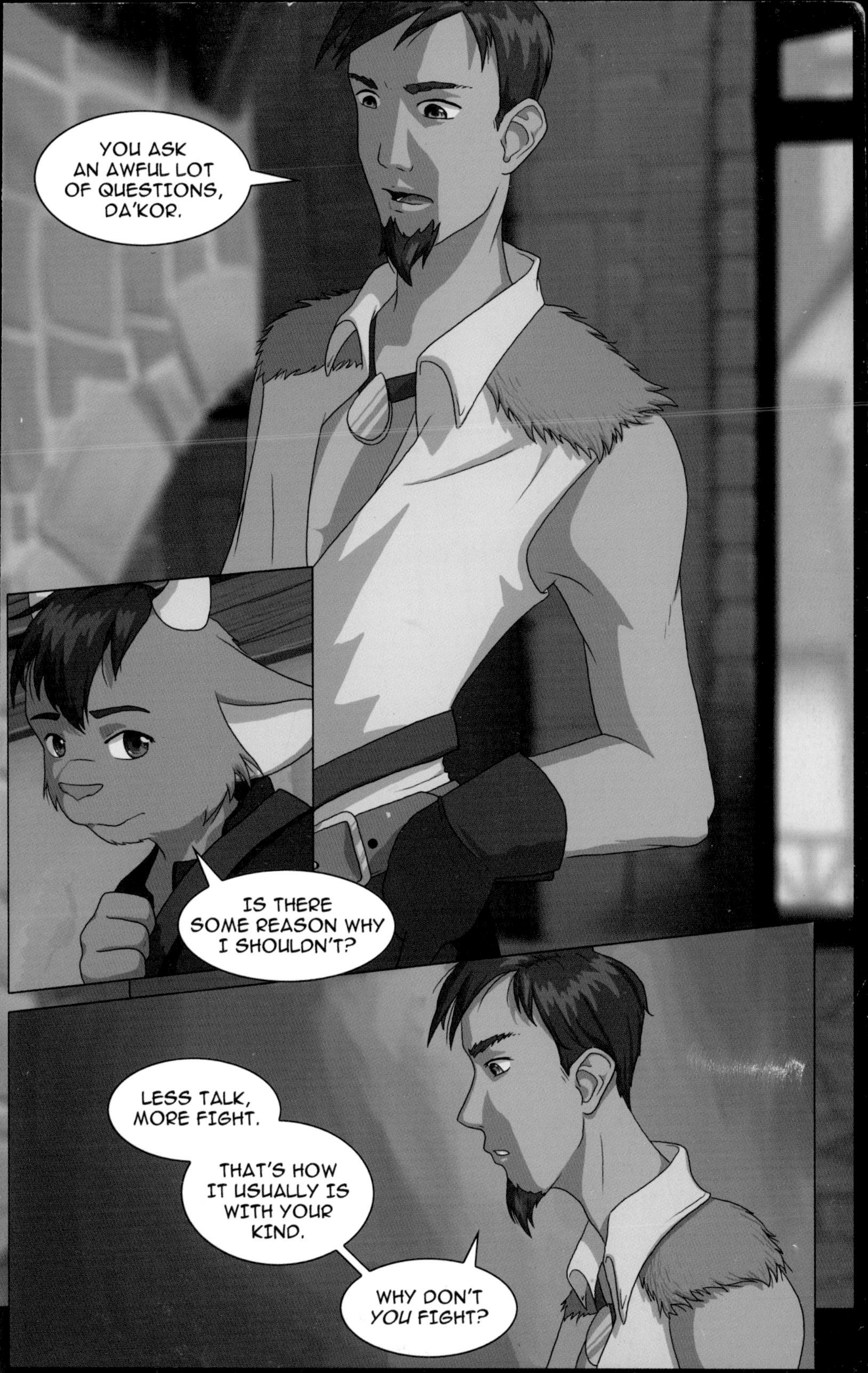
YOU ASK AN AWFUL LOT OF QUESTIONS, DA'KOR.
IS THERE SOME REASON WHY I SHOULDN'T?
LESS TALK, MORE FIGHT.
THAT'S HOW IT USUALLY IS WITH YOUR KIND.
WHY DON'T *YOU* FIGHT?

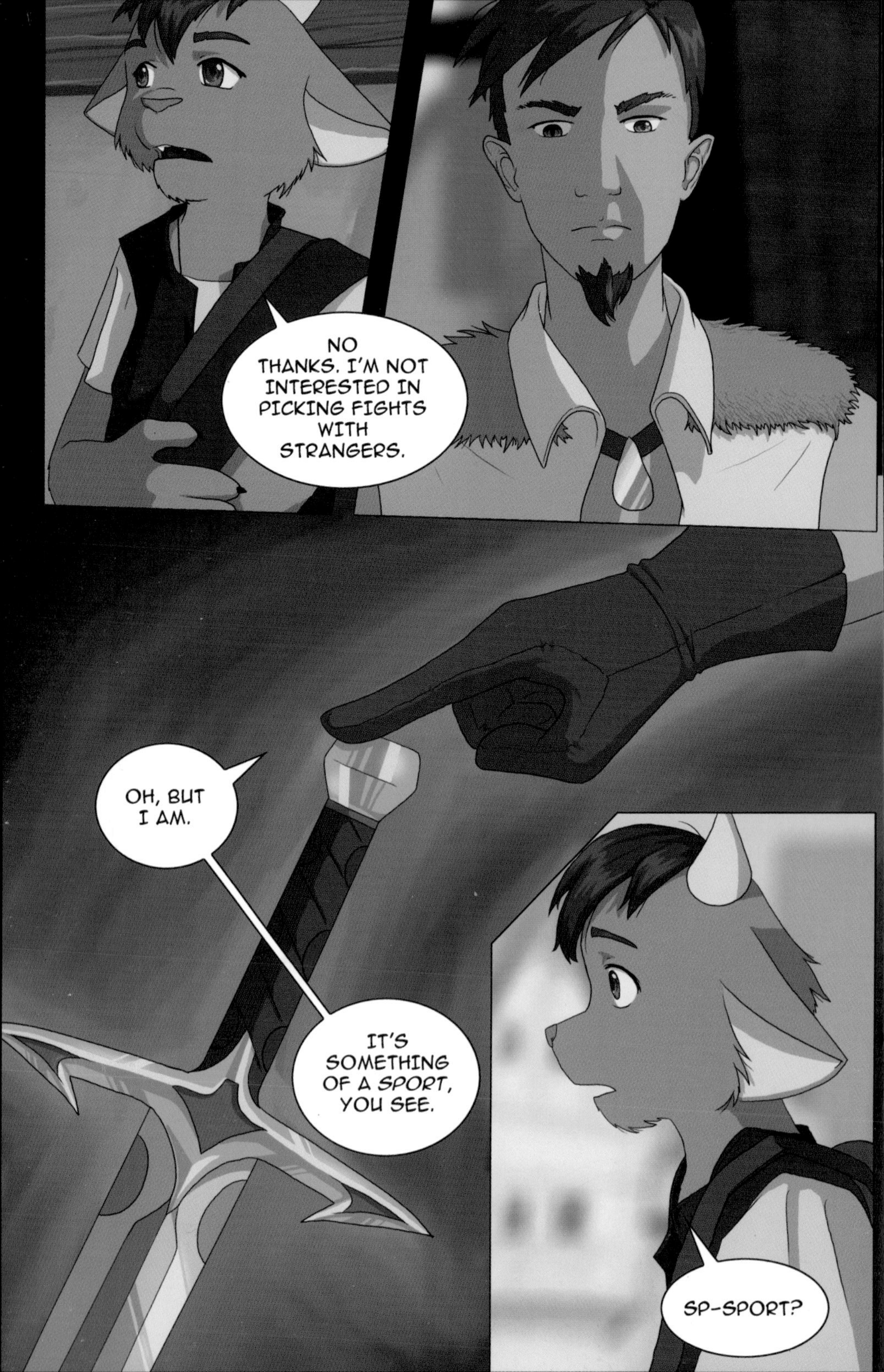
NO THANKS. I'M NOT INTERESTED IN PICKING FIGHTS WITH STRANGERS.
OH, BUT I AM.
IT'S SOMETHING OF A *SPORT*, YOU SEE.
SP-SPORT?

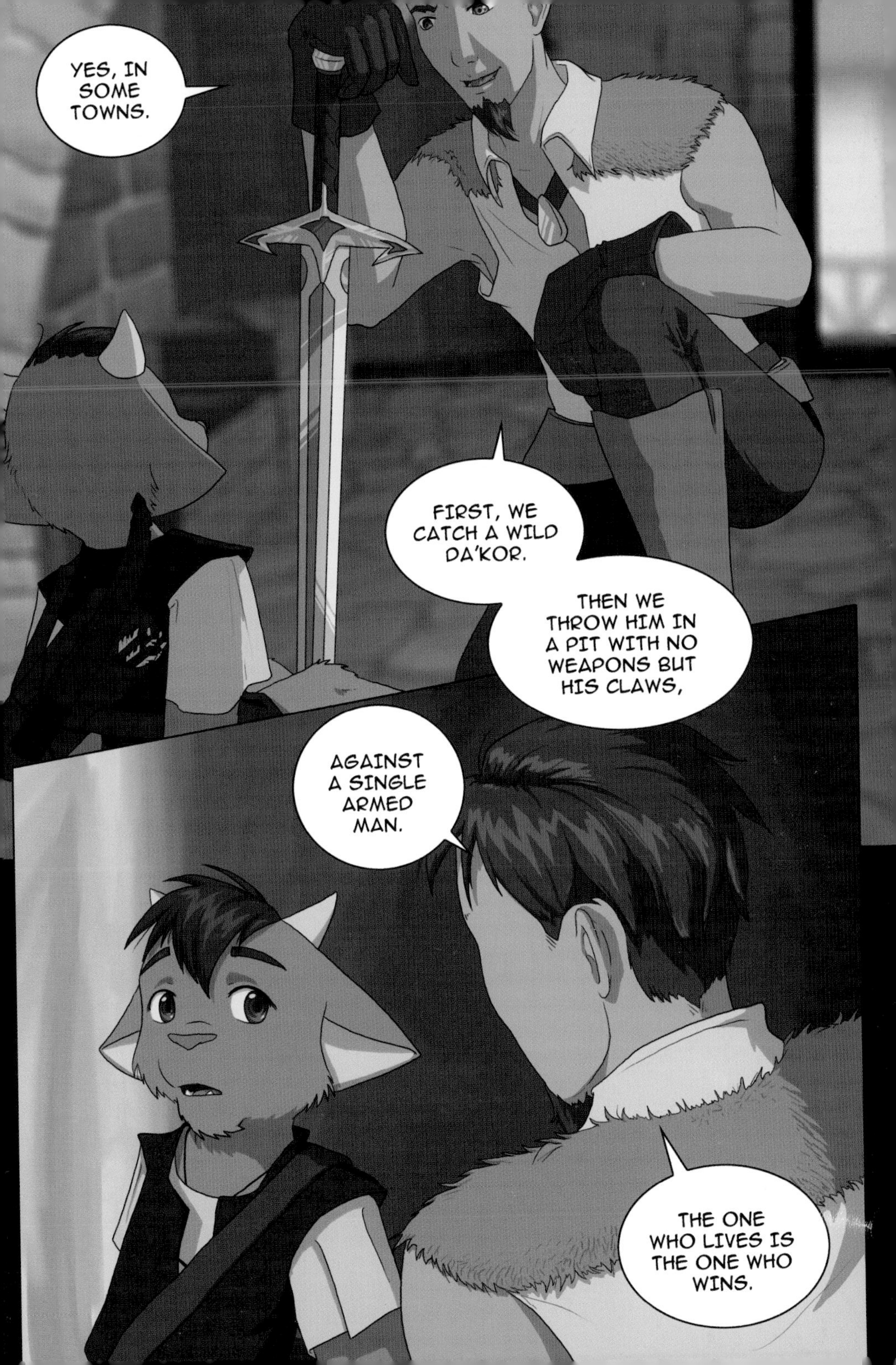
YES, IN SOME TOWNS.
FIRST, WE CATCH A WILD DA'KOR.
THEN WE THROW HIM IN A PIT WITH NO WEAPONS BUT HIS CLAWS,
AGAINST A SINGLE ARMED MAN.
THE ONE WHO LIVES IS THE ONE WHO WINS.

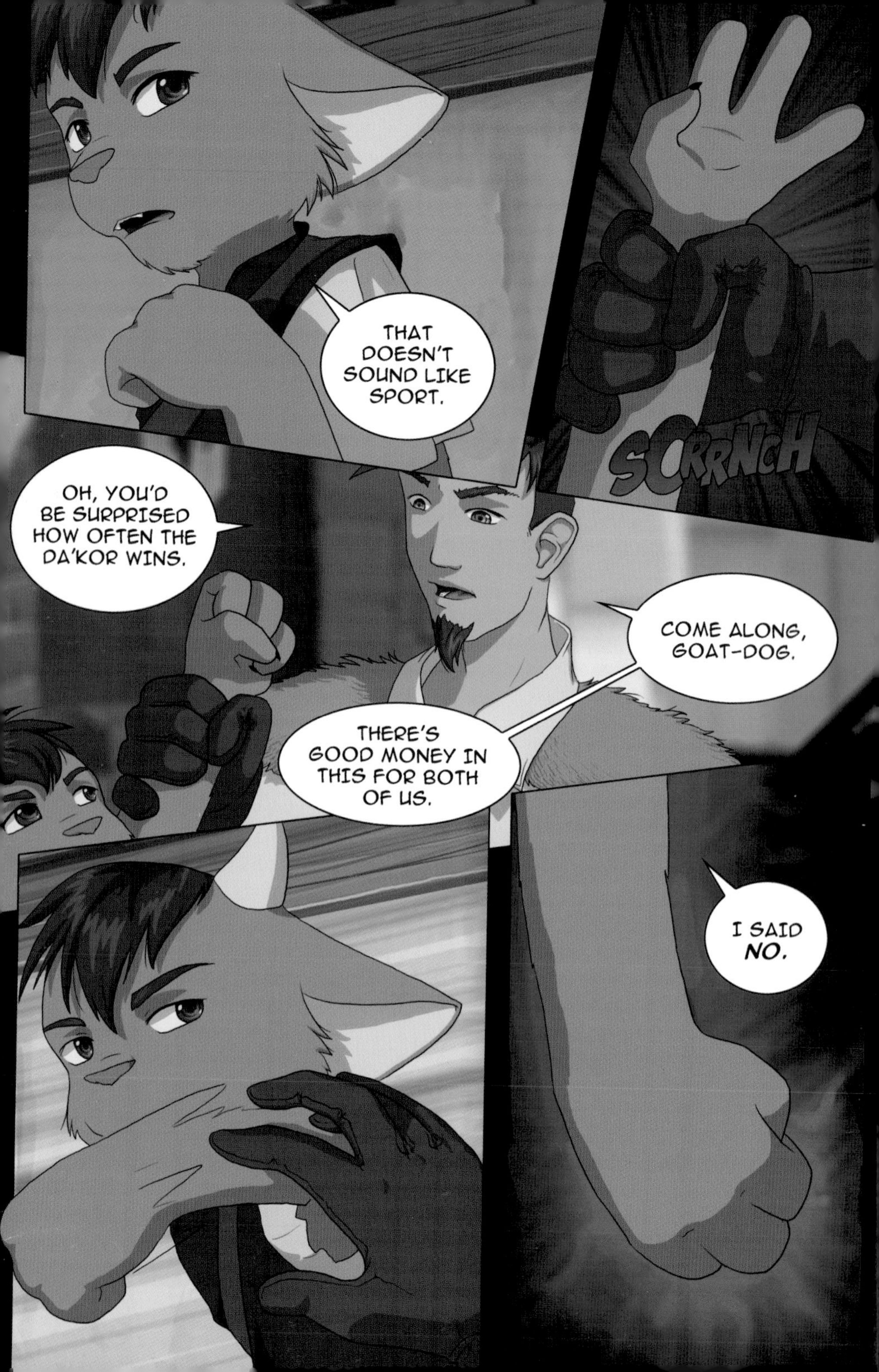
THAT DOESN'T SOUND LIKE SPORT.
SCRRNCH
OH, YOU'D BE SURPRISED HOW OFTEN THE DA'KOR WINS.
COME ALONG, GOAT-DOG.
THERE'S GOOD MONEY IN THIS FOR BOTH OF US.
I SAID NO.

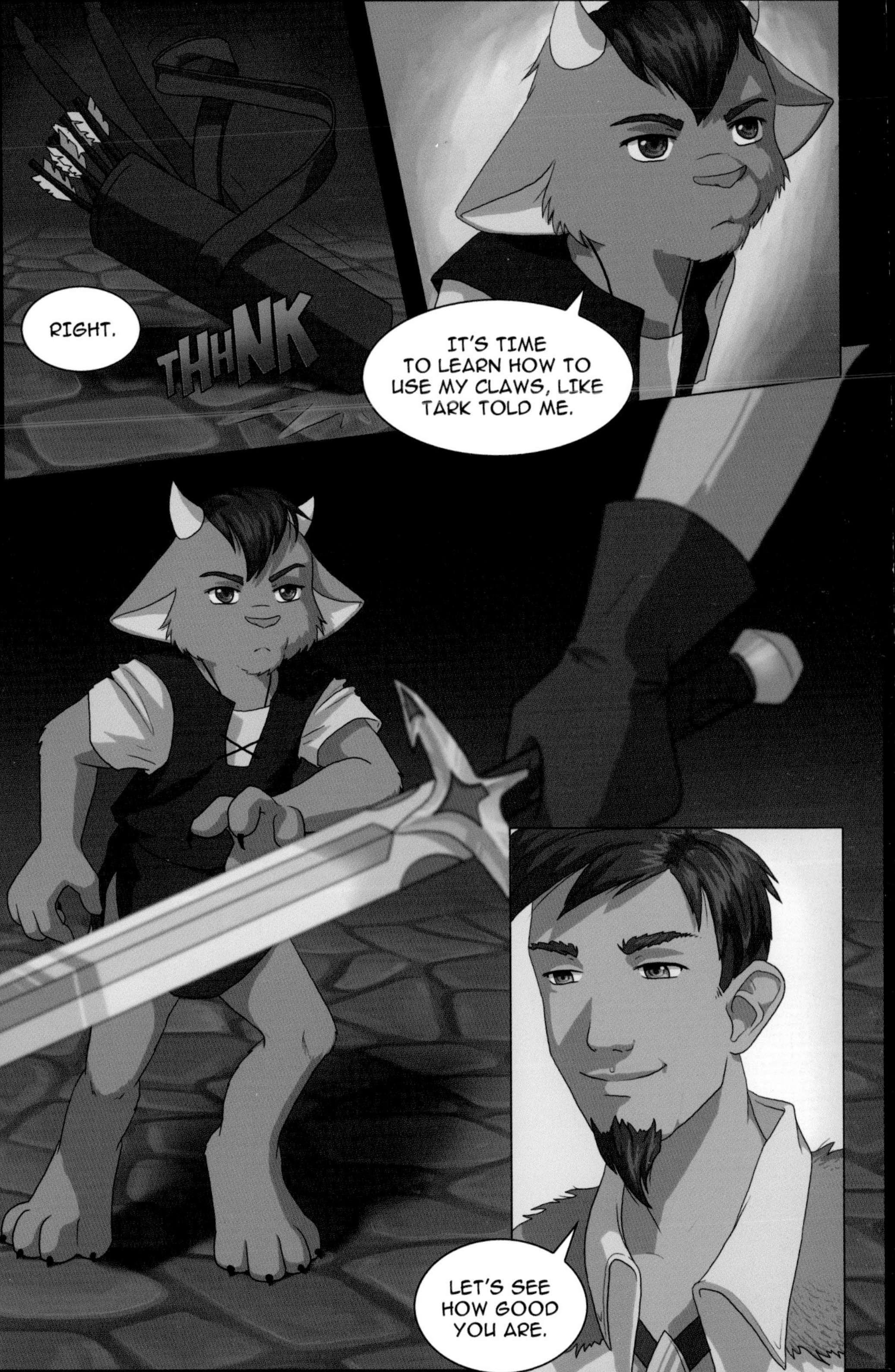
RIGHT.
THHNK
IT'S TIME TO LEARN HOW TO USE MY CLAWS, LIKE TARK TOLD ME.
LET'S SEE HOW GOOD YOU ARE.

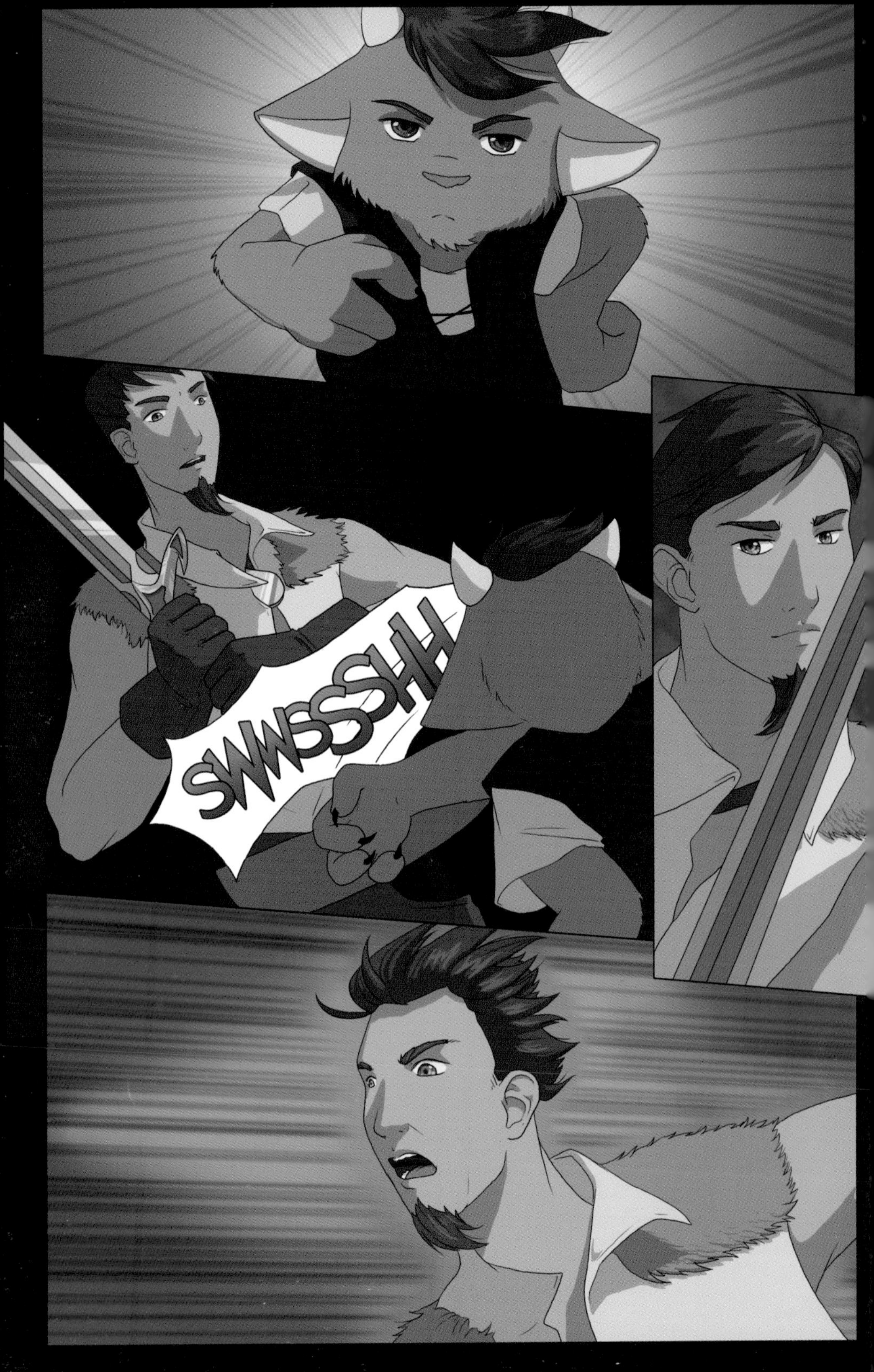
SWWSSHH

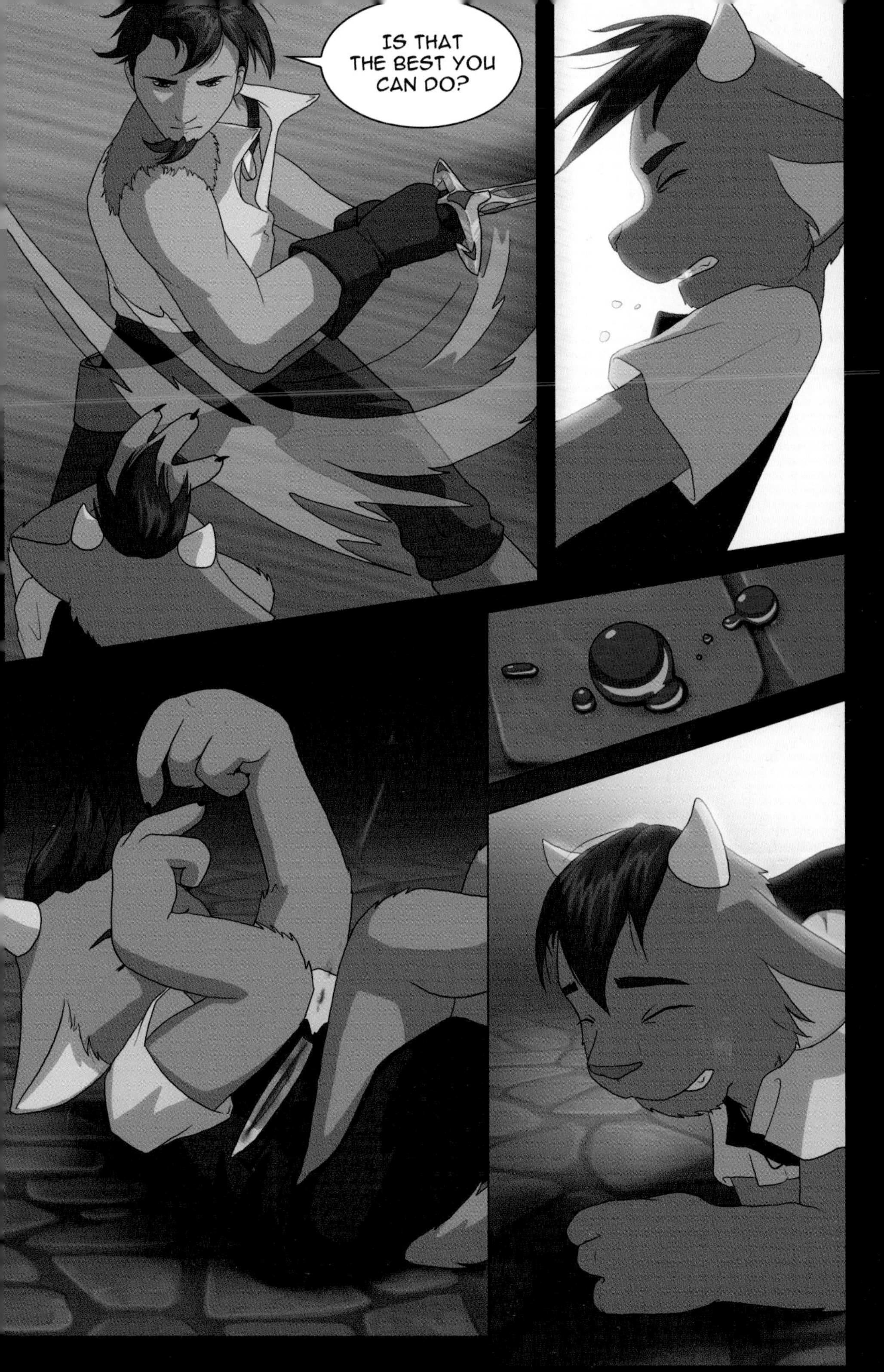
IS THAT THE BEST YOU CAN DO?

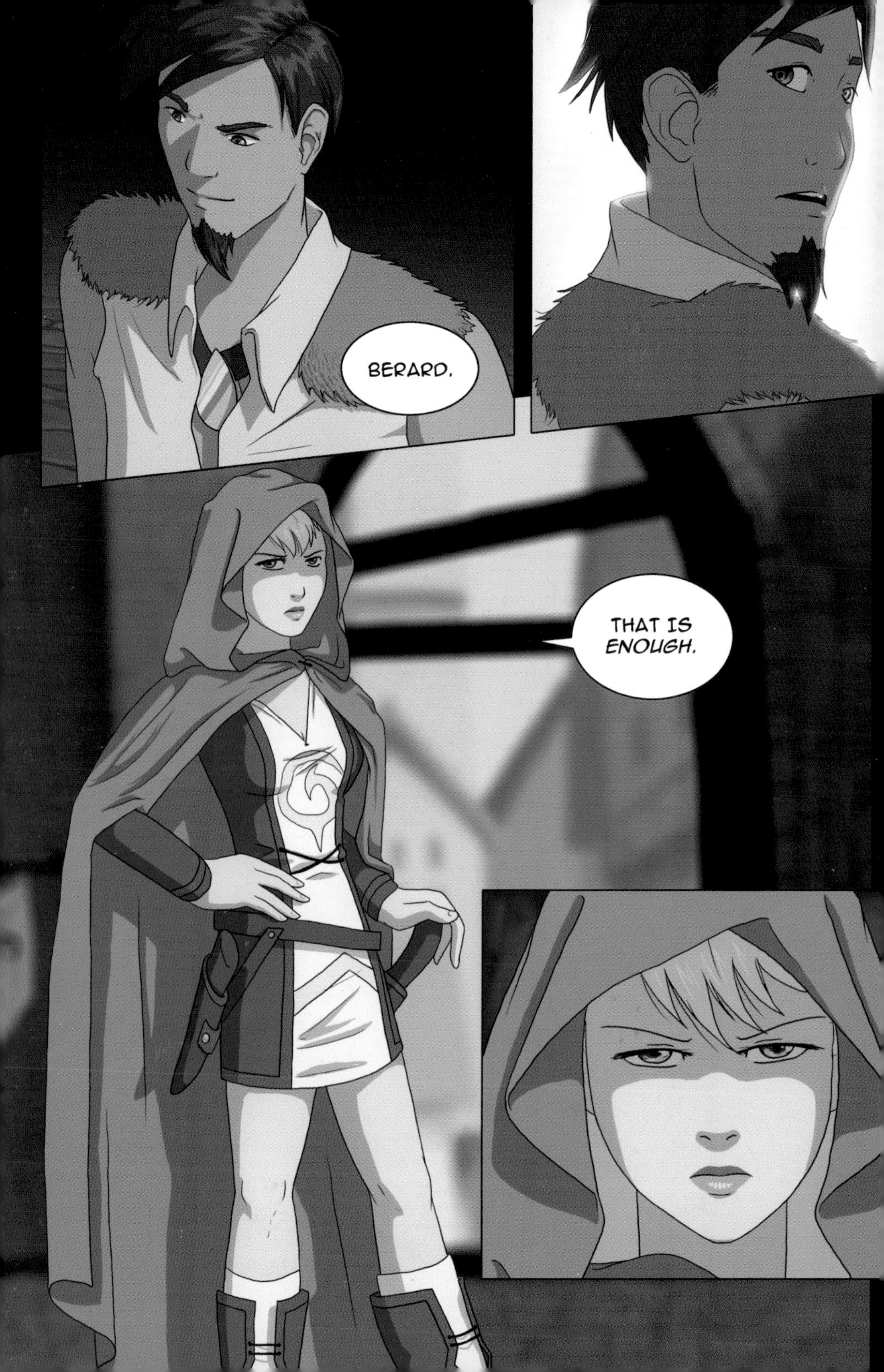
BERARD.
THAT IS ENOUGH.

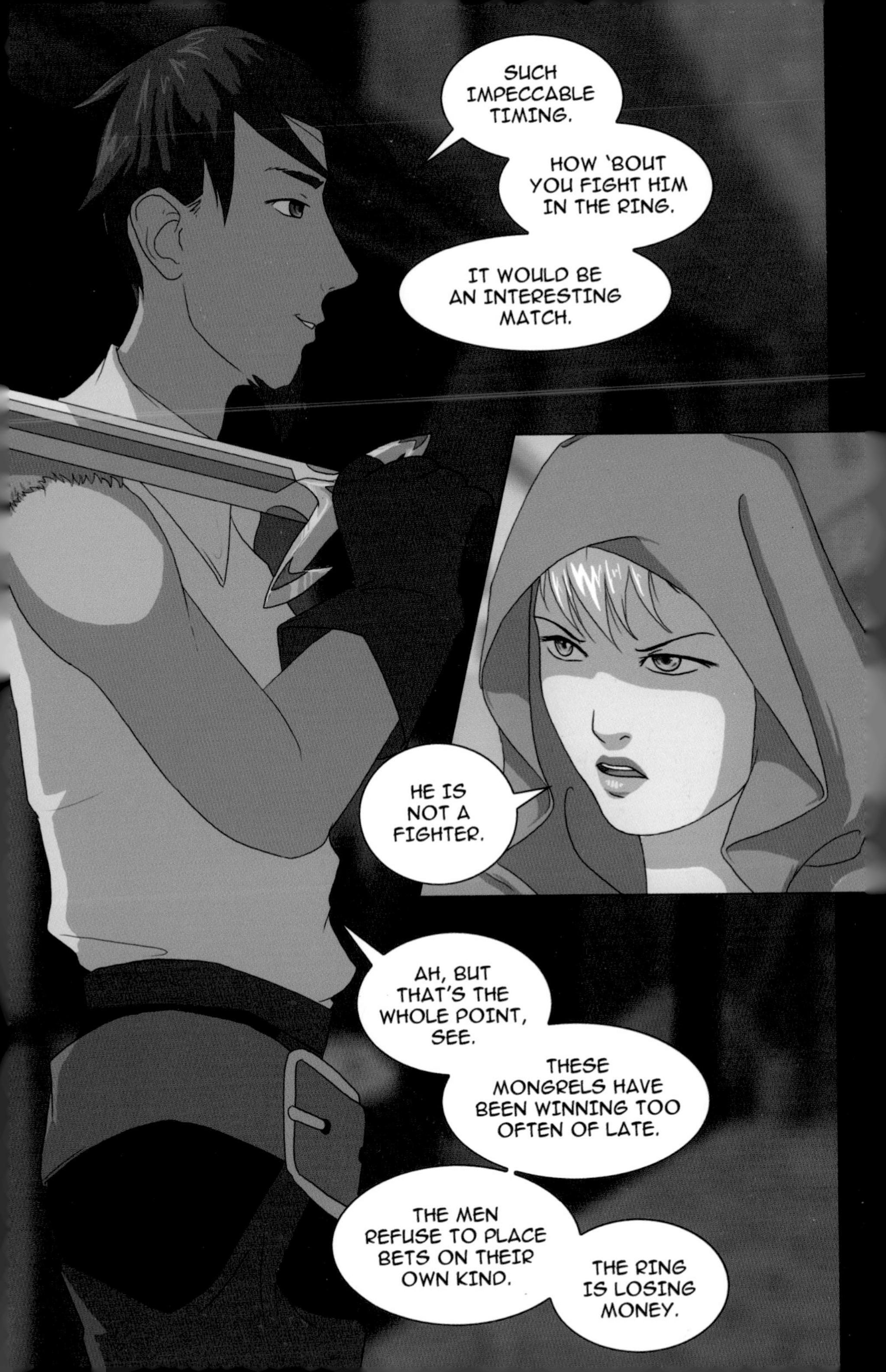
SUCH IMPECCABLE TIMING.
HOW 'BOUT YOU FIGHT HIM IN THE RING.
IT WOULD BE AN INTERESTING MATCH.
HE IS NOT A FIGHTER.
AH, BUT THAT'S THE WHOLE POINT, SEE.
THESE MONGRELS HAVE BEEN WINNING TOO OFTEN OF LATE.
THE MEN REFUSE TO PLACE BETS ON THEIR OWN KIND.
THE RING IS LOSING MONEY.

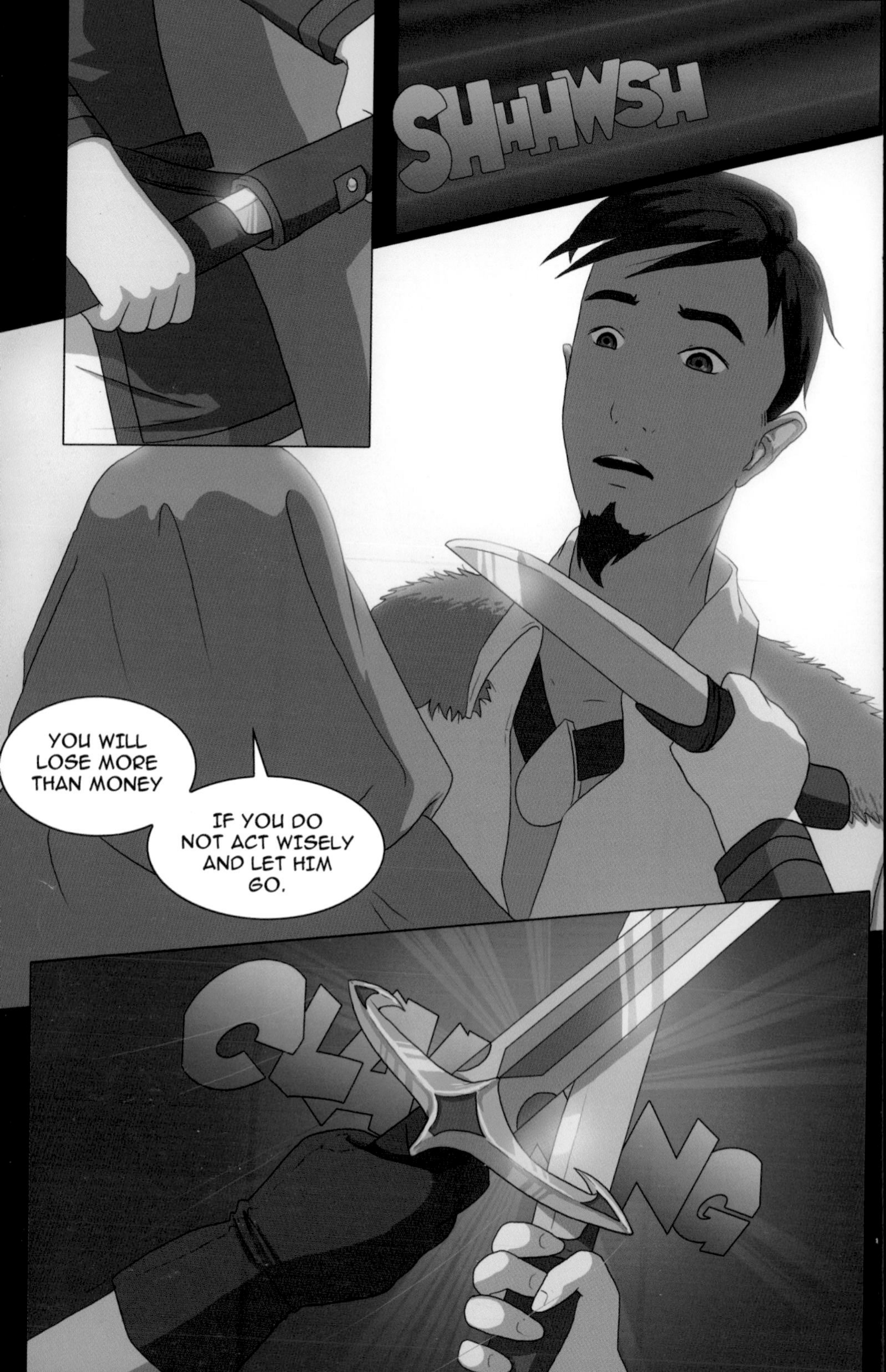
SHHHWSH
YOU WILL LOSE MORE THAN MONEY
IF YOU DO NOT ACT WISELY AND LET HIM GO.
CLANG

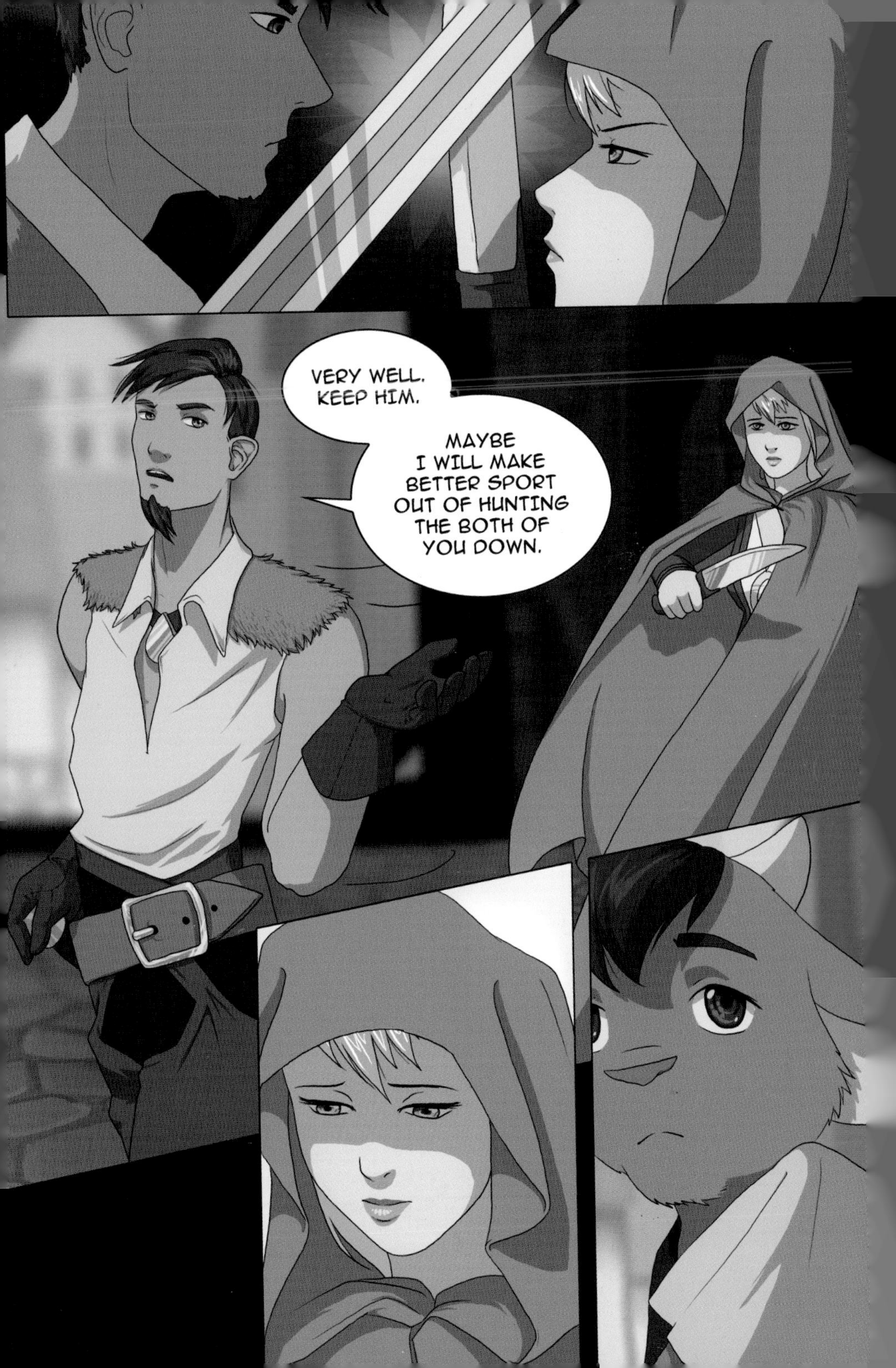
VERY WELL. KEEP HIM.
MAYBE I WILL MAKE BETTER SPORT OUT OF HUNTING THE BOTH OF YOU DOWN.

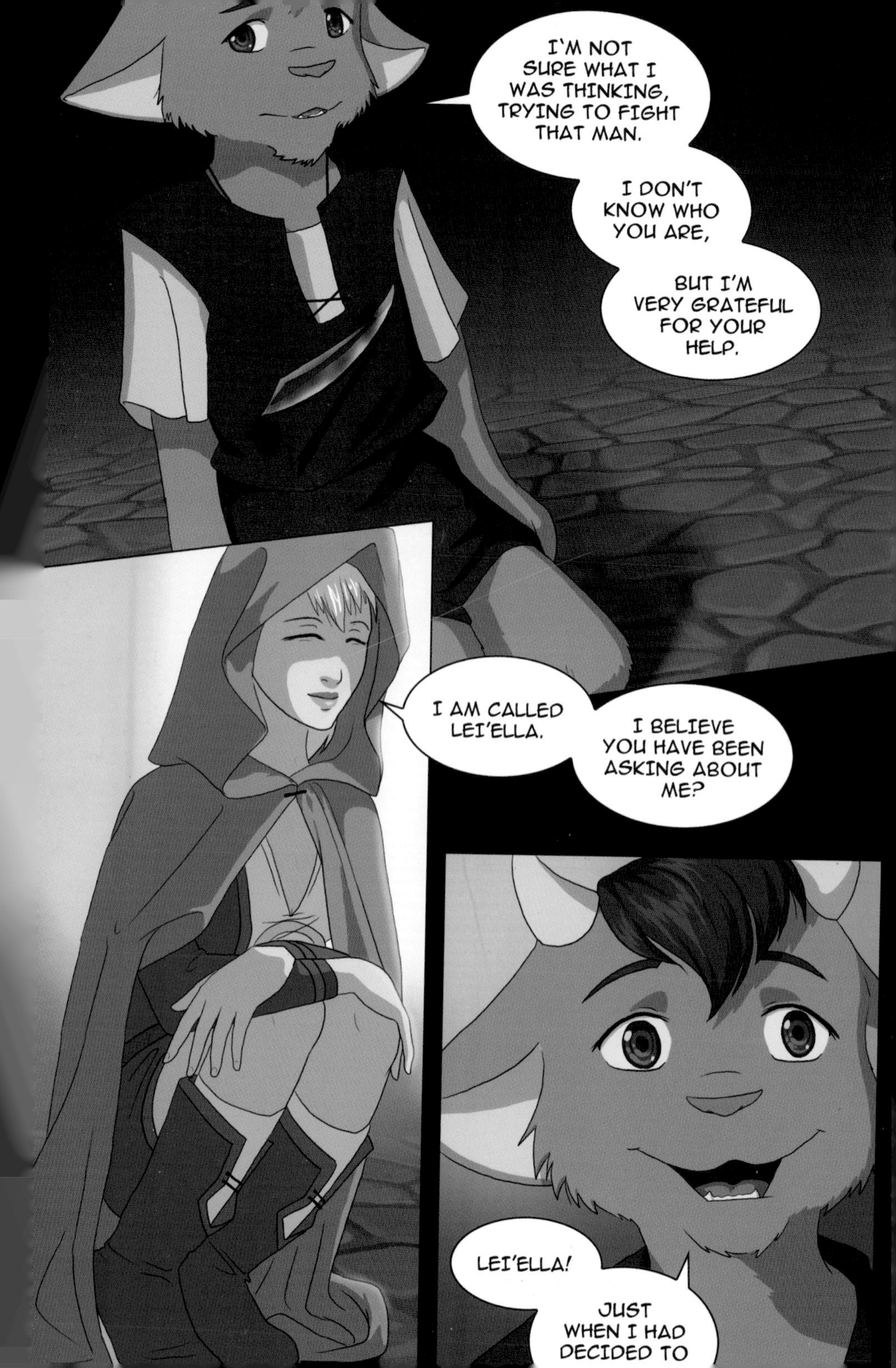
I'M NOT SURE WHAT I WAS THINKING, TRYING TO FIGHT THAT MAN.
I DON'T KNOW WHO YOU ARE,
BUT I'M VERY GRATEFUL FOR YOUR HELP.
I AM CALLED LEI'ELLA.
I BELIEVE YOU HAVE BEEN ASKING ABOUT ME?
LEI'ELLA!
JUST WHEN I HAD DECIDED TO

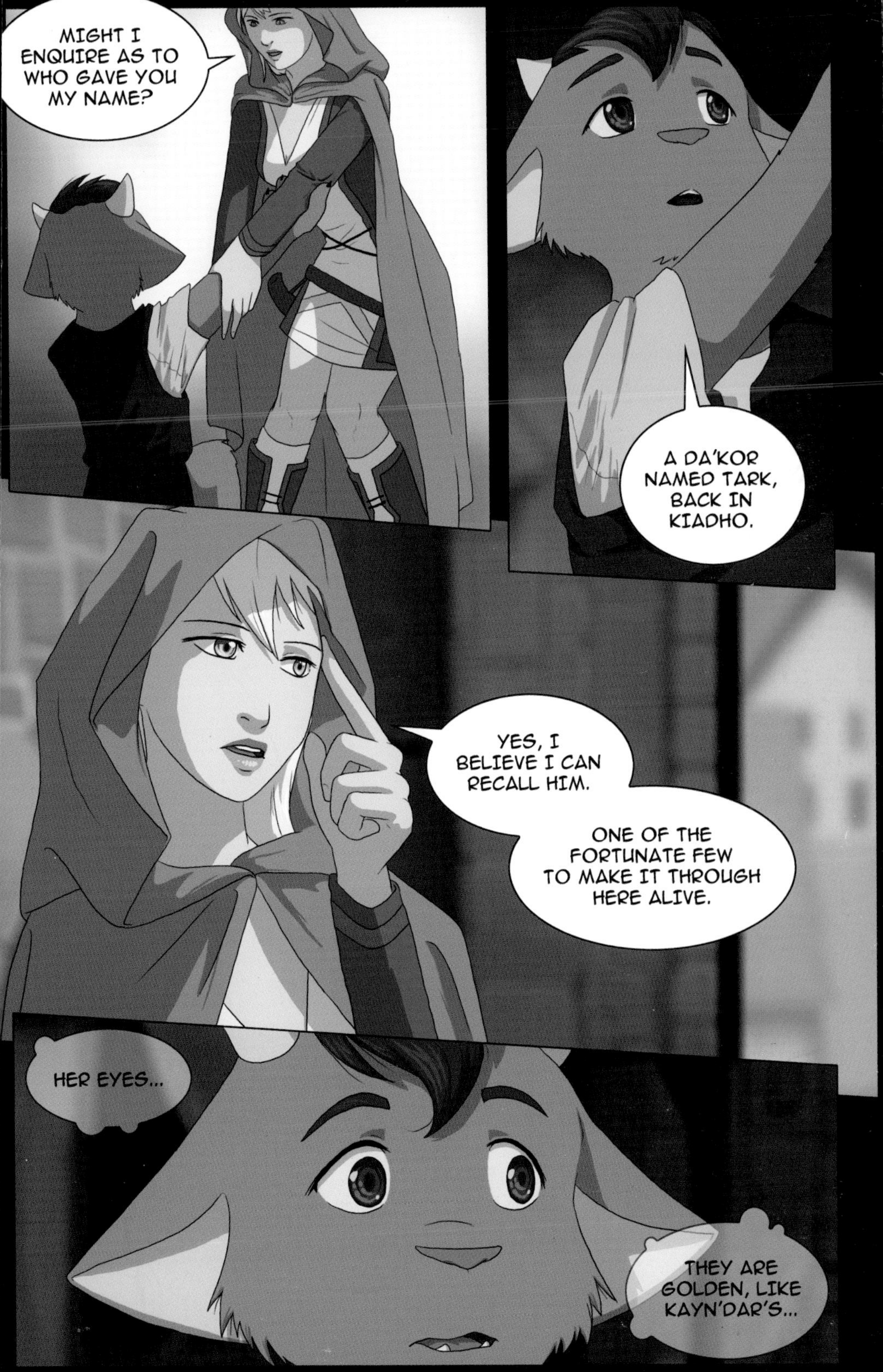
MIGHT I ENQUIRE AS TO WHO GAVE YOU MY NAME?
A DA'KOR NAMED TARK, BACK IN KIADHO.
YES, I BELIEVE I CAN RECALL HIM.
ONE OF THE FORTUNATE FEW TO MAKE IT THROUGH HERE ALIVE.
HER EYES...
THEY ARE GOLDEN, LIKE KAYN'DAR'S...

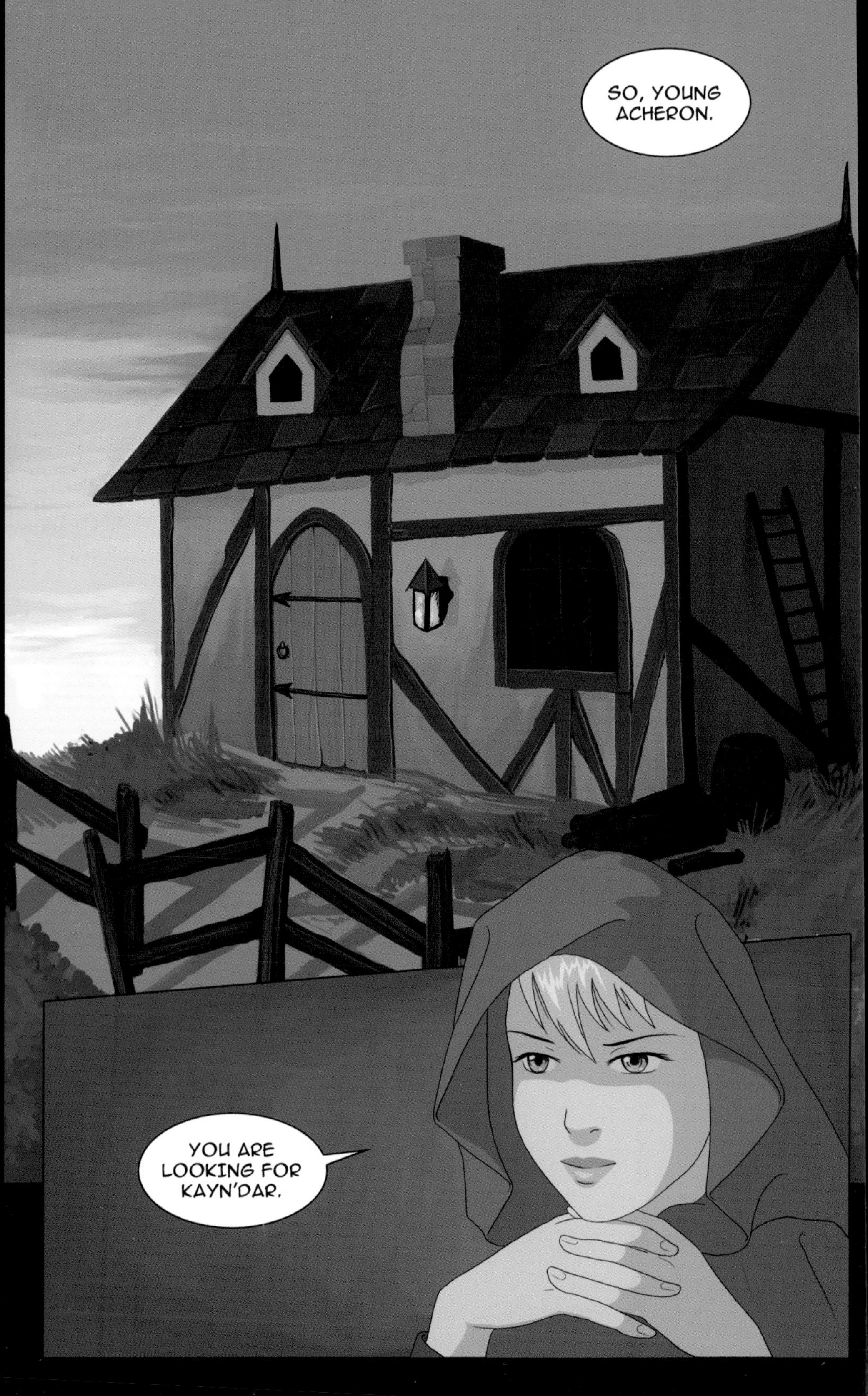
SO, YOUNG ACHERON.
YOU ARE LOOKING FOR KAYN'DAR.

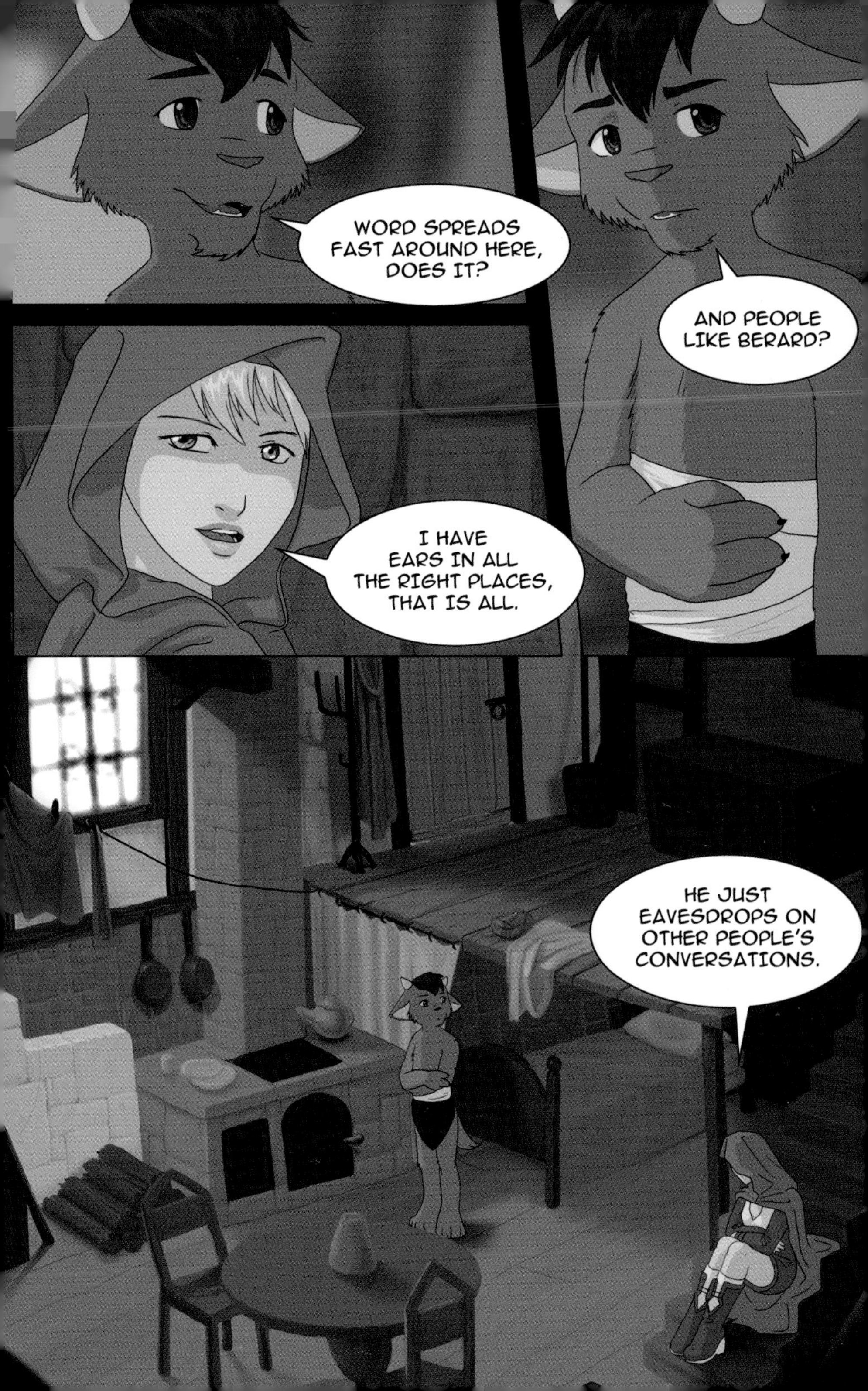
WORD SPREADS FAST AROUND HERE, DOES IT?
I HAVE EARS IN ALL THE RIGHT PLACES, THAT IS ALL.
AND PEOPLE LIKE BERARD?
HE JUST EAVESDROPS ON OTHER PEOPLE'S CONVERSATIONS.

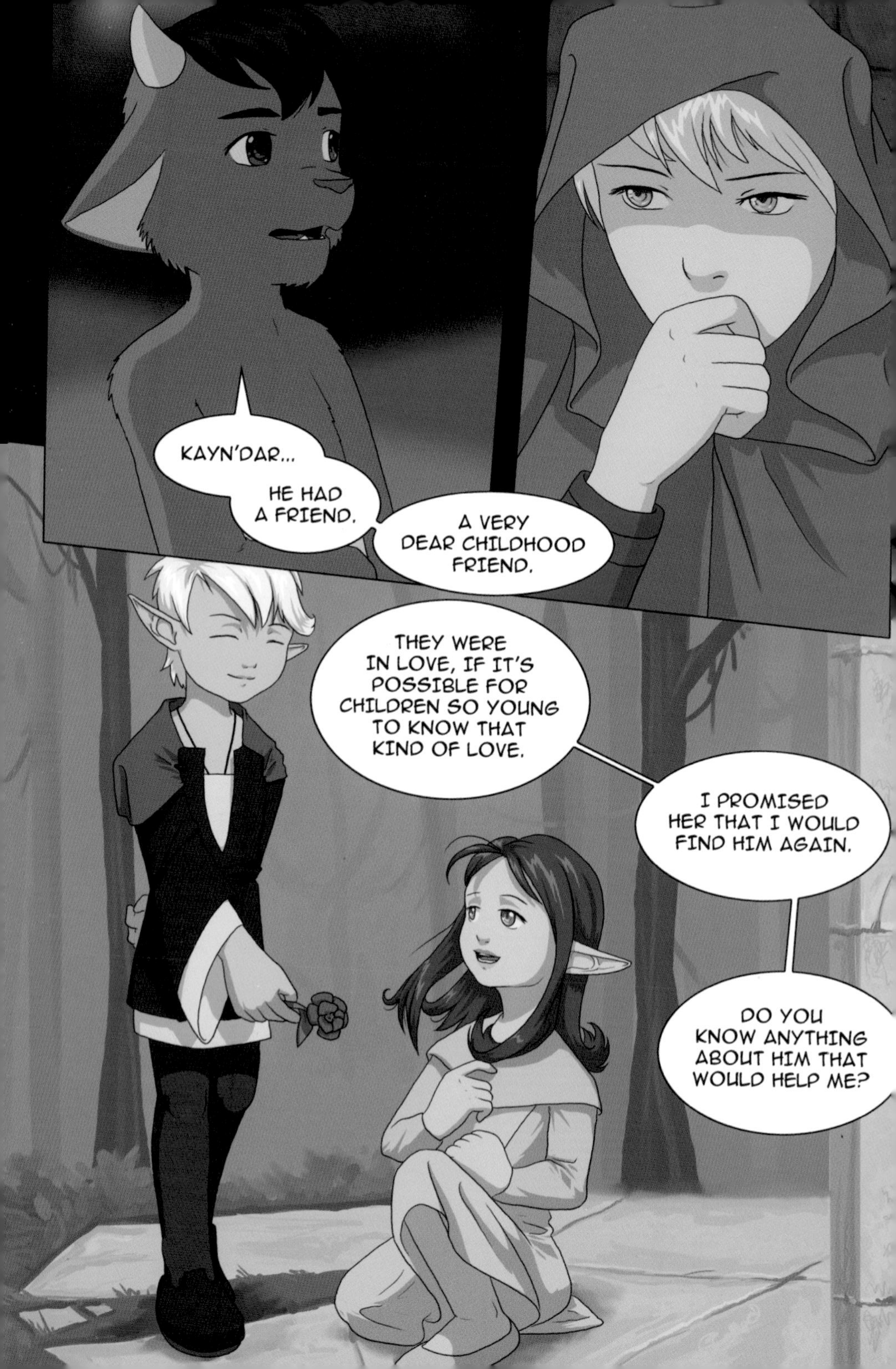
KAYN'DAR...
HE HAD A FRIEND.
A VERY DEAR CHILDHOOD FRIEND.
THEY WERE IN LOVE, IF IT'S POSSIBLE FOR CHILDREN SO YOUNG TO KNOW THAT KIND OF LOVE.
I PROMISED HER THAT I WOULD FIND HIM AGAIN.
DO YOU KNOW ANYTHING ABOUT HIM THAT WOULD HELP ME?

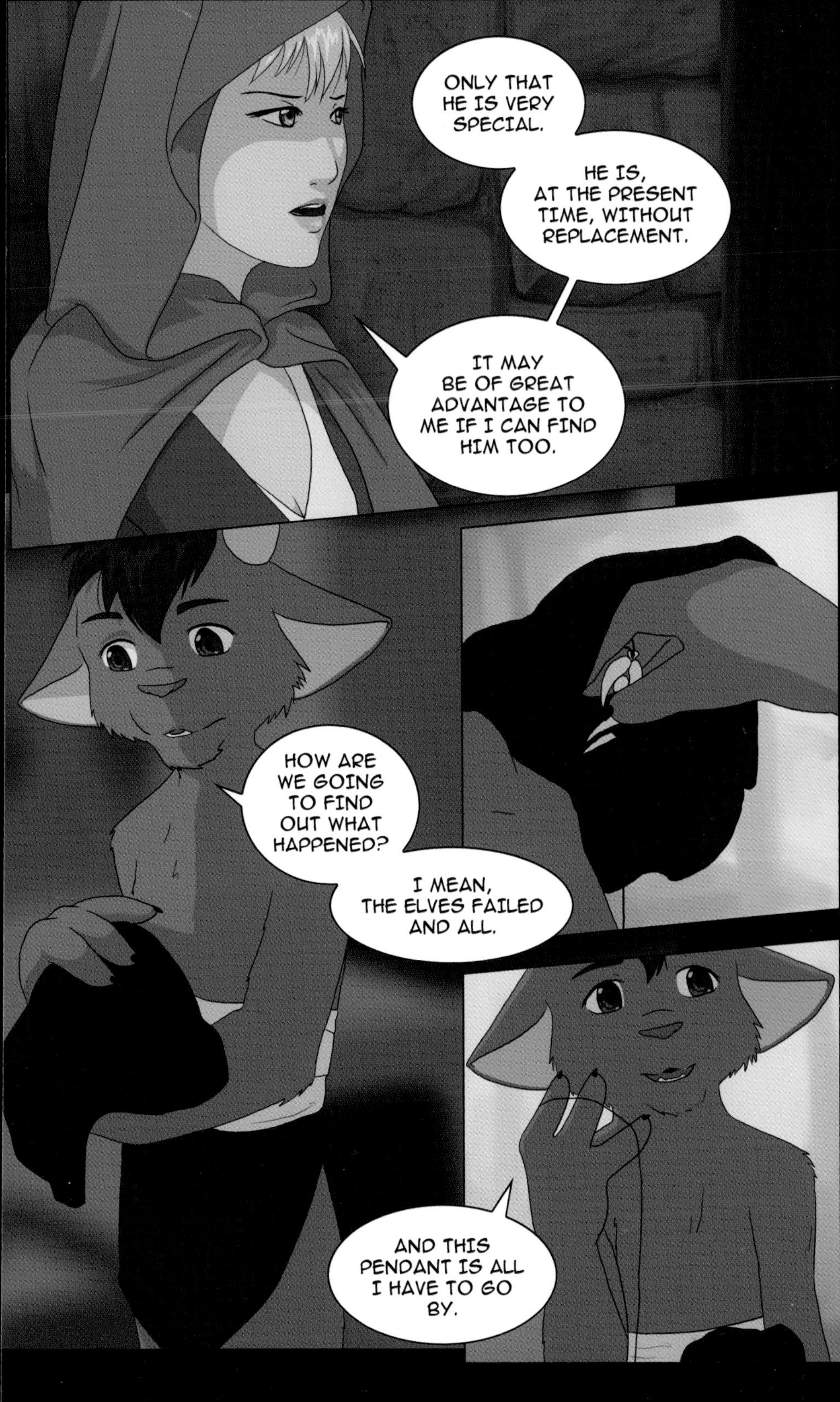
ONLY THAT HE IS VERY SPECIAL.
HE IS, AT THE PRESENT TIME, WITHOUT REPLACEMENT.
IT MAY BE OF GREAT ADVANTAGE TO ME IF I CAN FIND HIM TOO.
HOW ARE WE GOING TO FIND OUT WHAT HAPPENED?
I MEAN, THE ELVES FAILED AND ALL.
AND THIS PENDANT IS ALL I HAVE TO GO BY.

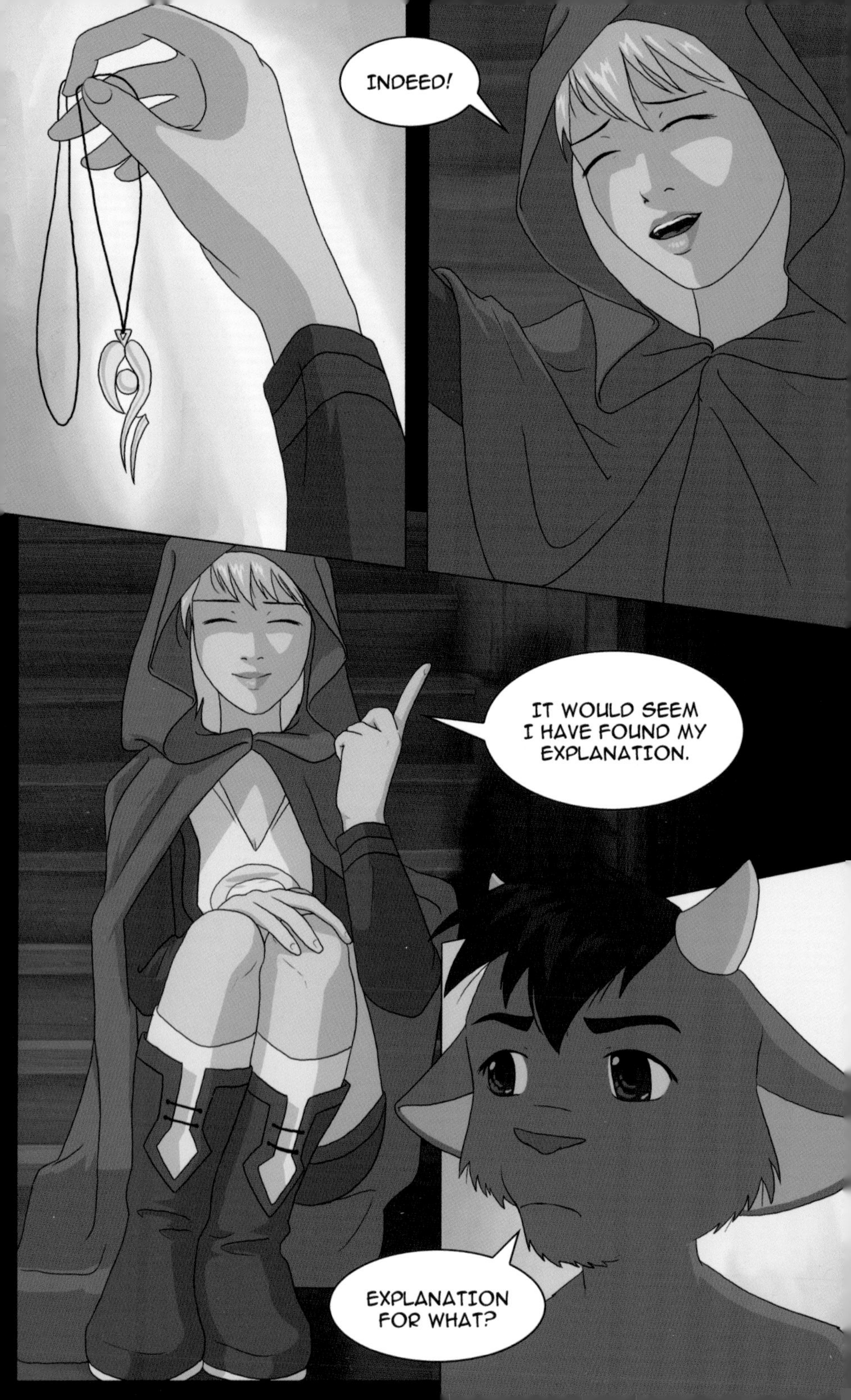
INDEED!
IT WOULD SEEM I HAVE FOUND MY EXPLANATION.
EXPLANATION FOR WHAT?

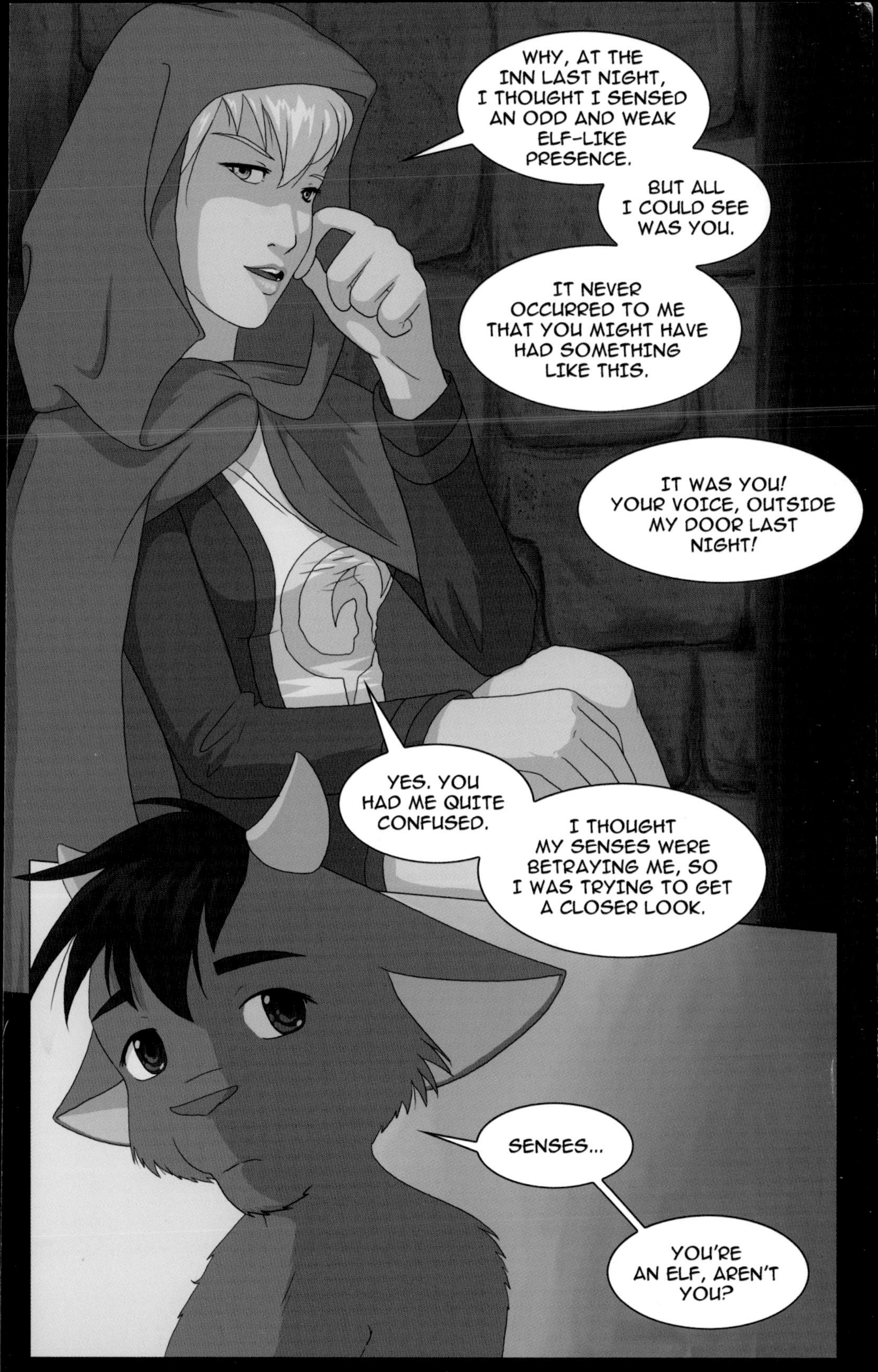
WHY, AT THE INN LAST NIGHT, I THOUGHT I SENSED AN ODD AND WEAK ELF-LIKE PRESENCE.
BUT ALL I COULD SEE WAS YOU.
IT NEVER OCCURRED TO ME THAT YOU MIGHT HAVE HAD SOMETHING LIKE THIS.
IT WAS YOU! YOUR VOICE, OUTSIDE MY DOOR LAST NIGHT!
YES. YOU HAD ME QUITE CONFUSED.
I THOUGHT MY SENSES WERE BETRAYING ME, SO I WAS TRYING TO GET A CLOSER LOOK.
SENSES...
YOU'RE AN ELF, AREN'T YOU?

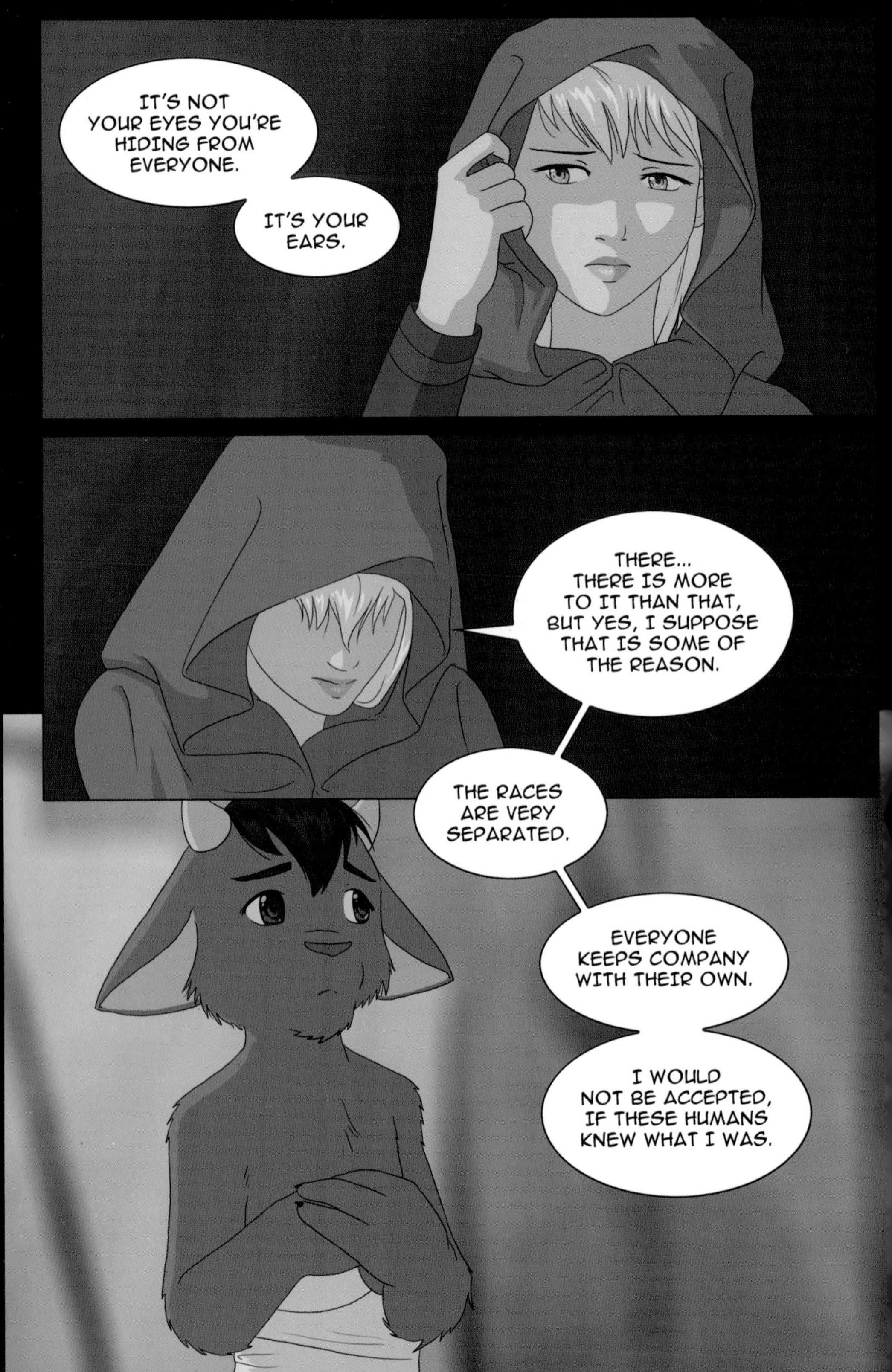
IT'S NOT YOUR EYES YOU'RE HIDING FROM EVERYONE.
IT'S YOUR EARS.
THERE... THERE IS MORE TO IT THAN THAT, BUT YES, I SUPPOSE THAT IS SOME OF THE REASON.
THE RACES ARE VERY SEPARATED.
EVERYONE KEEPS COMPANY WITH THEIR OWN.
I WOULD NOT BE ACCEPTED, IF THESE HUMANS KNEW WHAT I WAS.

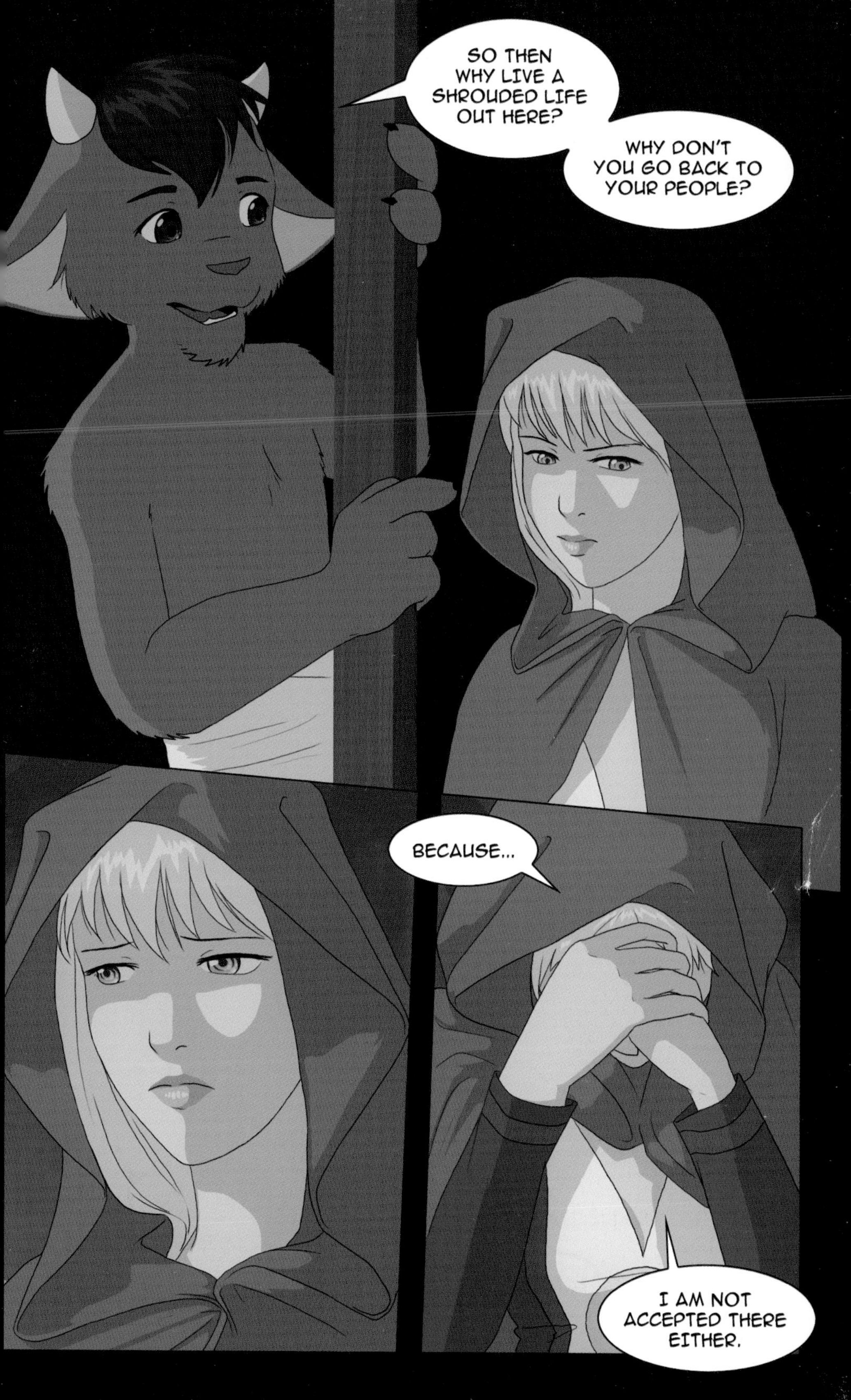
SO THEN WHY LIVE A SHROUDED LIFE OUT HERE?
WHY DON'T YOU GO BACK TO YOUR PEOPLE?
BECAUSE...
I AM NOT ACCEPTED THERE EITHER.

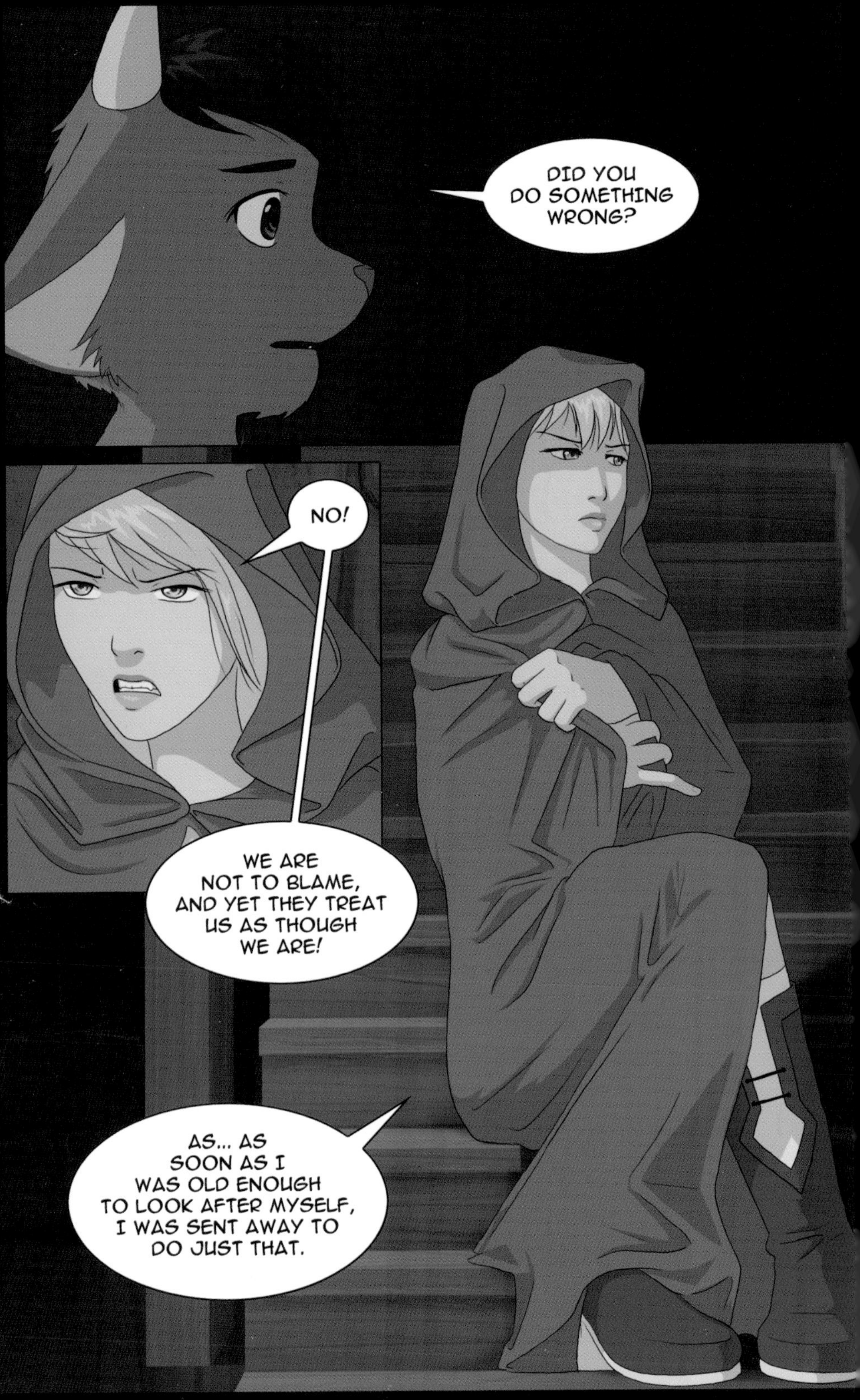

DID YOU DO SOMETHING WRONG?
NO!
WE ARE NOT TO BLAME, AND YET THEY TREAT US AS THOUGH WE ARE!
AS... AS SOON AS I WAS OLD ENOUGH TO LOOK AFTER MYSELF, I WAS SENT AWAY TO DO JUST THAT.

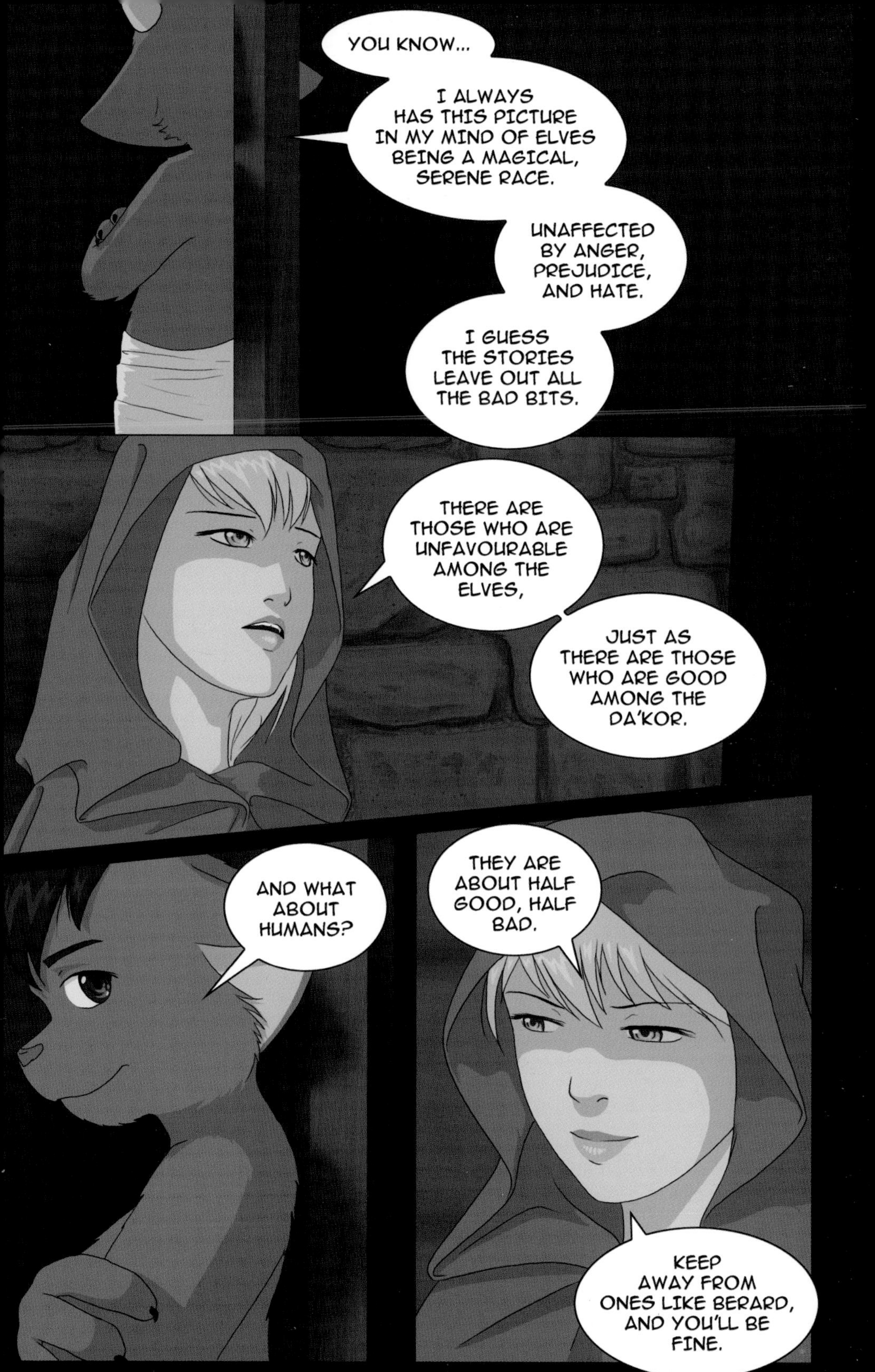
YOU KNOW...
I ALWAYS HAS THIS PICTURE IN MY MIND OF ELVES BEING A MAGICAL, SERENE RACE.
UNAFFECTED BY ANGER, PREJUDICE, AND HATE.
I GUESS THE STORIES LEAVE OUT ALL THE BAD BITS.
THERE ARE THOSE WHO ARE UNFAVOURABLE AMONG THE ELVES,
JUST AS THERE ARE THOSE WHO ARE GOOD AMONG THE DA'KOR.
AND WHAT ABOUT HUMANS?
THEY ARE ABOUT HALF GOOD, HALF BAD.
KEEP AWAY FROM ONES LIKE BERARD, AND YOU'LL BE FINE.

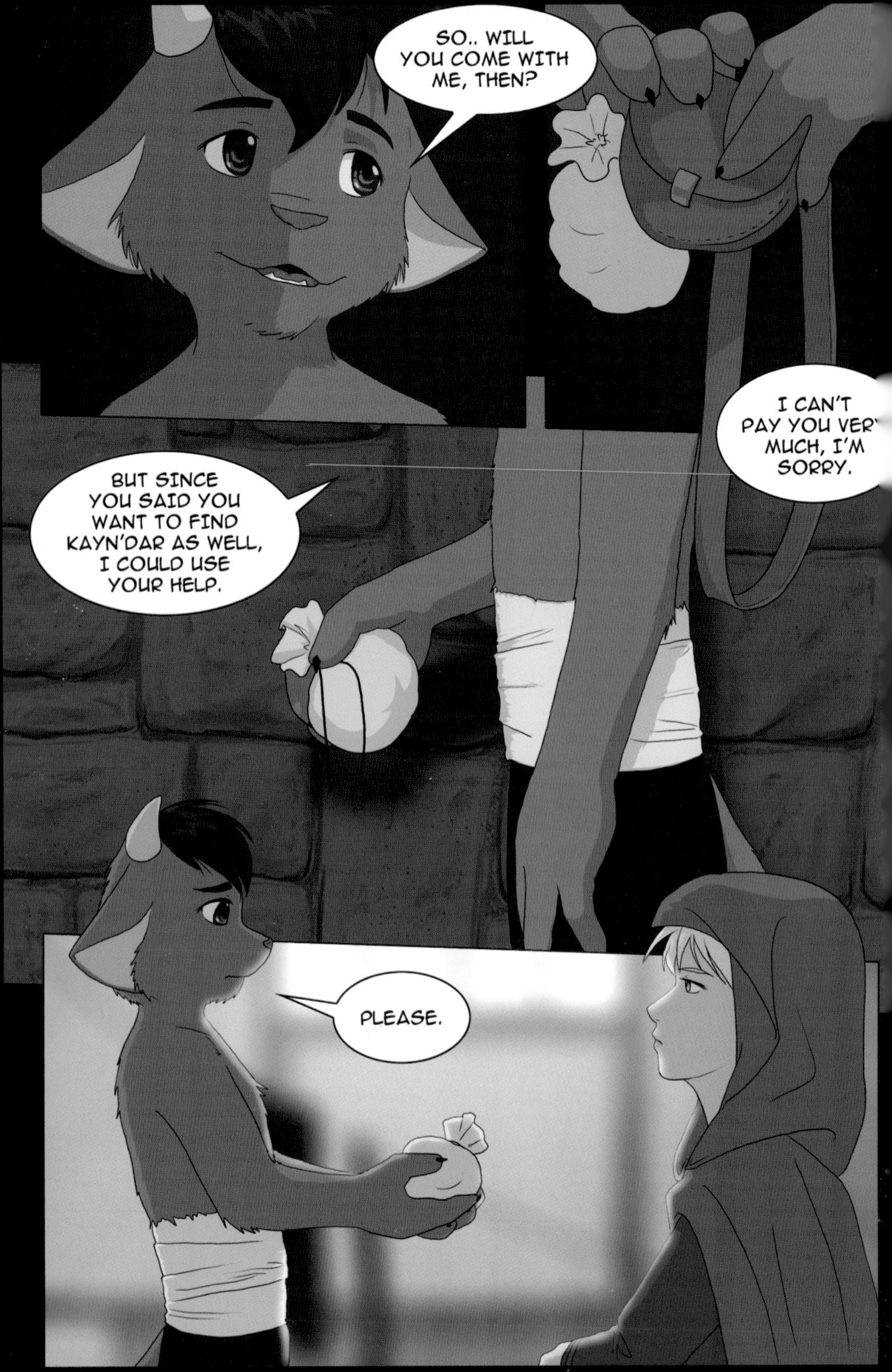
SO.. WILL YOU COME WITH ME, THEN?
I CAN'T PAY YOU VER MUCH, I'M SORRY.
BUT SINCE YOU SAID YOU WANT TO FIND KAYN'DAR AS WELL, I COULD USE YOUR HELP.
PLEASE.

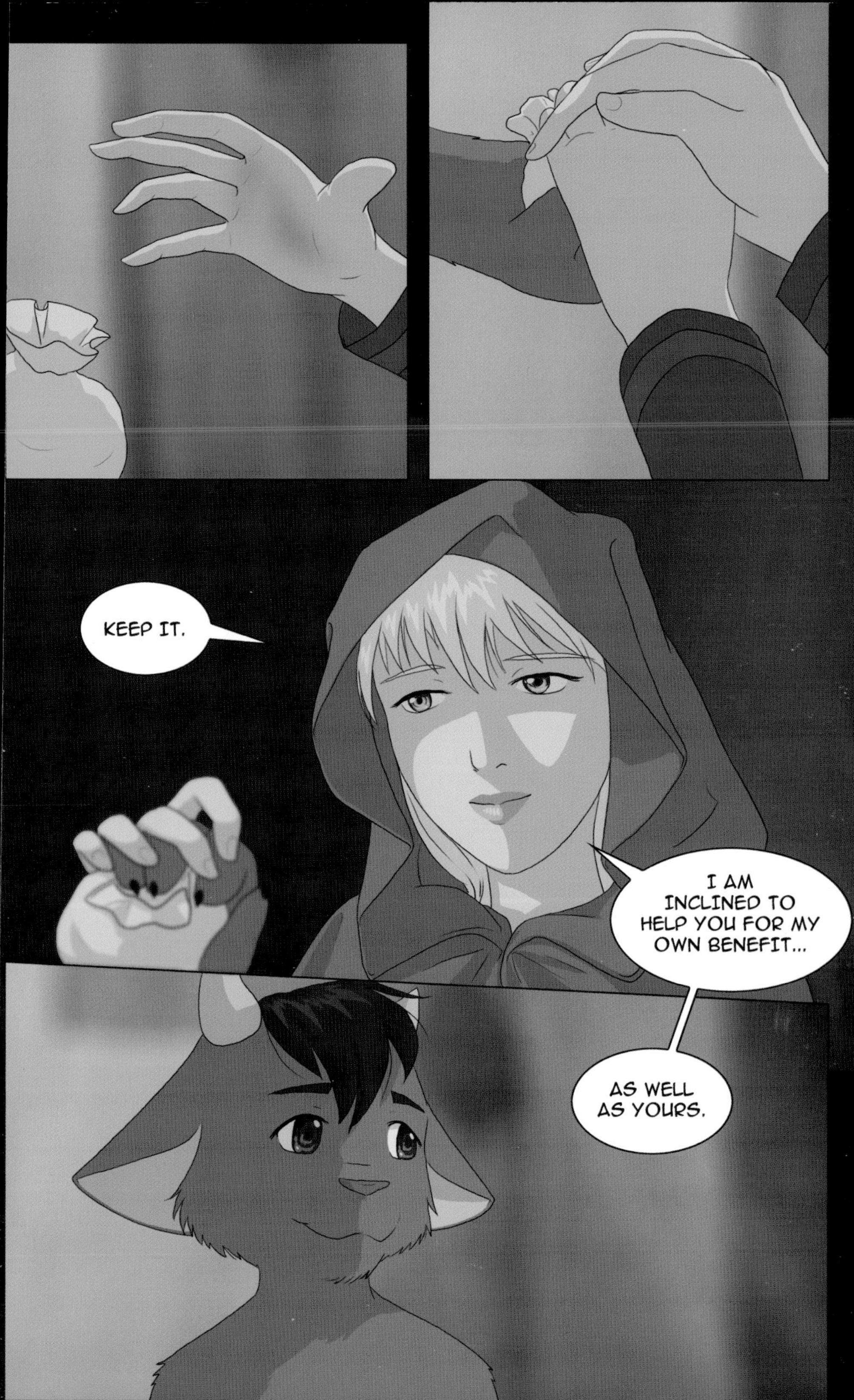
KEEP IT.
I AM INCLINED TO HELP YOU FOR MY OWN BENEFIT...
AS WELL AS YOURS.

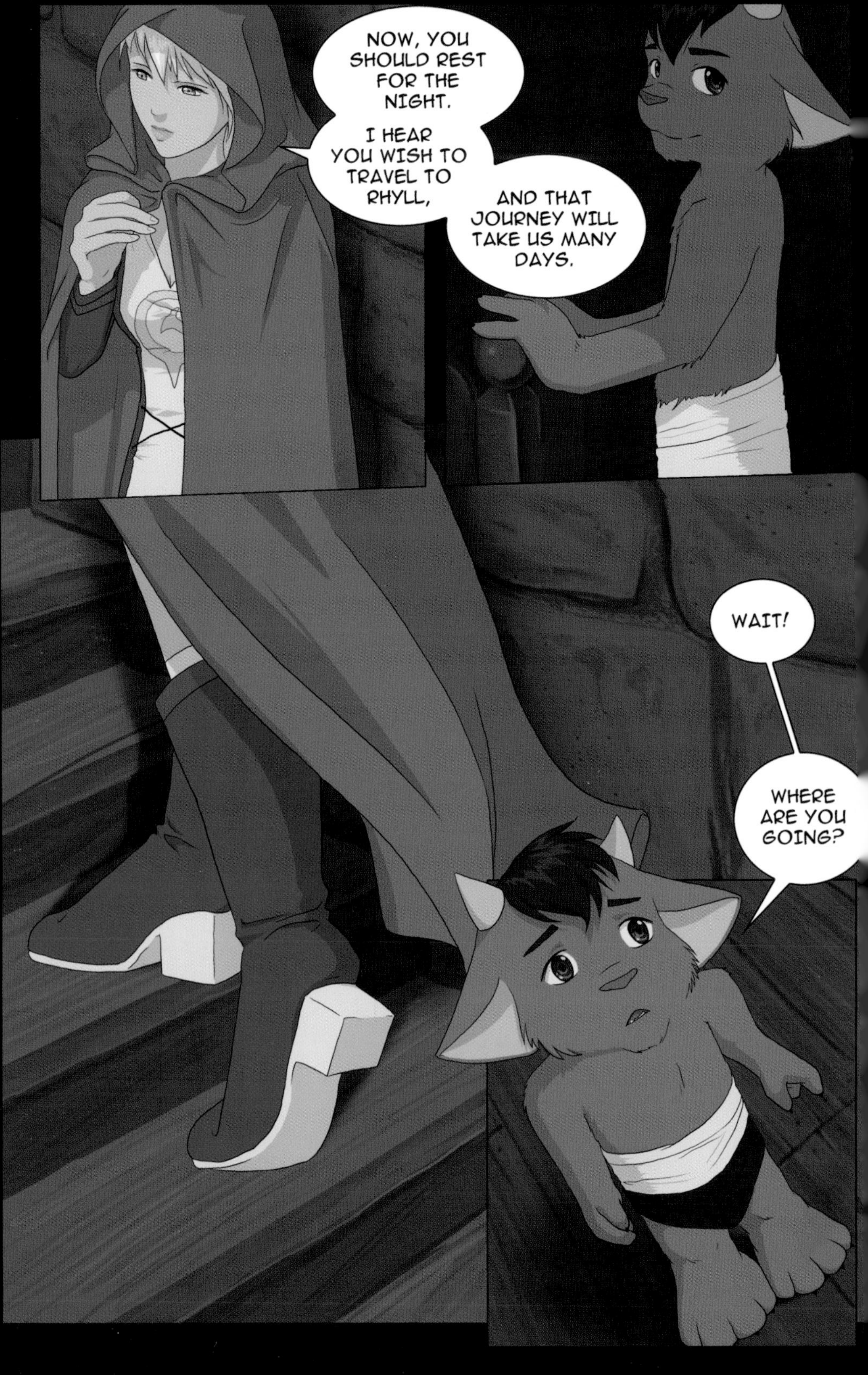
NOW, YOU SHOULD REST FOR THE NIGHT.
I HEAR YOU WISH TO TRAVEL TO RHYLL,
AND THAT JOURNEY WILL TAKE US MANY DAYS.
WAIT!
WHERE ARE YOU GOING?

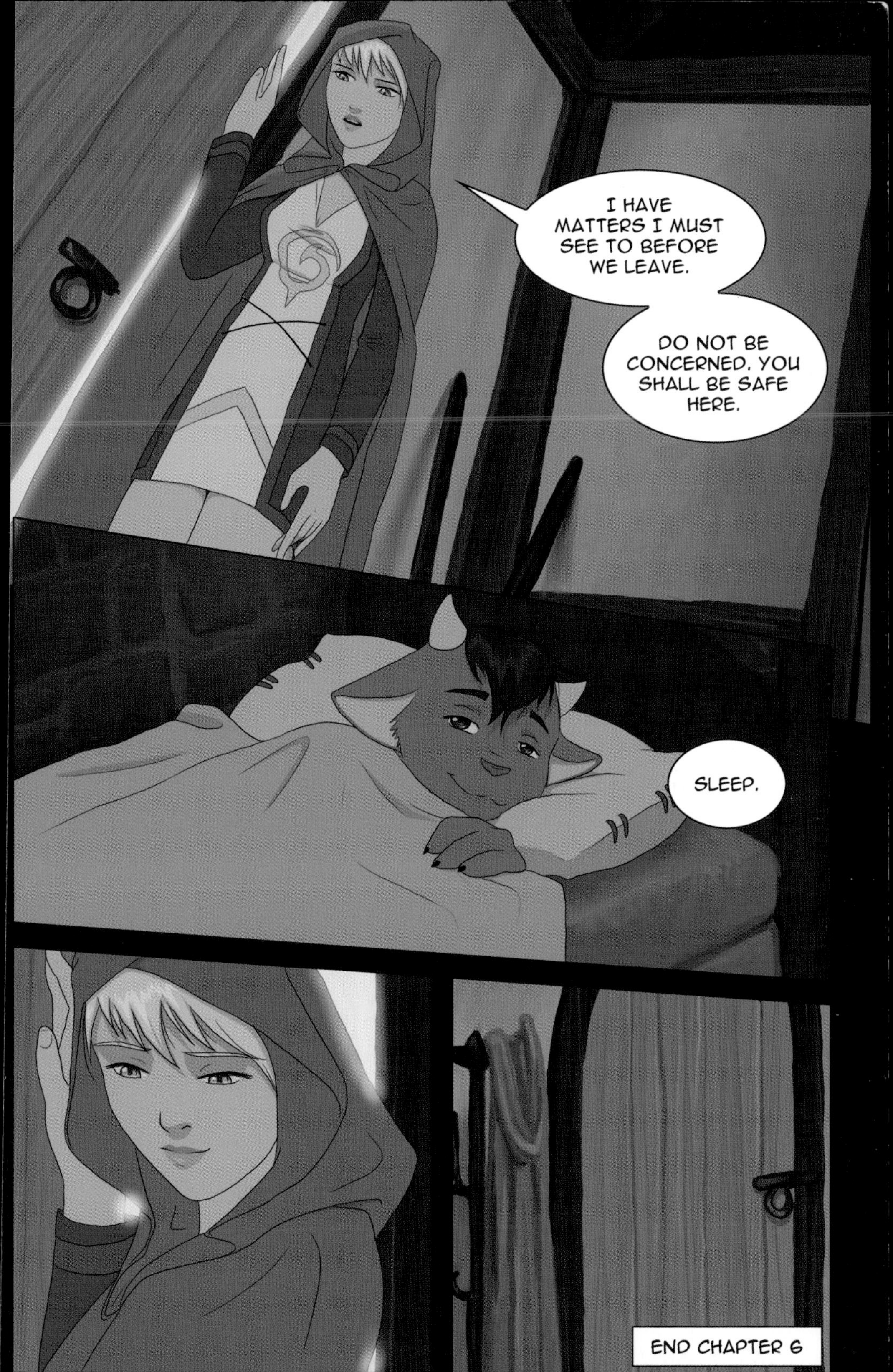
I HAVE MATTERS I MUST SEE TO BEFORE WE LEAVE.
DO NOT BE CONCERNED. YOU SHALL BE SAFE HERE.
SLEEP.
END CHAPTER 6

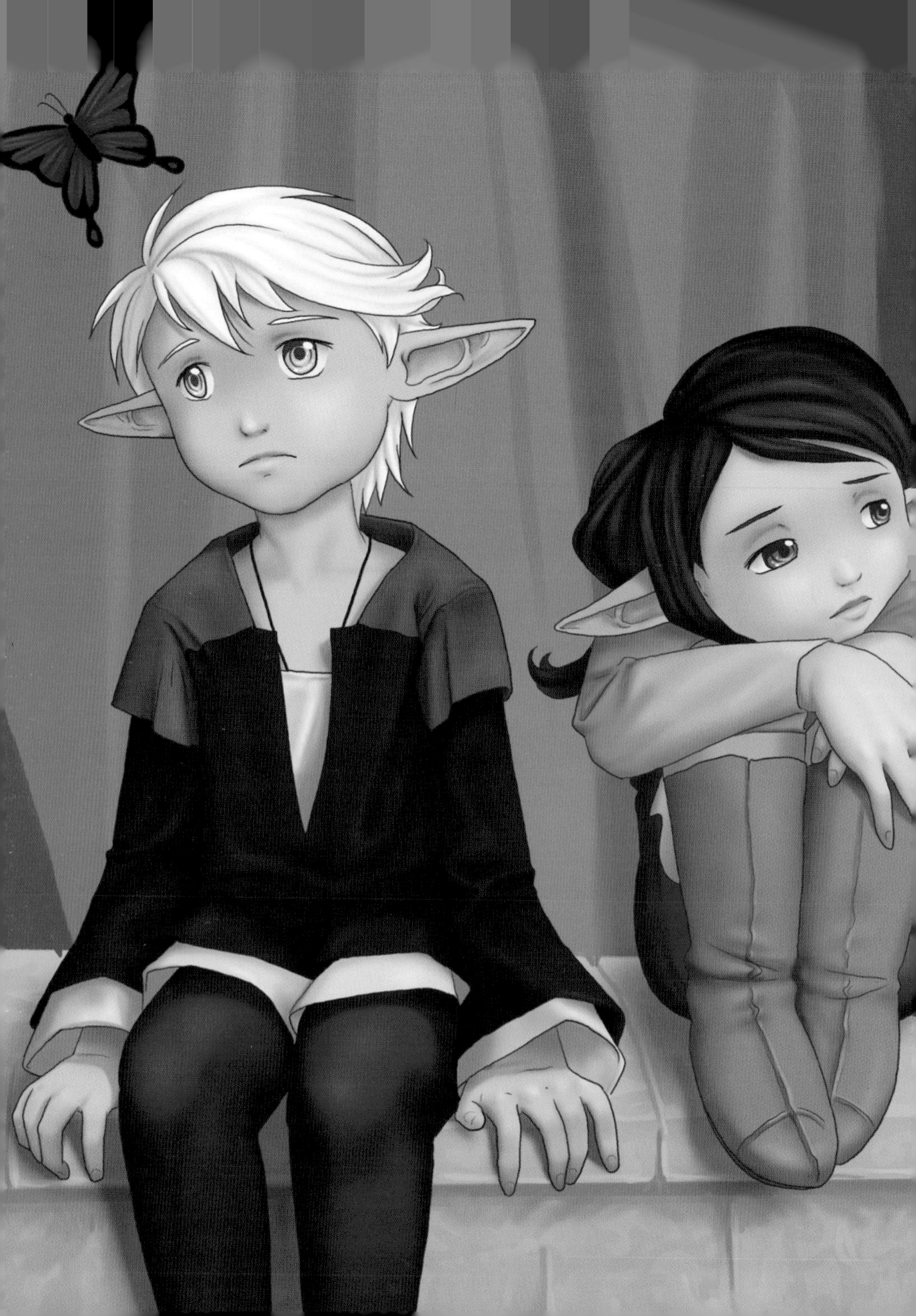

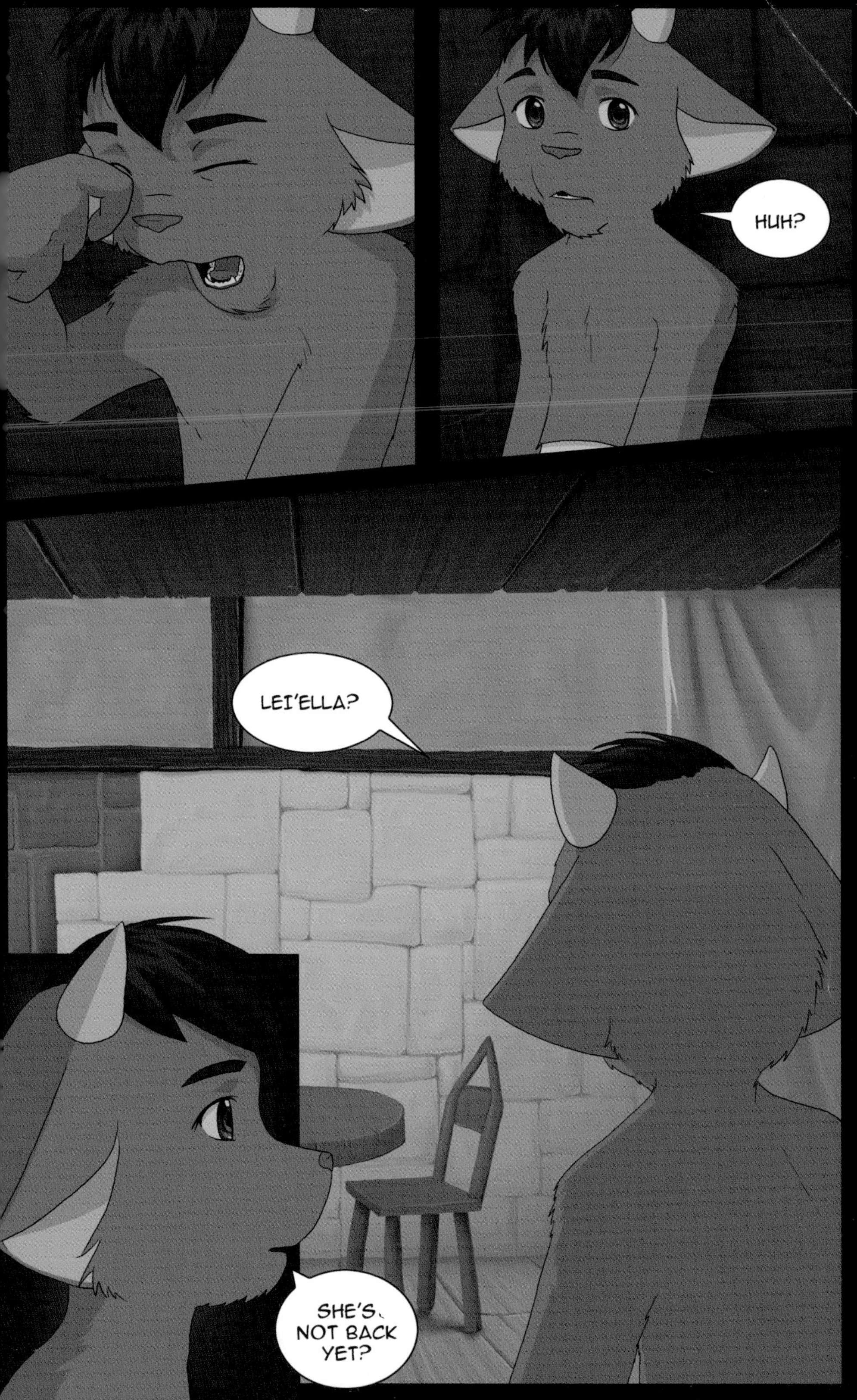
HUH?
LEI'ELLA?
SHE'S... NOT BACK YET?

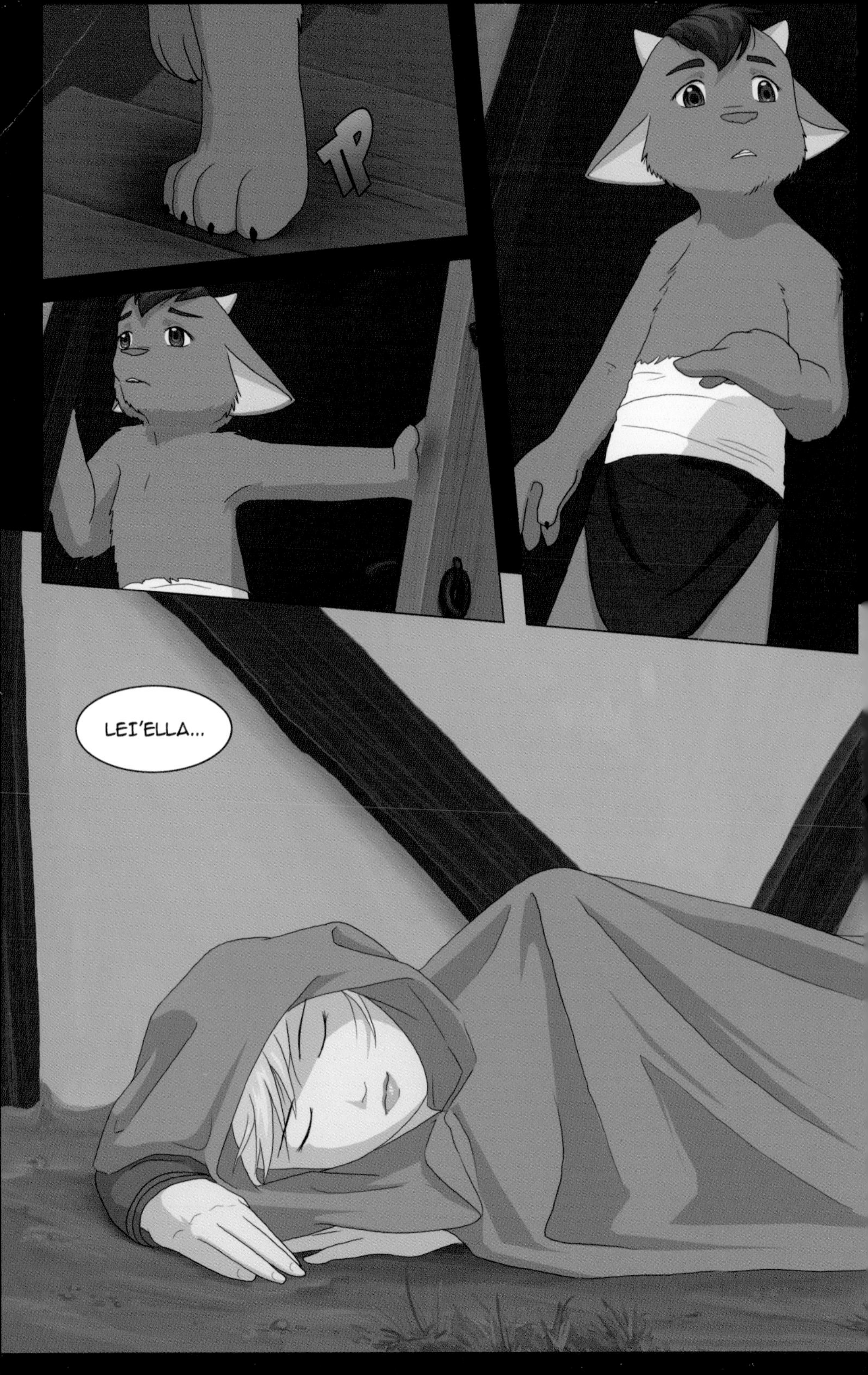

TP
LEI'ELLA...

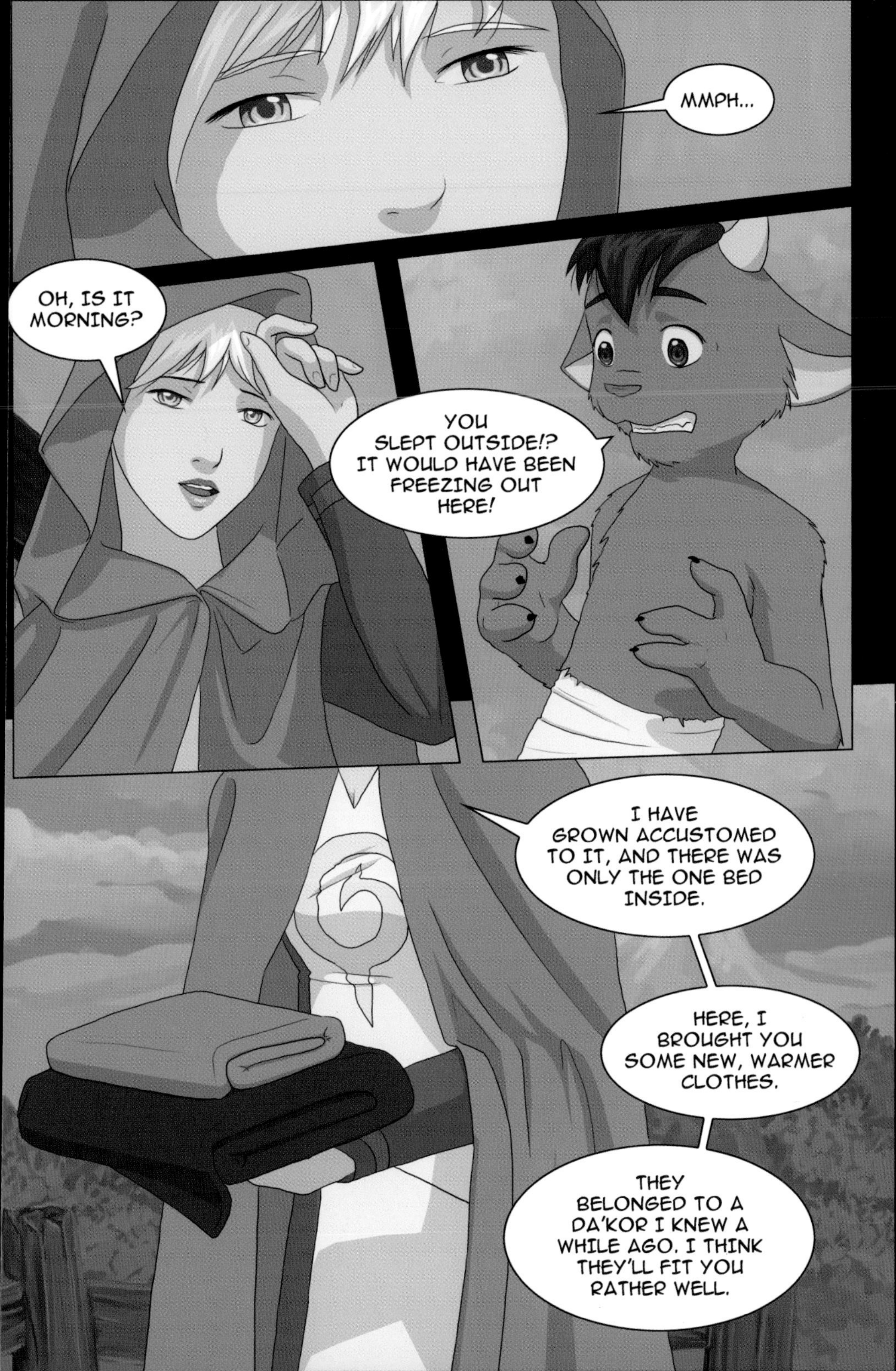
MMPH...
OH, IS IT MORNING?
YOU SLEPT OUTSIDE!? IT WOULD HAVE BEEN FREEZING OUT HERE!
I HAVE GROWN ACCUSTOMED TO IT, AND THERE WAS ONLY THE ONE BED INSIDE.
HERE, I BROUGHT YOU SOME NEW, WARMER CLOTHES.
THEY BELONGED TO A DA'KOR I KNEW A WHILE AGO. I THINK THEY'LL FIT YOU RATHER WELL.

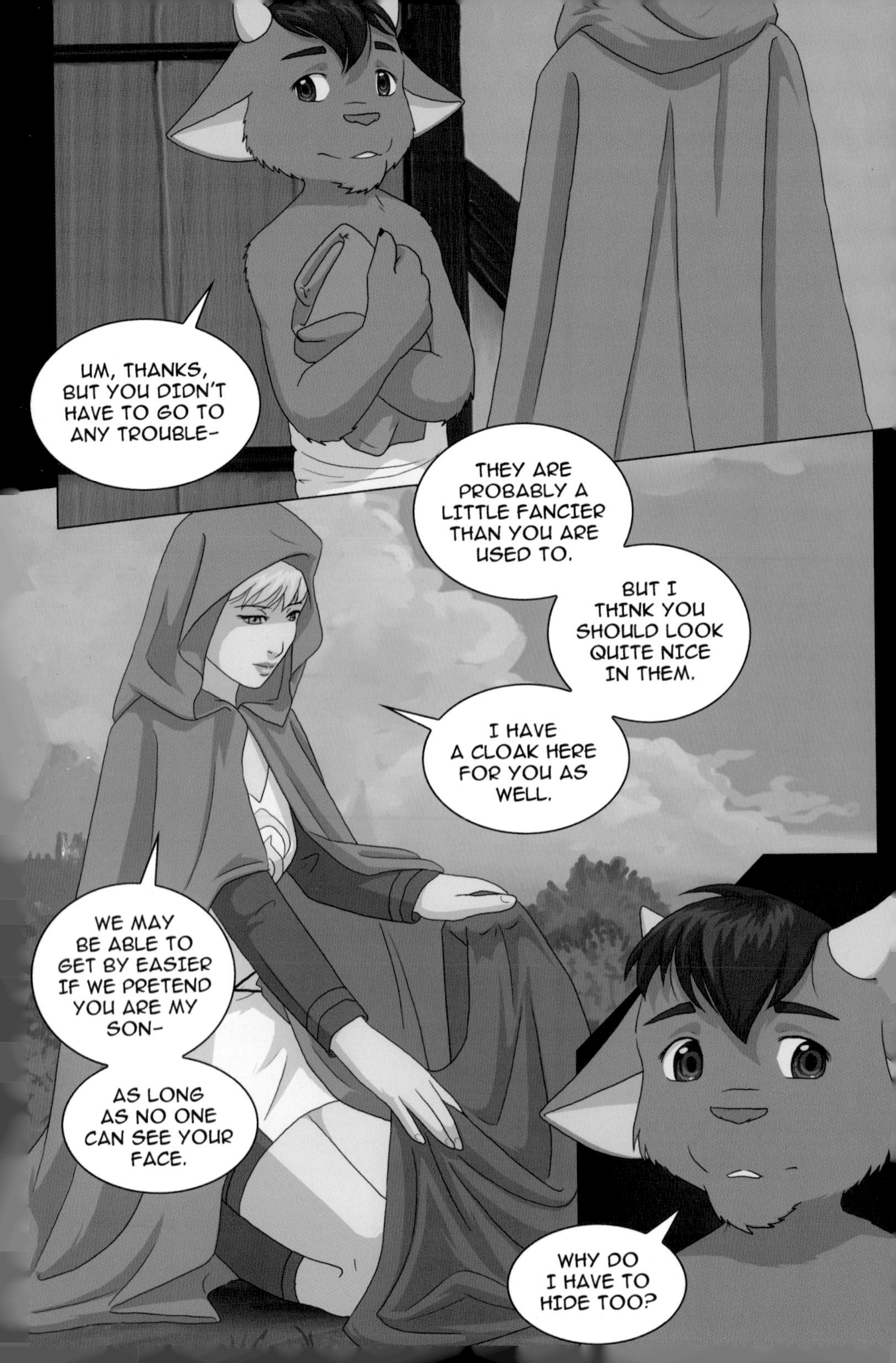
UM, THANKS, BUT YOU DIDN'T HAVE TO GO TO ANY TROUBLE-
THEY ARE PROBABLY A LITTLE FANCIER THAN YOU ARE USED TO.
BUT I THINK YOU SHOULD LOOK QUITE NICE IN THEM.
I HAVE A CLOAK HERE FOR YOU AS WELL.
WE MAY BE ABLE TO GET BY EASIER IF WE PRETEND YOU ARE MY SON-
AS LONG AS NO ONE CAN SEE YOUR FACE.
WHY DO I HAVE TO HIDE TOO?

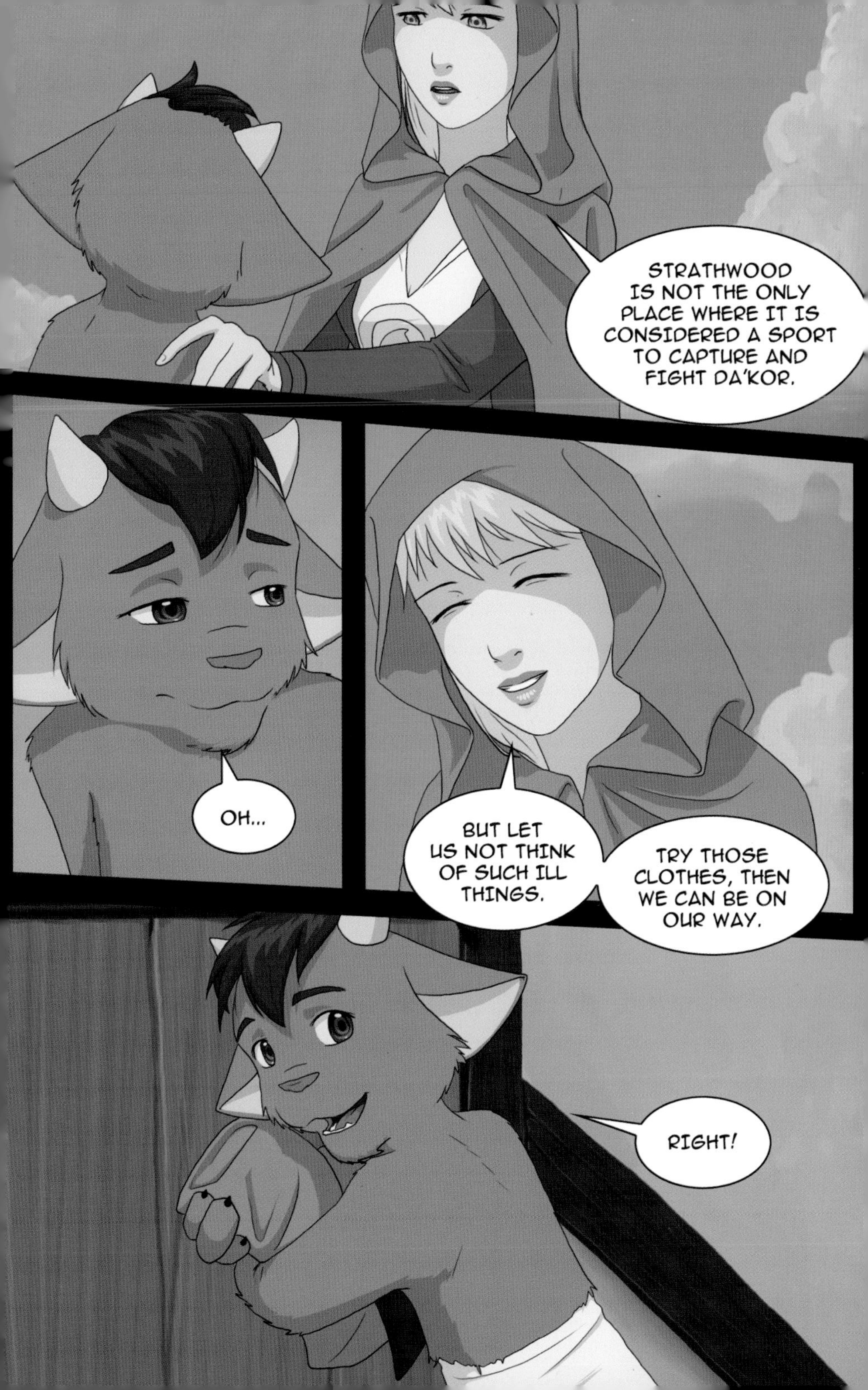
STRATHWOOD IS NOT THE ONLY PLACE WHERE IT IS CONSIDERED A SPORT TO CAPTURE AND FIGHT DA'KOR.
OH...
BUT LET US NOT THINK OF SUCH ILL THINGS.
TRY THOSE CLOTHES, THEN WE CAN BE ON OUR WAY.
RIGHT!

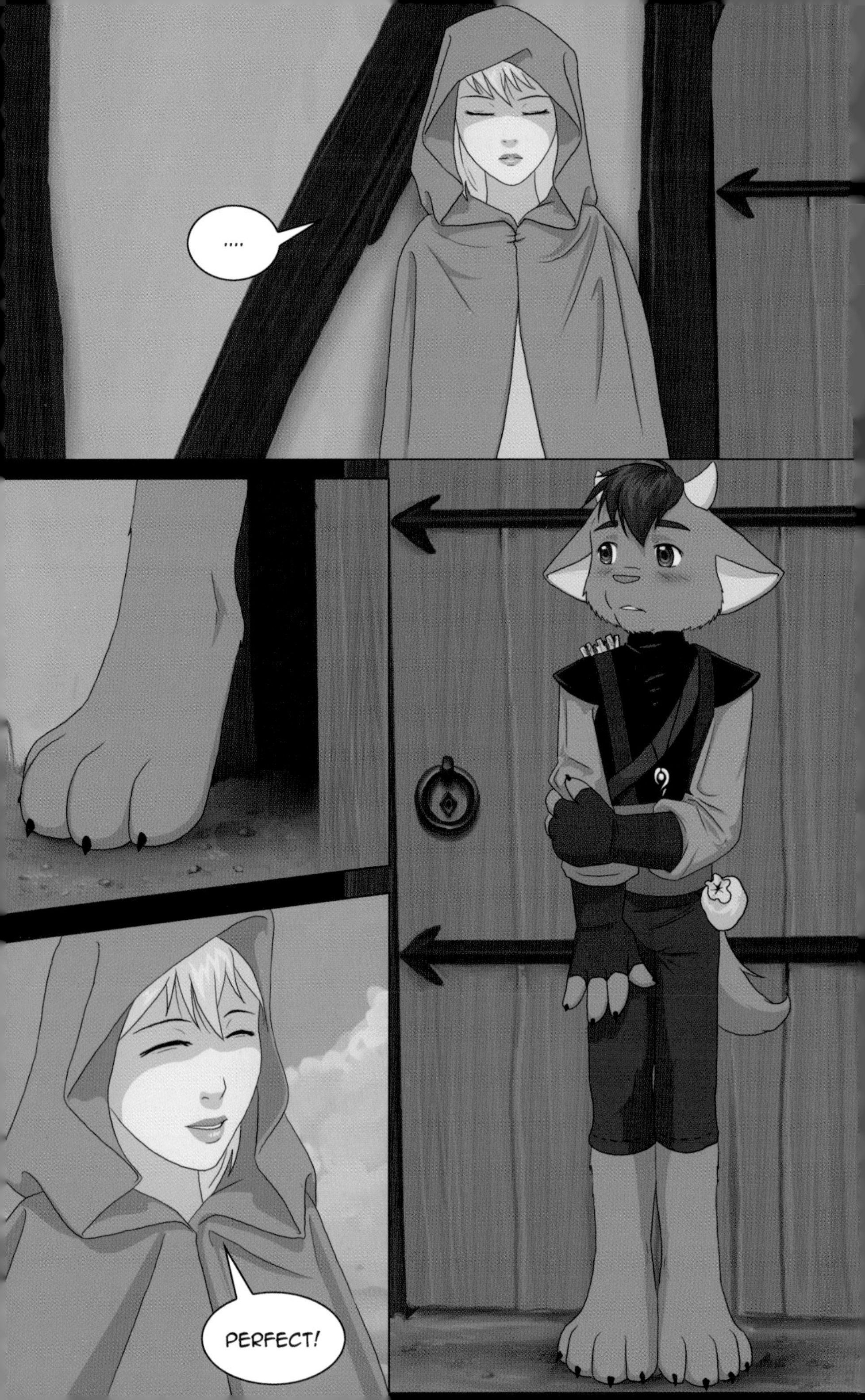
....
PERFECT!

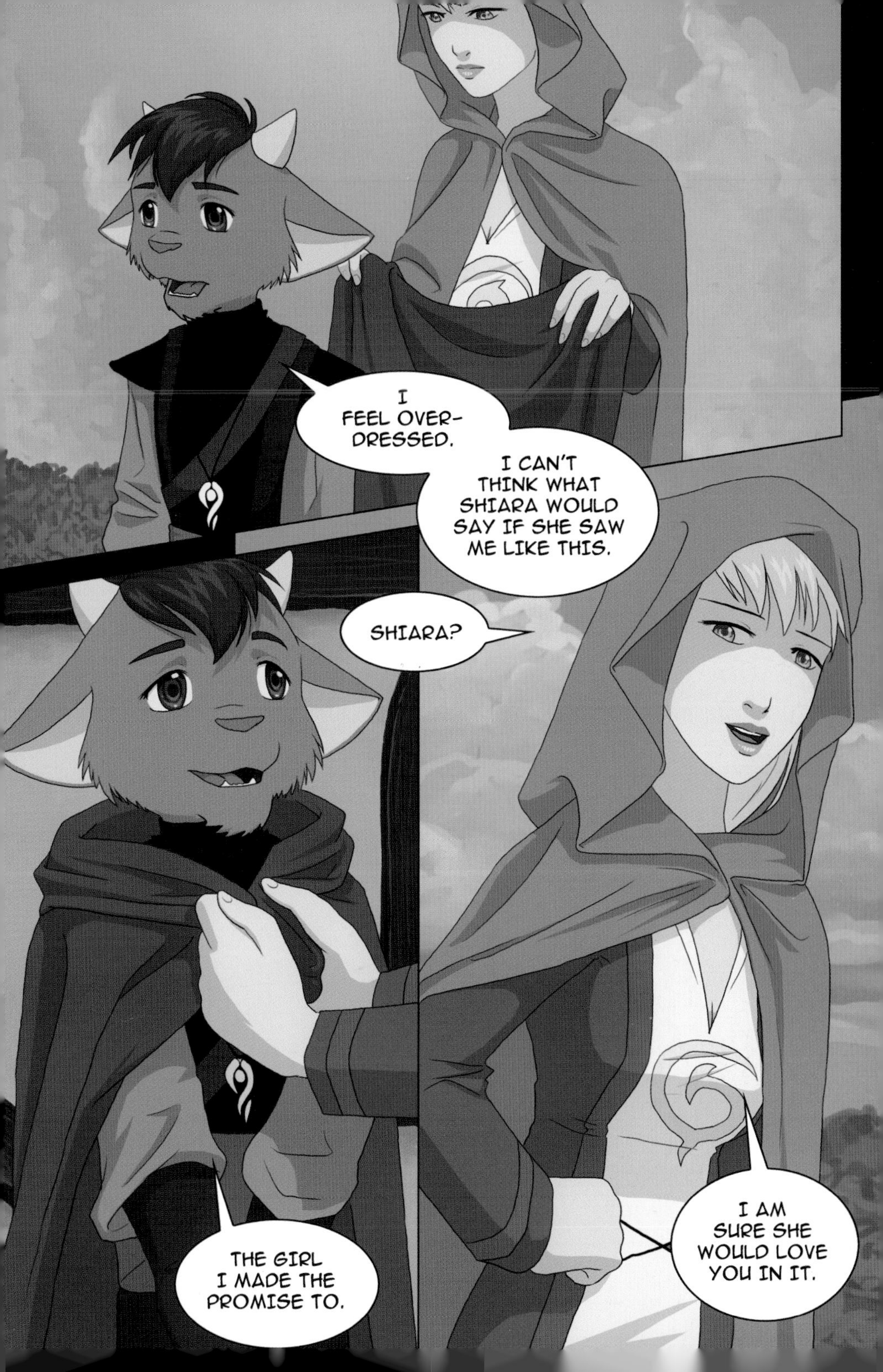
I FEEL OVER-DRESSED.
I CAN'T THINK WHAT SHIARA WOULD SAY IF SHE SAW ME LIKE THIS.
SHIARA?
THE GIRL I MADE THE PROMISE TO.
I AM SURE SHE WOULD LOVE YOU IN IT.

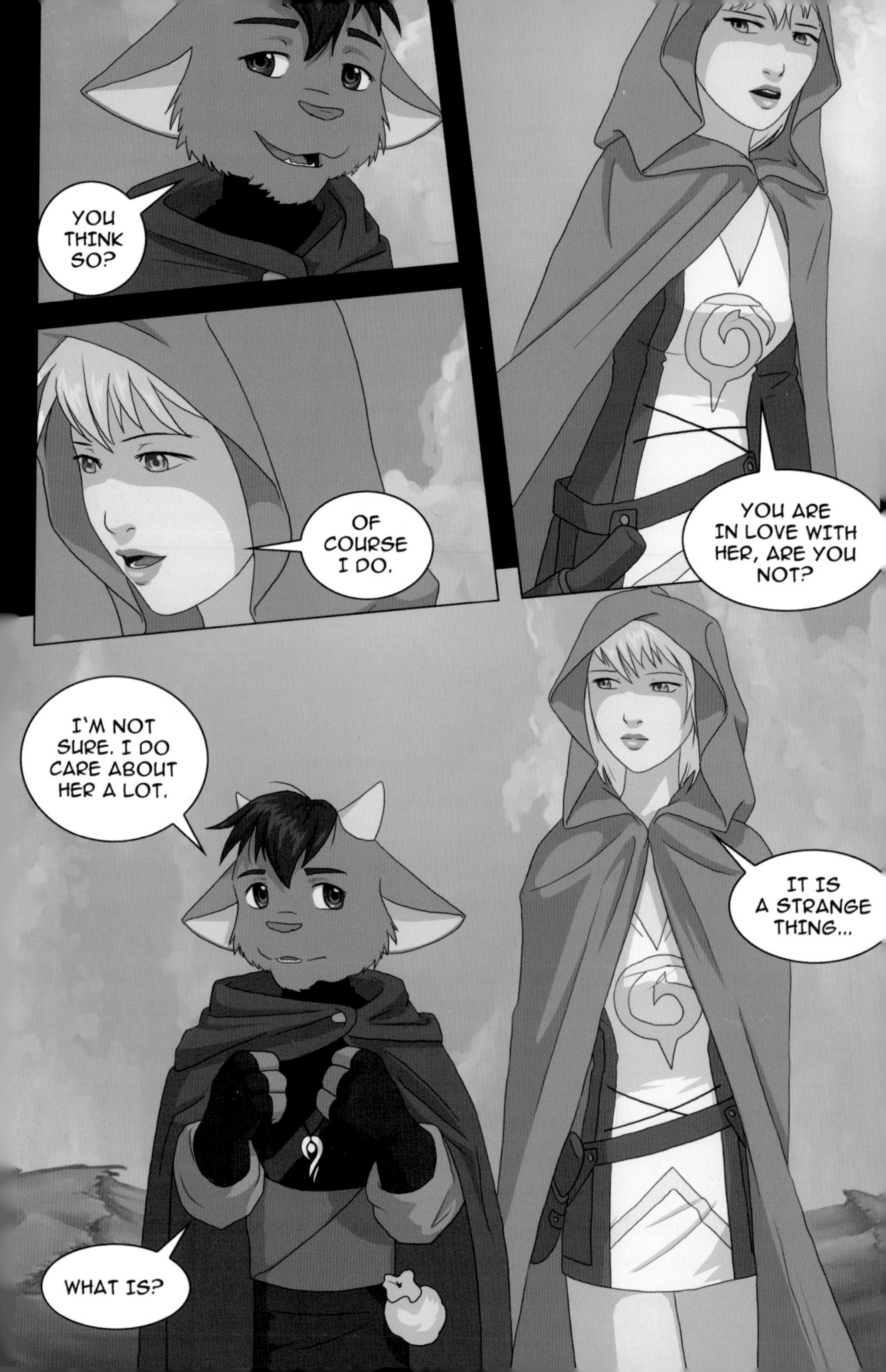
YOU THINK SO?
OF COURSE I DO.
YOU ARE IN LOVE WITH HER, ARE YOU NOT?
I'M NOT SURE. I DO CARE ABOUT HER A LOT.
IT IS A STRANGE THING...
WHAT IS?

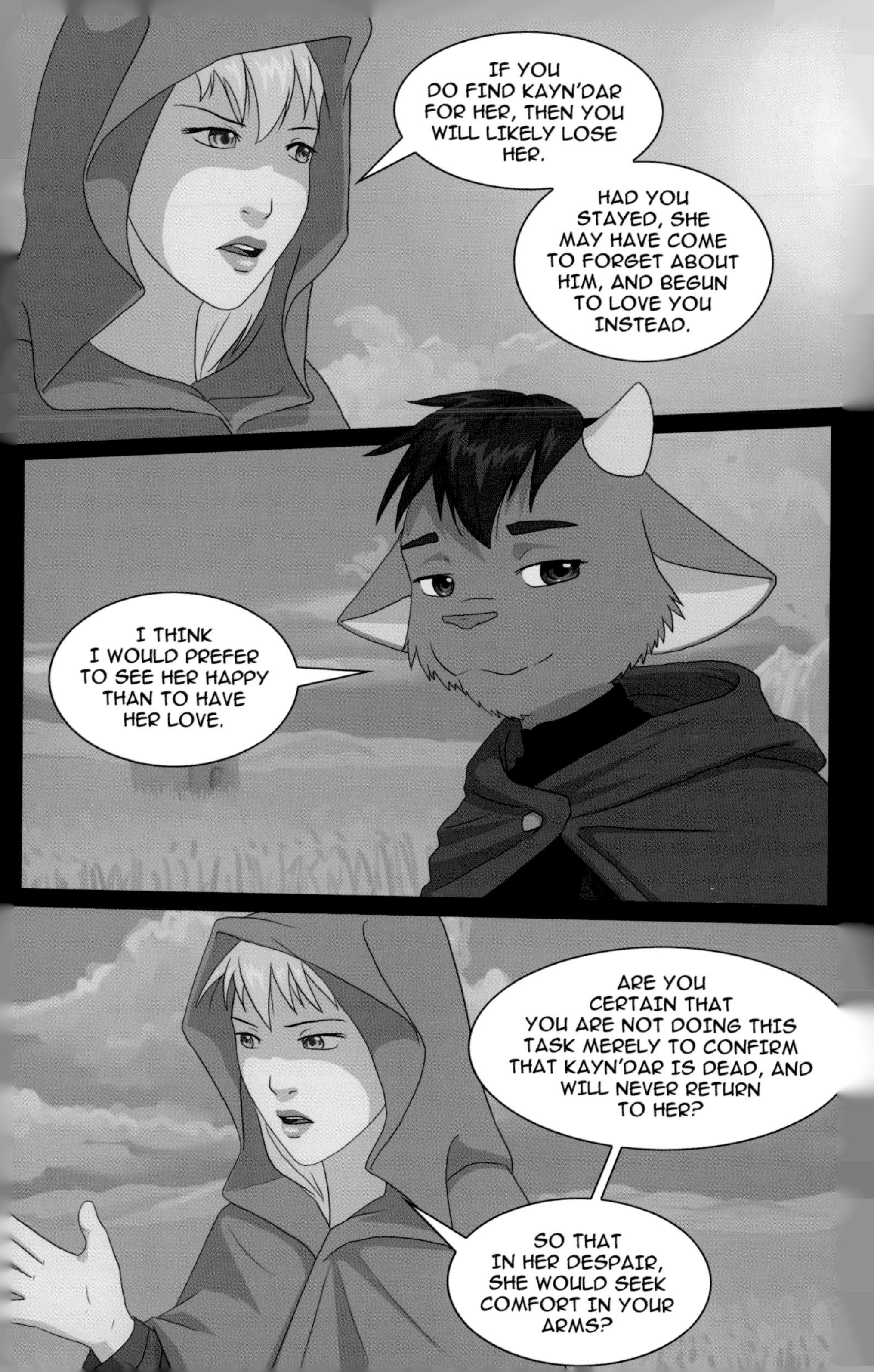
IF YOU DO FIND KAYN'DAR FOR HER, THEN YOU WILL LIKELY LOSE HER.
HAD YOU STAYED, SHE MAY HAVE COME TO FORGET ABOUT HIM, AND BEGUN TO LOVE YOU INSTEAD.
I THINK I WOULD PREFER TO SEE HER HAPPY THAN TO HAVE HER LOVE.
ARE YOU CERTAIN THAT YOU ARE NOT DOING THIS TASK MERELY TO CONFIRM THAT KAYN'DAR IS DEAD, AND WILL NEVER RETURN TO HER?
SO THAT IN HER DESPAIR, SHE WOULD SEEK COMFORT IN YOUR ARMS?

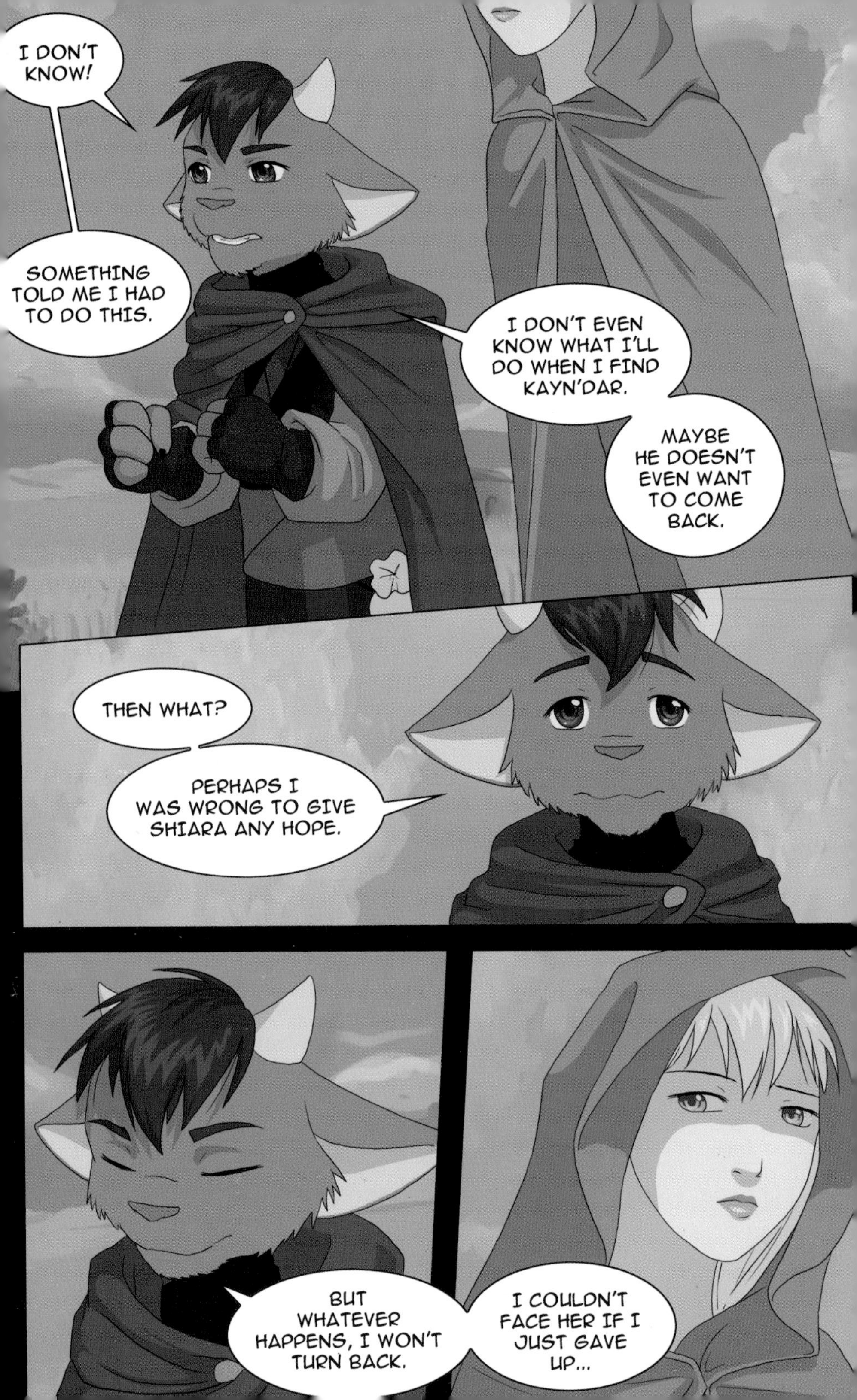
I DON'T KNOW!
SOMETHING TOLD ME I HAD TO DO THIS.
I DON'T EVEN KNOW WHAT I'LL DO WHEN I FIND KAYN'DAR.
MAYBE HE DOESN'T EVEN WANT TO COME BACK.
THEN WHAT?
PERHAPS I WAS WRONG TO GIVE SHIARA ANY HOPE.
BUT WHATEVER HAPPENS, I WON'T TURN BACK.
I COULDN'T FACE HER IF I JUST GAVE UP...

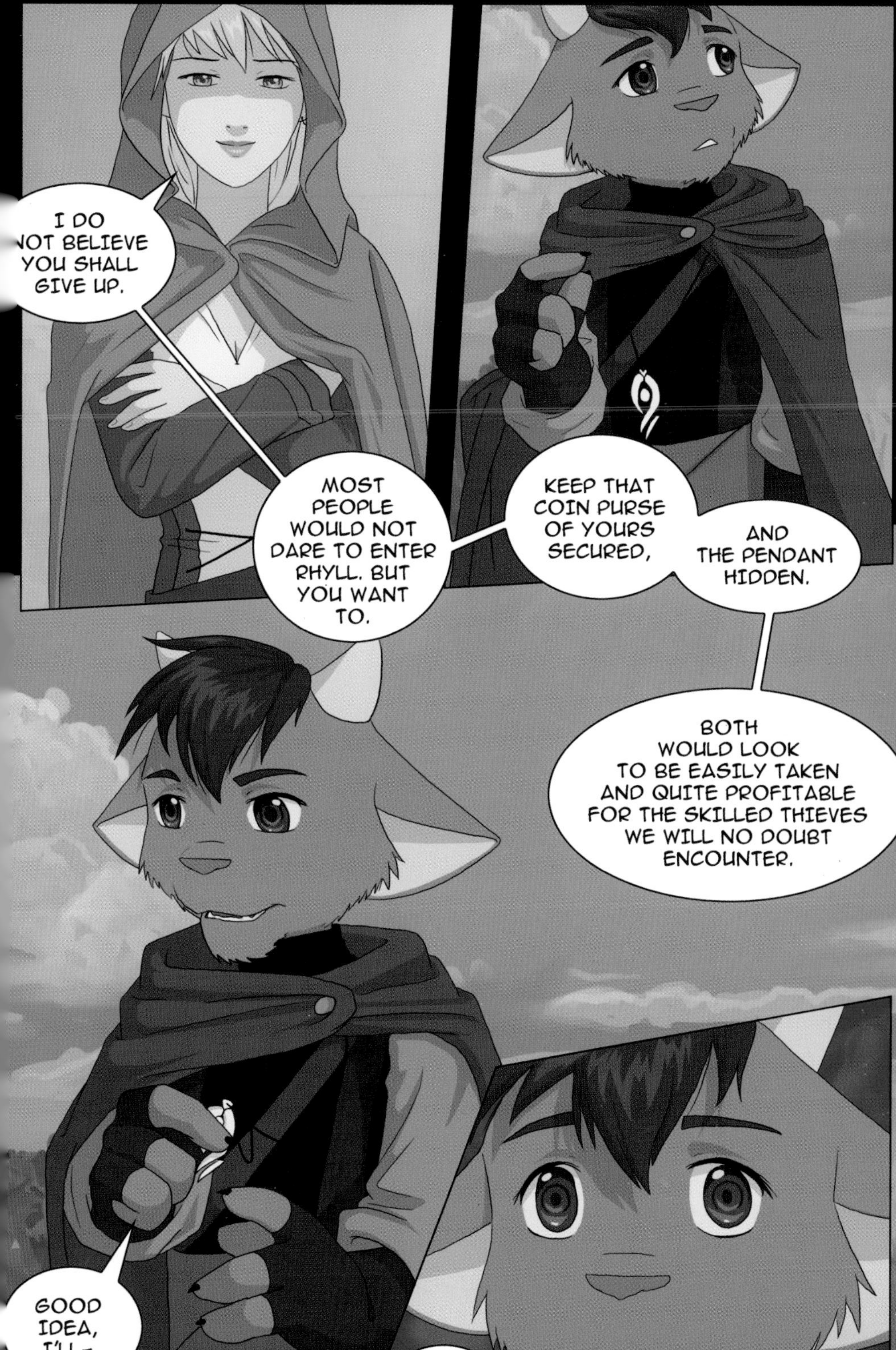
I DO NOT BELIEVE YOU SHALL GIVE UP.
MOST PEOPLE WOULD NOT DARE TO ENTER RHYLL. BUT YOU WANT TO.
KEEP THAT COIN PURSE OF YOURS SECURED,
AND THE PENDANT HIDDEN.
BOTH WOULD LOOK TO BE EASILY TAKEN AND QUITE PROFITABLE FOR THE SKILLED THIEVES WE WILL NO DOUBT ENCOUNTER.
GOOD IDEA, I'LL-
HUH?

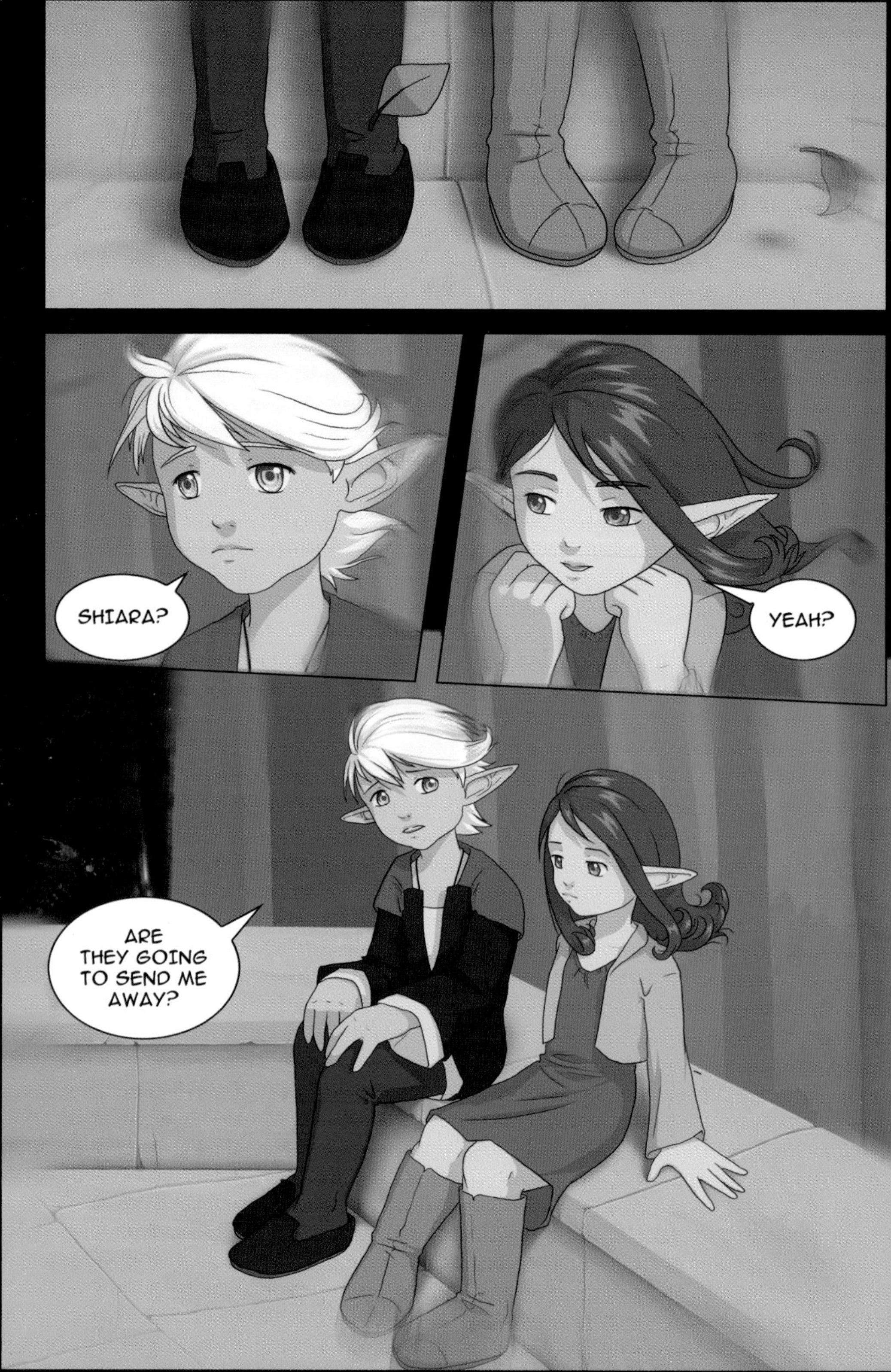
SHIARA?
YEAH?
ARE THEY GOING TO SEND ME AWAY?

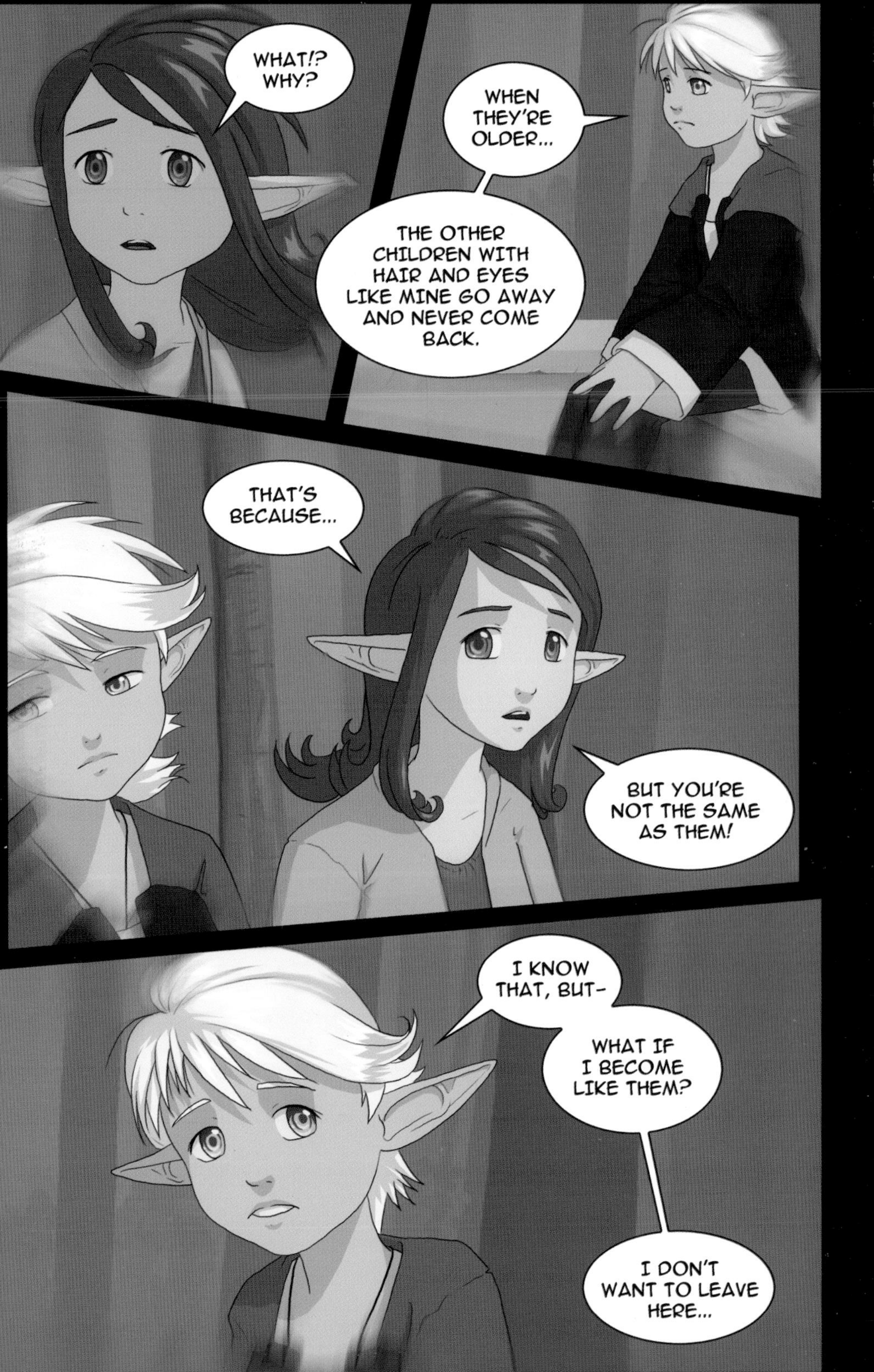
WHAT!? WHY?
WHEN THEY'RE OLDER...
THE OTHER CHILDREN WITH HAIR AND EYES LIKE MINE GO AWAY AND NEVER COME BACK.
THAT'S BECAUSE...
BUT YOU'RE NOT THE SAME AS THEM!
I KNOW THAT, BUT-
WHAT IF I BECOME LIKE THEM?
I DON'T WANT TO LEAVE HERE...

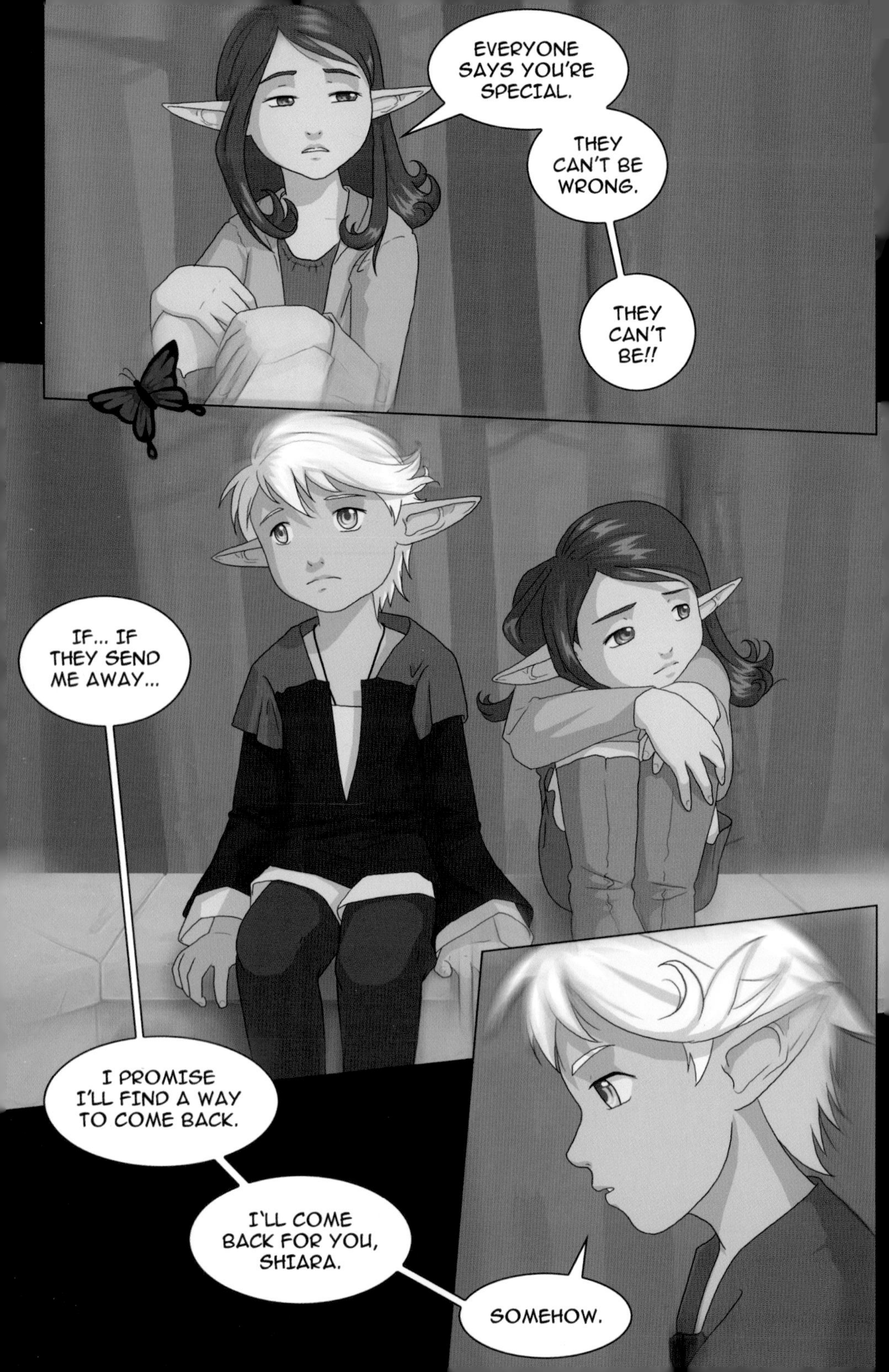
EVERYONE SAYS YOU'RE SPECIAL.
THEY CAN'T BE WRONG.
THEY CAN'T BE!!
IF... IF THEY SEND ME AWAY...
I PROMISE I'LL FIND A WAY TO COME BACK.
I'LL COME BACK FOR YOU, SHIARA.
SOMEHOW.

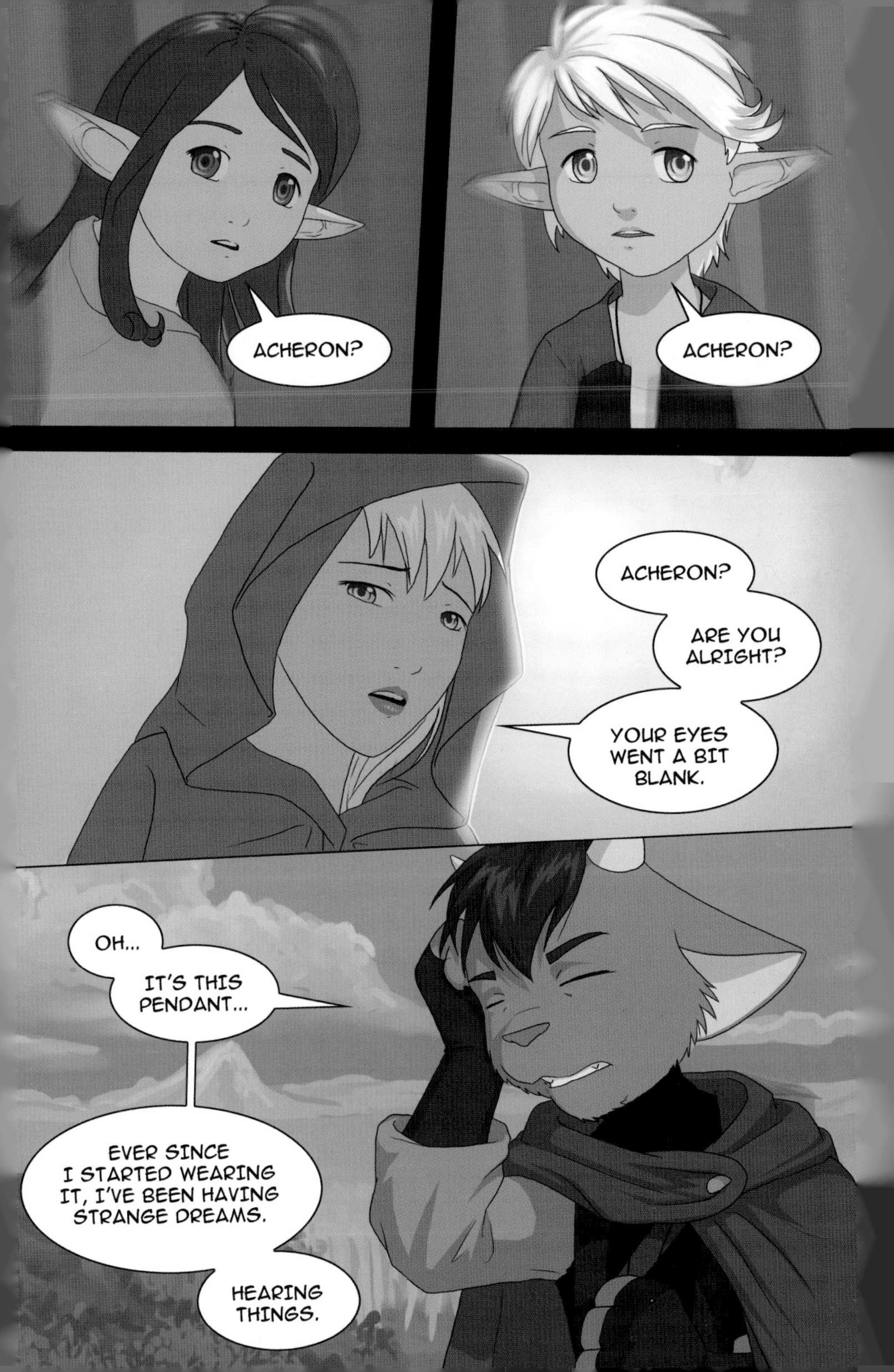
ACHERON?
ACHERON?
ACHERON?
ARE YOU ALRIGHT?
YOUR EYES WENT A BIT BLANK.
OH...
IT'S THIS PENDANT...
EVER SINCE I STARTED WEARING IT, I'VE BEEN HAVING STRANGE DREAMS.
HEARING THINGS.

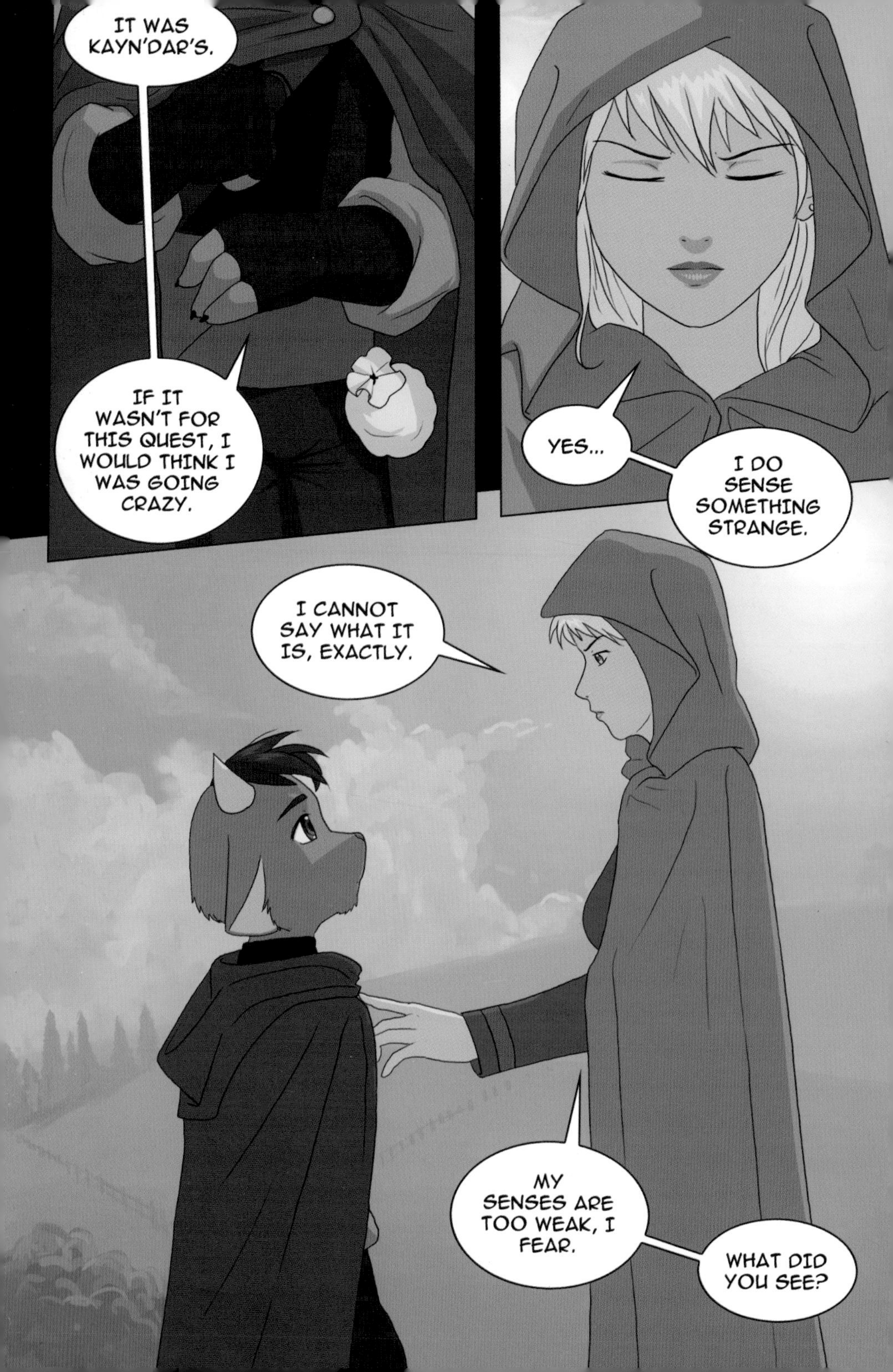
IT WAS KAYN'DAR'S.
IF IT WASN'T FOR THIS QUEST, I WOULD THINK I WAS GOING CRAZY.
YES...
I DO SENSE SOMETHING STRANGE.
I CANNOT SAY WHAT IT IS, EXACTLY.
MY SENSES ARE TOO WEAK, I FEAR.
WHAT DID YOU SEE?

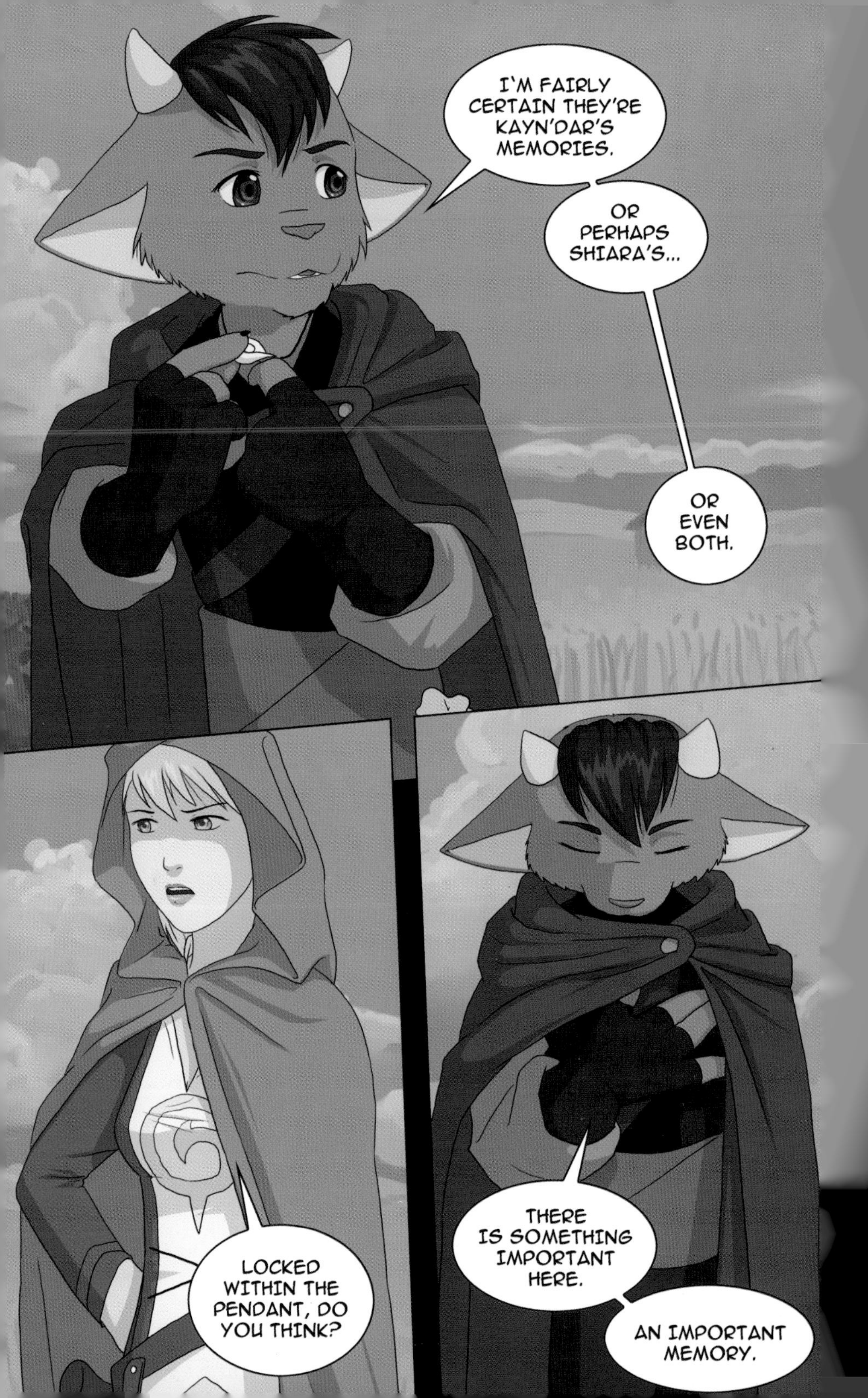
I'M FAIRLY CERTAIN THEY'RE KAYN'DAR'S MEMORIES.
OR PERHAPS SHIARA'S...
OR EVEN BOTH.
LOCKED WITHIN THE PENDANT, DO YOU THINK?
THERE IS SOMETHING IMPORTANT HERE.
AN IMPORTANT MEMORY.

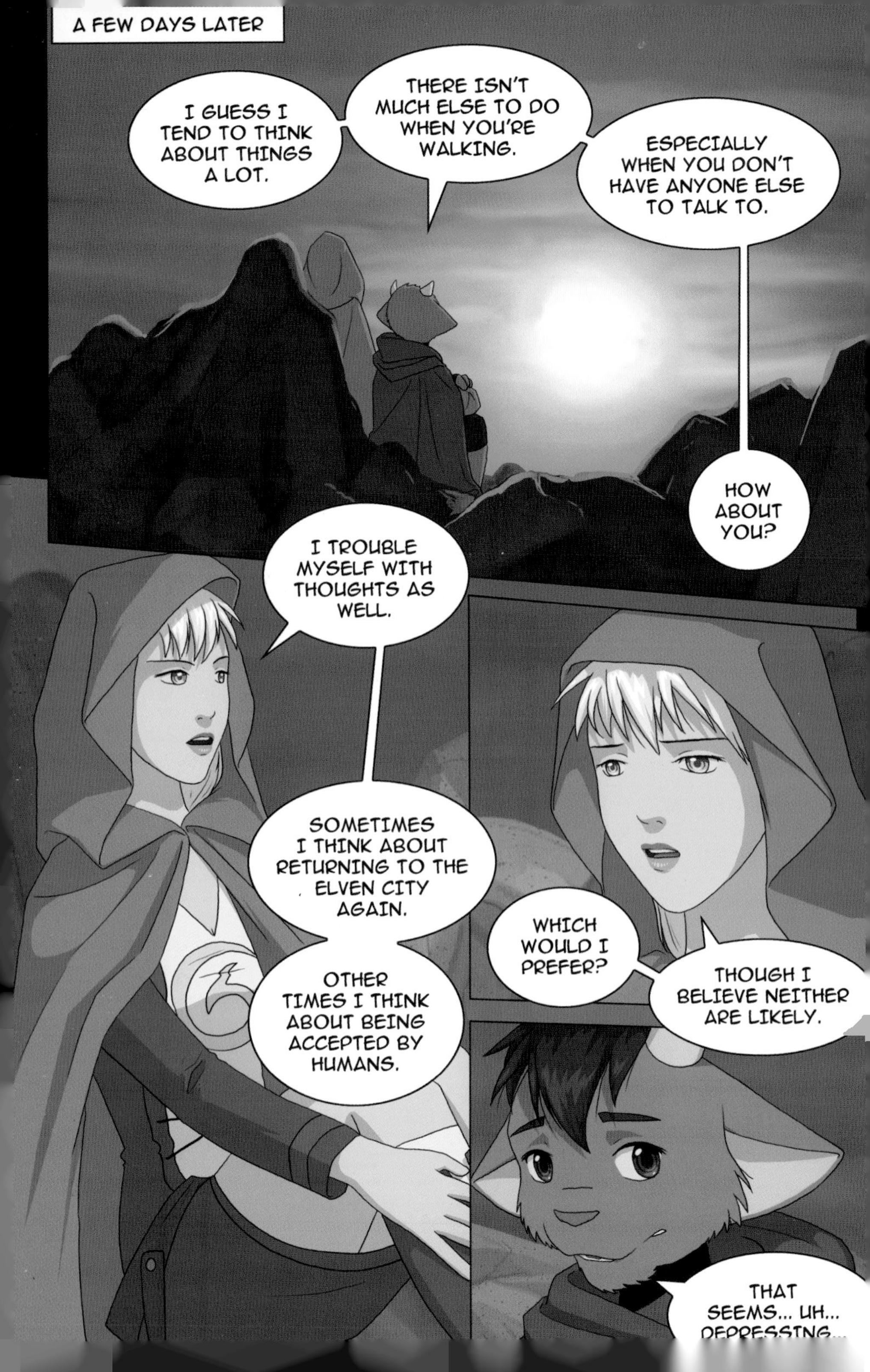
A FEW DAYS LATER
I GUESS I TEND TO THINK ABOUT THINGS A LOT.
THERE ISN'T MUCH ELSE TO DO WHEN YOU'RE WALKING.
ESPECIALLY WHEN YOU DON'T HAVE ANYONE ELSE TO TALK TO.
HOW ABOUT YOU?
I TROUBLE MYSELF WITH THOUGHTS AS WELL.
SOMETIMES I THINK ABOUT RETURNING TO THE ELVEN CITY AGAIN.
OTHER TIMES I THINK ABOUT BEING ACCEPTED BY HUMANS.
WHICH WOULD I PREFER?
THOUGH I BELIEVE NEITHER ARE LIKELY.
THAT SEEMS... UH...

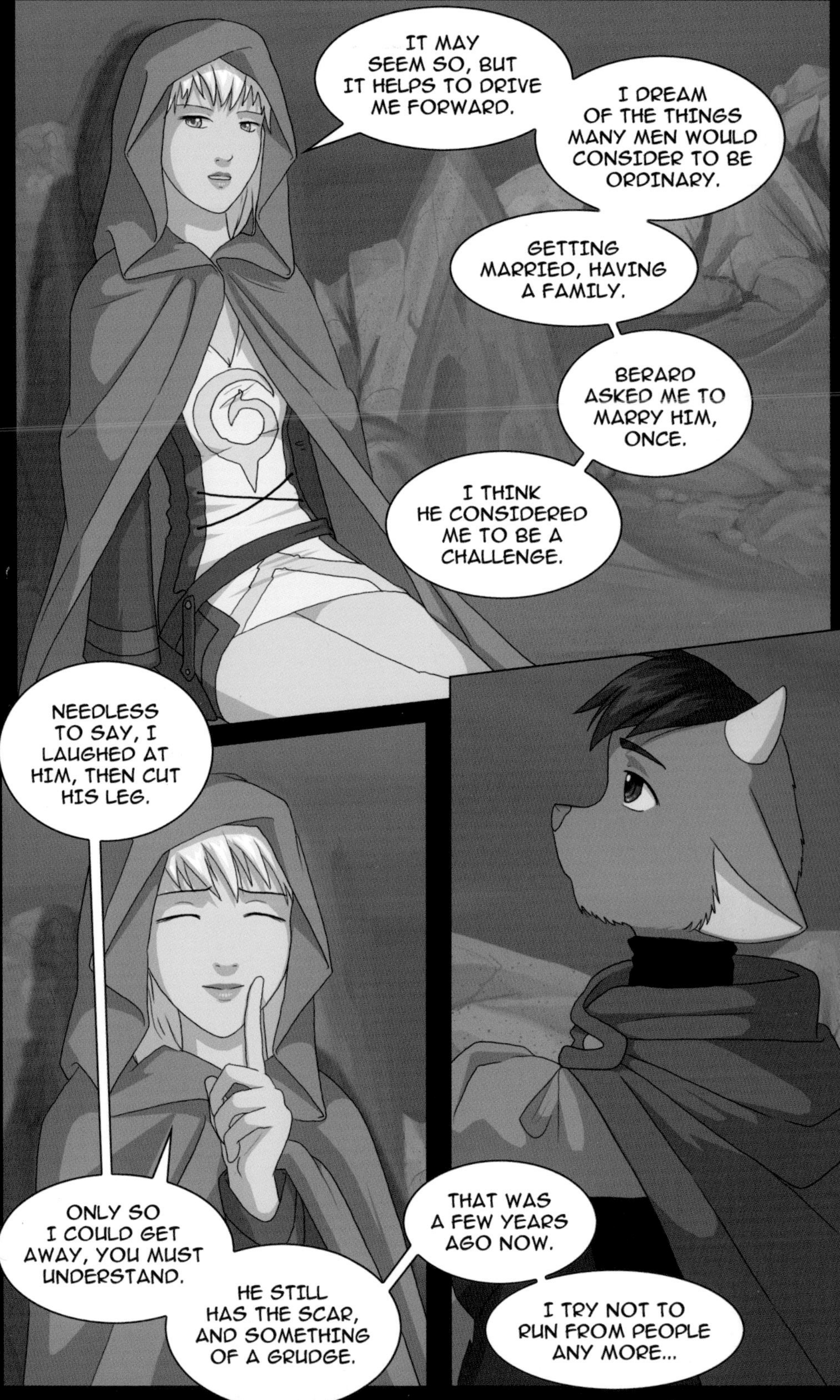
IT MAY SEEM SO, BUT IT HELPS TO DRIVE ME FORWARD.
I DREAM OF THE THINGS MANY MEN WOULD CONSIDER TO BE ORDINARY.
GETTING MARRIED, HAVING A FAMILY.
BERARD ASKED ME TO MARRY HIM, ONCE.
I THINK HE CONSIDERED ME TO BE A CHALLENGE.
NEEDLESS TO SAY, I LAUGHED AT HIM, THEN CUT HIS LEG.
ONLY SO I COULD GET AWAY, YOU MUST UNDERSTAND.
HE STILL HAS THE SCAR, AND SOMETHING OF A GRUDGE.
THAT WAS A FEW YEARS AGO NOW.
I TRY NOT TO RUN FROM PEOPLE ANY MORE...

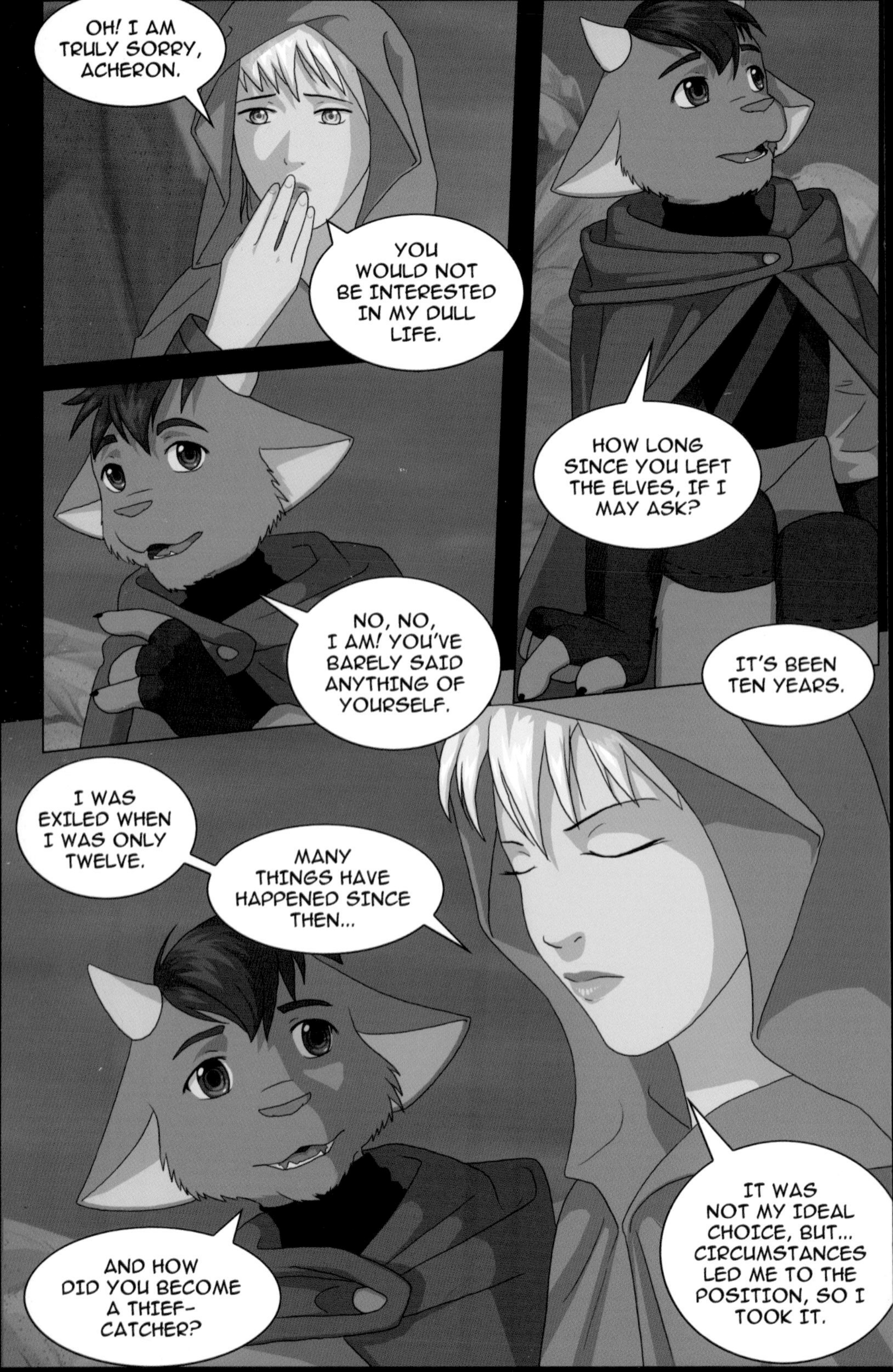
OH! I AM TRULY SORRY, ACHERON.
YOU WOULD NOT BE INTERESTED IN MY DULL LIFE.
NO, NO, I AM! YOU'VE BARELY SAID ANYTHING OF YOURSELF.
HOW LONG SINCE YOU LEFT THE ELVES, IF I MAY ASK?
IT'S BEEN TEN YEARS.
I WAS EXILED WHEN I WAS ONLY TWELVE.
MANY THINGS HAVE HAPPENED SINCE THEN...
AND HOW DID YOU BECOME A THIEF-CATCHER?
IT WAS NOT MY IDEAL CHOICE, BUT... CIRCUMSTANCES LED ME TO THE POSITION, SO I TOOK IT.

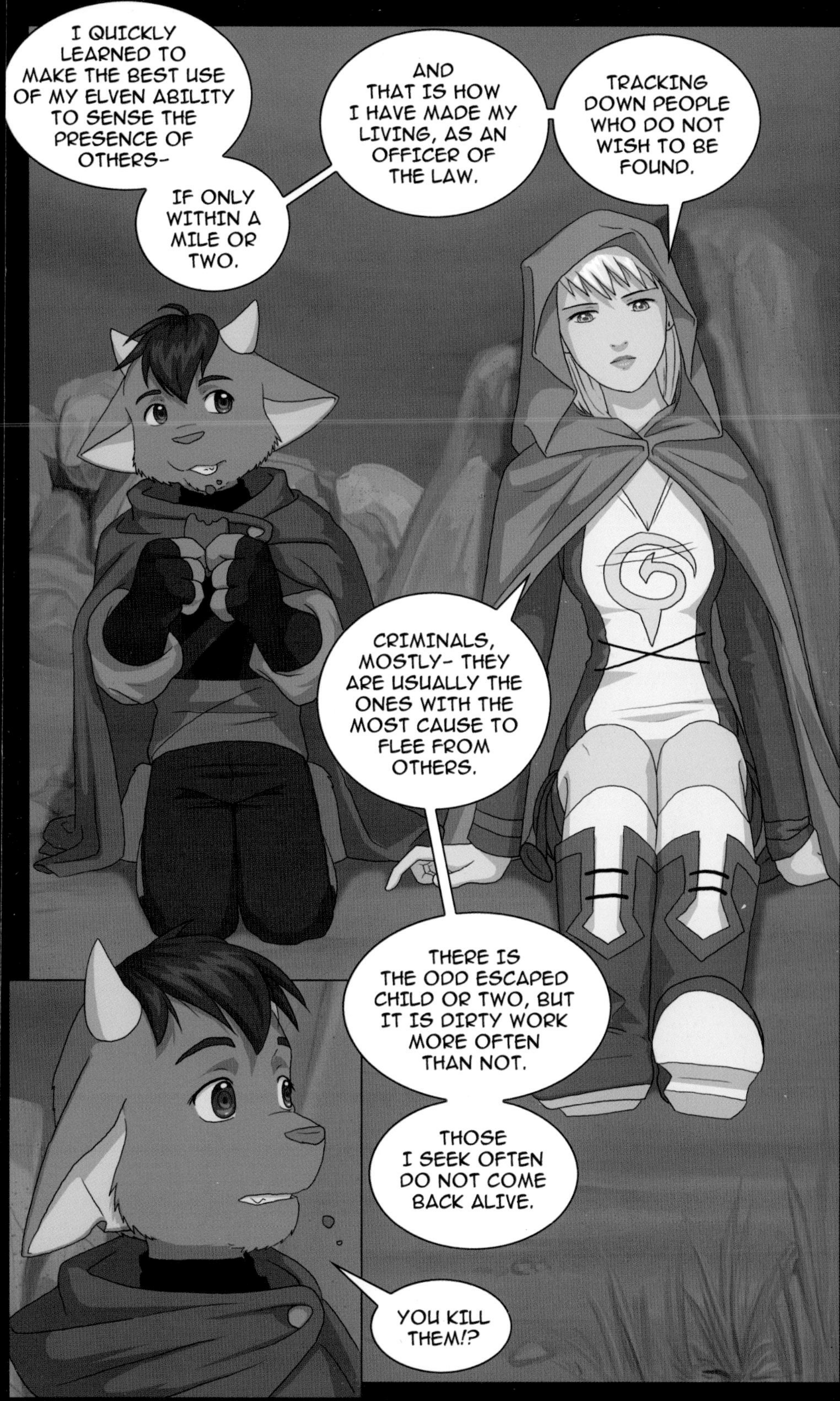
I QUICKLY LEARNED TO MAKE THE BEST USE OF MY ELVEN ABILITY TO SENSE THE PRESENCE OF OTHERS-
IF ONLY WITHIN A MILE OR TWO.
AND THAT IS HOW I HAVE MADE MY LIVING, AS AN OFFICER OF THE LAW.
TRACKING DOWN PEOPLE WHO DO NOT WISH TO BE FOUND.
CRIMINALS, MOSTLY- THEY ARE USUALLY THE ONES WITH THE MOST CAUSE TO FLEE FROM OTHERS.
THERE IS THE ODD ESCAPED CHILD OR TWO, BUT IT IS DIRTY WORK MORE OFTEN THAN NOT.
THOSE I SEEK OFTEN DO NOT COME BACK ALIVE.
YOU KILL THEM!?

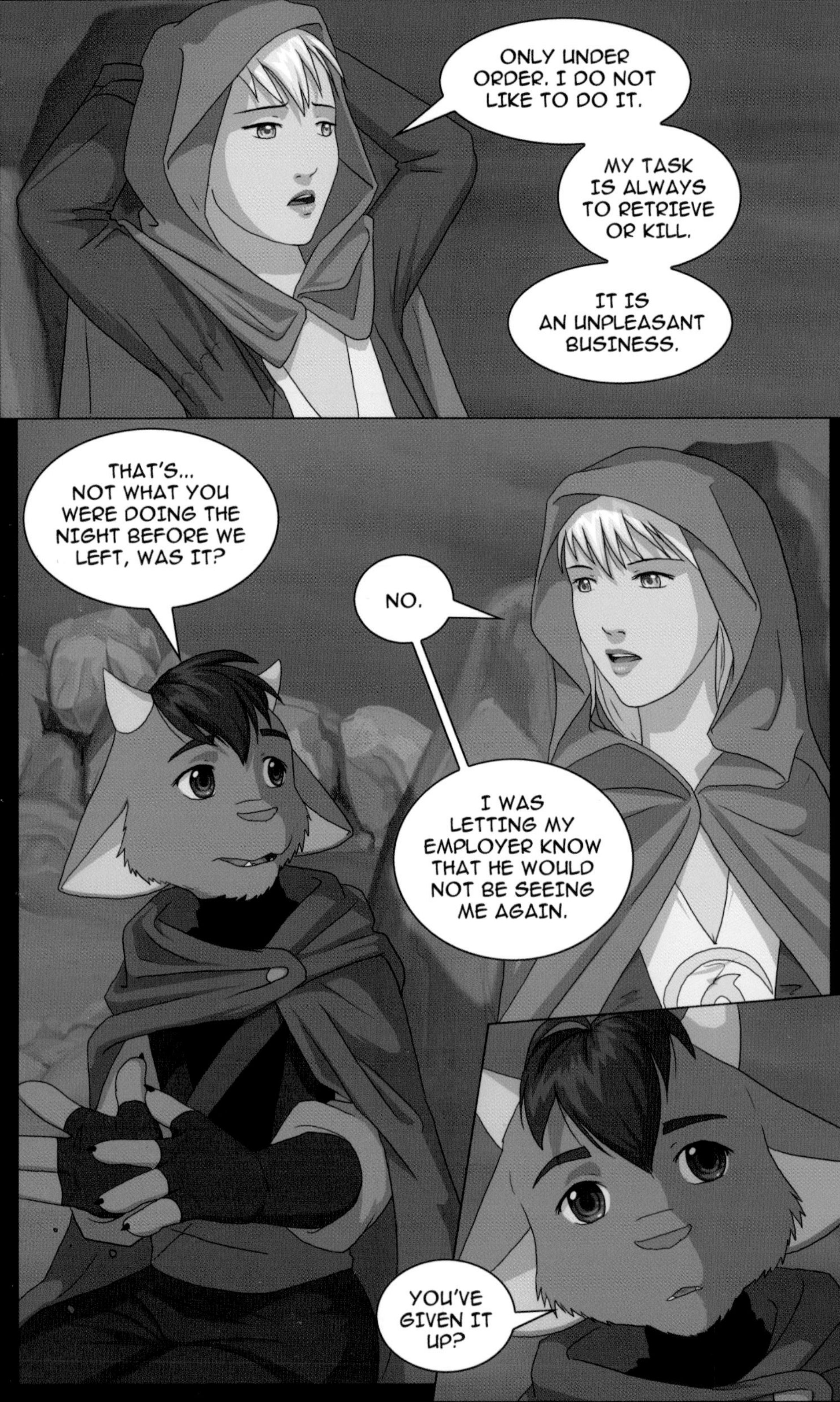
ONLY UNDER ORDER. I DO NOT LIKE TO DO IT.
MY TASK IS ALWAYS TO RETRIEVE OR KILL.
IT IS AN UNPLEASANT BUSINESS.
THAT'S... NOT WHAT YOU WERE DOING THE NIGHT BEFORE WE LEFT, WAS IT?
NO.
I WAS LETTING MY EMPLOYER KNOW THAT HE WOULD NOT BE SEEING ME AGAIN.
YOU'VE GIVEN IT UP?

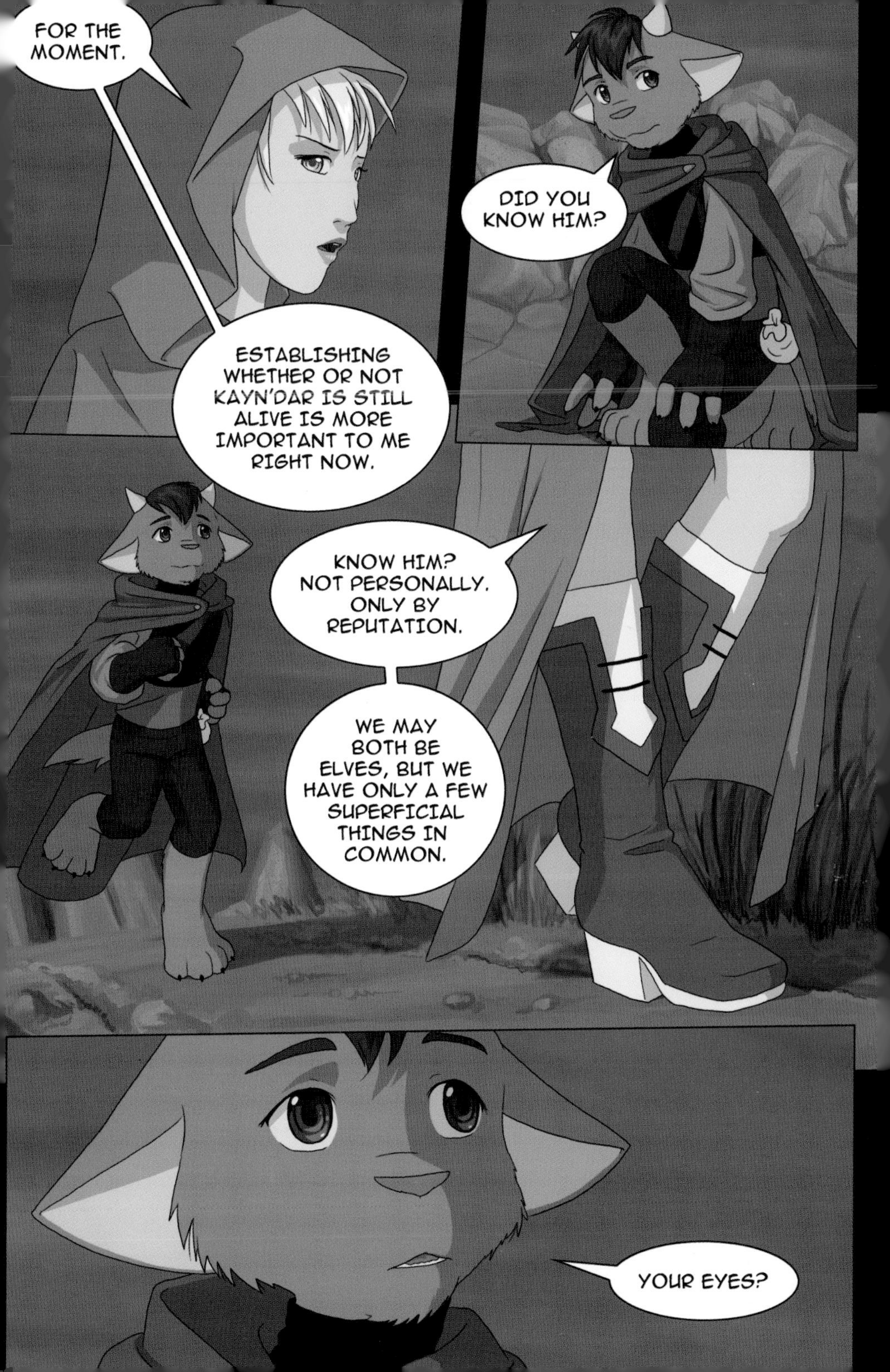
FOR THE MOMENT.
ESTABLISHING WHETHER OR NOT KAYN'DAR IS STILL ALIVE IS MORE IMPORTANT TO ME RIGHT NOW.
DID YOU KNOW HIM?
KNOW HIM? NOT PERSONALLY. ONLY BY REPUTATION.
WE MAY BOTH BE ELVES, BUT WE HAVE ONLY A FEW SUPERFICIAL THINGS IN COMMON.
YOUR EYES?

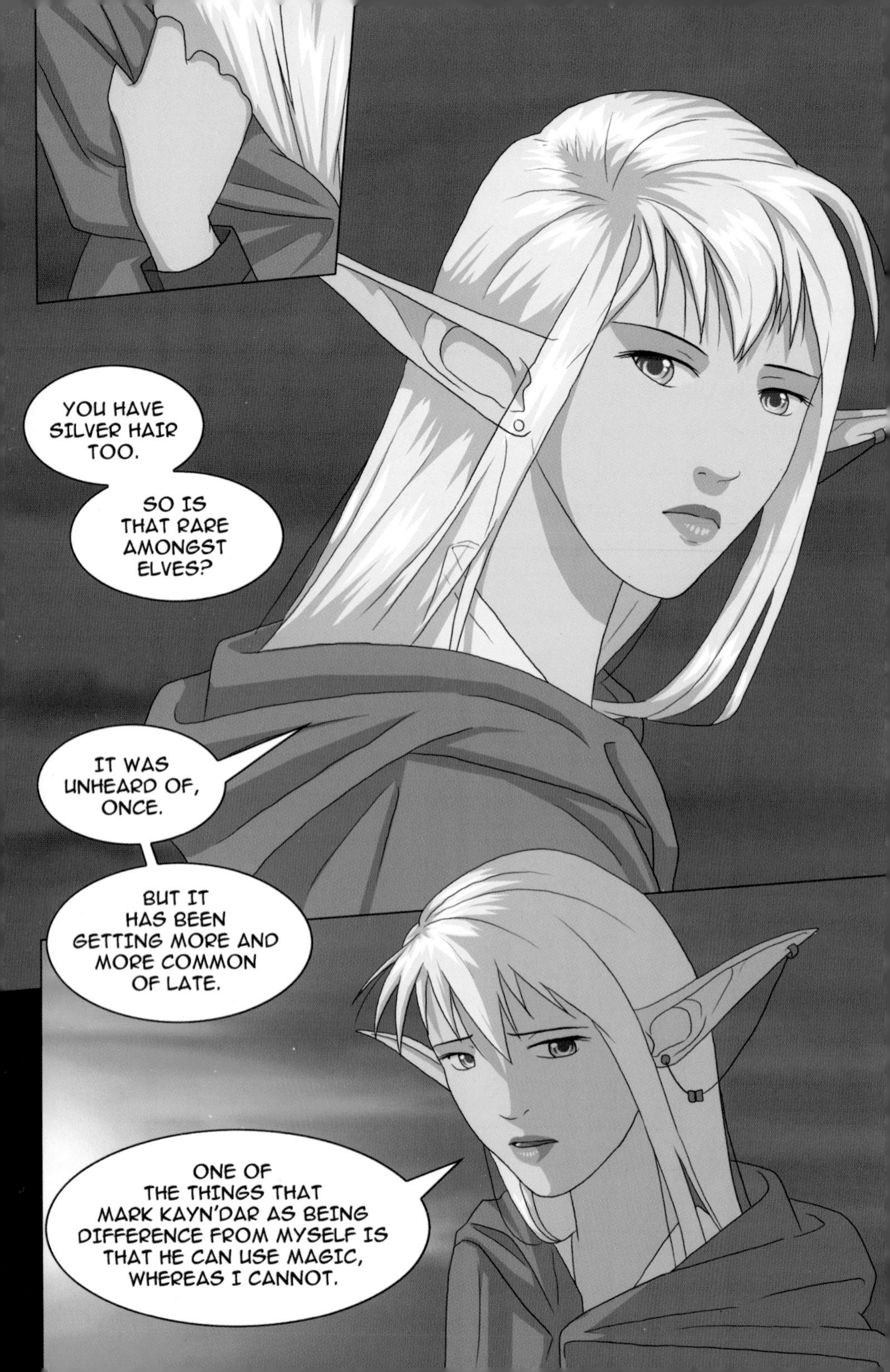
YOU HAVE SILVER HAIR TOO.
SO IS THAT RARE AMONGST ELVES?
IT WAS UNHEARD OF, ONCE.
BUT IT HAS BEEN GETTING MORE AND MORE COMMON OF LATE.
ONE OF THE THINGS THAT MARK KAYN'DAR AS BEING DIFFERENCE FROM MYSELF IS THAT HE CAN USE MAGIC, WHEREAS I CANNOT.

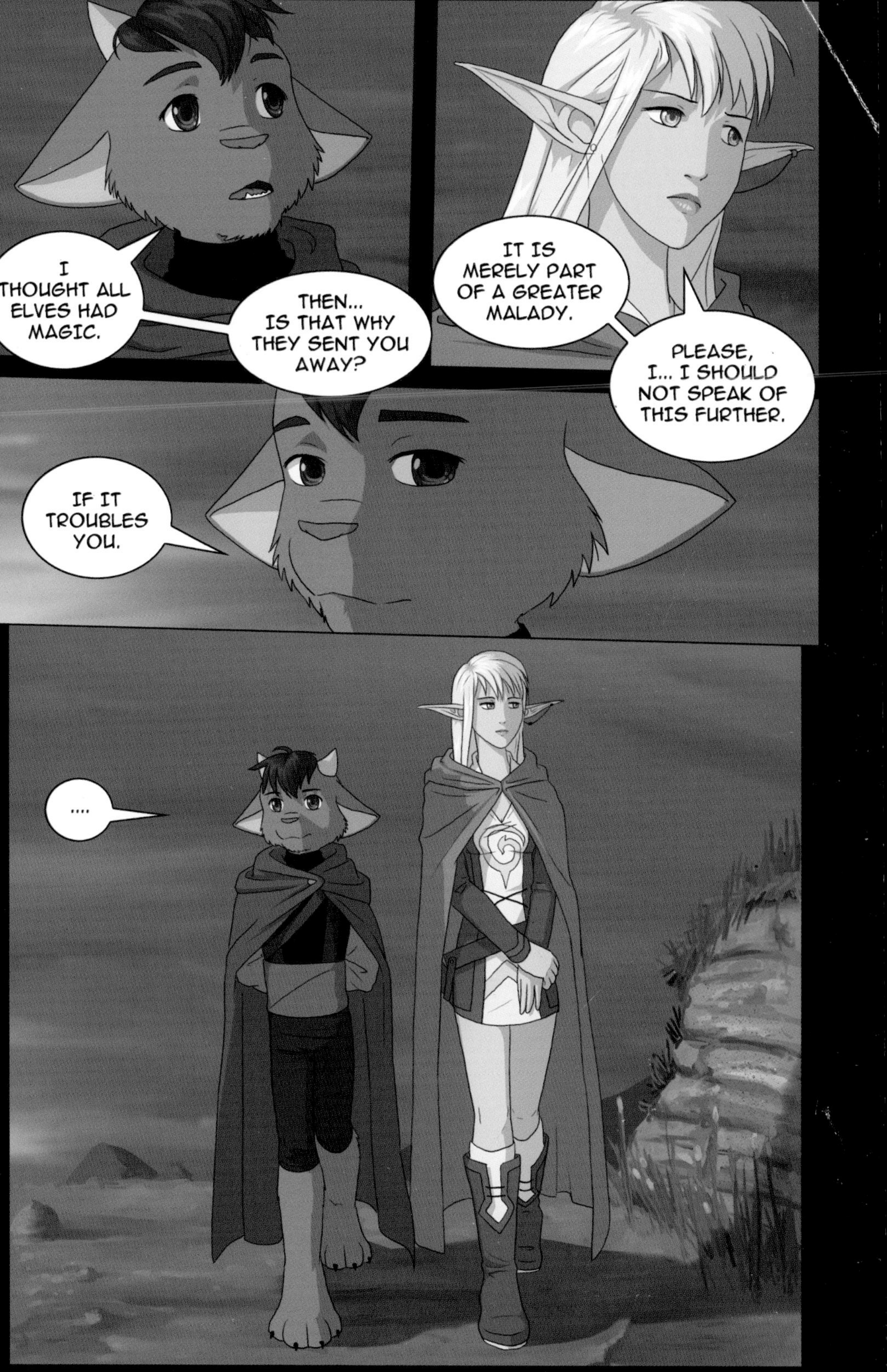
I THOUGHT ALL ELVES HAD MAGIC.
THEN... IS THAT WHY THEY SENT YOU AWAY?
IT IS MERELY PART OF A GREATER MALADY.
PLEASE, I... I SHOULD NOT SPEAK OF THIS FURTHER.
IF IT TROUBLES YOU.
....

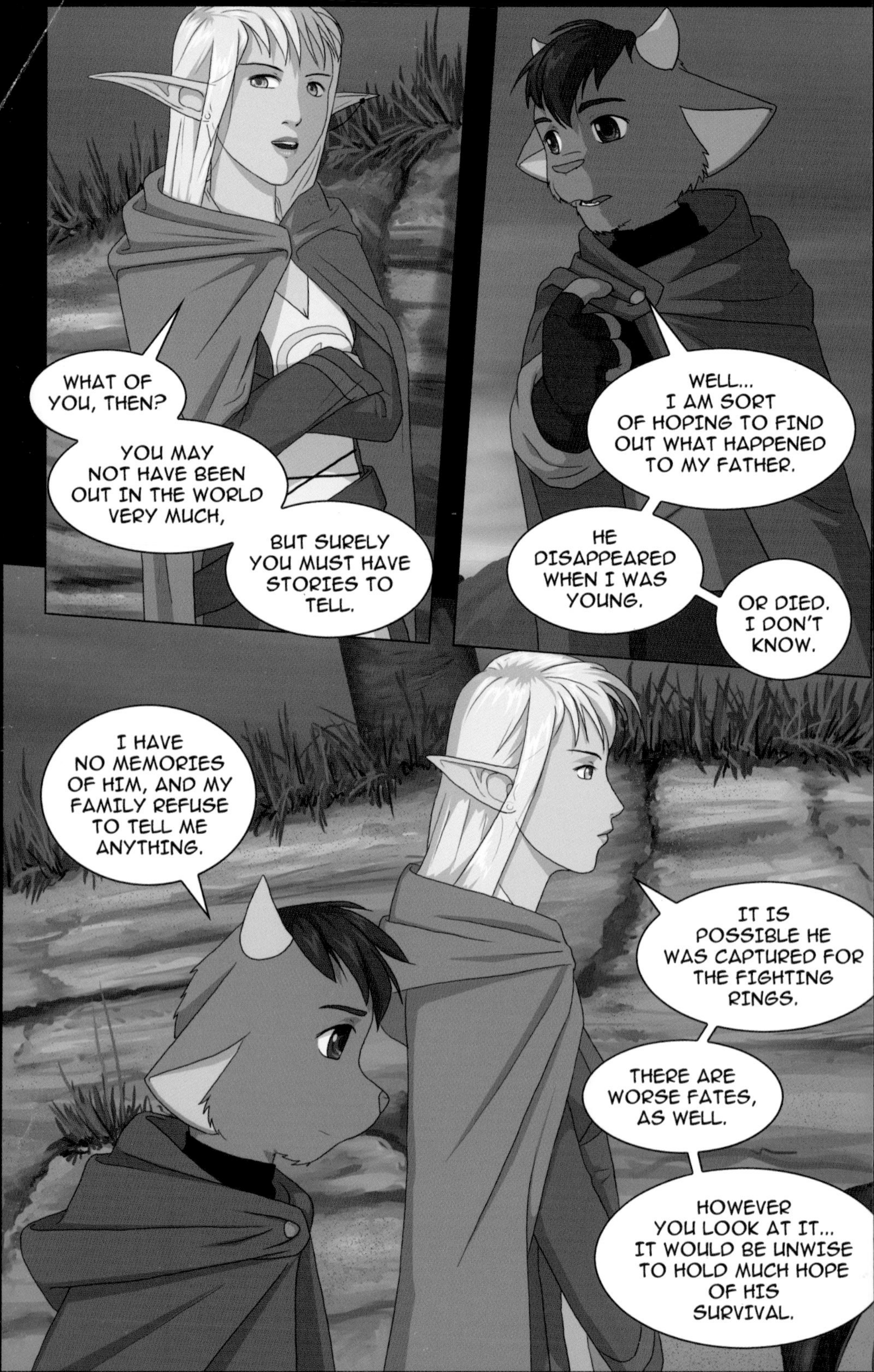
WHAT OF YOU, THEN?
YOU MAY NOT HAVE BEEN OUT IN THE WORLD VERY MUCH,
BUT SURELY YOU MUST HAVE STORIES TO TELL.
WELL... I AM SORT OF HOPING TO FIND OUT WHAT HAPPENED TO MY FATHER.
HE DISAPPEARED WHEN I WAS YOUNG.
OR DIED. I DON'T KNOW.
I HAVE NO MEMORIES OF HIM, AND MY FAMILY REFUSE TO TELL ME ANYTHING.
IT IS POSSIBLE HE WAS CAPTURED FOR THE FIGHTING RINGS.
THERE ARE WORSE FATES, AS WELL.
HOWEVER YOU LOOK AT IT... IT WOULD BE UNWISE TO HOLD MUCH HOPE OF HIS SURVIVAL.

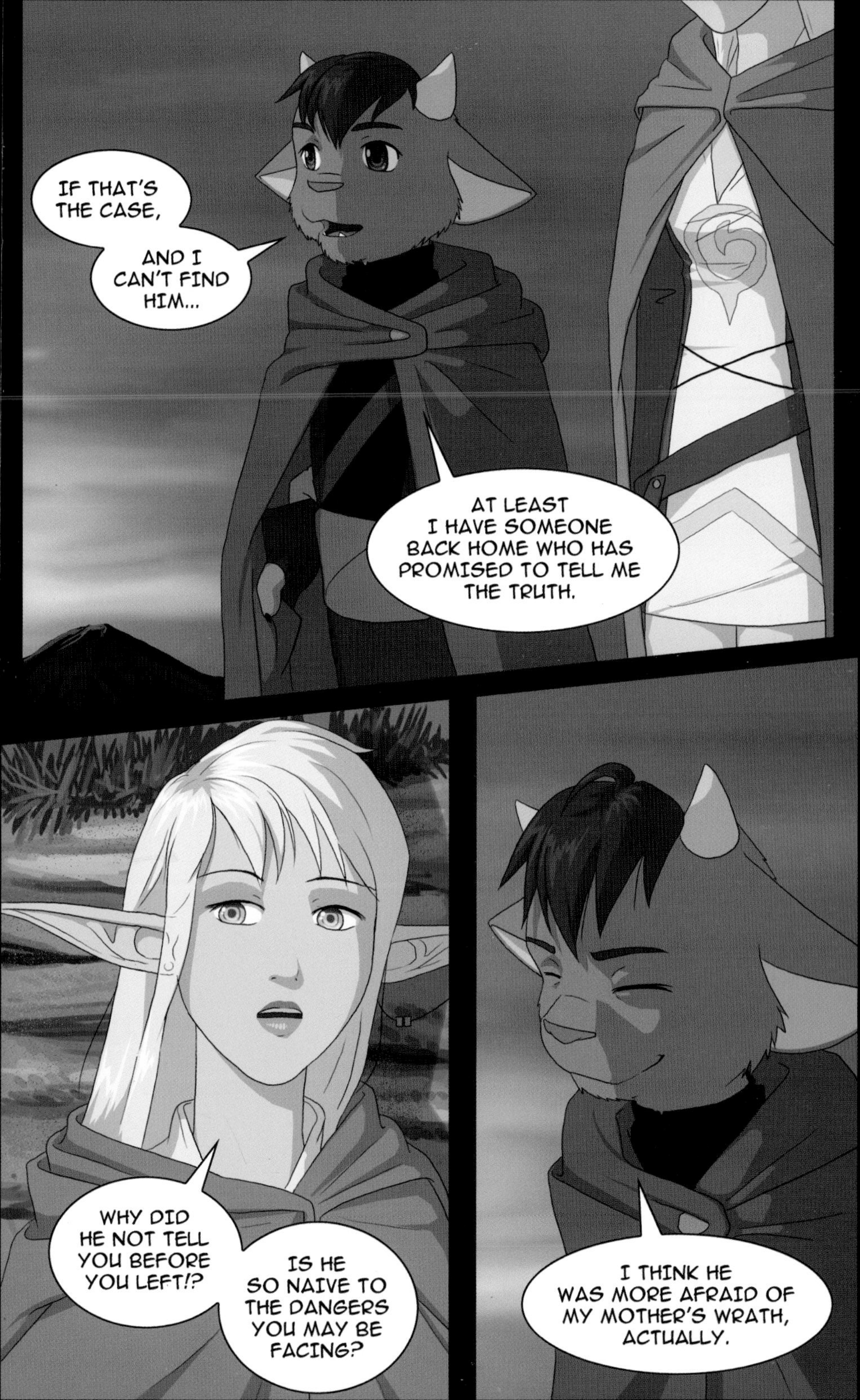
IF THAT'S THE CASE,
AND I CAN'T FIND HIM...
AT LEAST I HAVE SOMEONE BACK HOME WHO HAS PROMISED TO TELL ME THE TRUTH.
WHY DID HE NOT TELL YOU BEFORE YOU LEFT!?
IS HE SO NAIVE TO THE DANGERS YOU MAY BE FACING?
I THINK HE WAS MORE AFRAID OF MY MOTHER'S WRATH, ACTUALLY.

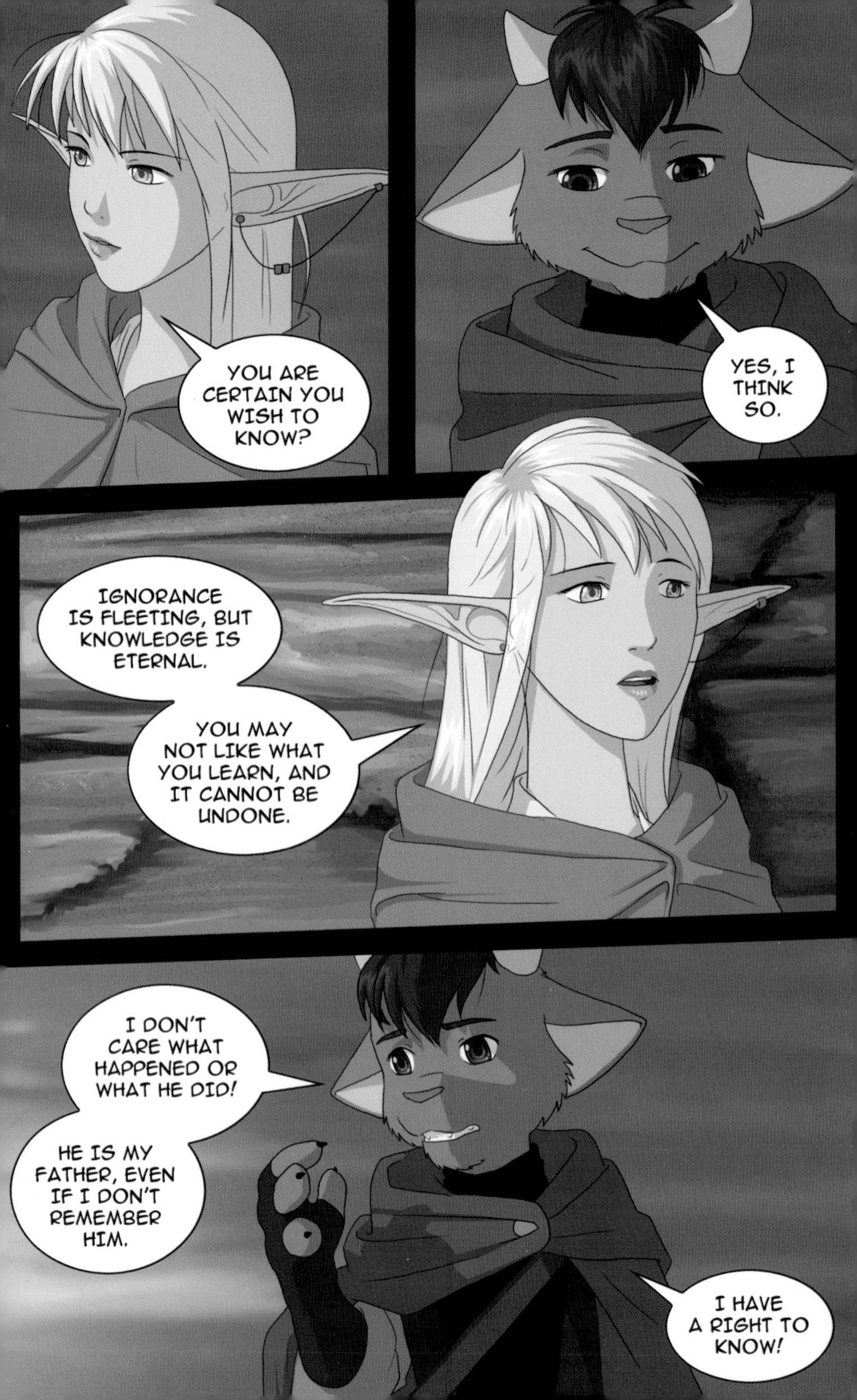
YOU ARE CERTAIN YOU WISH TO KNOW?
YES, I THINK SO.
IGNORANCE IS FLEETING, BUT KNOWLEDGE IS ETERNAL.
YOU MAY NOT LIKE WHAT YOU LEARN, AND IT CANNOT BE UNDONE.
I DON'T CARE WHAT HAPPENED OR WHAT HE DID!
HE IS MY FATHER, EVEN IF I DON'T REMEMBER HIM.
I HAVE A RIGHT TO KNOW!

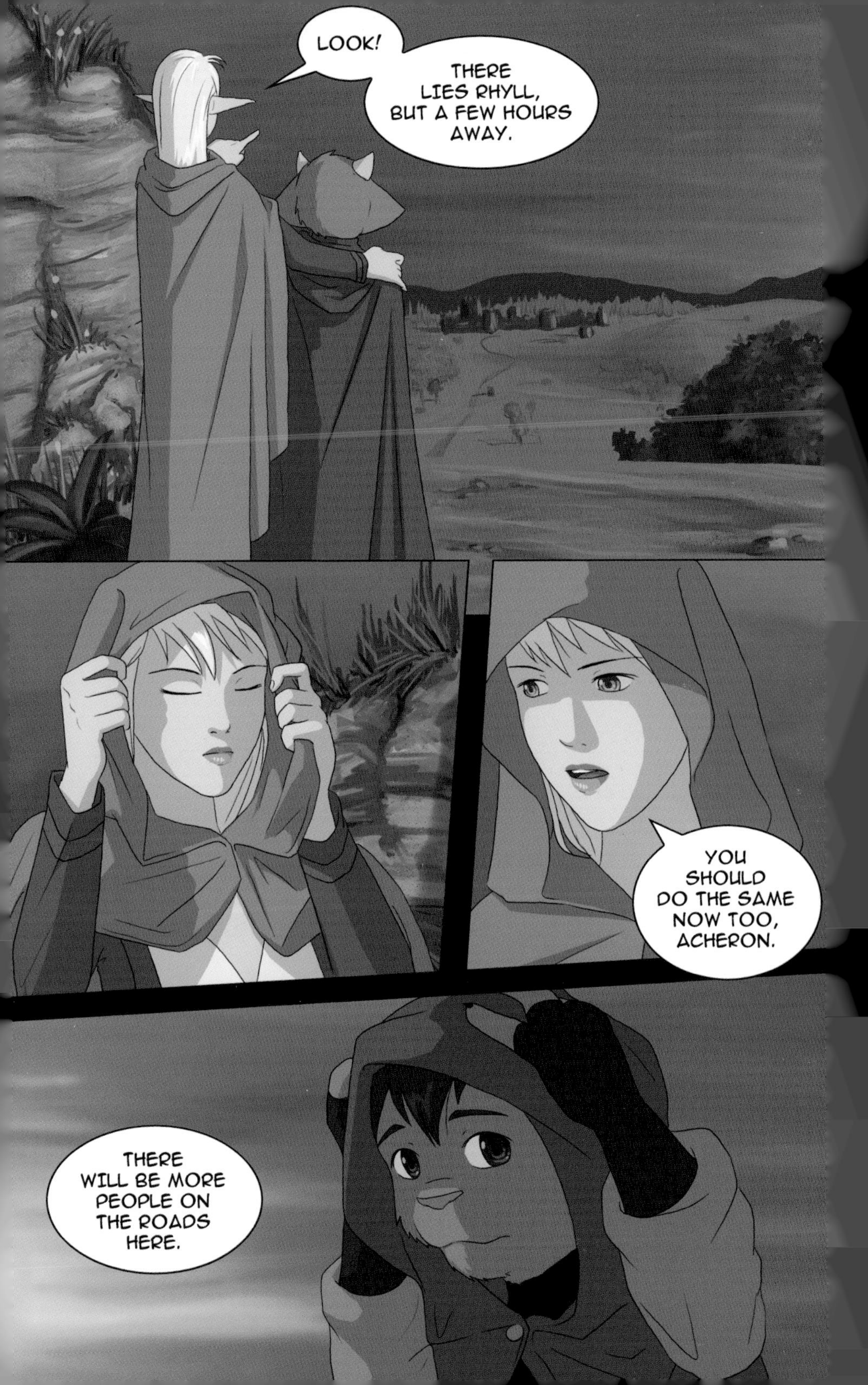
LOOK!
THERE LIES RHYLL, BUT A FEW HOURS AWAY.
YOU SHOULD DO THE SAME NOW TOO, ACHERON.
THERE WILL BE MORE PEOPLE ON THE ROADS HERE.

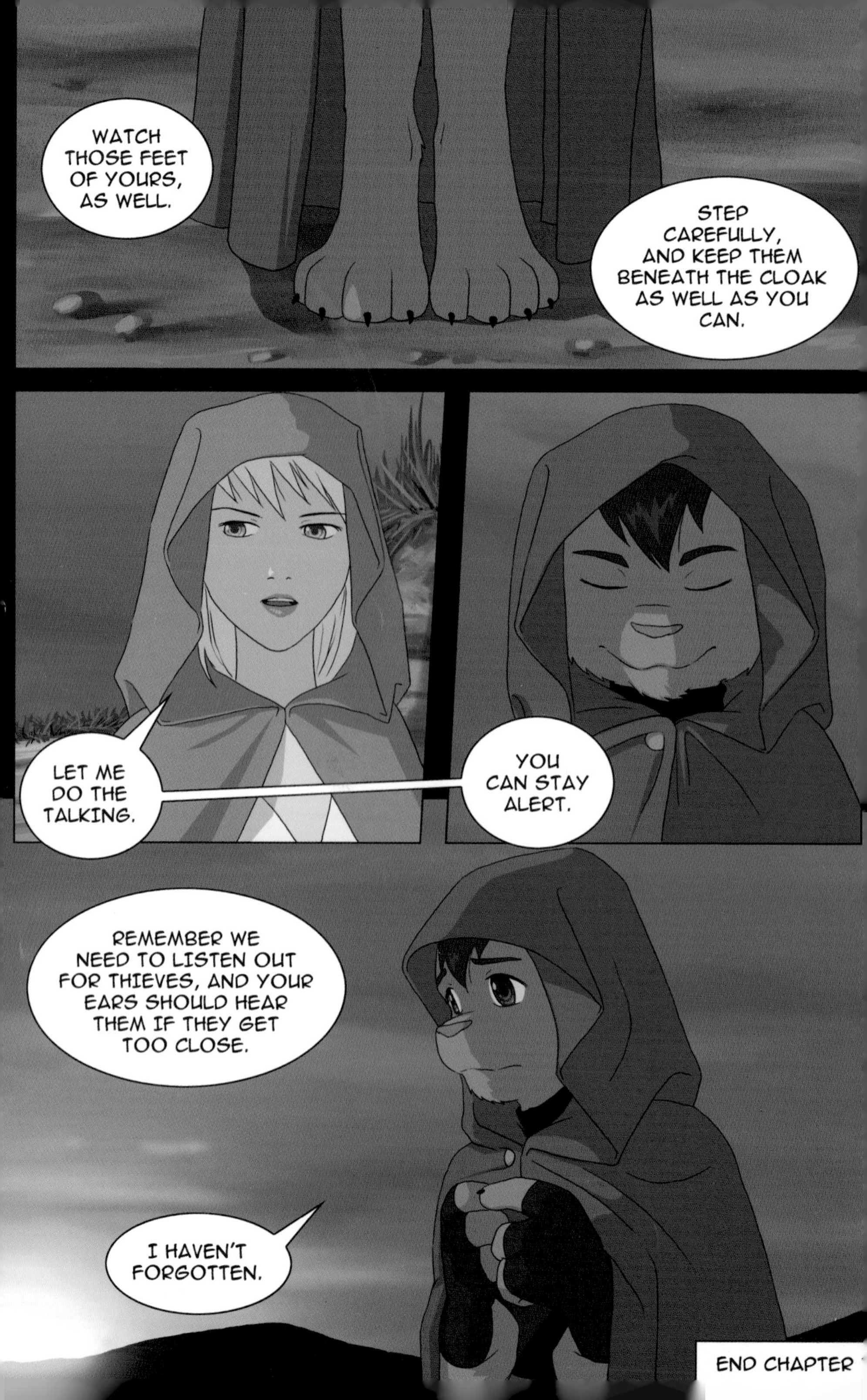
WATCH THOSE FEET OF YOURS, AS WELL.
STEP CAREFULLY, AND KEEP THEM BENEATH THE CLOAK AS WELL AS YOU CAN.
LET ME DO THE TALKING.
YOU CAN STAY ALERT.
REMEMBER WE NEED TO LISTEN OUT FOR THIEVES, AND YOUR EARS SHOULD HEAR THEM IF THEY GET TOO CLOSE.
I HAVEN'T FORGOTTEN.
END CHAPTER

CHAPTER 8 :CRYPTIC CLUES

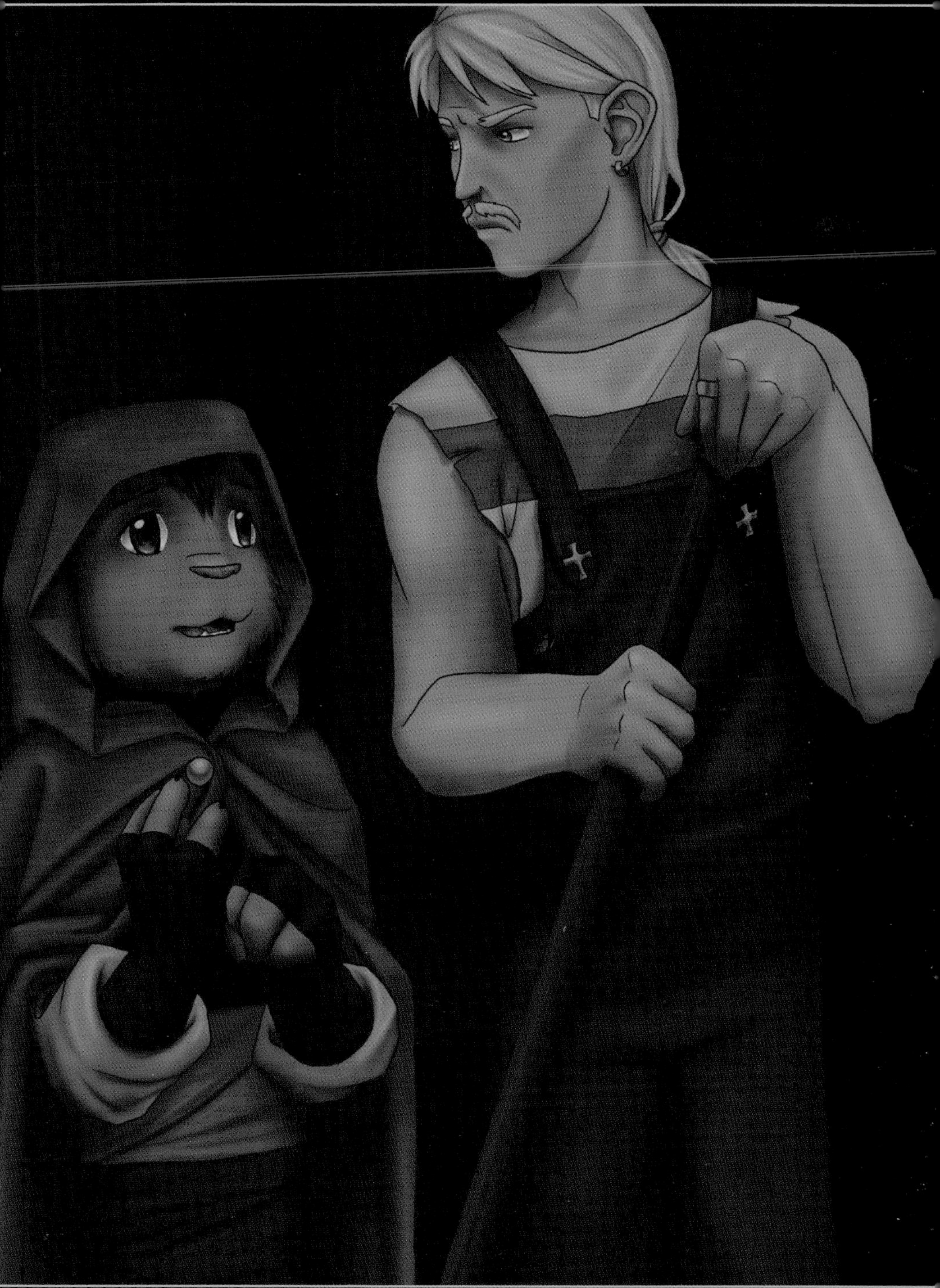

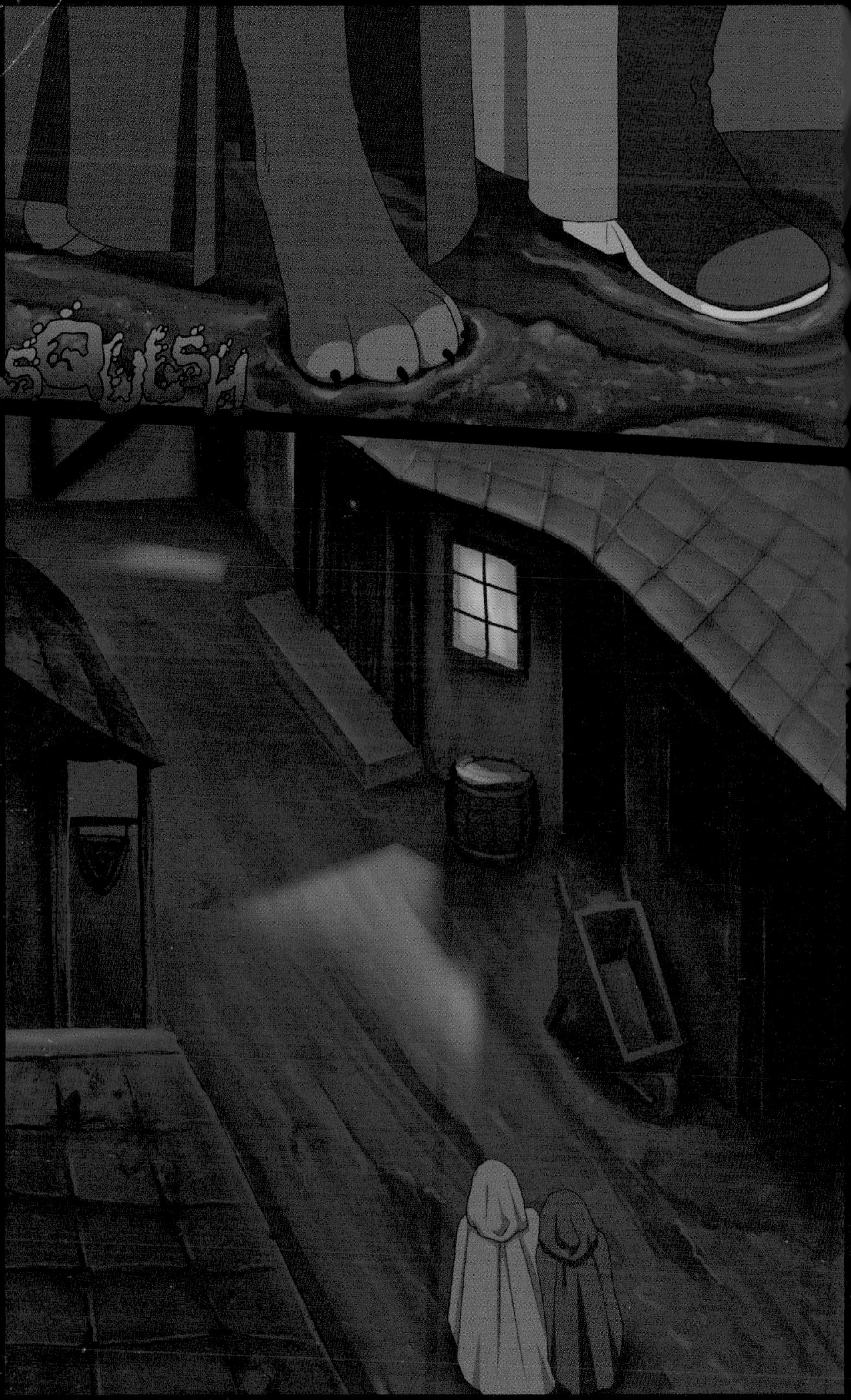
SQUISH

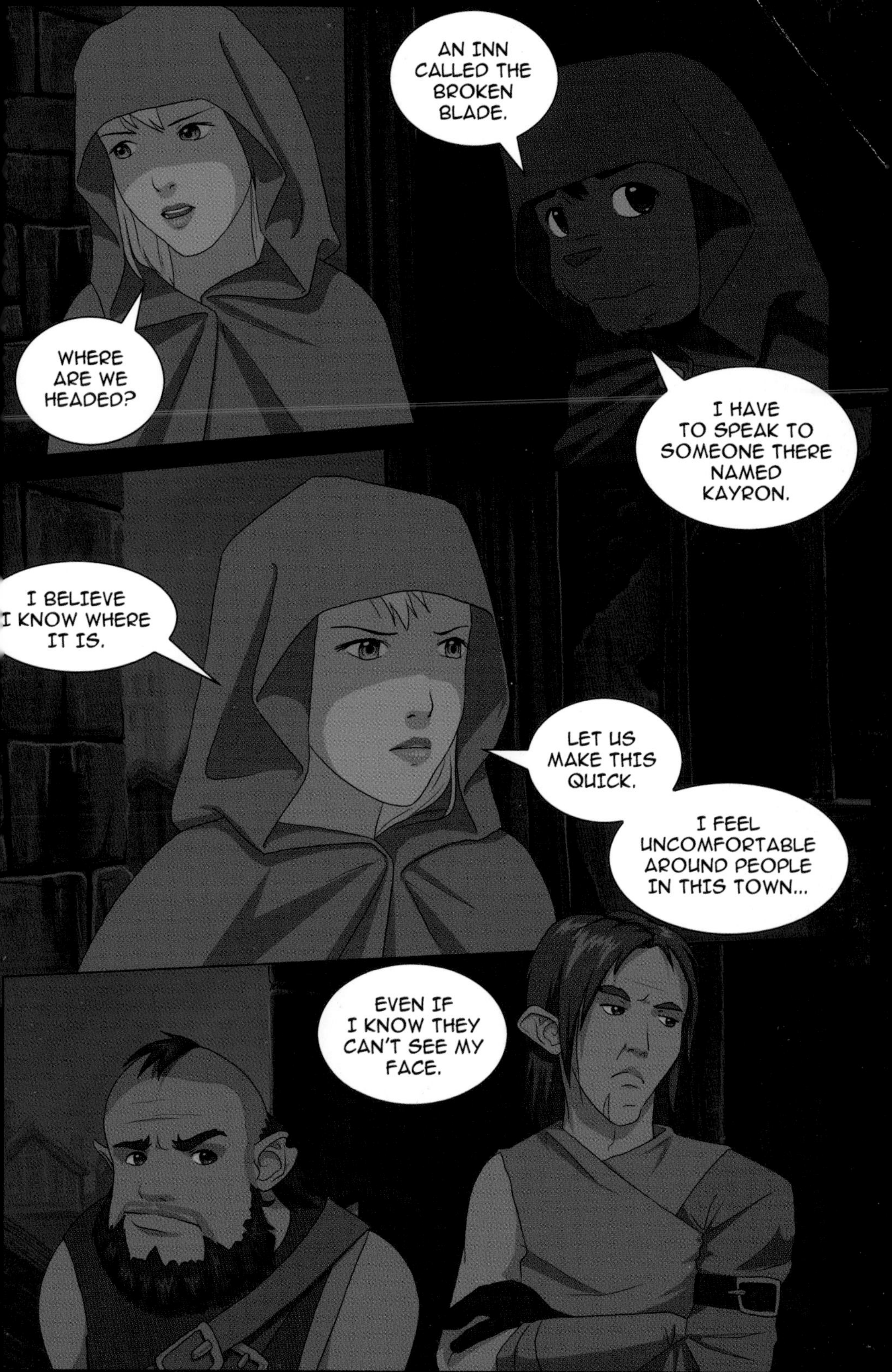
WHERE ARE WE HEADED?
AN INN CALLED THE BROKEN BLADE.
I HAVE TO SPEAK TO SOMEONE THERE NAMED KAYRON.
I BELIEVE I KNOW WHERE IT IS.
LET US MAKE THIS QUICK.
I FEEL UNCOMFORTABLE AROUND PEOPLE IN THIS TOWN...
EVEN IF I KNOW THEY CAN'T SEE MY FACE.

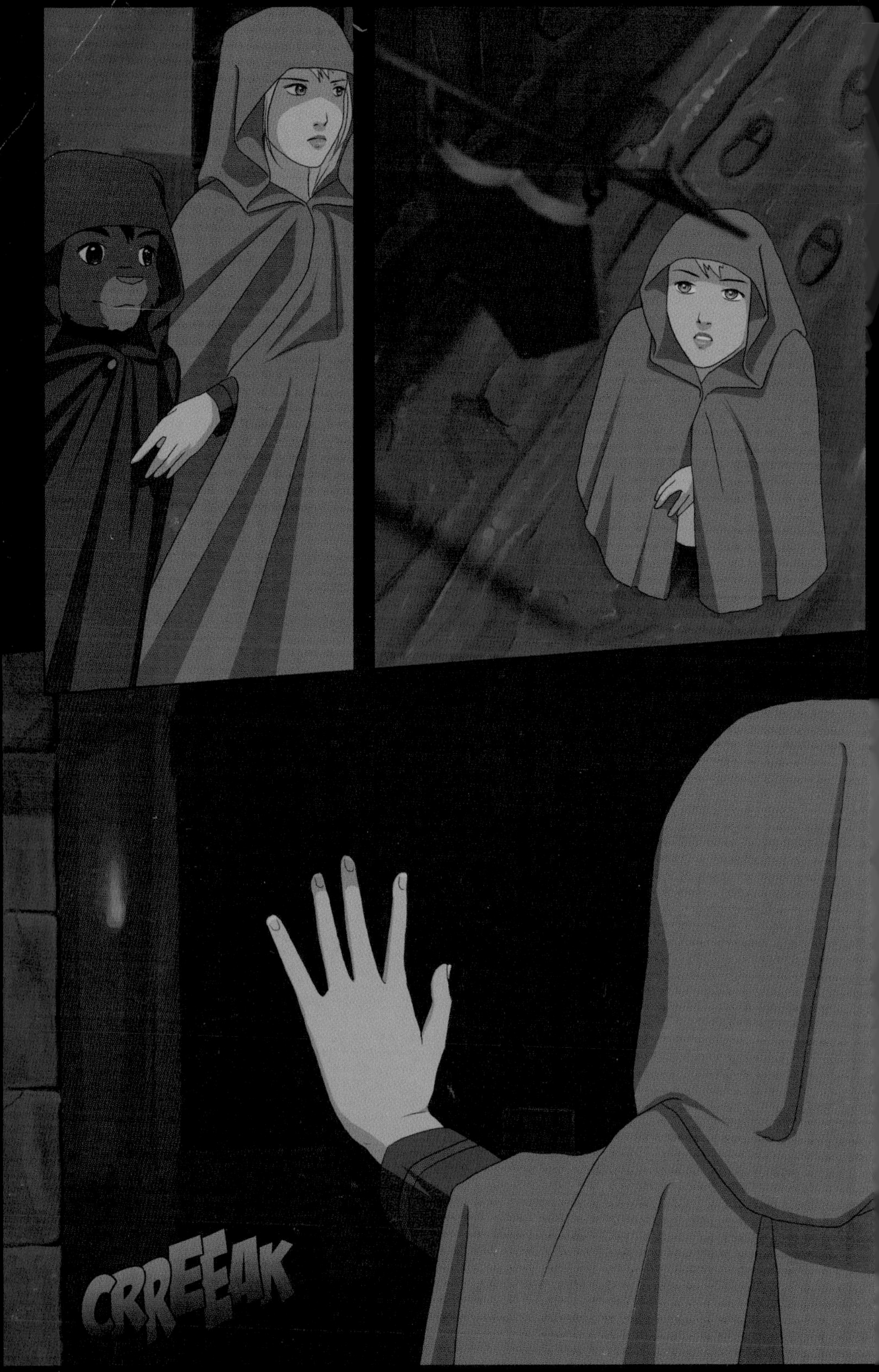
CRREEAK

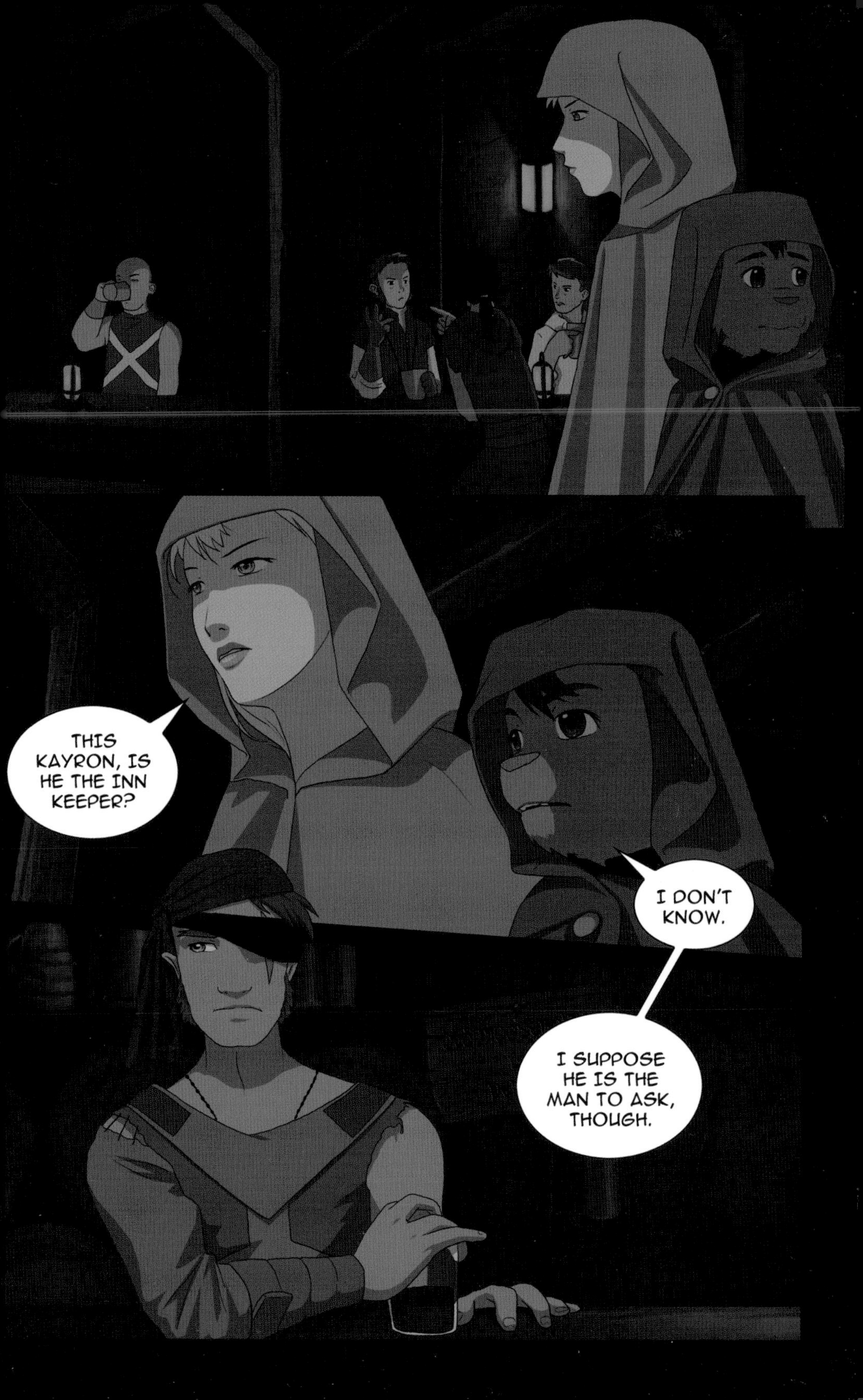
THIS KAYRON, IS HE THE INN KEEPER?
I DON'T KNOW.
I SUPPOSE HE IS THE MAN TO ASK, THOUGH.

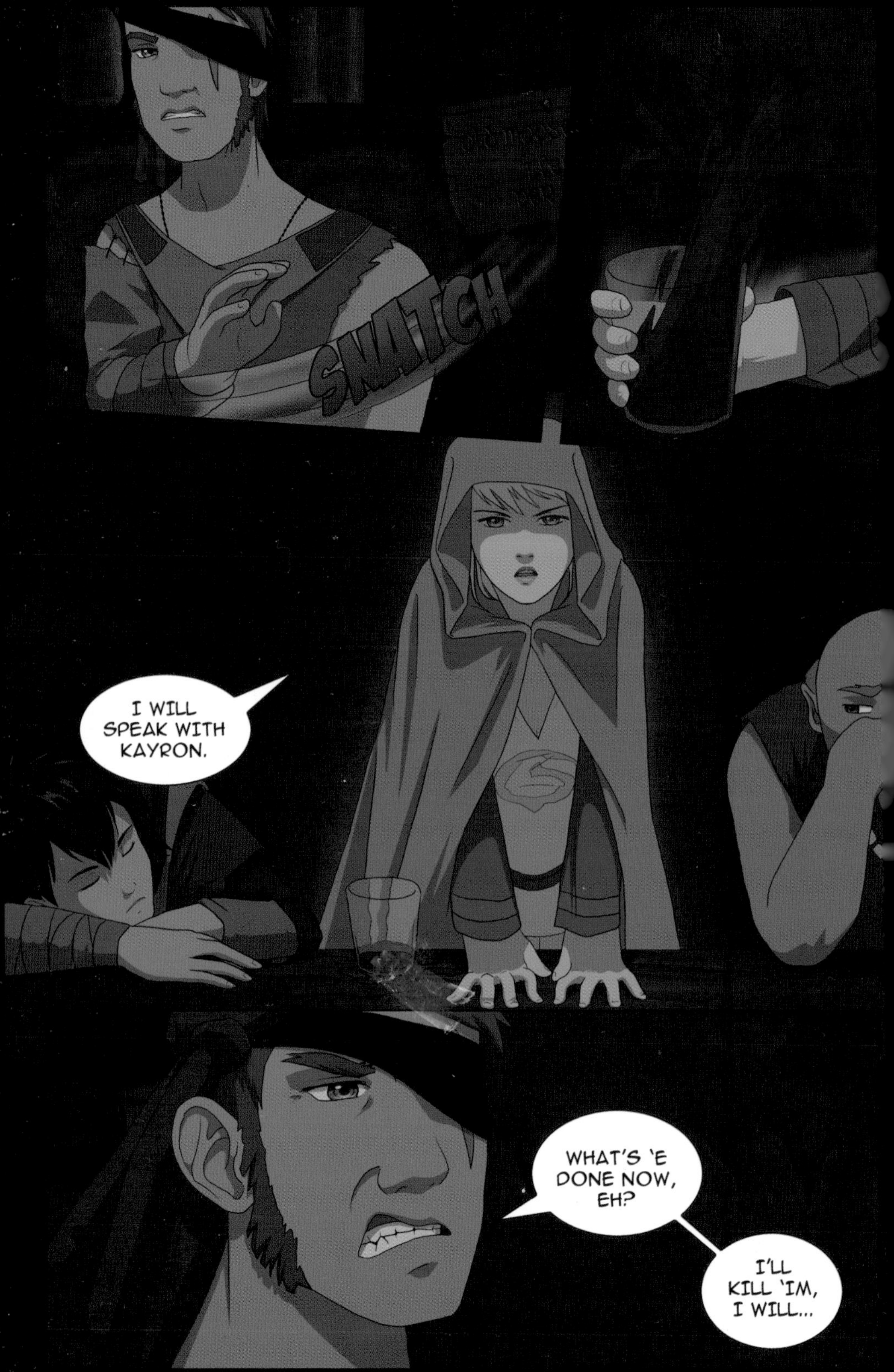
SNATCH
I WILL SPEAK WITH KAYRON.
WHAT'S 'E DONE NOW, EH?
I'LL KILL 'IM, I WILL...

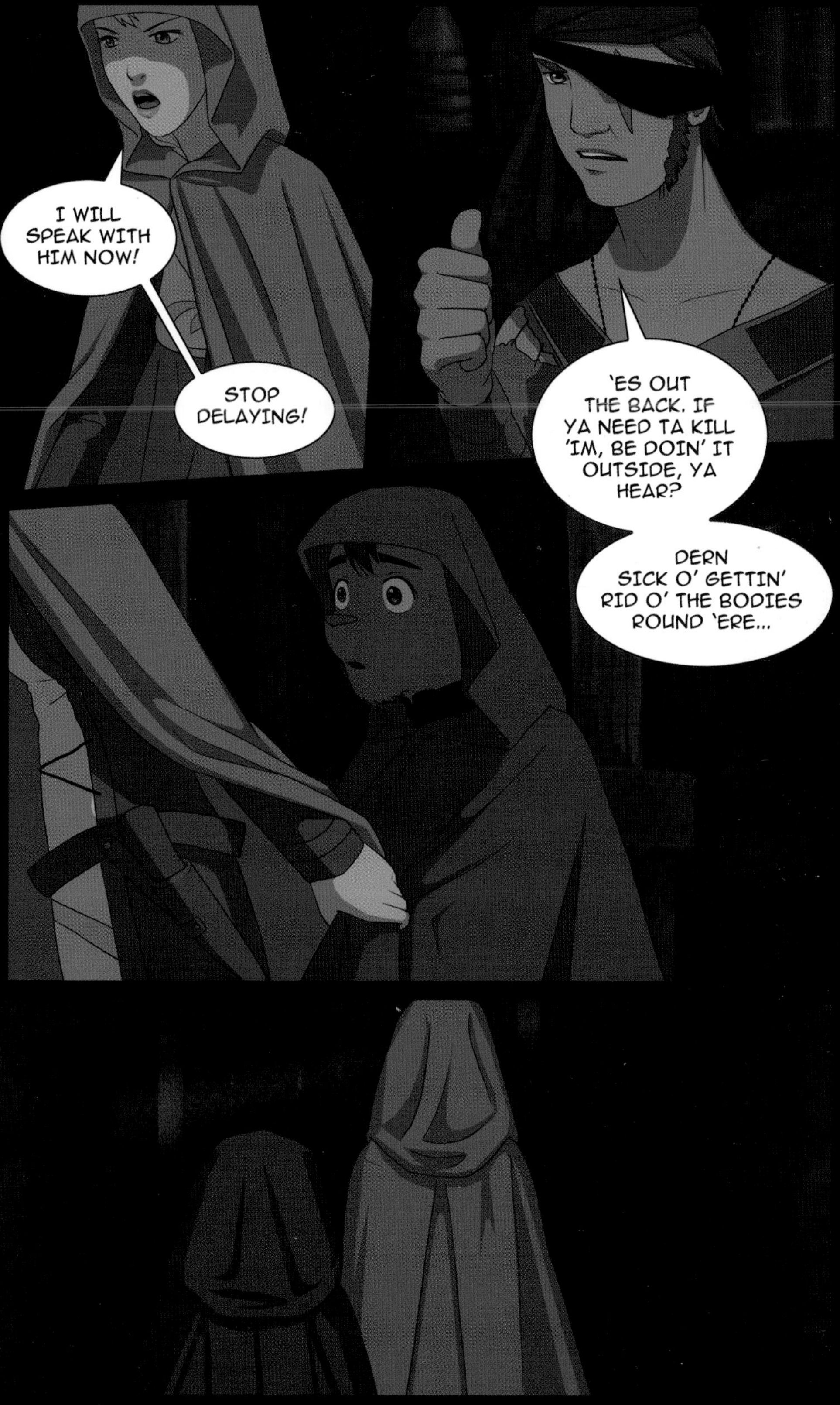
I WILL SPEAK WITH HIM NOW!
STOP DELAYING!
'ES OUT THE BACK. IF YA NEED TA KILL 'IM, BE DOIN' IT OUTSIDE, YA HEAR?
DERN SICK O' GETTIN' RID O' THE BODIES ROUND 'ERE...

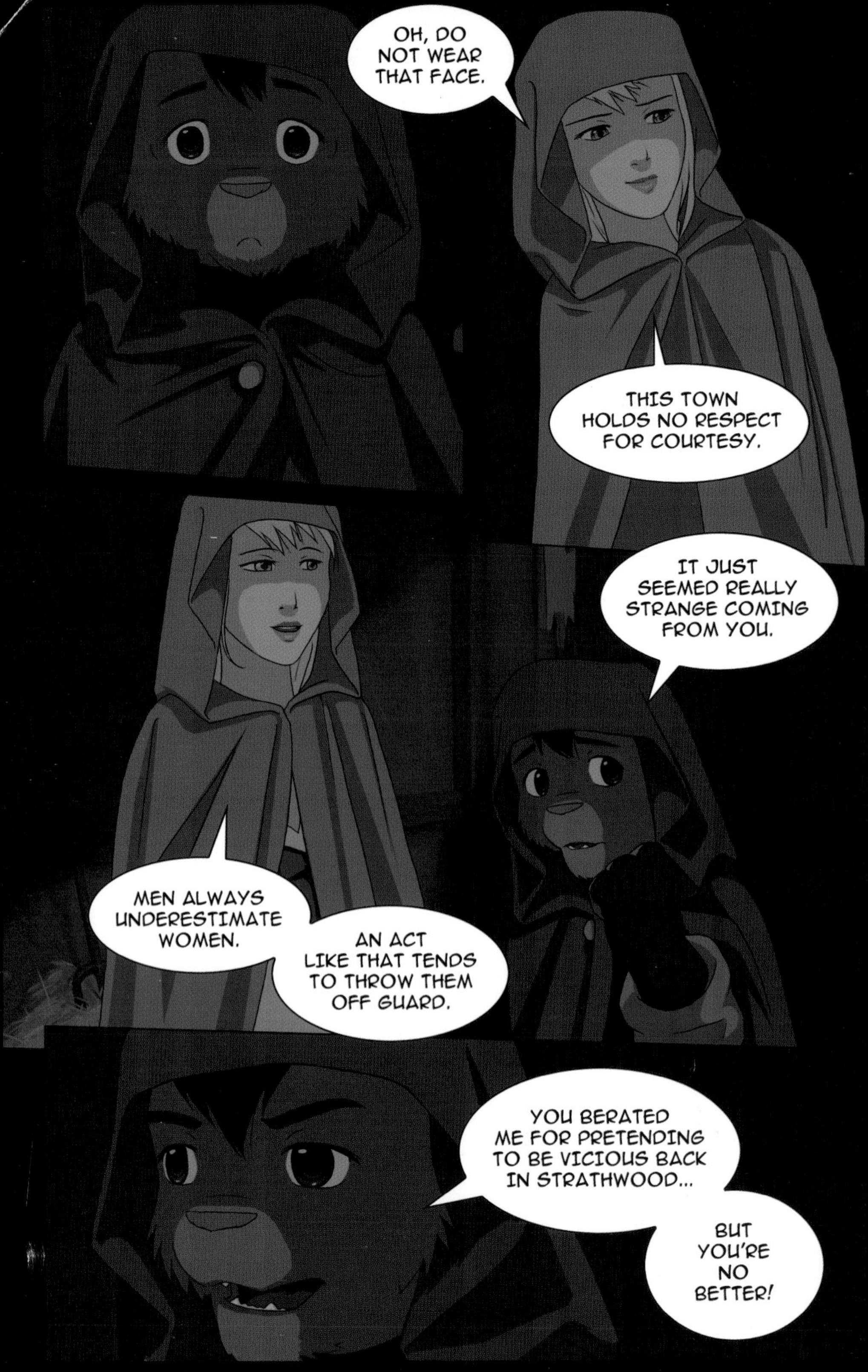
OH, DO NOT WEAR THAT FACE.
THIS TOWN HOLDS NO RESPECT FOR COURTESY.
IT JUST SEEMED REALLY STRANGE COMING FROM YOU.
MEN ALWAYS UNDERESTIMATE WOMEN.
AN ACT LIKE THAT TENDS TO THROW THEM OFF GUARD.
YOU BERATED ME FOR PRETENDING TO BE VICIOUS BACK IN STRATHWOOD...
BUT YOU'RE NO BETTER!

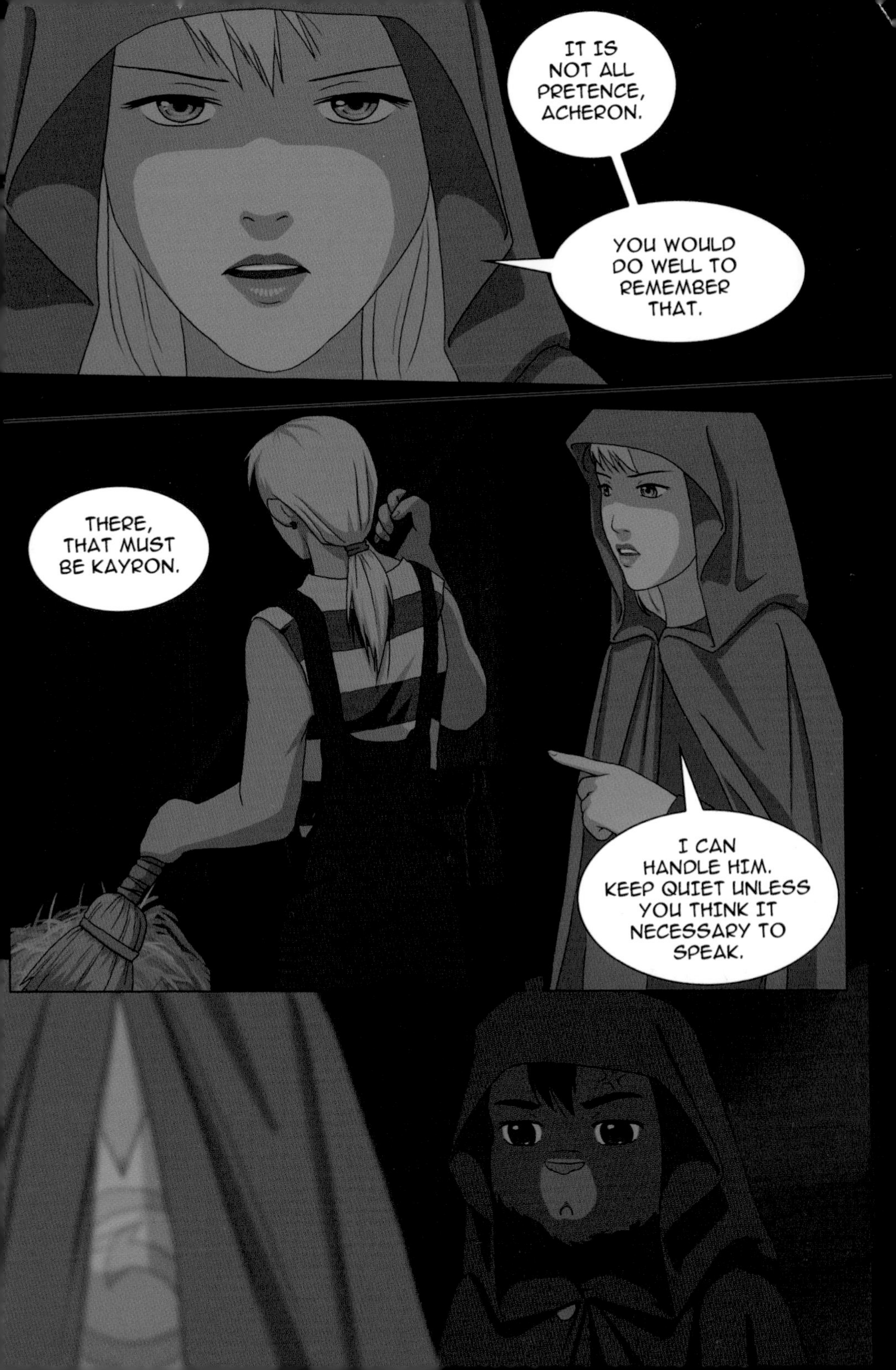
IT IS NOT ALL PRETENCE, ACHERON.
YOU WOULD DO WELL TO REMEMBER THAT.
THERE, THAT MUST BE KAYRON.
I CAN HANDLE HIM. KEEP QUIET UNLESS YOU THINK IT NECESSARY TO SPEAK.

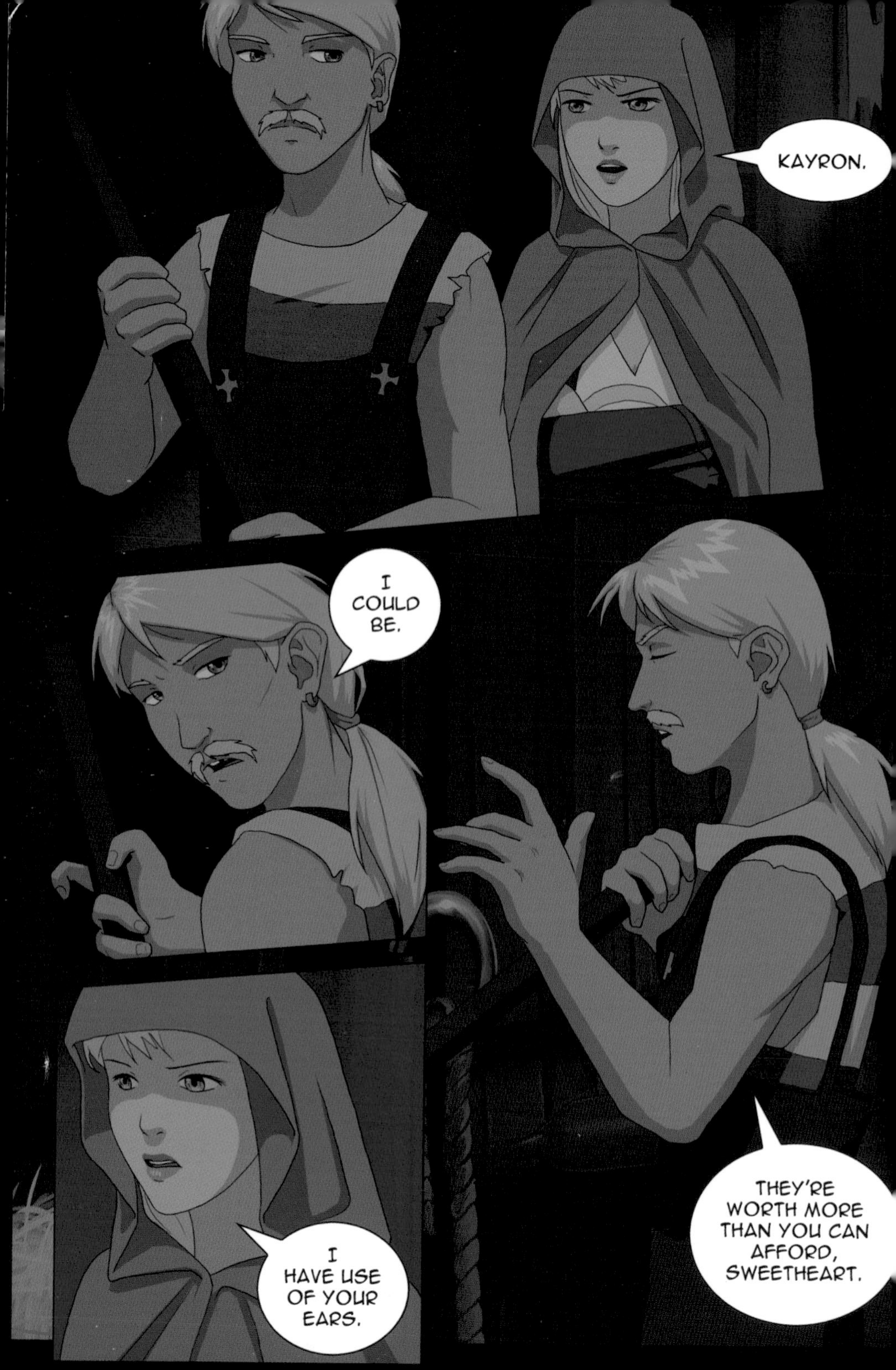
KAYRON.
I COULD BE.
THEY'RE WORTH MORE THAN YOU CAN AFFORD, SWEETHEART.
I HAVE USE OF YOUR EARS.

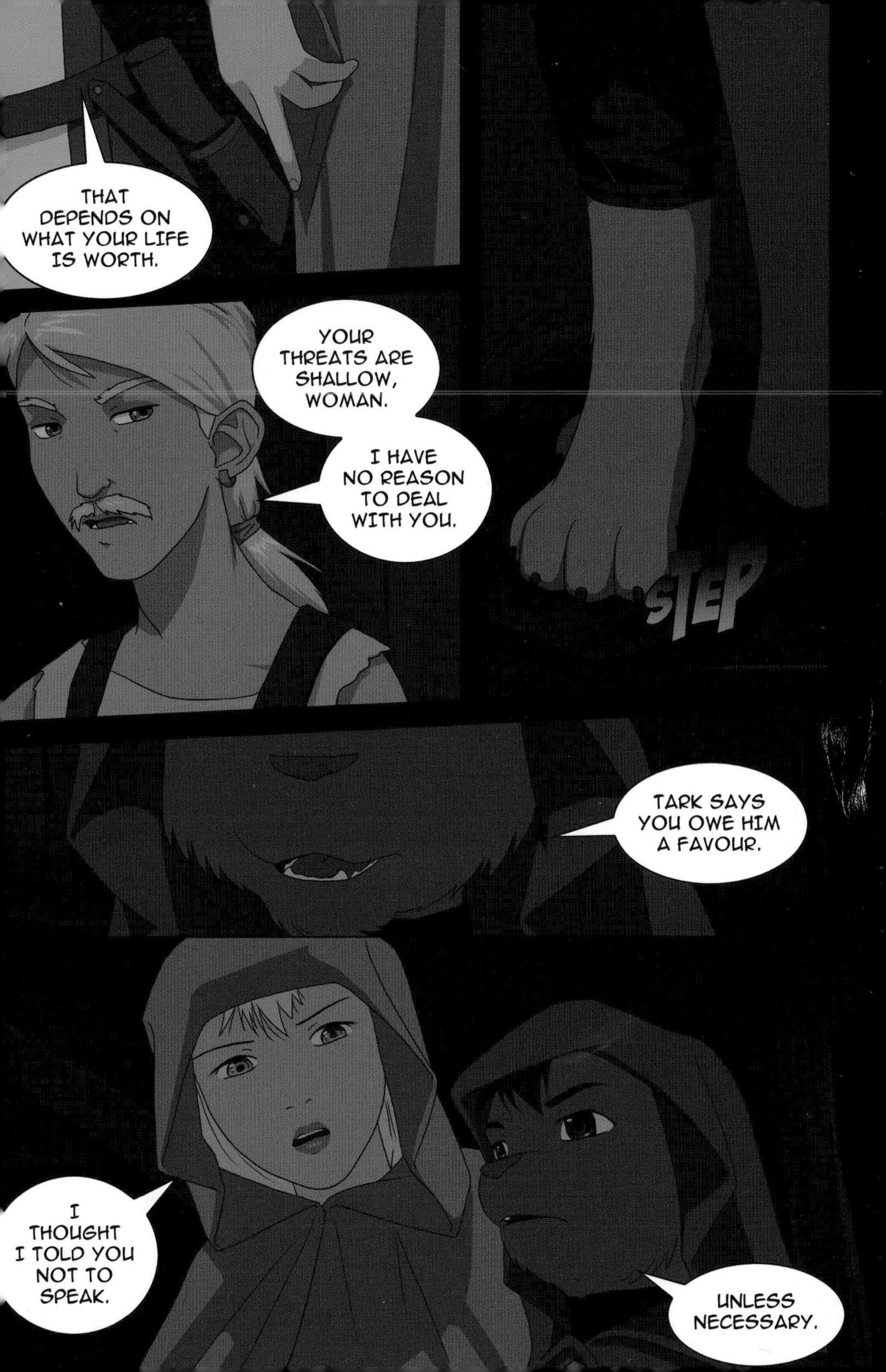
THAT DEPENDS ON WHAT YOUR LIFE IS WORTH.
YOUR THREATS ARE SHALLOW, WOMAN.
I HAVE NO REASON TO DEAL WITH YOU.
STEP
TARK SAYS YOU OWE HIM A FAVOUR.
I THOUGHT I TOLD YOU NOT TO SPEAK.
UNLESS NECESSARY.

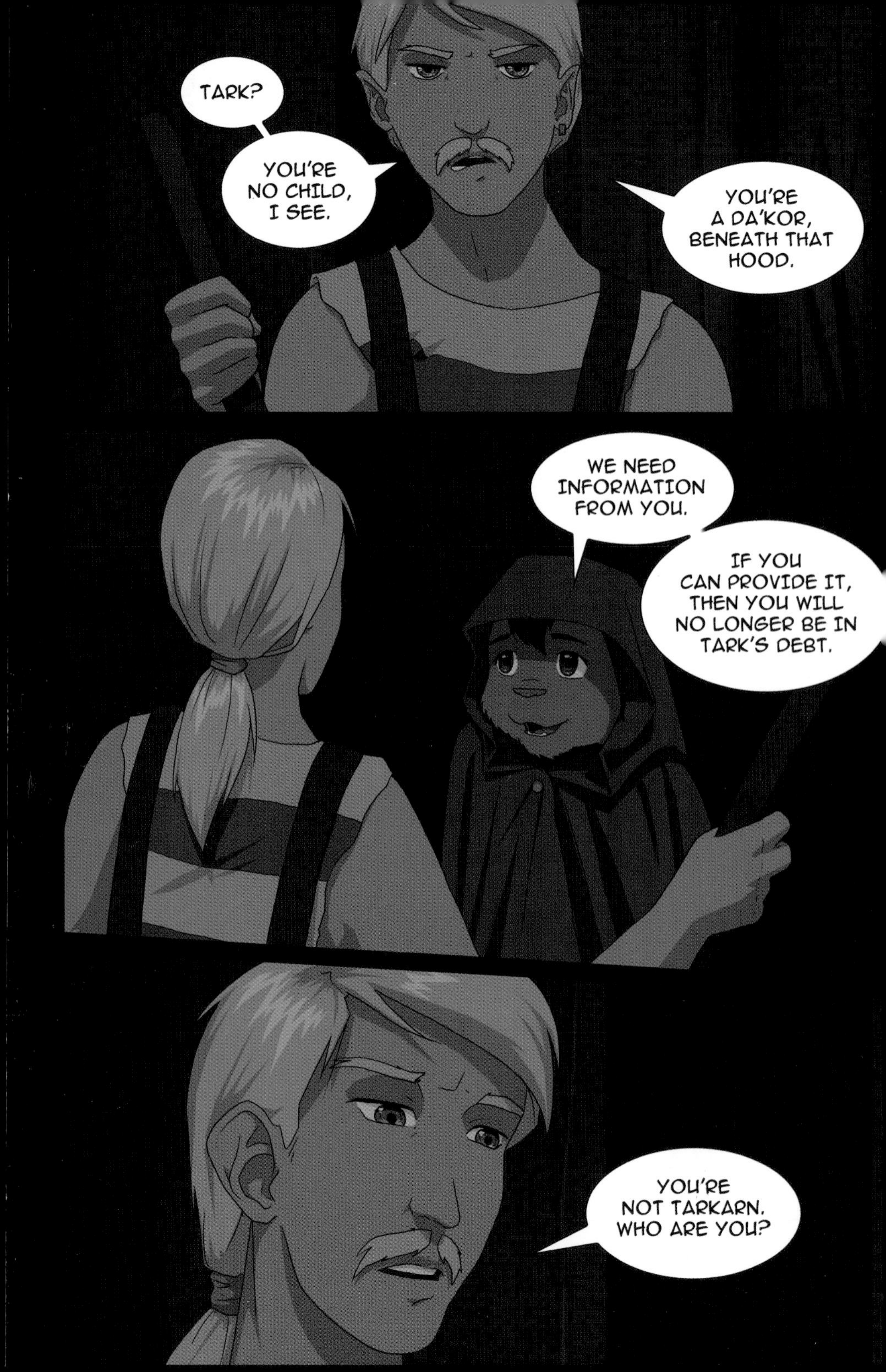
TARK?
YOU'RE NO CHILD, I SEE.
YOU'RE A DA'KOR, BENEATH THAT HOOD.
WE NEED INFORMATION FROM YOU.
IF YOU CAN PROVIDE IT, THEN YOU WILL NO LONGER BE IN TARK'S DEBT.
YOU'RE NOT TARKARN. WHO ARE YOU?

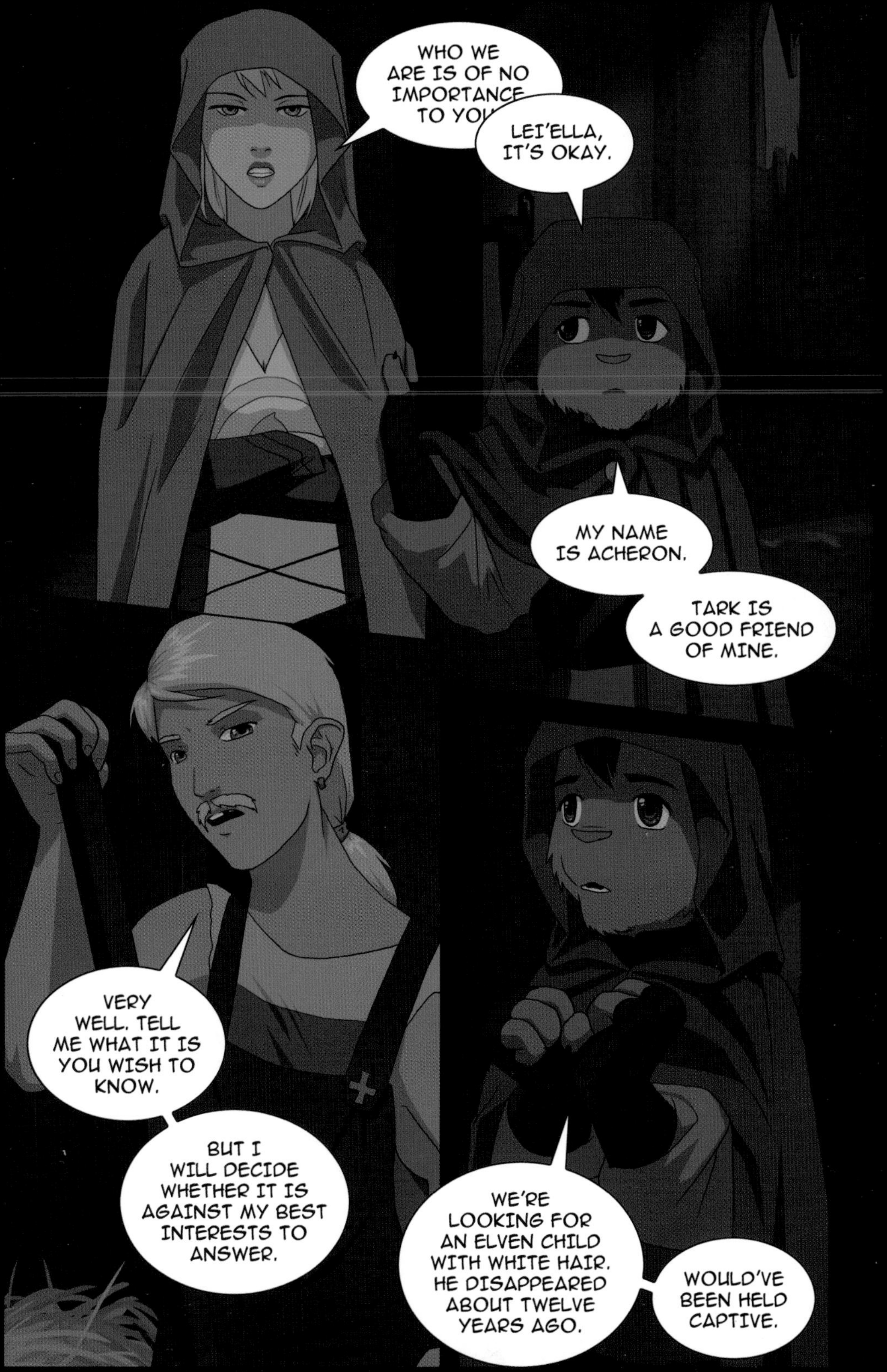
WHO WE ARE IS OF NO IMPORTANCE TO YOU.
LEI'ELLA, IT'S OKAY.
MY NAME IS ACHERON.
TARK IS A GOOD FRIEND OF MINE.
VERY WELL. TELL ME WHAT IT IS YOU WISH TO KNOW.
BUT I WILL DECIDE WHETHER IT IS AGAINST MY BEST INTERESTS TO ANSWER.
WE'RE LOOKING FOR AN ELVEN CHILD WITH WHITE HAIR. HE DISAPPEARED ABOUT TWELVE YEARS AGO.
WOULD'VE BEEN HELD CAPTIVE.

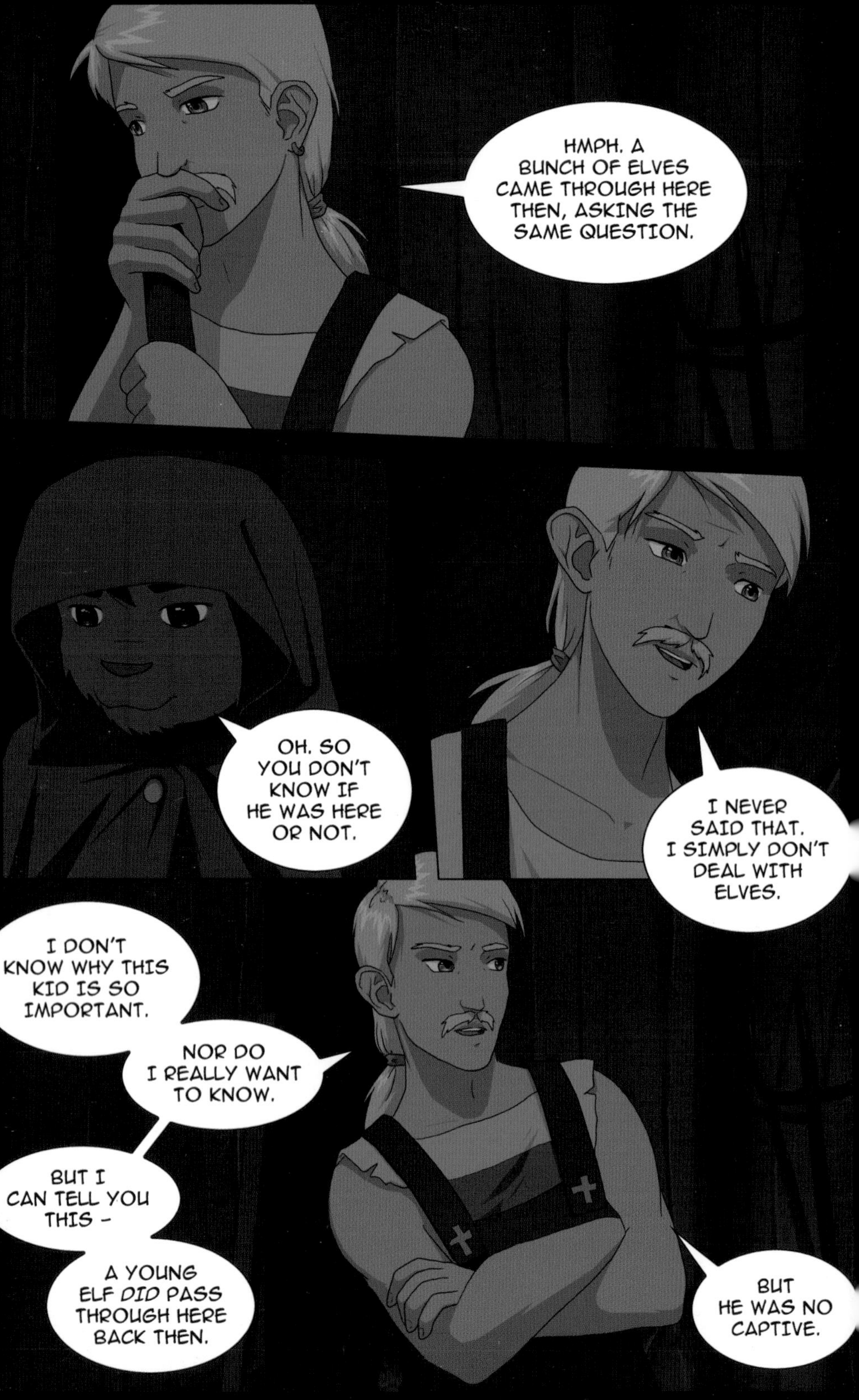

HMPH. A BUNCH OF ELVES CAME THROUGH HERE THEN, ASKING THE SAME QUESTION.
OH. SO YOU DON'T KNOW IF HE WAS HERE OR NOT.
I NEVER SAID THAT. I SIMPLY DON'T DEAL WITH ELVES.
I DON'T KNOW WHY THIS KID IS SO IMPORTANT.
NOR DO I REALLY WANT TO KNOW.
BUT I CAN TELL YOU THIS -
A YOUNG ELF *DID* PASS THROUGH HERE BACK THEN.
BUT HE WAS NO CAPTIVE.

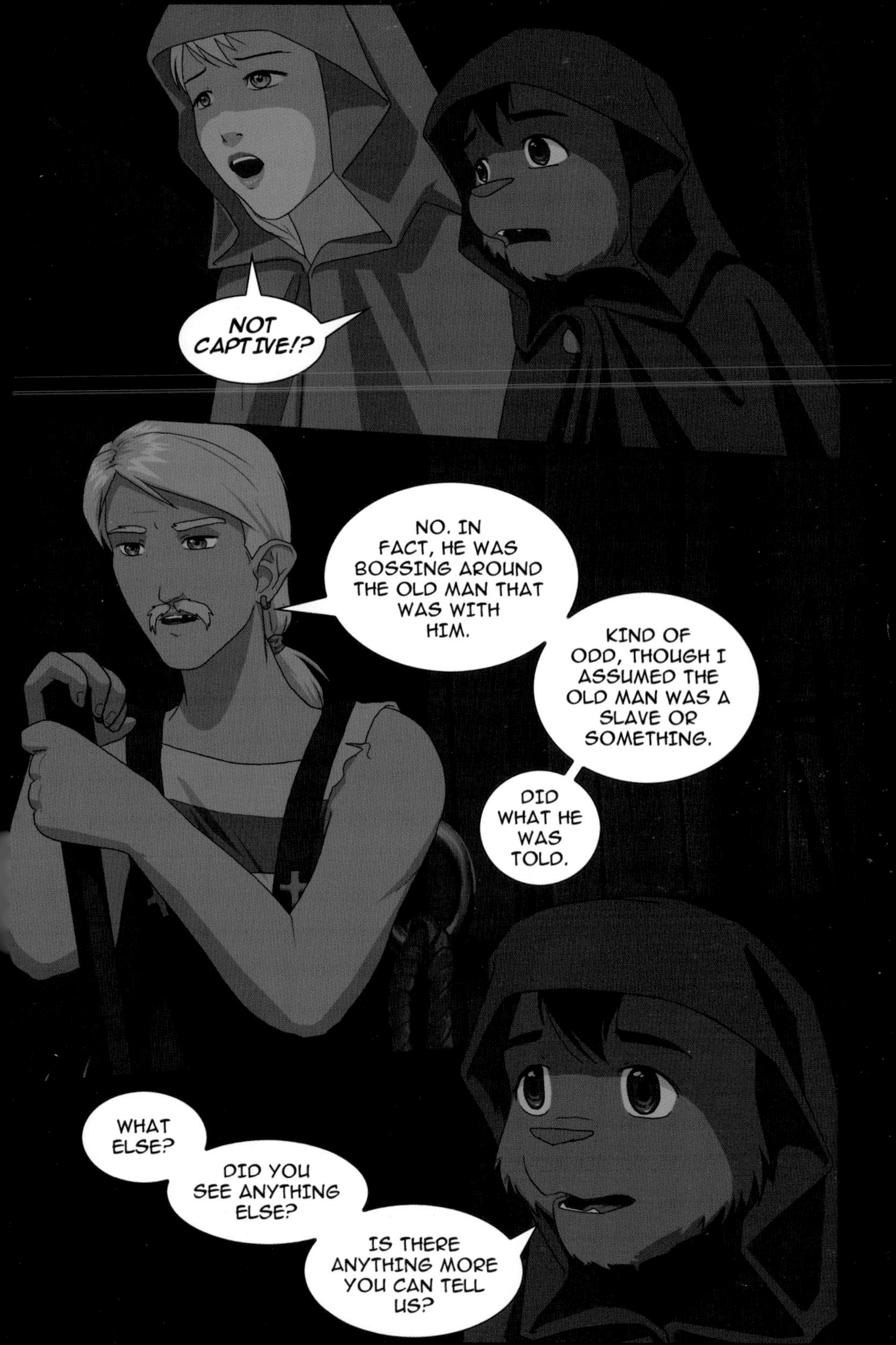
NOT CAPTIVE!?
NO. IN FACT, HE WAS BOSSING AROUND THE OLD MAN THAT WAS WITH HIM.
KIND OF ODD, THOUGH I ASSUMED THE OLD MAN WAS A SLAVE OR SOMETHING.
DID WHAT HE WAS TOLD.
WHAT ELSE?
DID YOU SEE ANYTHING ELSE?
IS THERE ANYTHING MORE YOU CAN TELL US?

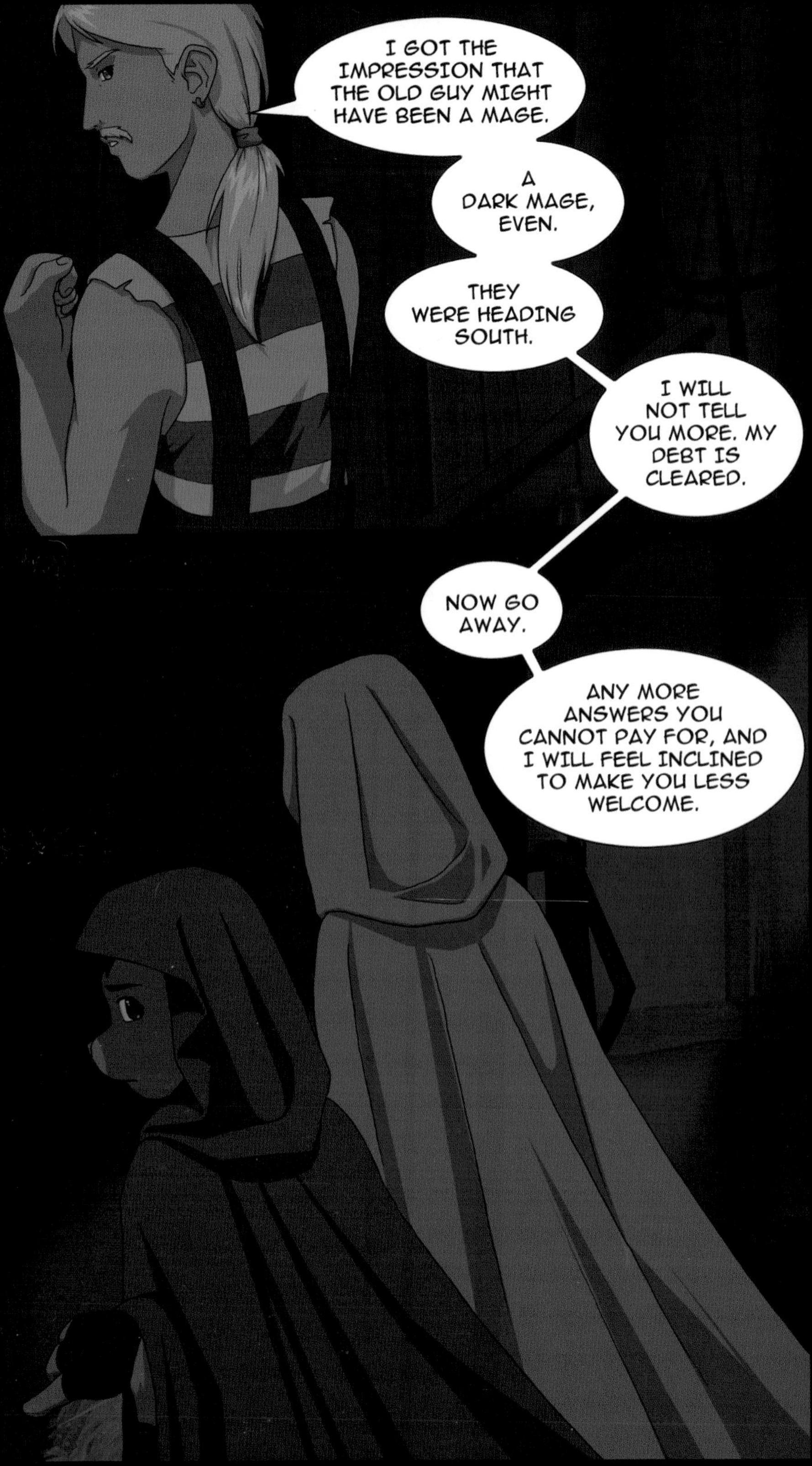
I GOT THE IMPRESSION THAT THE OLD GUY MIGHT HAVE BEEN A MAGE.
A DARK MAGE, EVEN.
THEY WERE HEADING SOUTH.
I WILL NOT TELL YOU MORE. MY DEBT IS CLEARED.
NOW GO AWAY.
ANY MORE ANSWERS YOU CANNOT PAY FOR, AND I WILL FEEL INCLINED TO MAKE YOU LESS WELCOME.

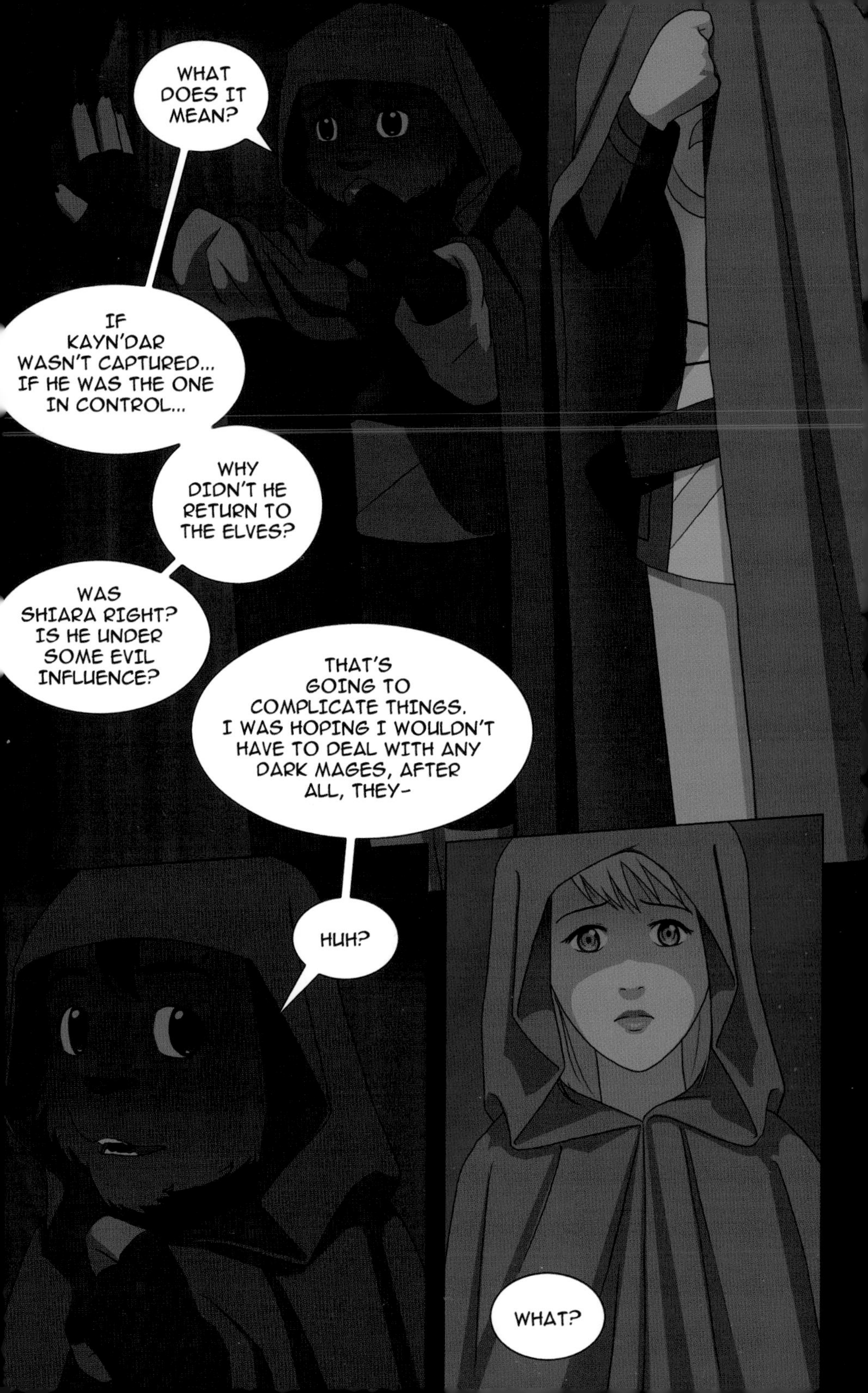
WHAT DOES IT MEAN?
IF KAYN'DAR WASN'T CAPTURED... IF HE WAS THE ONE IN CONTROL...
WHY DIDN'T HE RETURN TO THE ELVES?
WAS SHIARA RIGHT? IS HE UNDER SOME EVIL INFLUENCE?
THAT'S GOING TO COMPLICATE THINGS. I WAS HOPING I WOULDN'T HAVE TO DEAL WITH ANY DARK MAGES, AFTER ALL, THEY-
HUH?
WHAT?

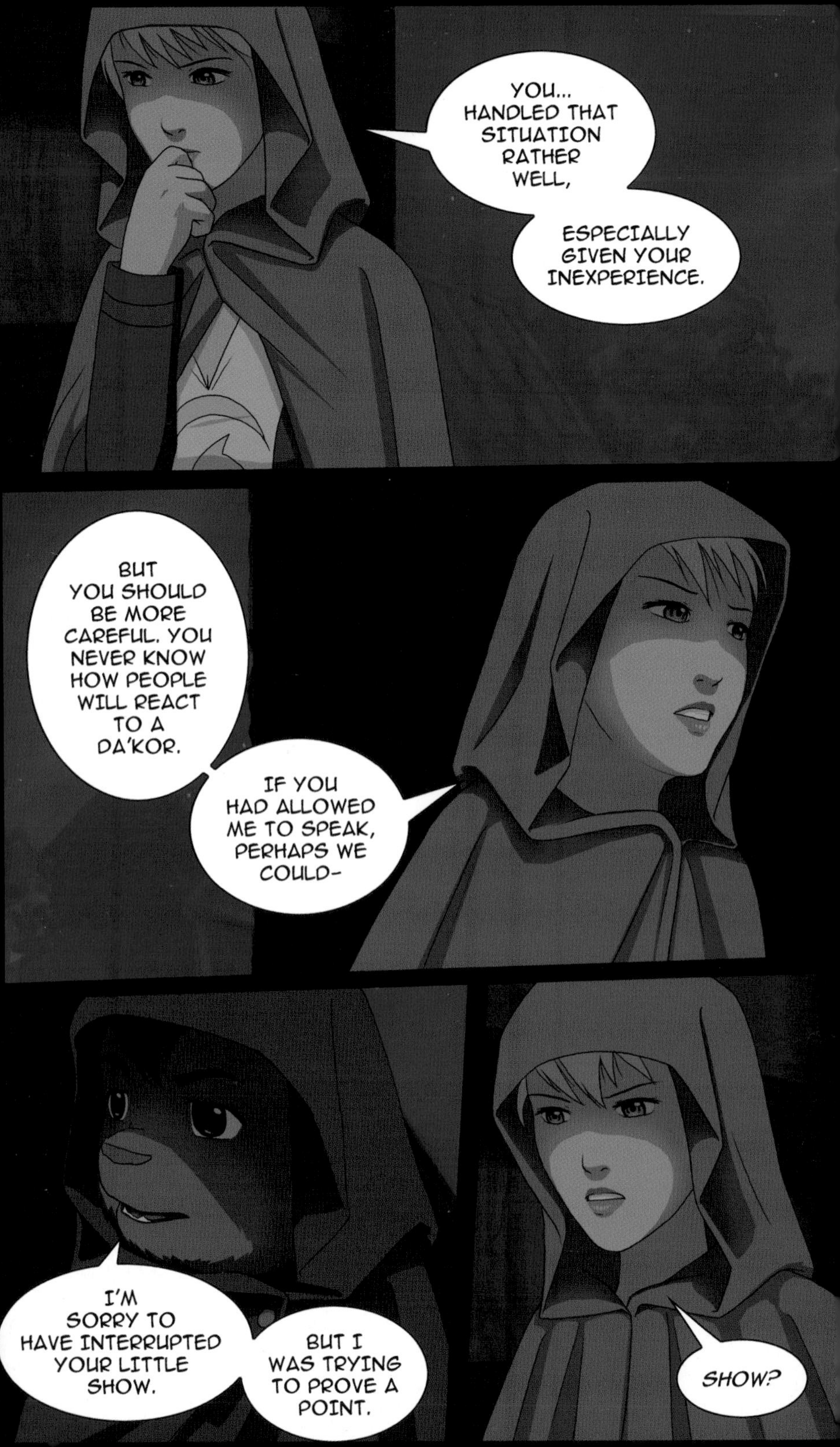
YOU... HANDLED THAT SITUATION RATHER WELL,
ESPECIALLY GIVEN YOUR INEXPERIENCE.
BUT YOU SHOULD BE MORE CAREFUL. YOU NEVER KNOW HOW PEOPLE WILL REACT TO A DA'KOR.
IF YOU HAD ALLOWED ME TO SPEAK, PERHAPS WE COULD-
I'M SORRY TO HAVE INTERRUPTED YOUR LITTLE SHOW.
BUT I WAS TRYING TO PROVE A POINT.
SHOW?

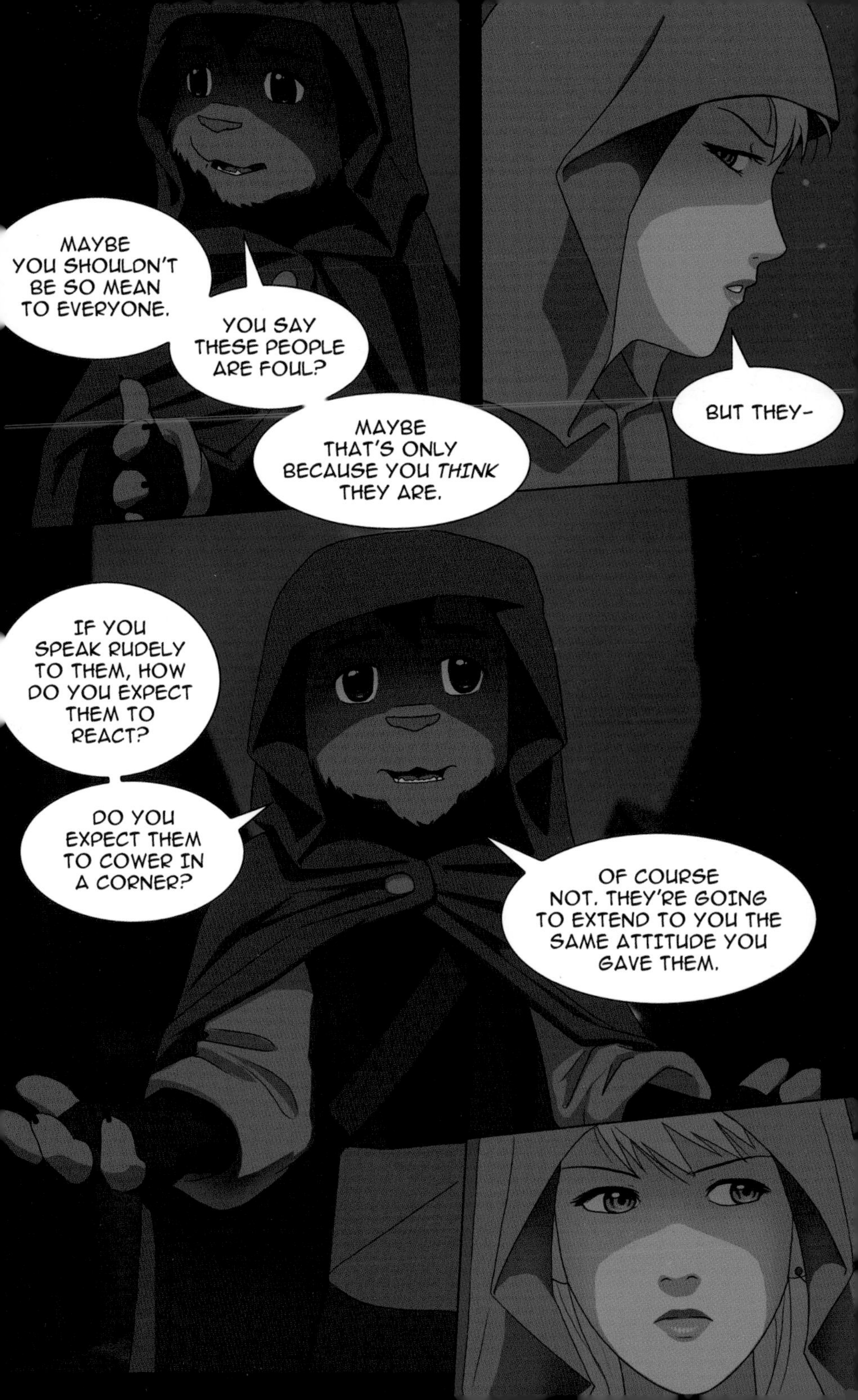
MAYBE YOU SHOULDN'T BE SO MEAN TO EVERYONE.
YOU SAY THESE PEOPLE ARE FOUL?
BUT THEY-
MAYBE THAT'S ONLY BECAUSE YOU *THINK* THEY ARE.
IF YOU SPEAK RUDELY TO THEM, HOW DO YOU EXPECT THEM TO REACT?
DO YOU EXPECT THEM TO COWER IN A CORNER?
OF COURSE NOT. THEY'RE GOING TO EXTEND TO YOU THE SAME ATTITUDE YOU GAVE THEM.

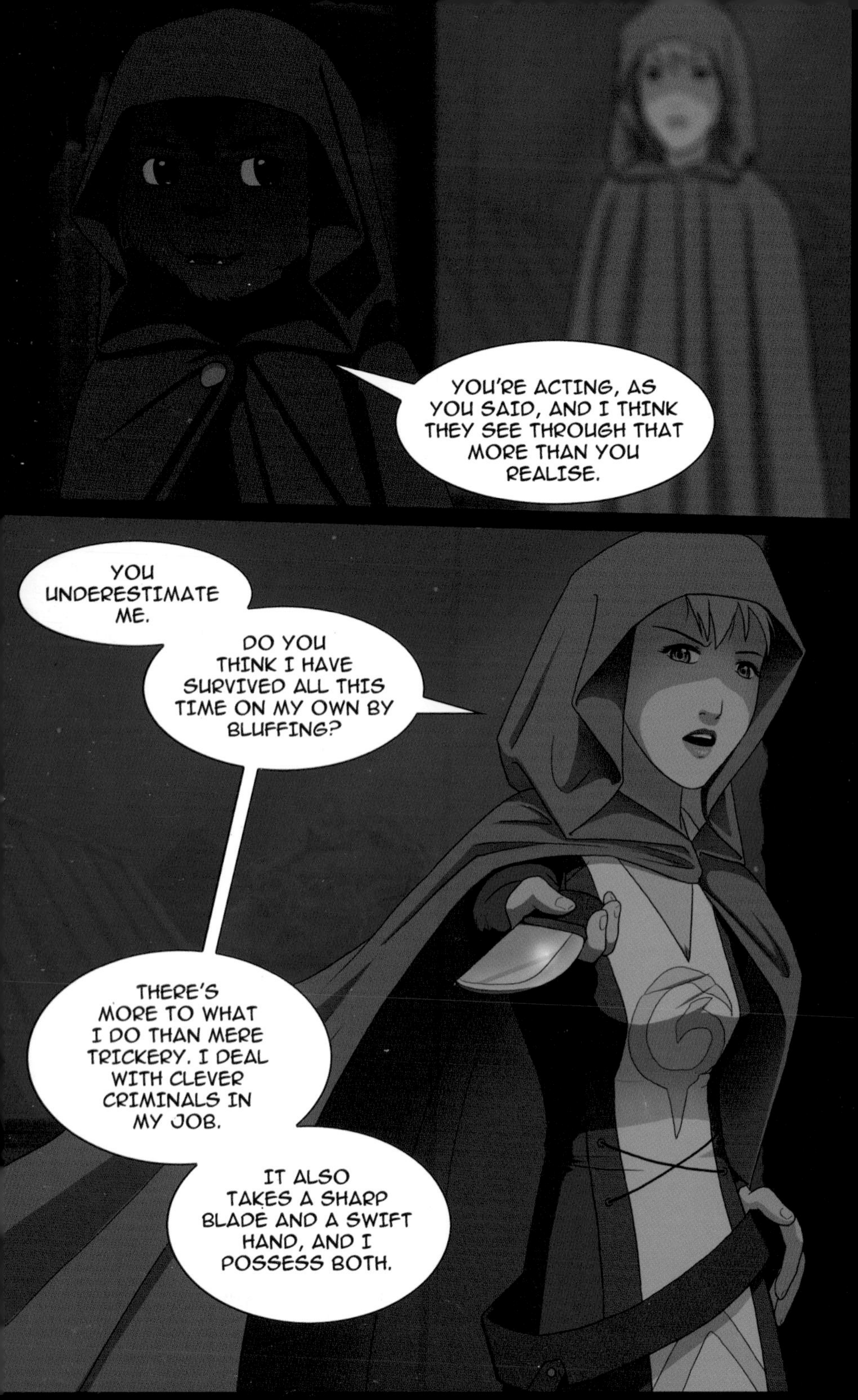
YOU'RE ACTING, AS YOU SAID, AND I THINK THEY SEE THROUGH THAT MORE THAN YOU REALISE.
YOU UNDERESTIMATE ME.
DO YOU THINK I HAVE SURVIVED ALL THIS TIME ON MY OWN BY BLUFFING?
THERE'S MORE TO WHAT I DO THAN MERE TRICKERY. I DEAL WITH CLEVER CRIMINALS IN MY JOB.
IT ALSO TAKES A SHARP BLADE AND A SWIFT HAND, AND I POSSESS BOTH.

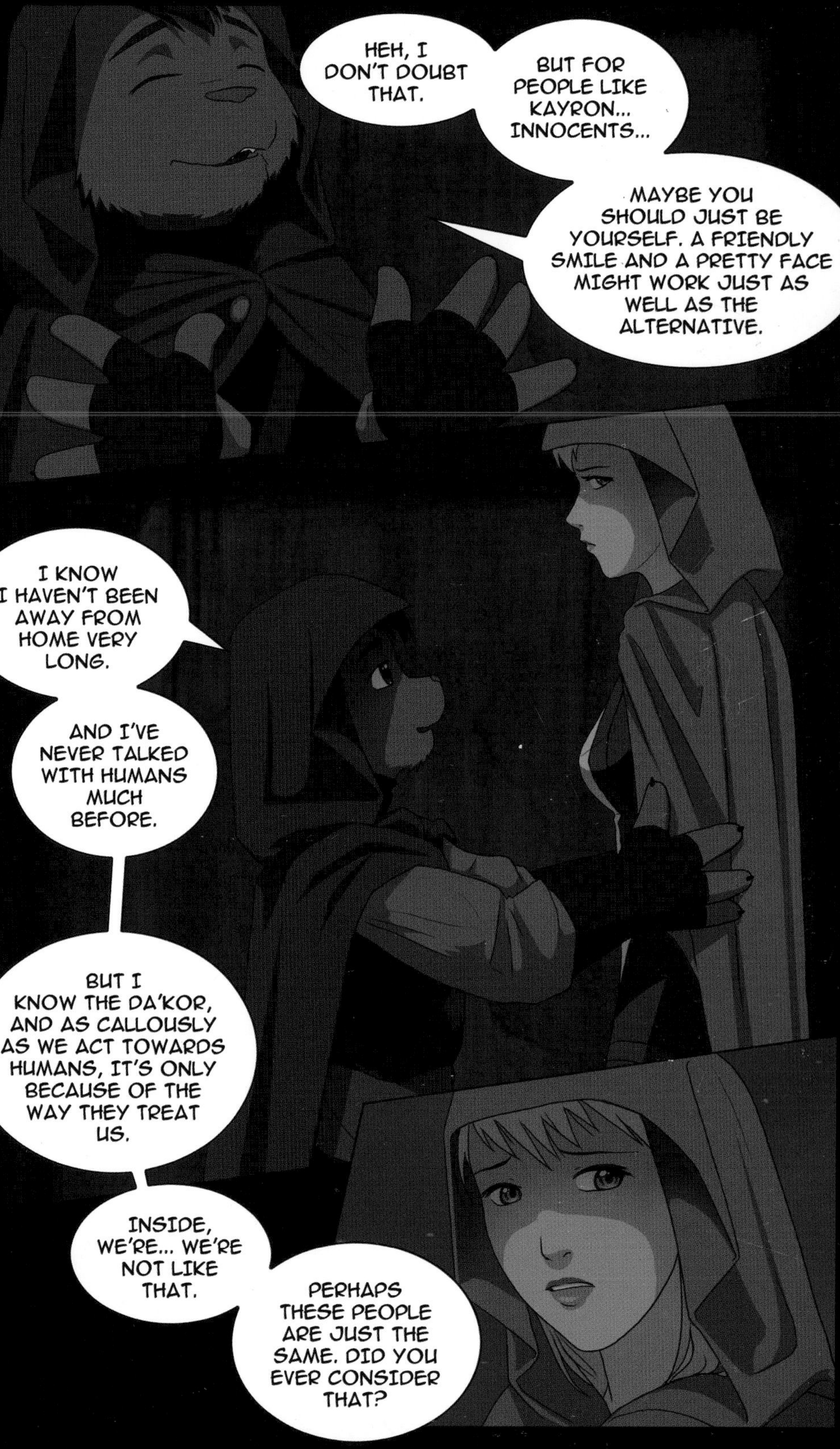
HEH, I DON'T DOUBT THAT.
BUT FOR PEOPLE LIKE KAYRON... INNOCENTS...
MAYBE YOU SHOULD JUST BE YOURSELF. A FRIENDLY SMILE AND A PRETTY FACE MIGHT WORK JUST AS WELL AS THE ALTERNATIVE.
I KNOW I HAVEN'T BEEN AWAY FROM HOME VERY LONG.
AND I'VE NEVER TALKED WITH HUMANS MUCH BEFORE.
BUT I KNOW THE DA'KOR, AND AS CALLOUSLY AS WE ACT TOWARDS HUMANS, IT'S ONLY BECAUSE OF THE WAY THEY TREAT US.
INSIDE, WE'RE... WE'RE NOT LIKE THAT.
PERHAPS THESE PEOPLE ARE JUST THE SAME. DID YOU EVER CONSIDER THAT?

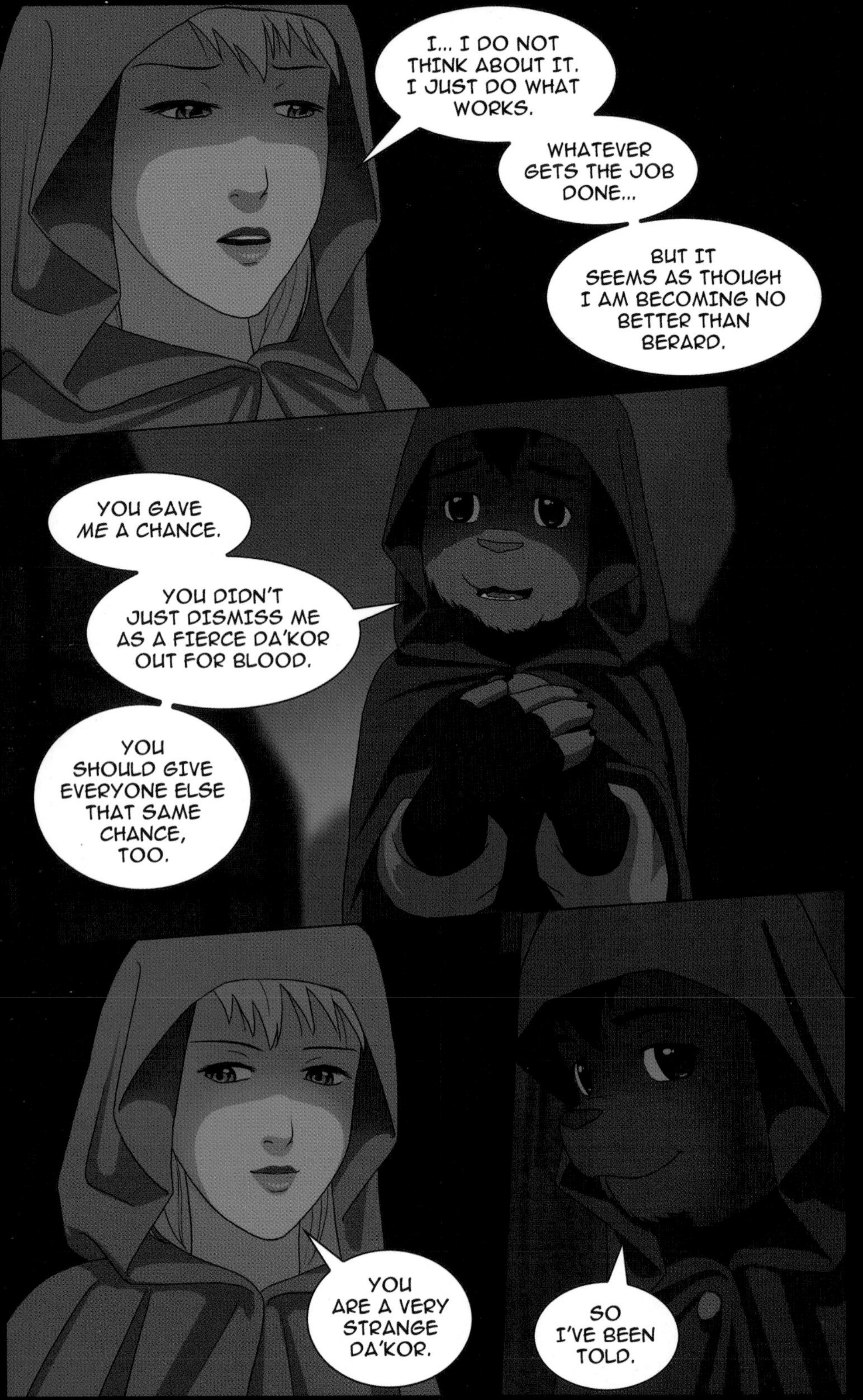
I... I DO NOT THINK ABOUT IT. I JUST DO WHAT WORKS.
WHATEVER GETS THE JOB DONE...
BUT IT SEEMS AS THOUGH I AM BECOMING NO BETTER THAN BERARD.
YOU GAVE ME A CHANCE.
YOU DIDN'T JUST DISMISS ME AS A FIERCE DA'KOR OUT FOR BLOOD.
YOU SHOULD GIVE EVERYONE ELSE THAT SAME CHANCE, TOO.
YOU ARE A VERY STRANGE DA'KOR.
SO I'VE BEEN TOLD.

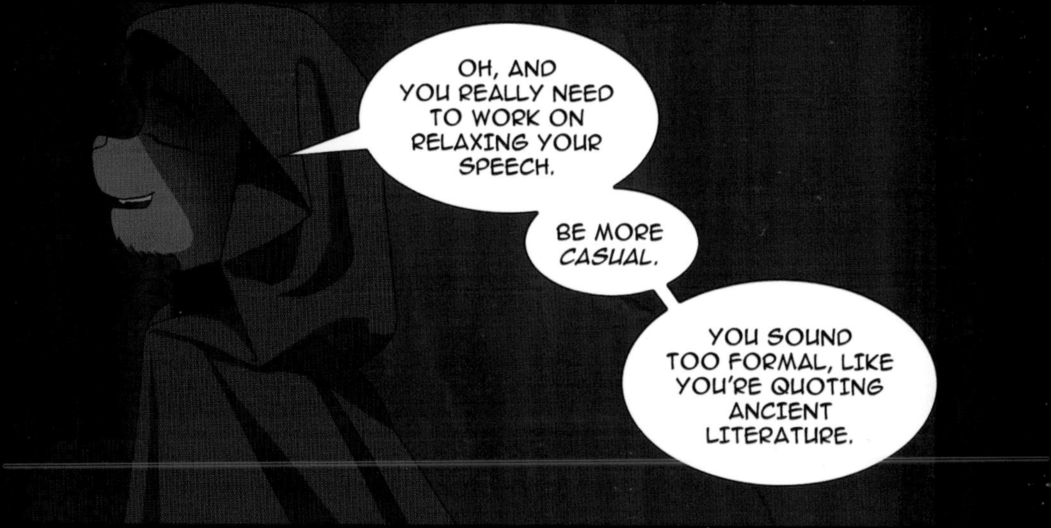
OH, AND YOU REALLY NEED TO WORK ON RELAXING YOUR SPEECH.
BE MORE *CASUAL*.
YOU SOUND TOO FORMAL, LIKE YOU'RE QUOTING ANCIENT LITERATURE.

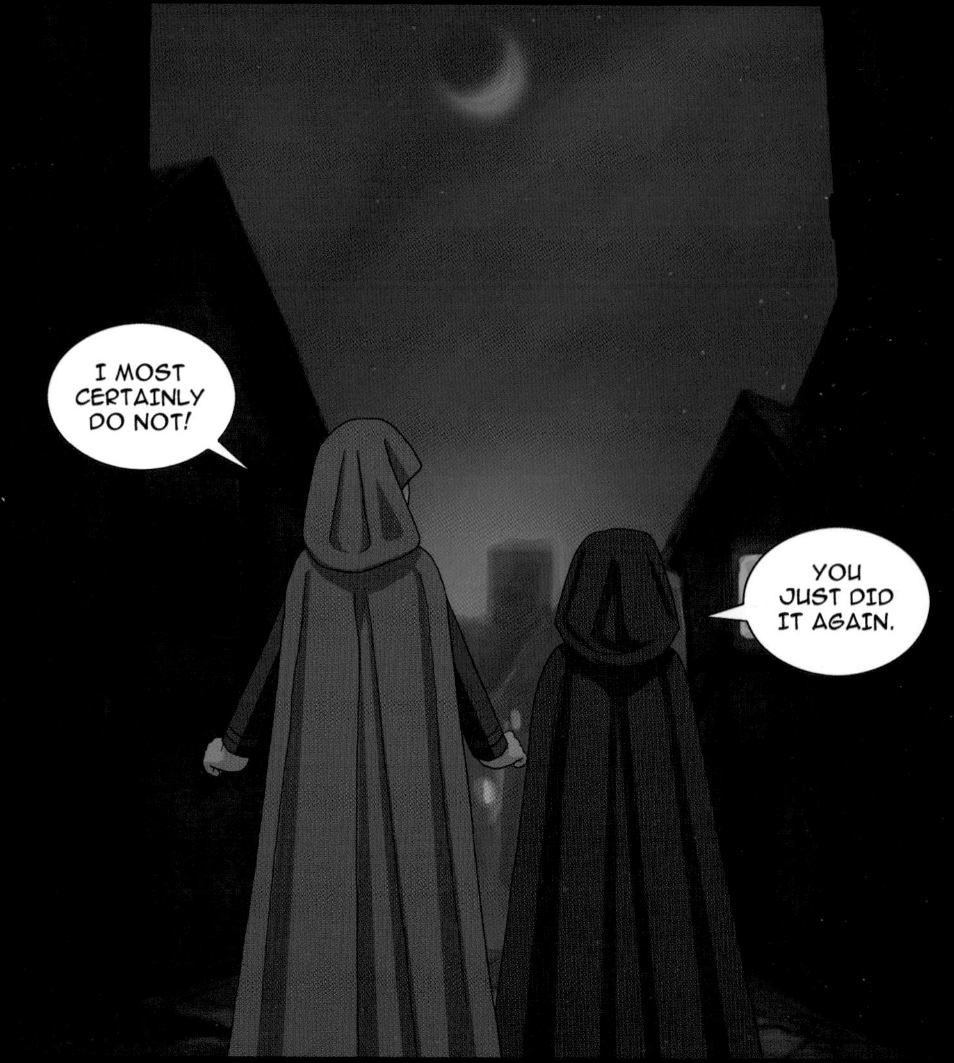
I MOST CERTAINLY DO NOT!
YOU JUST DID IT AGAIN.

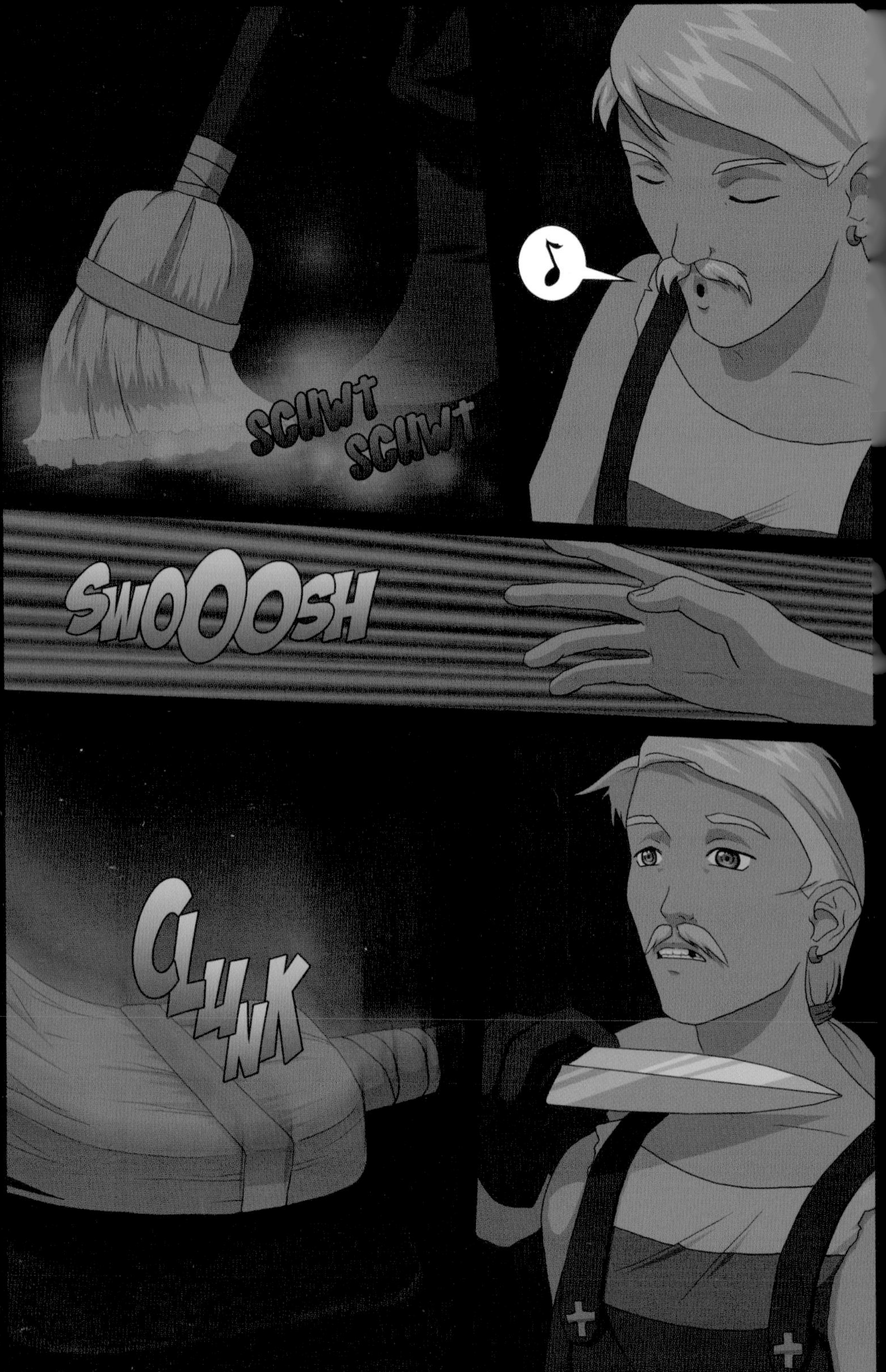

SCHWT SCHWT
♪
SWOOOSH
CLUNK

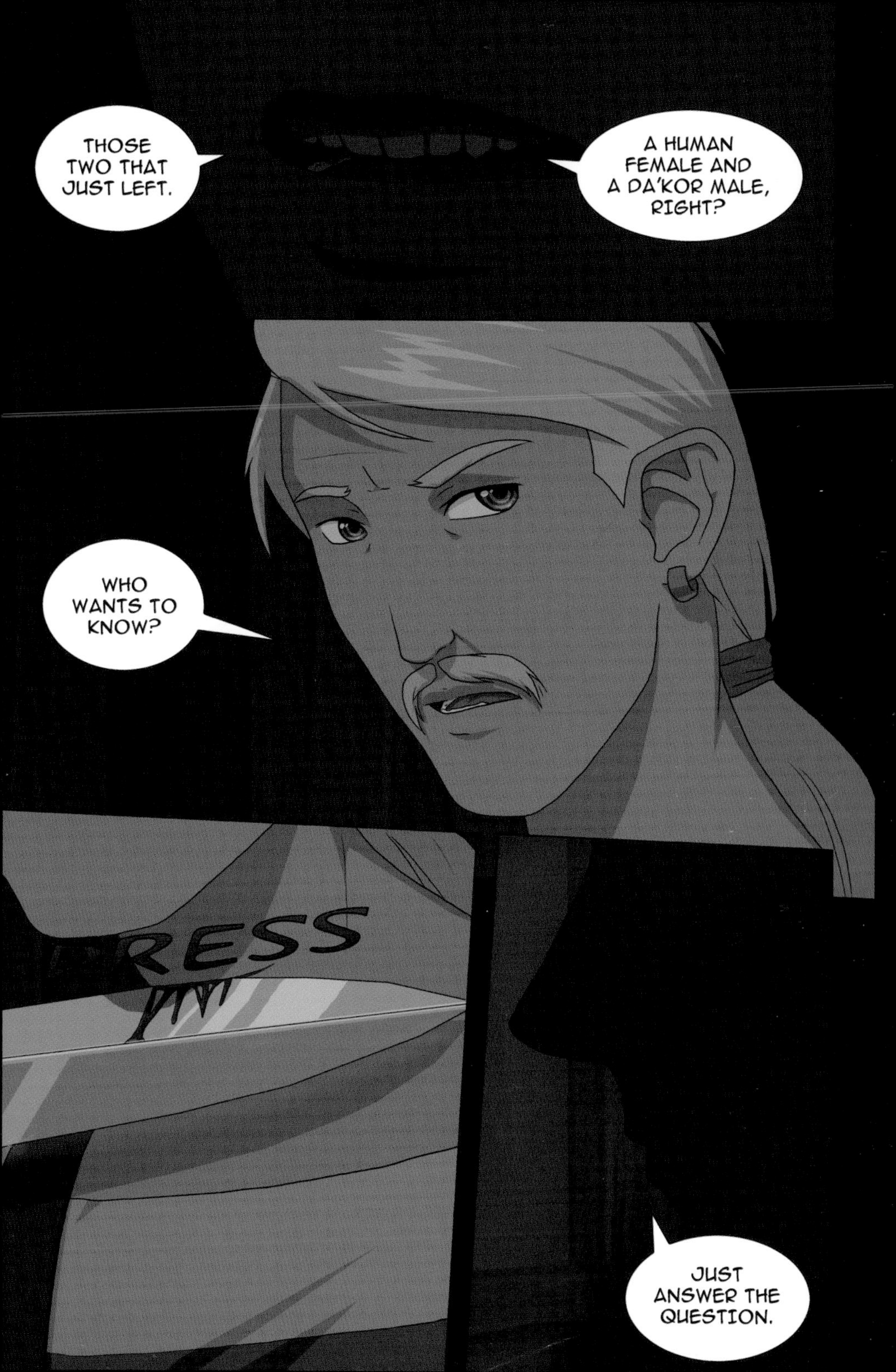
THOSE TWO THAT JUST LEFT.
A HUMAN FEMALE AND A DA'KOR MALE, RIGHT?
WHO WANTS TO KNOW?
JUST ANSWER THE QUESTION.

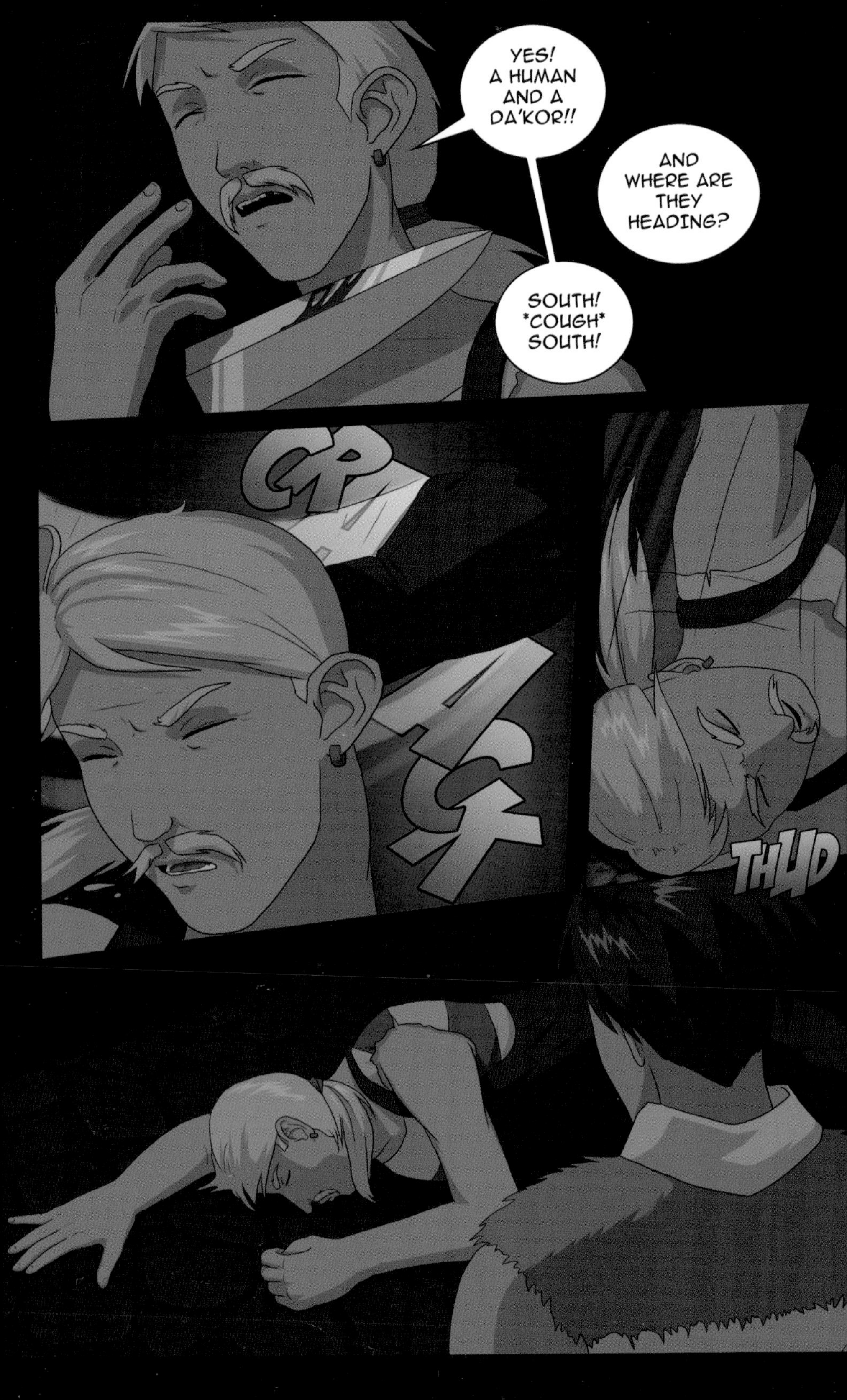
YES! A HUMAN AND A DA'KOR!!
AND WHERE ARE THEY HEADING?
SOUTH! *COUGH* SOUTH!
CRACK
THUD

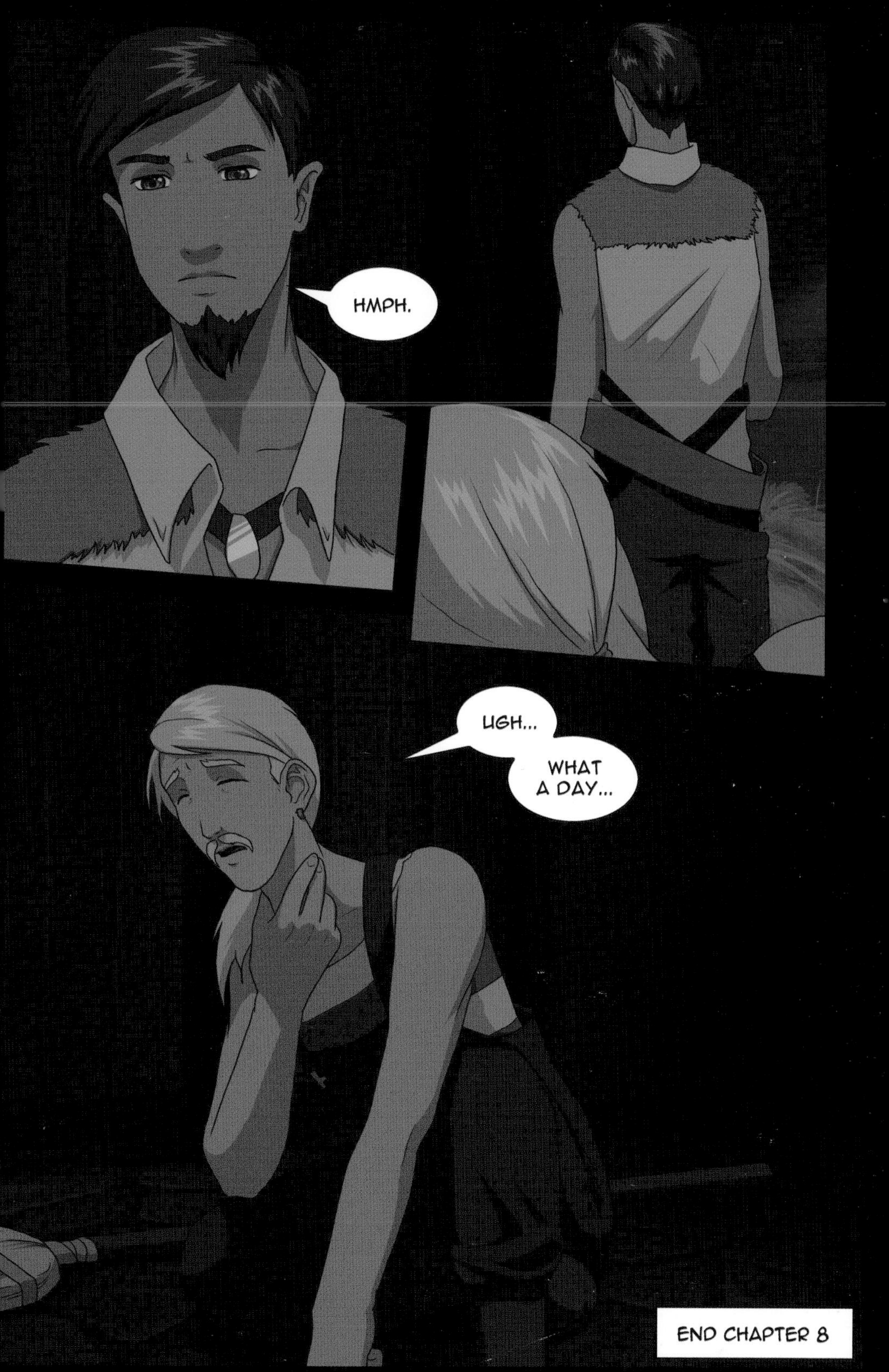
HMPH.
UGH...
WHAT A DAY...
END CHAPTER 8

CHAPTER 9 :DUPLICITY

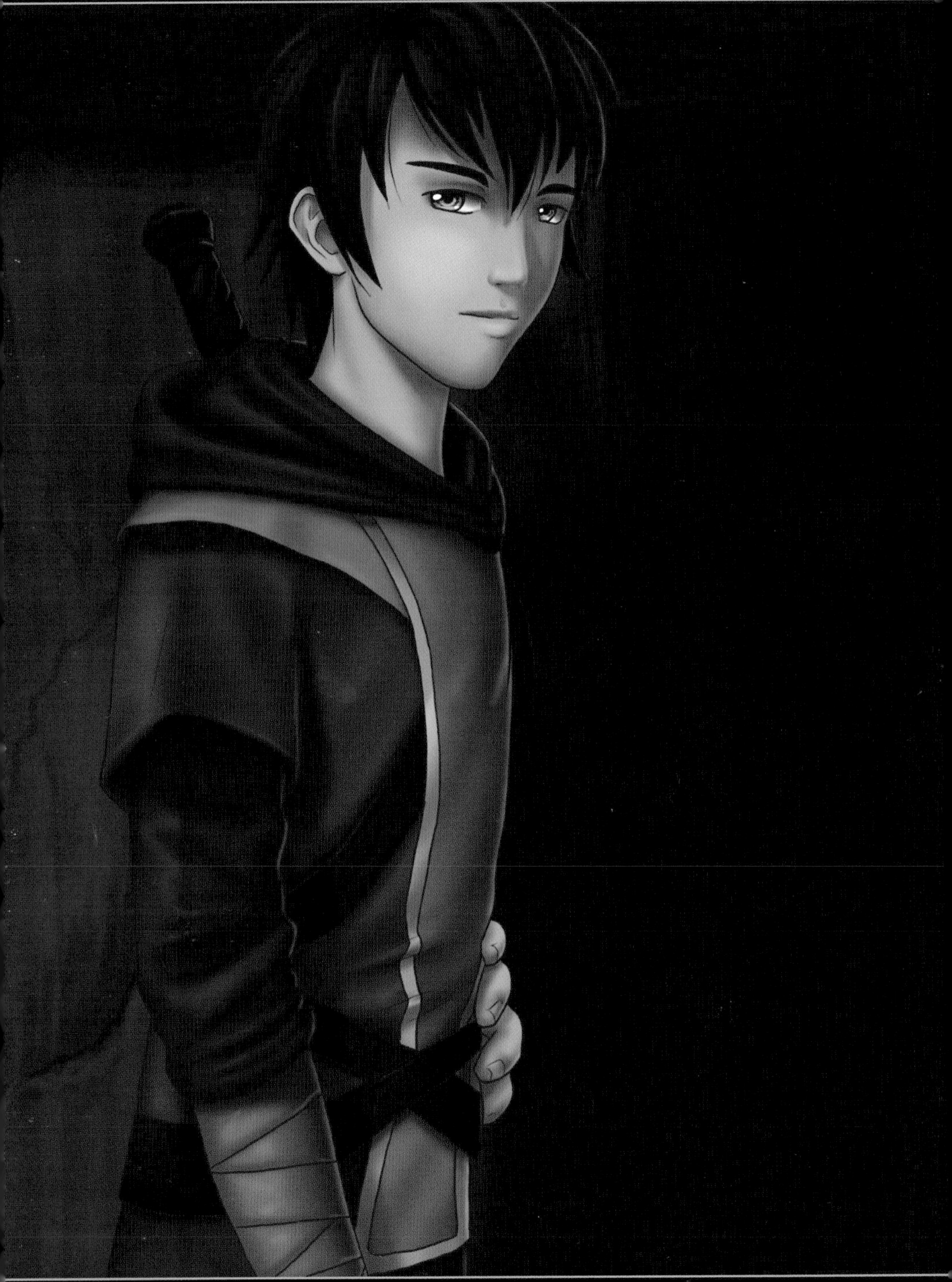

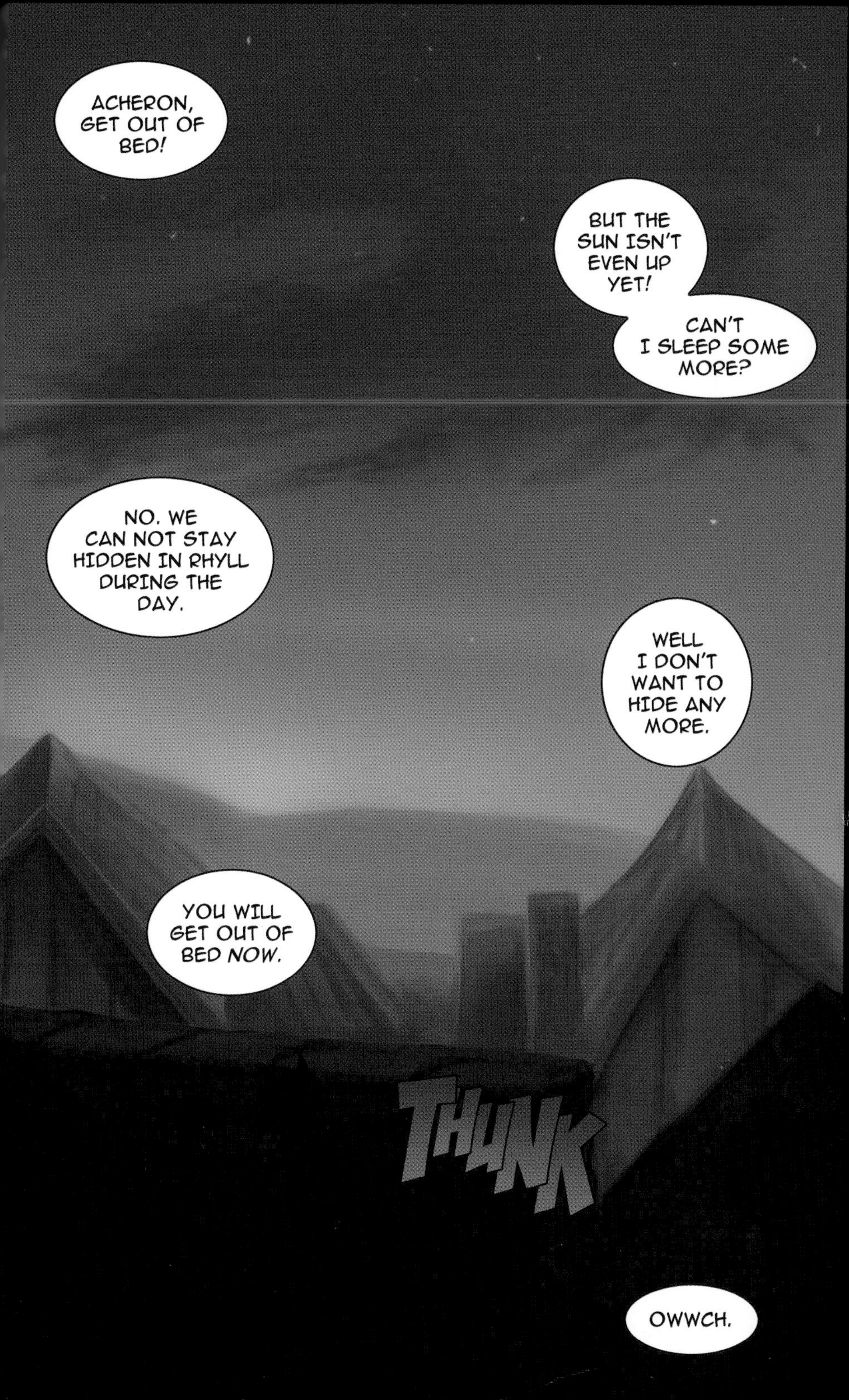
ACHERON, GET OUT OF BED!
BUT THE SUN ISN'T EVEN UP YET!
CAN'T I SLEEP SOME MORE?
NO. WE CAN NOT STAY HIDDEN IN RHYLL DURING THE DAY.
WELL I DON'T WANT TO HIDE ANY MORE.
YOU WILL GET OUT OF BED NOW.
THUNK
OWWCH.

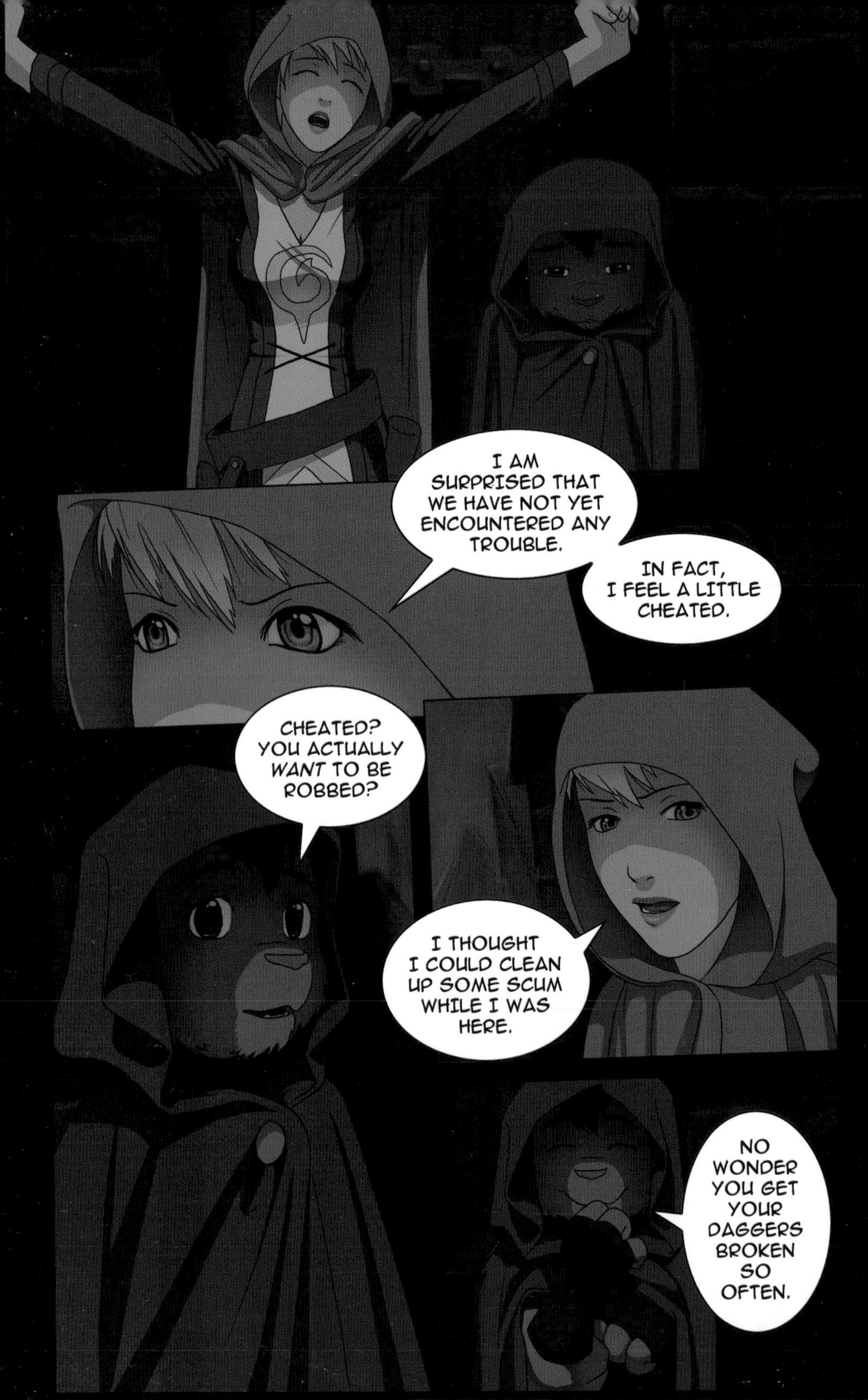
I AM SURPRISED THAT WE HAVE NOT YET ENCOUNTERED ANY TROUBLE.
IN FACT, I FEEL A LITTLE CHEATED.
CHEATED? YOU ACTUALLY WANT TO BE ROBBED?
I THOUGHT I COULD CLEAN UP SOME SCUM WHILE I WAS HERE.
NO WONDER YOU GET YOUR DAGGERS BROKEN SO OFTEN.

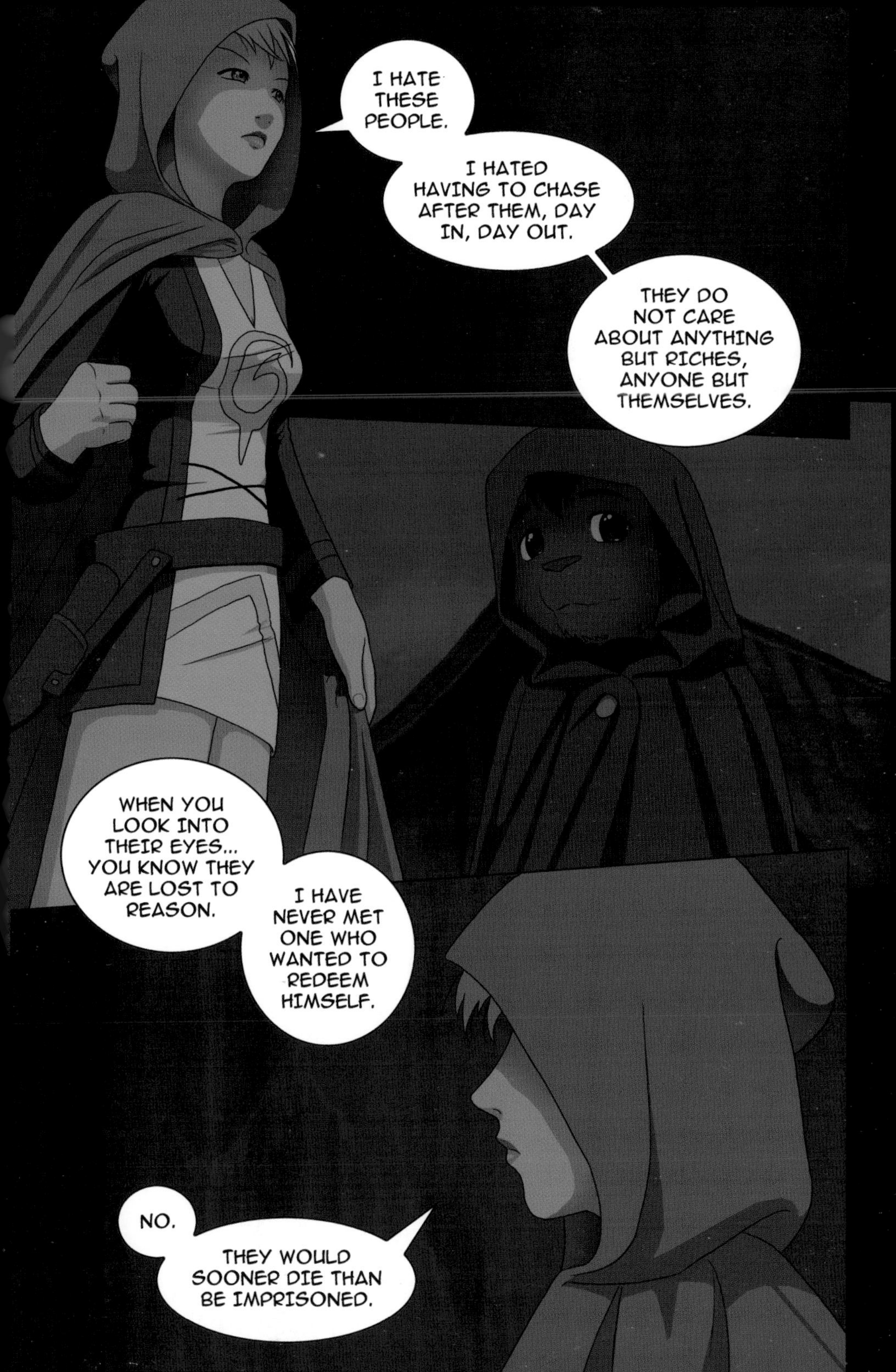
I HATE THESE PEOPLE.
I HATED HAVING TO CHASE AFTER THEM, DAY IN, DAY OUT.
THEY DO NOT CARE ABOUT ANYTHING BUT RICHES, ANYONE BUT THEMSELVES.
WHEN YOU LOOK INTO THEIR EYES... YOU KNOW THEY ARE LOST TO REASON.
I HAVE NEVER MET ONE WHO WANTED TO REDEEM HIMSELF.
NO.
THEY WOULD SOONER DIE THAN BE IMPRISONED.

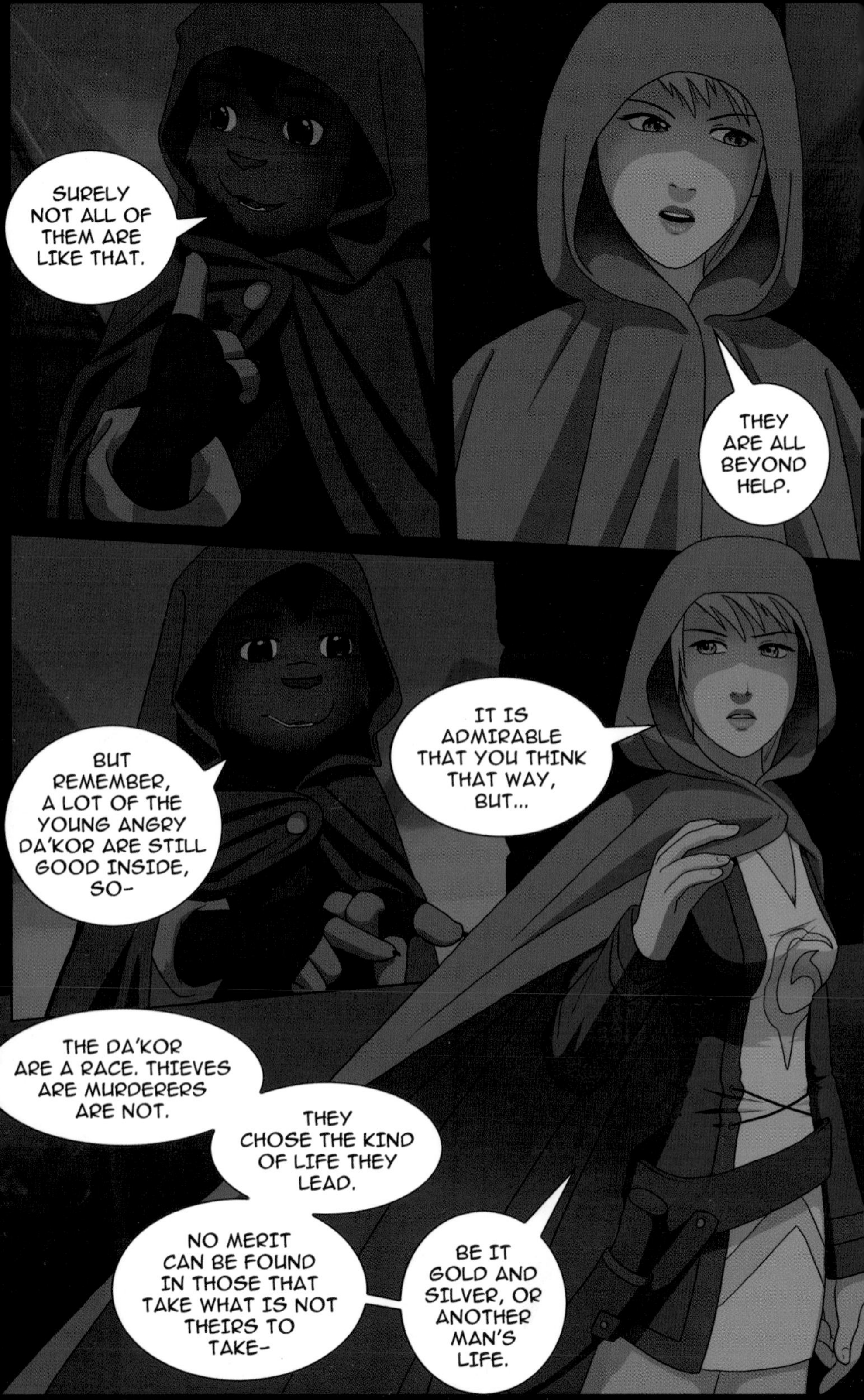
SURELY NOT ALL OF THEM ARE LIKE THAT.
THEY ARE ALL BEYOND HELP.
BUT REMEMBER, A LOT OF THE YOUNG ANGRY DA'KOR ARE STILL GOOD INSIDE, SO-
IT IS ADMIRABLE THAT YOU THINK THAT WAY, BUT...
THE DA'KOR ARE A RACE. THIEVES ARE MURDERERS ARE NOT.
THEY CHOSE THE KIND OF LIFE THEY LEAD.
NO MERIT CAN BE FOUND IN THOSE THAT TAKE WHAT IS NOT THEIRS TO TAKE-
BE IT GOLD AND SILVER, OR ANOTHER MAN'S LIFE.

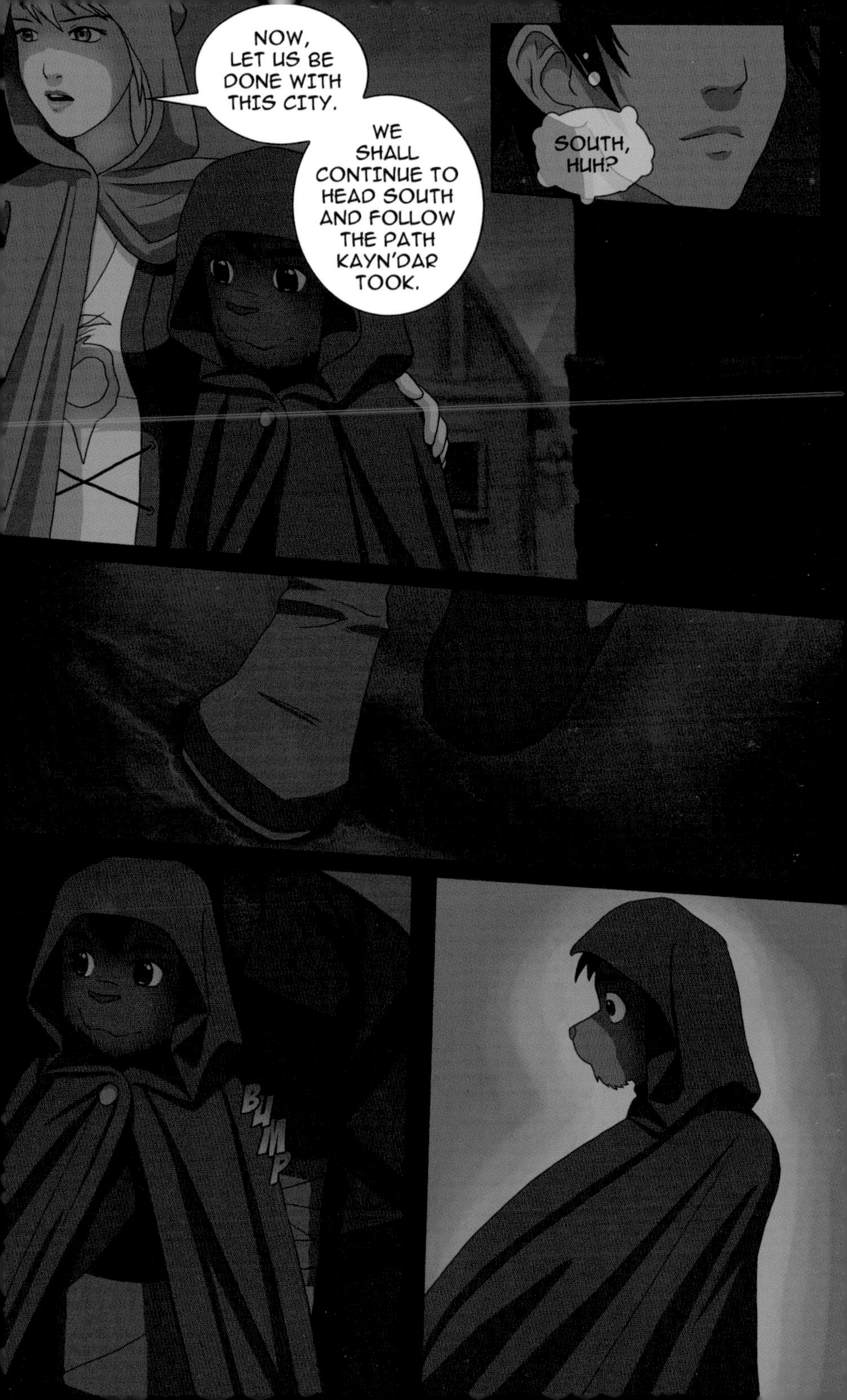
NOW, LET US BE DONE WITH THIS CITY.
WE SHALL CONTINUE TO HEAD SOUTH AND FOLLOW THE PATH KAYN'DAR TOOK.
SOUTH, HUH?
BUMP

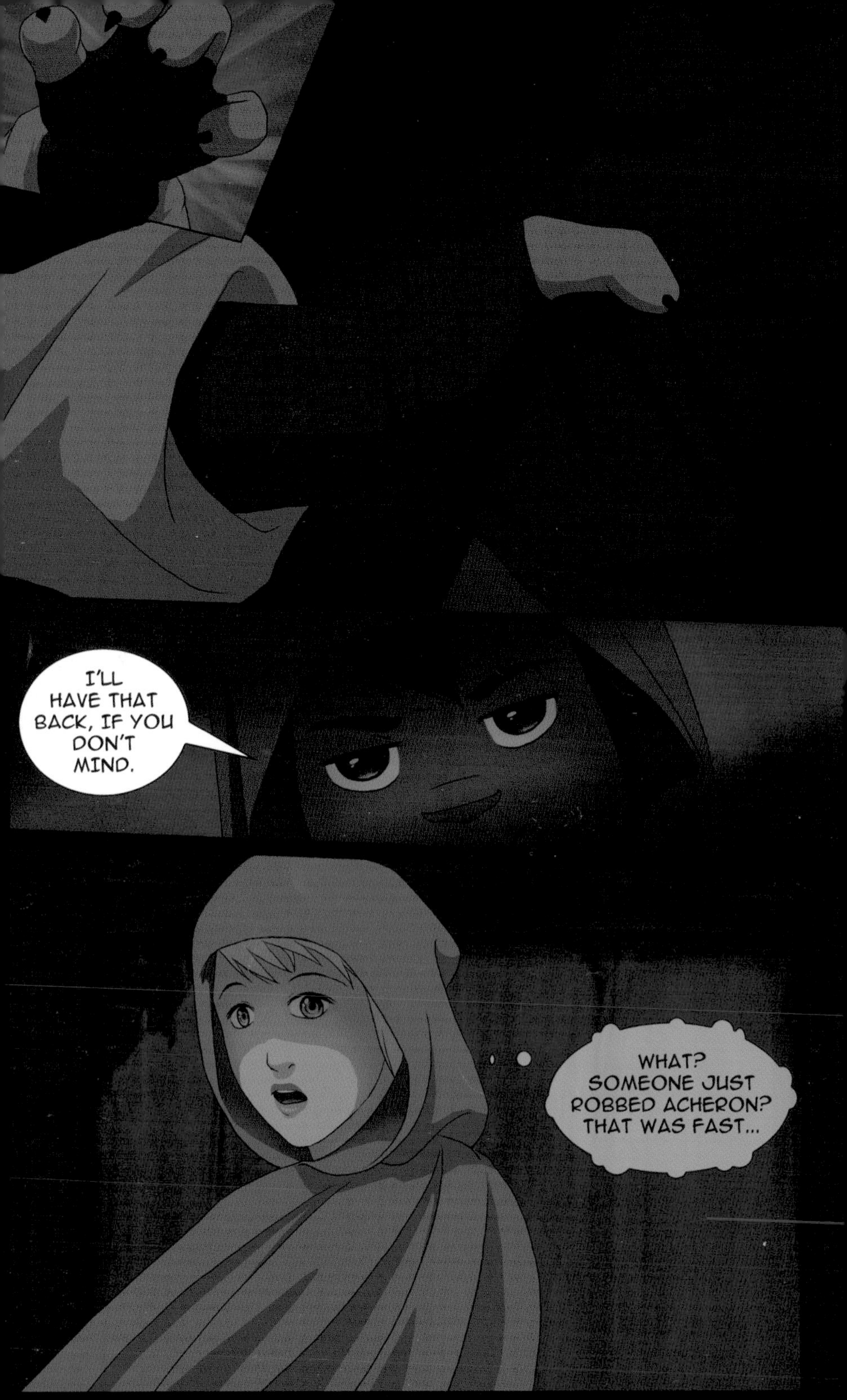
I'LL HAVE THAT BACK, IF YOU DON'T MIND.
WHAT? SOMEONE JUST ROBBED ACHERON? THAT WAS FAST...

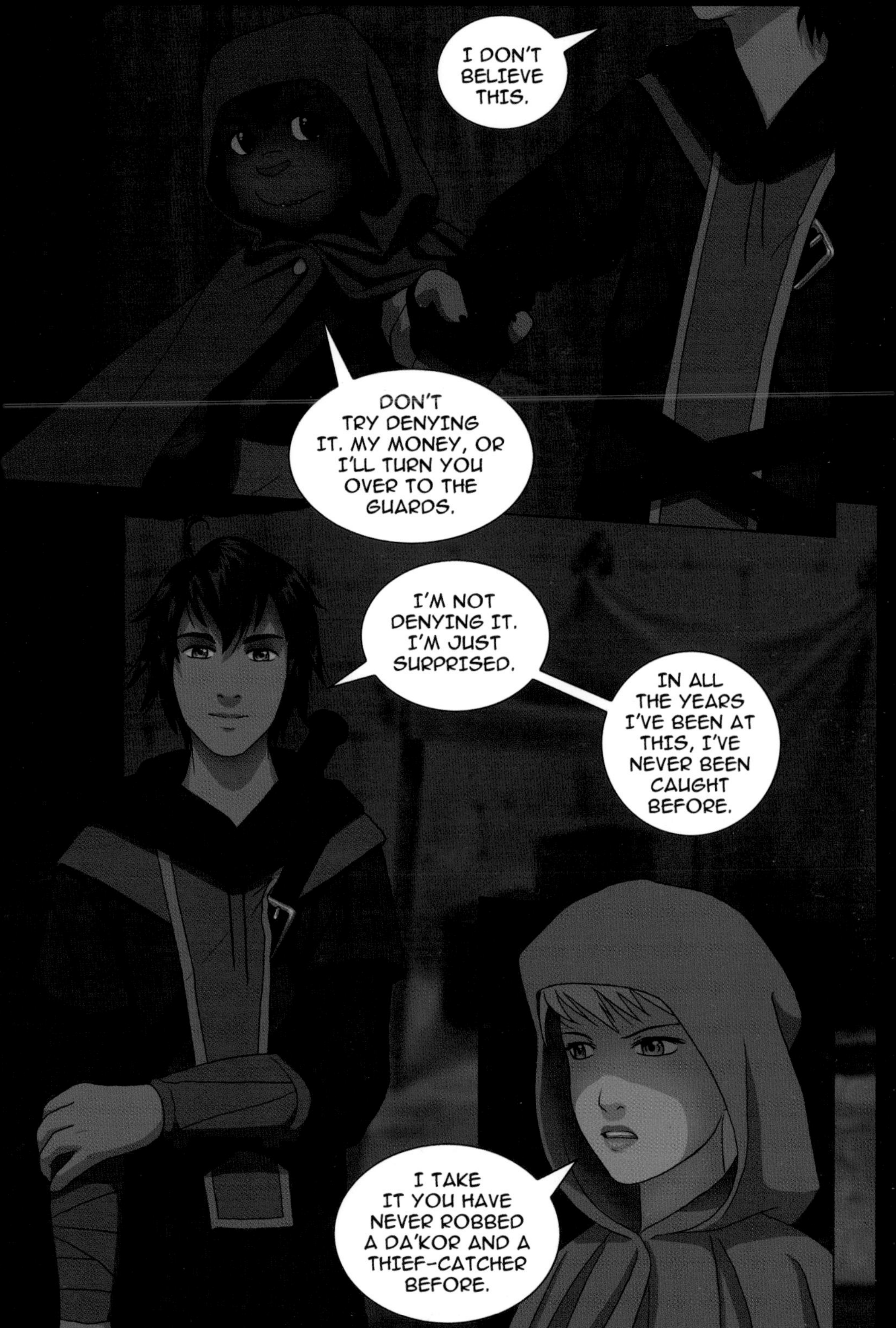
I DON'T BELIEVE THIS.
DON'T TRY DENYING IT. MY MONEY, OR I'LL TURN YOU OVER TO THE GUARDS.
I'M NOT DENYING IT. I'M JUST SURPRISED.
IN ALL THE YEARS I'VE BEEN AT THIS, I'VE NEVER BEEN CAUGHT BEFORE.
I TAKE IT YOU HAVE NEVER ROBBED A DA'KOR AND A THIEF-CATCHER BEFORE.

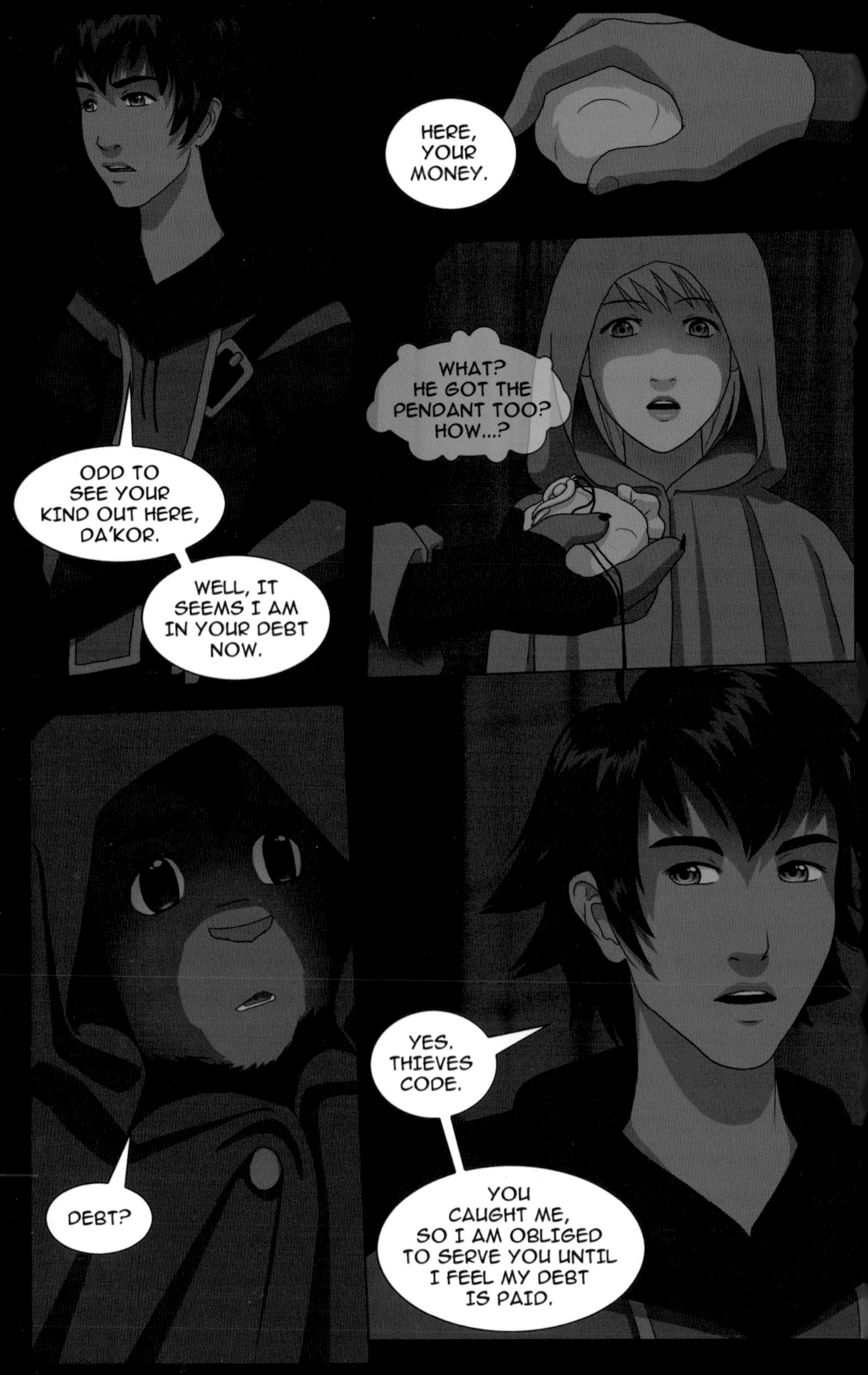
ODD TO SEE YOUR KIND OUT HERE, DA'KOR.
WELL, IT SEEMS I AM IN YOUR DEBT NOW.
HERE, YOUR MONEY.
WHAT? HE GOT THE PENDANT TOO? HOW...?
DEBT?
YES. THIEVES CODE.
YOU CAUGHT ME, SO I AM OBLIGED TO SERVE YOU UNTIL I FEEL MY DEBT IS PAID.

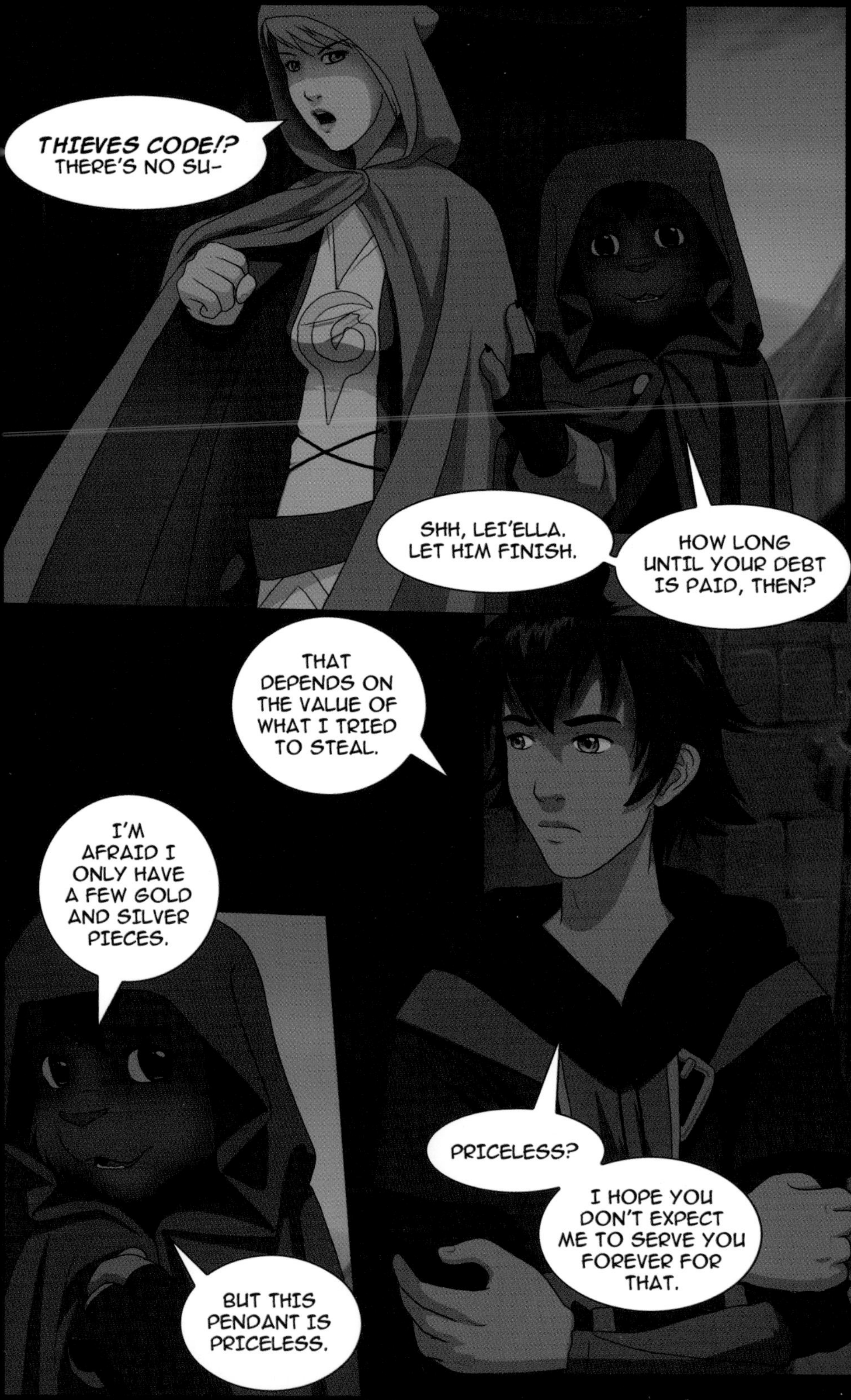
THIEVES CODE!? THERE'S NO SU-
SHH, LEI'ELLA. LET HIM FINISH.
HOW LONG UNTIL YOUR DEBT IS PAID, THEN?
THAT DEPENDS ON THE VALUE OF WHAT I TRIED TO STEAL.
I'M AFRAID I ONLY HAVE A FEW GOLD AND SILVER PIECES.
BUT THIS PENDANT IS PRICELESS.
PRICELESS?
I HOPE YOU DON'T EXPECT ME TO SERVE YOU FOREVER FOR THAT.

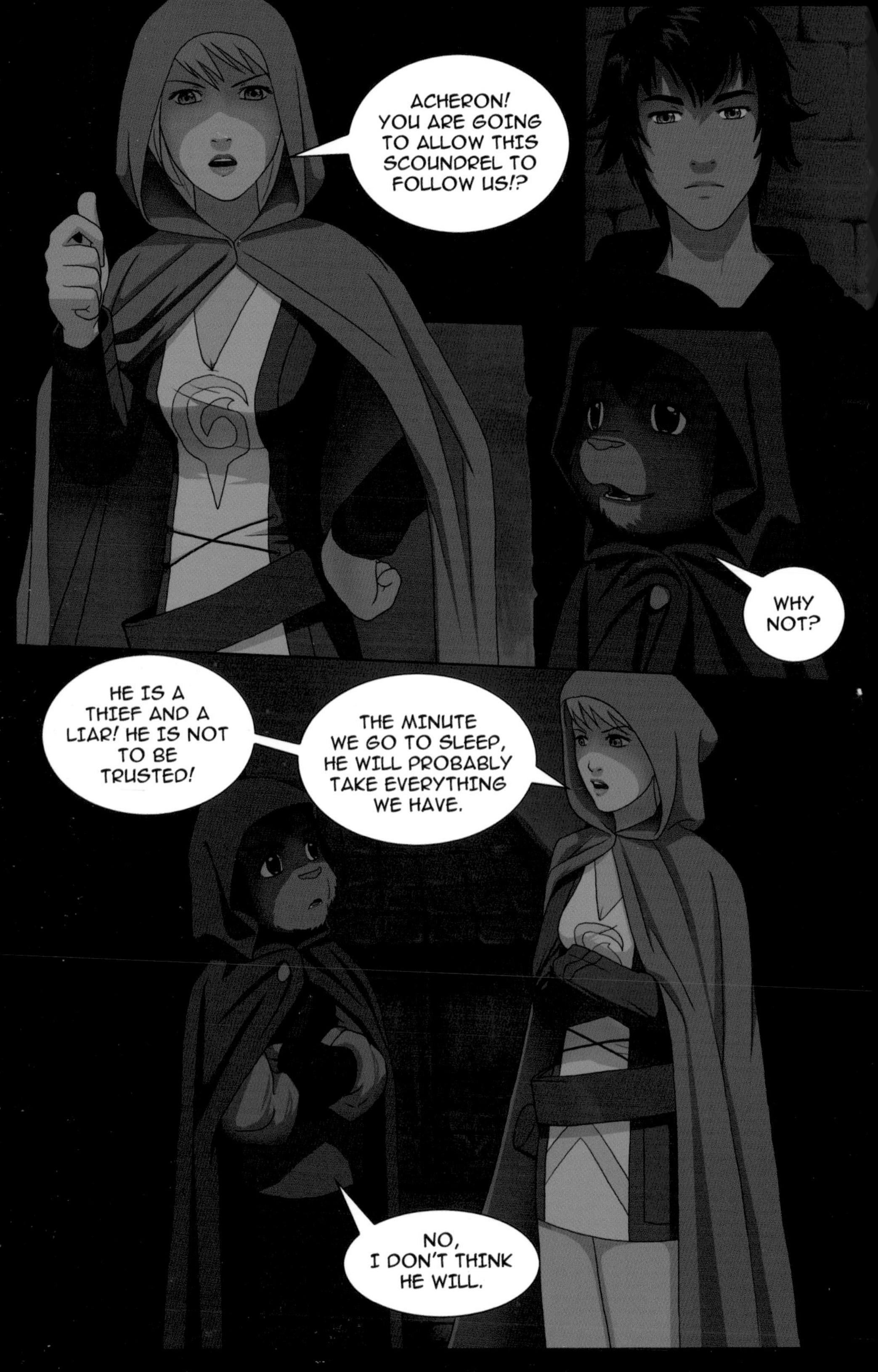
ACHERON! YOU ARE GOING TO ALLOW THIS SCOUNDREL TO FOLLOW US!?
WHY NOT?
HE IS A THIEF AND A LIAR! HE IS NOT TO BE TRUSTED!
THE MINUTE WE GO TO SLEEP, HE WILL PROBABLY TAKE EVERYTHING WE HAVE.
NO, I DON'T THINK HE WILL.

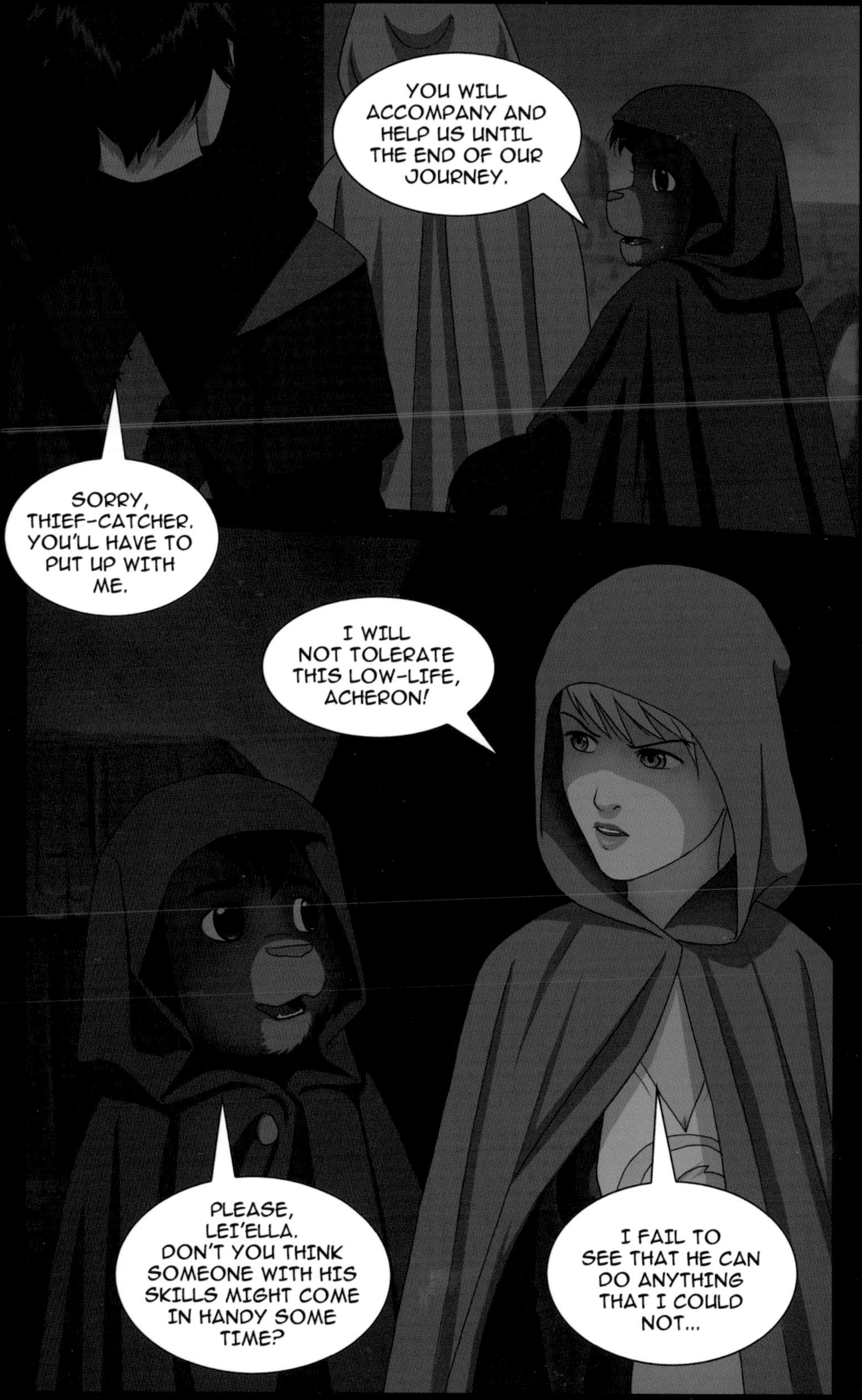
YOU WILL ACCOMPANY AND HELP US UNTIL THE END OF OUR JOURNEY.
SORRY, THIEF-CATCHER. YOU'LL HAVE TO PUT UP WITH ME.
I WILL NOT TOLERATE THIS LOW-LIFE, ACHERON!
PLEASE, LEI'ELLA. DON'T YOU THINK SOMEONE WITH HIS SKILLS MIGHT COME IN HANDY SOME TIME?
I FAIL TO SEE THAT HE CAN DO ANYTHING THAT I COULD NOT...

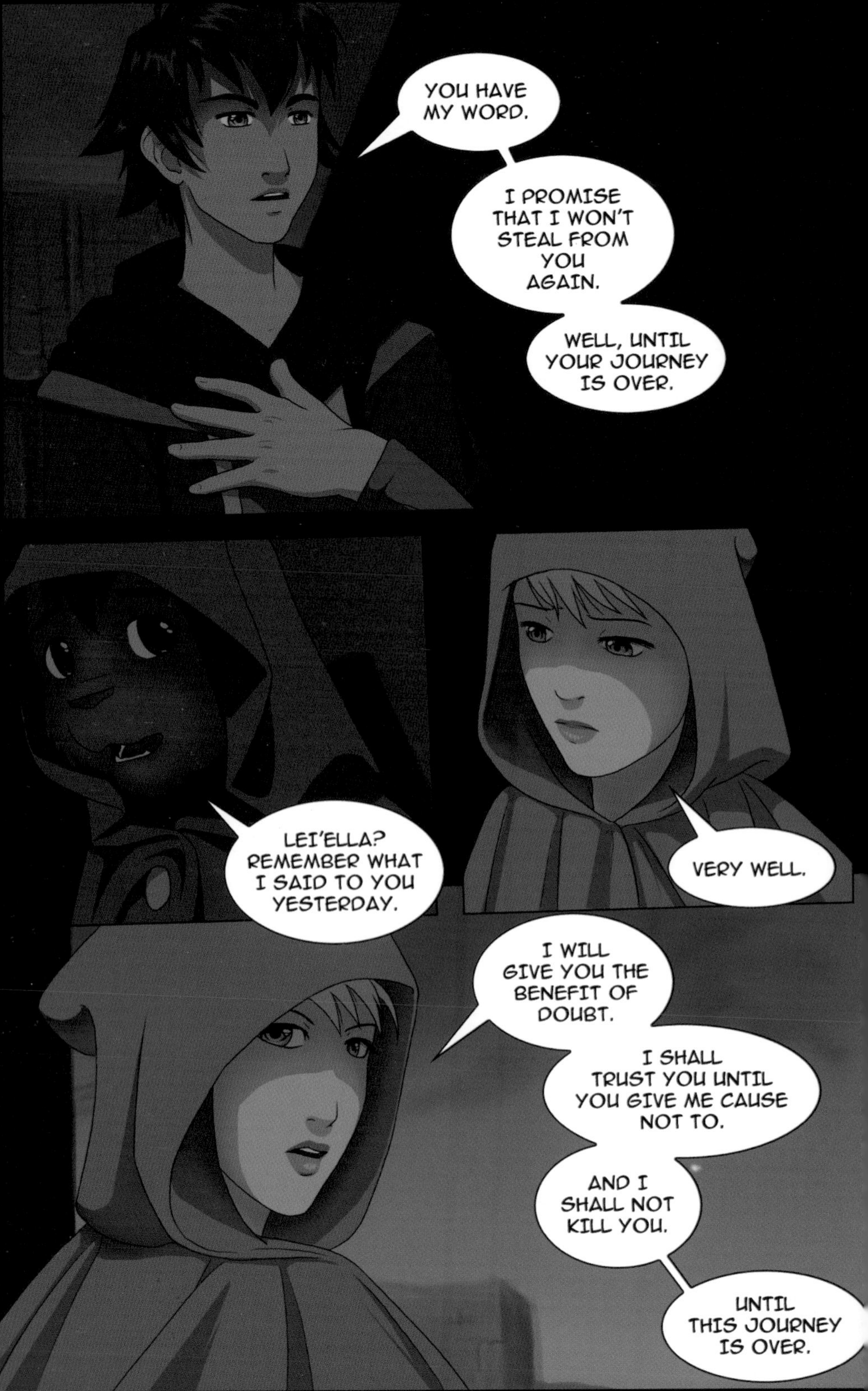
YOU HAVE MY WORD.
I PROMISE THAT I WON'T STEAL FROM YOU AGAIN.
WELL, UNTIL YOUR JOURNEY IS OVER.
LEI'ELLA? REMEMBER WHAT I SAID TO YOU YESTERDAY.
VERY WELL.
I WILL GIVE YOU THE BENEFIT OF DOUBT.
I SHALL TRUST YOU UNTIL YOU GIVE ME CAUSE NOT TO.
AND I SHALL NOT KILL YOU.
UNTIL THIS JOURNEY IS OVER.

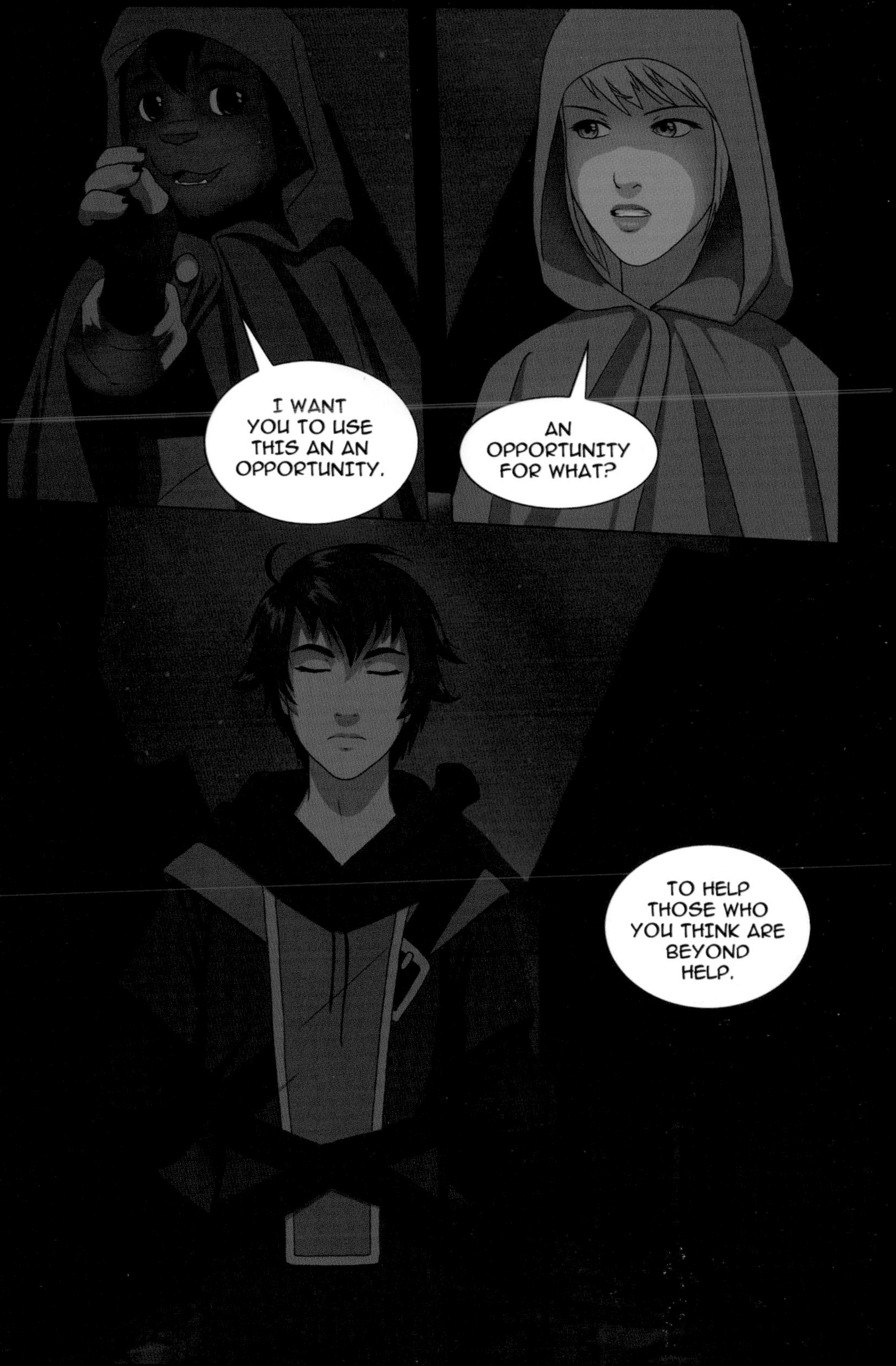
I WANT YOU TO USE THIS AN AN OPPORTUNITY.
AN OPPORTUNITY FOR WHAT?
TO HELP THOSE WHO YOU THINK ARE BEYOND HELP.

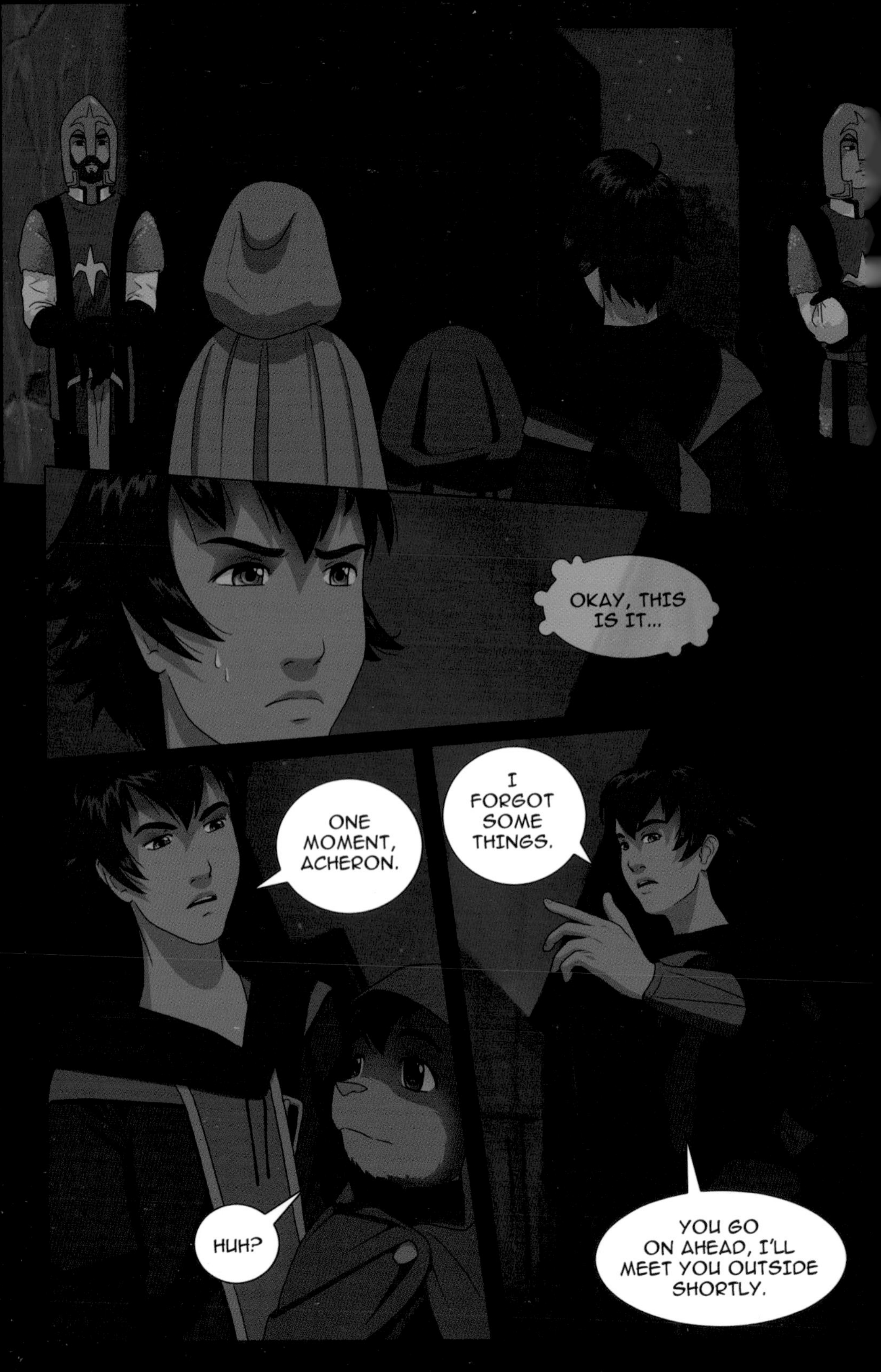
OKAY, THIS IS IT...
ONE MOMENT, ACHERON.
I FORGOT SOME THINGS.
HUH?
YOU GO ON AHEAD, I'LL MEET YOU OUTSIDE SHORTLY.

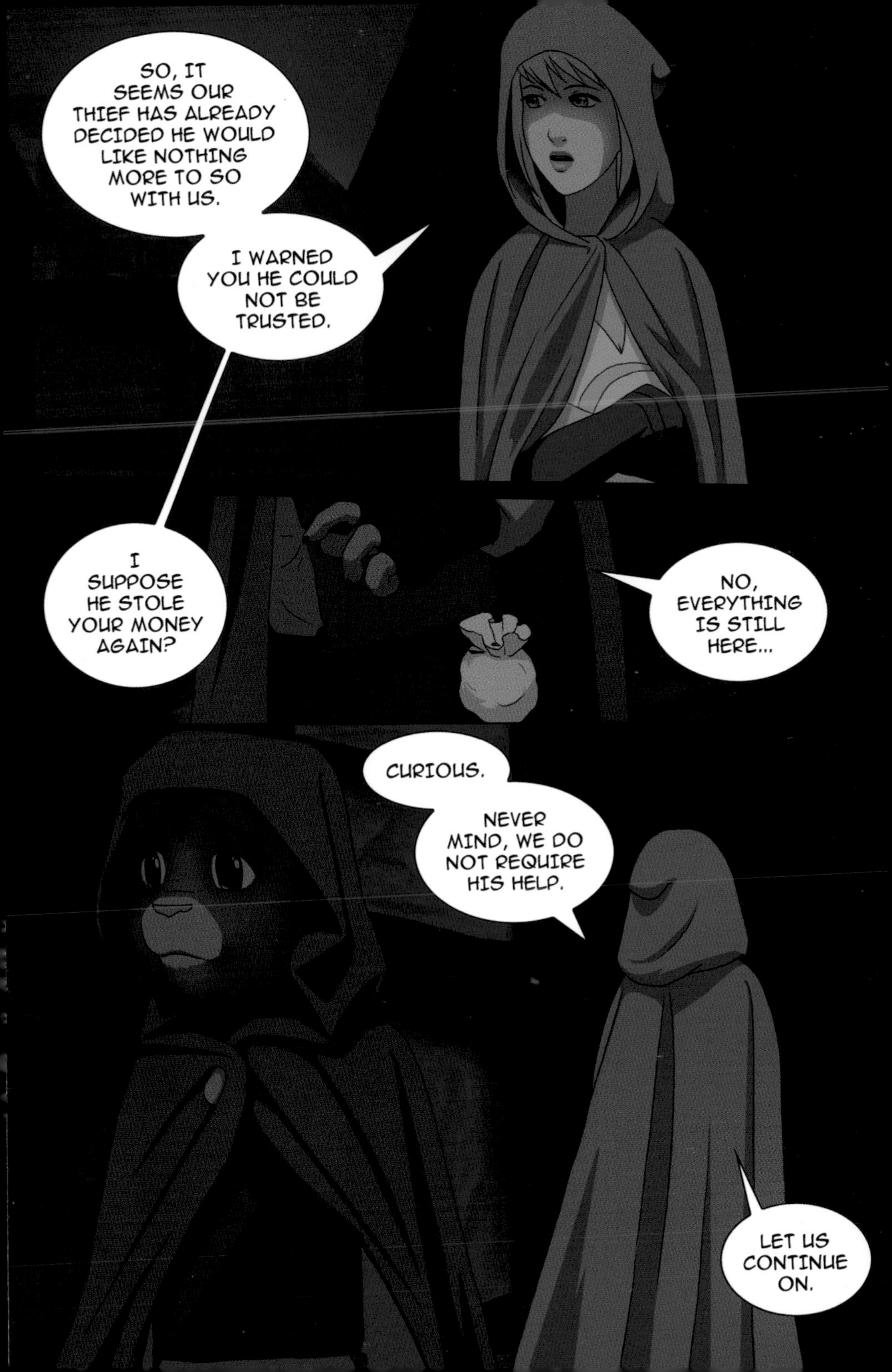
SO, IT SEEMS OUR THIEF HAS ALREADY DECIDED HE WOULD LIKE NOTHING MORE TO SO WITH US.
I WARNED YOU HE COULD NOT BE TRUSTED.
I SUPPOSE HE STOLE YOUR MONEY AGAIN?
NO, EVERYTHING IS STILL HERE...
CURIOUS.
NEVER MIND, WE DO NOT REQUIRE HIS HELP.
LET US CONTINUE ON.

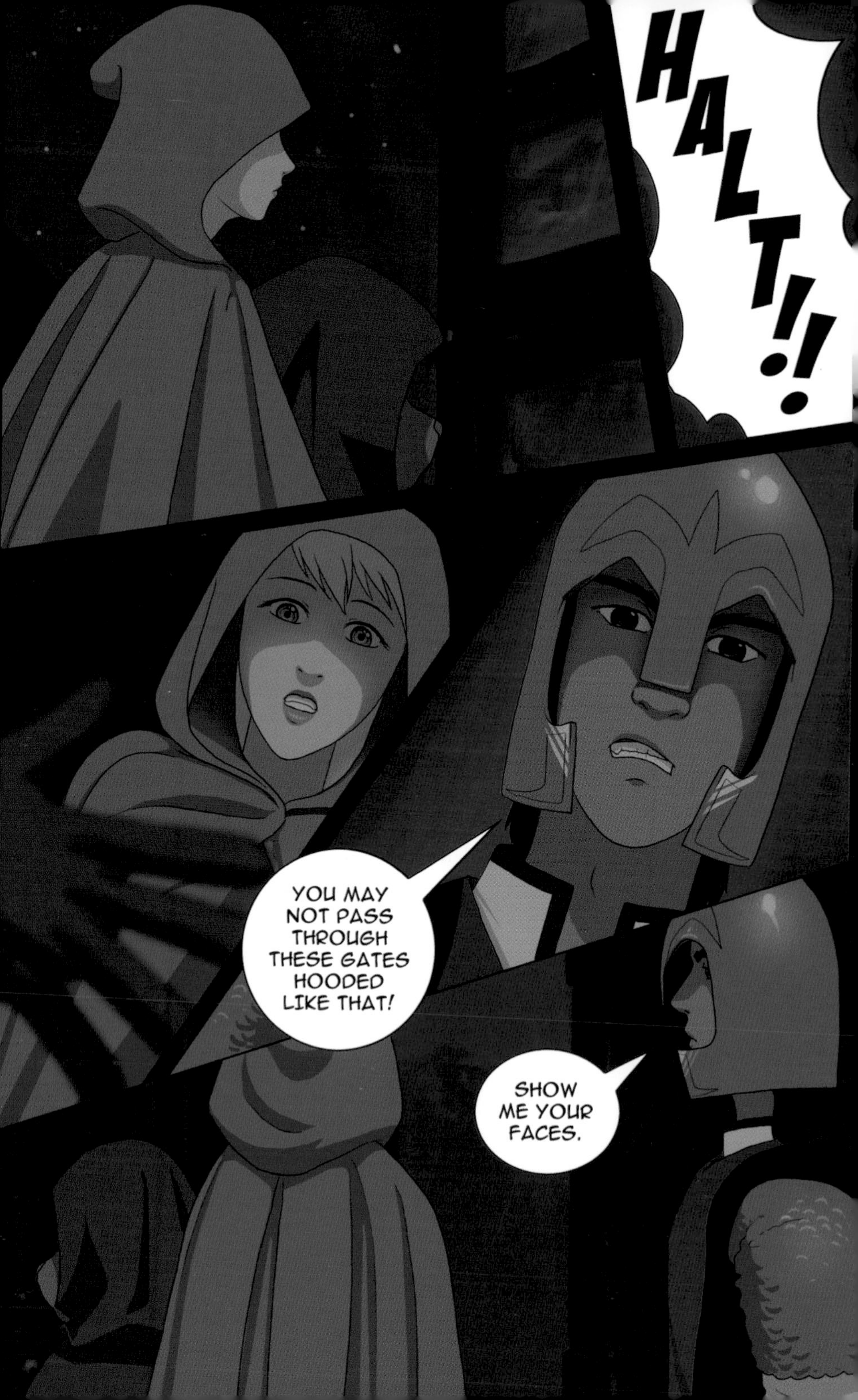
HALT!!
YOU MAY NOT PASS THROUGH THESE GATES HOODED LIKE THAT!
SHOW ME YOUR FACES.

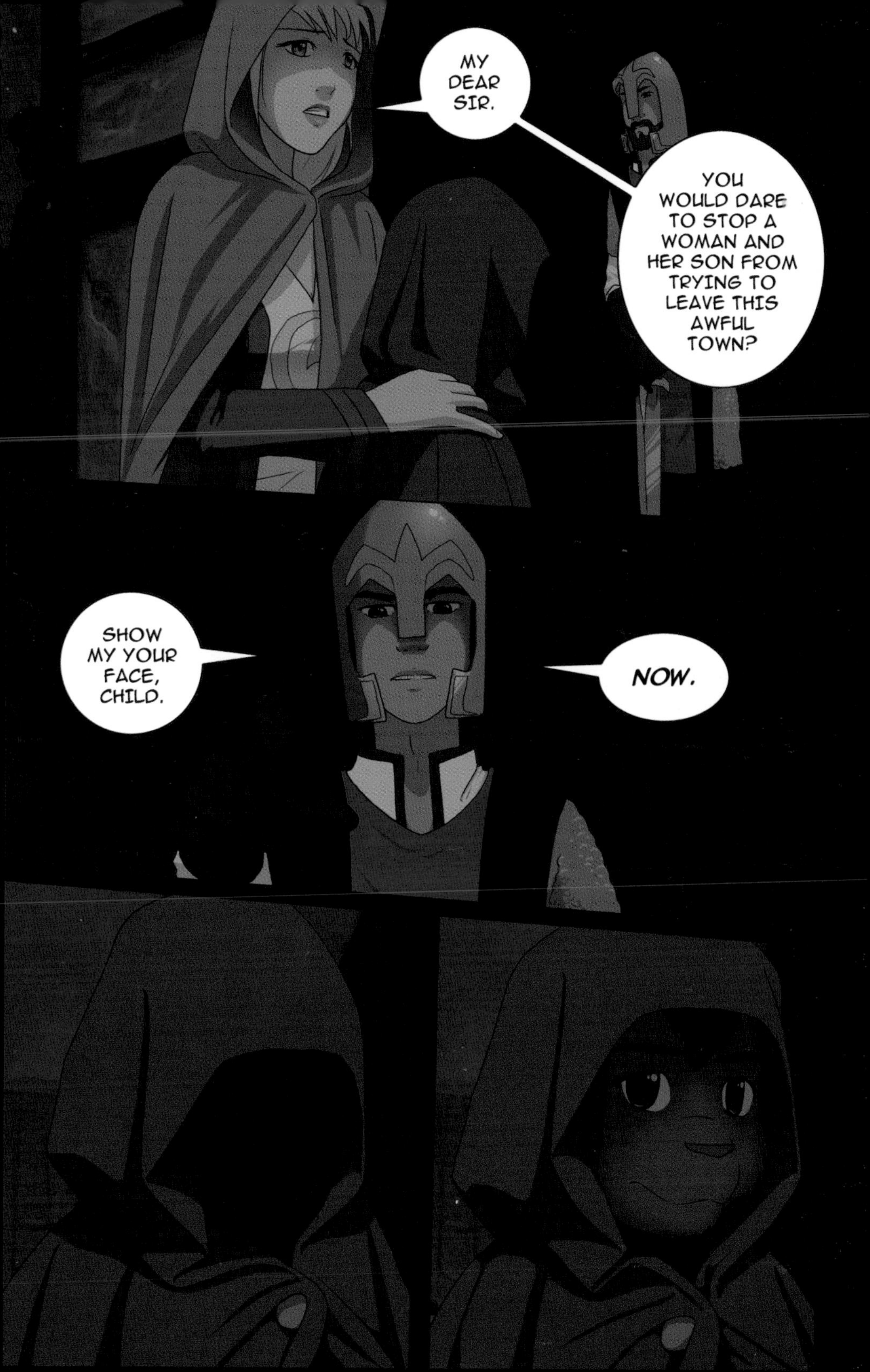
MY DEAR SIR.
YOU WOULD DARE TO STOP A WOMAN AND HER SON FROM TRYING TO LEAVE THIS AWFUL TOWN?
SHOW MY YOUR FACE, CHILD.
NOW.

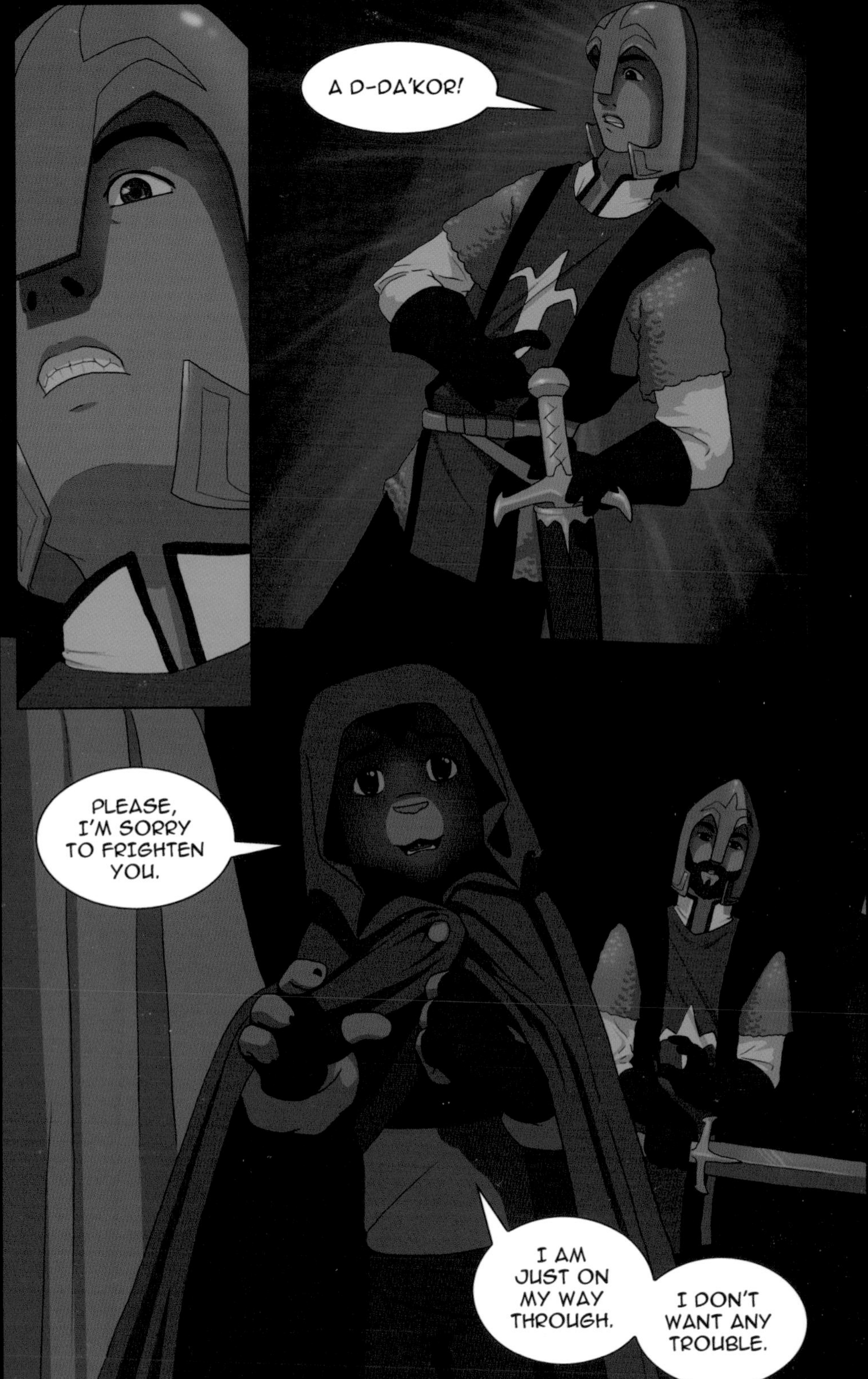
A D-DA'KOR!
PLEASE, I'M SORRY TO FRIGHTEN YOU.
I AM JUST ON MY WAY THROUGH.
I DON'T WANT ANY TROUBLE.

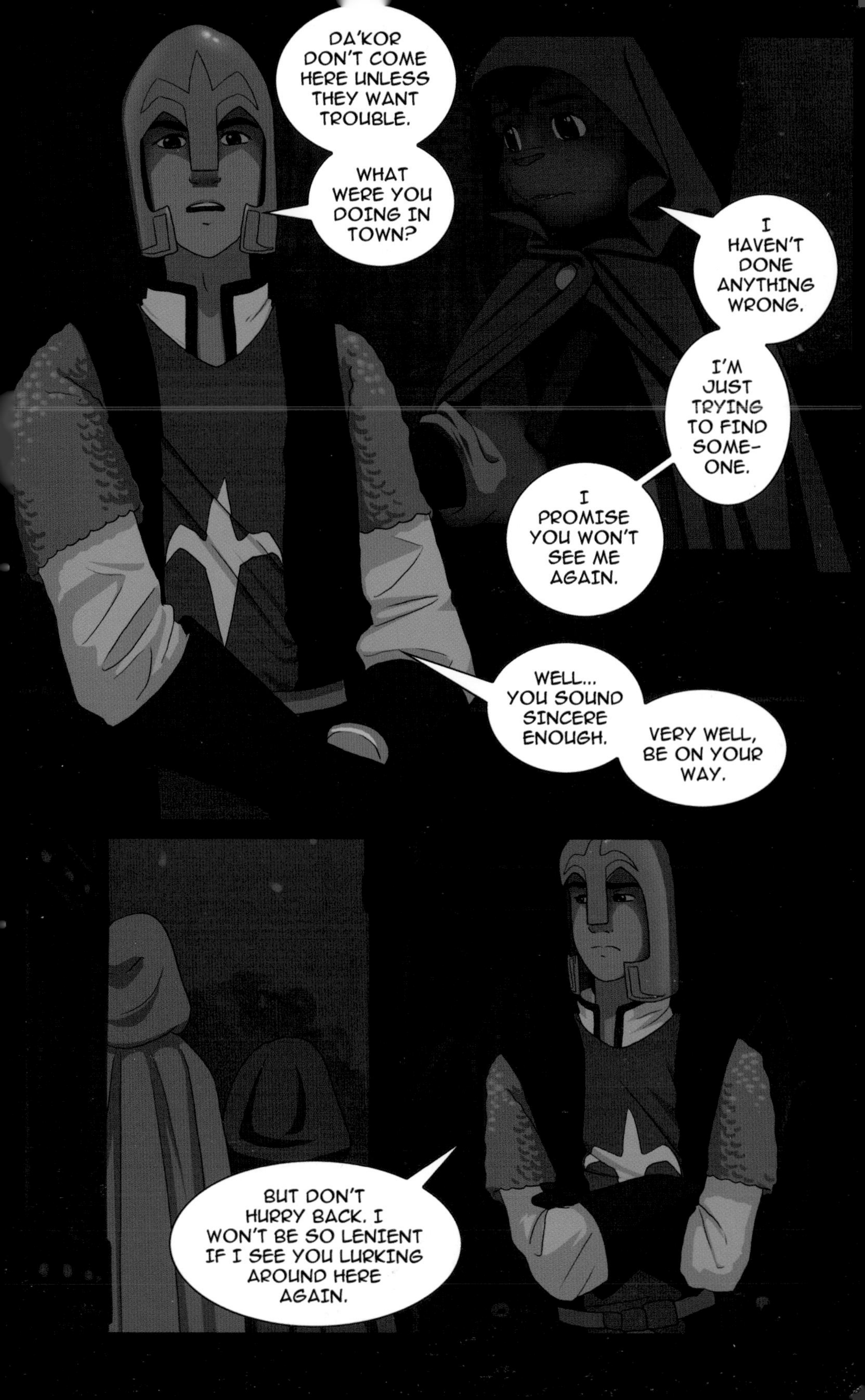
DA'KOR DON'T COME HERE UNLESS THEY WANT TROUBLE.
WHAT WERE YOU DOING IN TOWN?
I HAVEN'T DONE ANYTHING WRONG.
I'M JUST TRYING TO FIND SOME-ONE.
I PROMISE YOU WON'T SEE ME AGAIN.
WELL... YOU SOUND SINCERE ENOUGH.
VERY WELL, BE ON YOUR WAY.
BUT DON'T HURRY BACK. I WON'T BE SO LENIENT IF I SEE YOU LURKING AROUND HERE AGAIN.

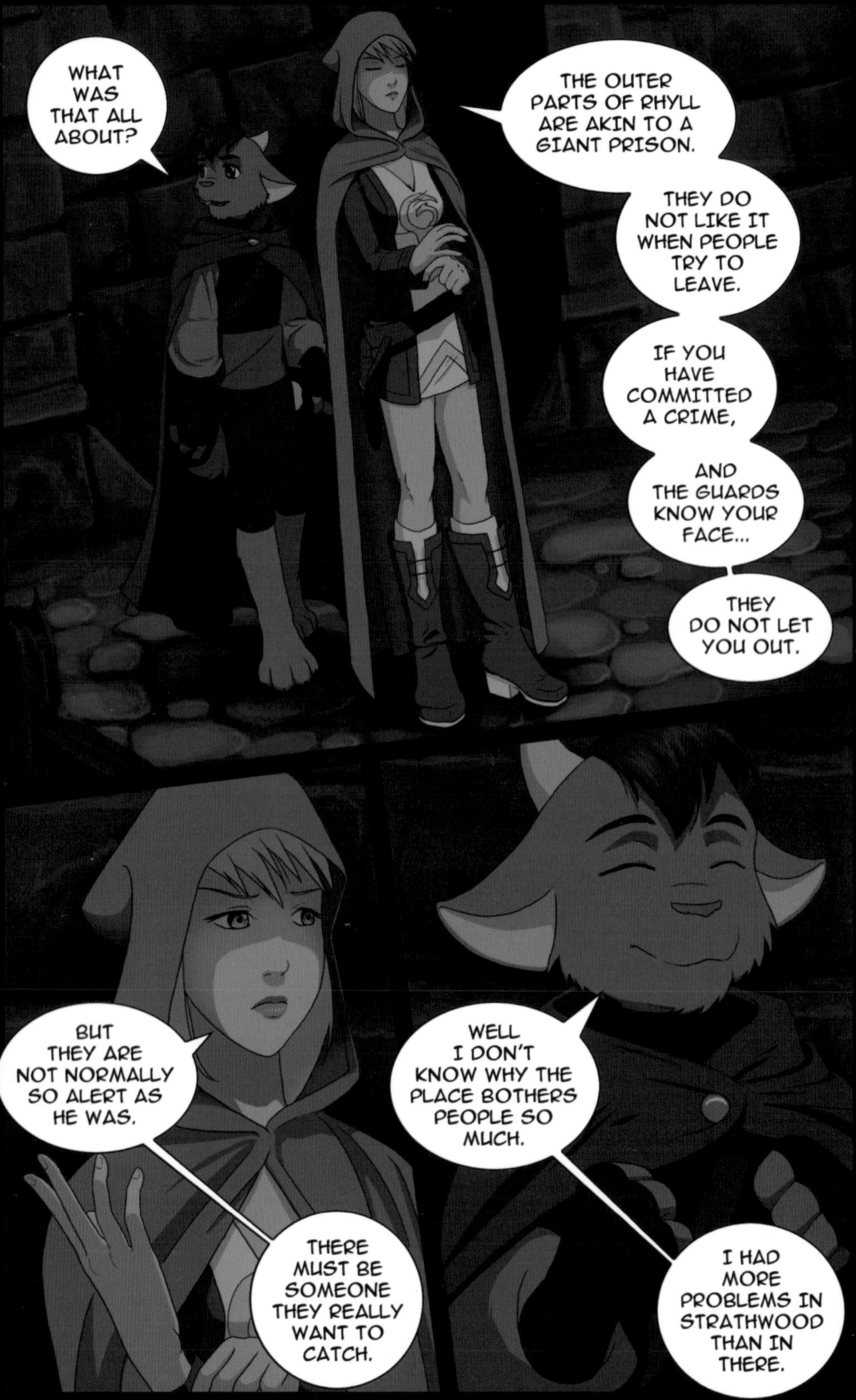
WHAT WAS THAT ALL ABOUT?
THE OUTER PARTS OF RHYLL ARE AKIN TO A GIANT PRISON.
THEY DO NOT LIKE IT WHEN PEOPLE TRY TO LEAVE.
IF YOU HAVE COMMITTED A CRIME,
AND THE GUARDS KNOW YOUR FACE...
THEY DO NOT LET YOU OUT.
BUT THEY ARE NOT NORMALLY SO ALERT AS HE WAS.
THERE MUST BE SOMEONE THEY REALLY WANT TO CATCH.
WELL I DON'T KNOW WHY THE PLACE BOTHERS PEOPLE SO MUCH.
I HAD MORE PROBLEMS IN STRATHWOOD THAN IN THERE.

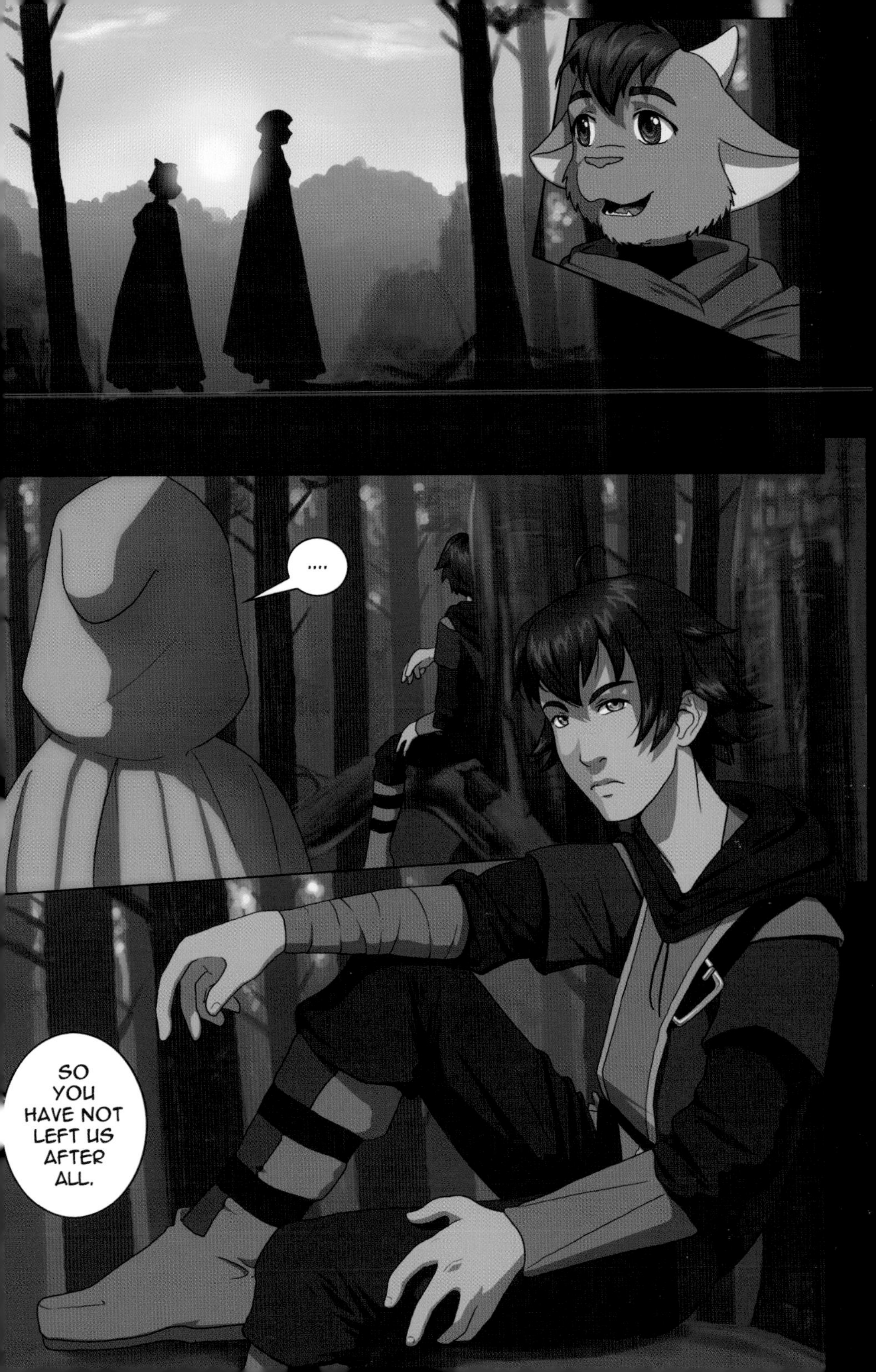
....
SO YOU HAVE NOT LEFT US AFTER ALL.

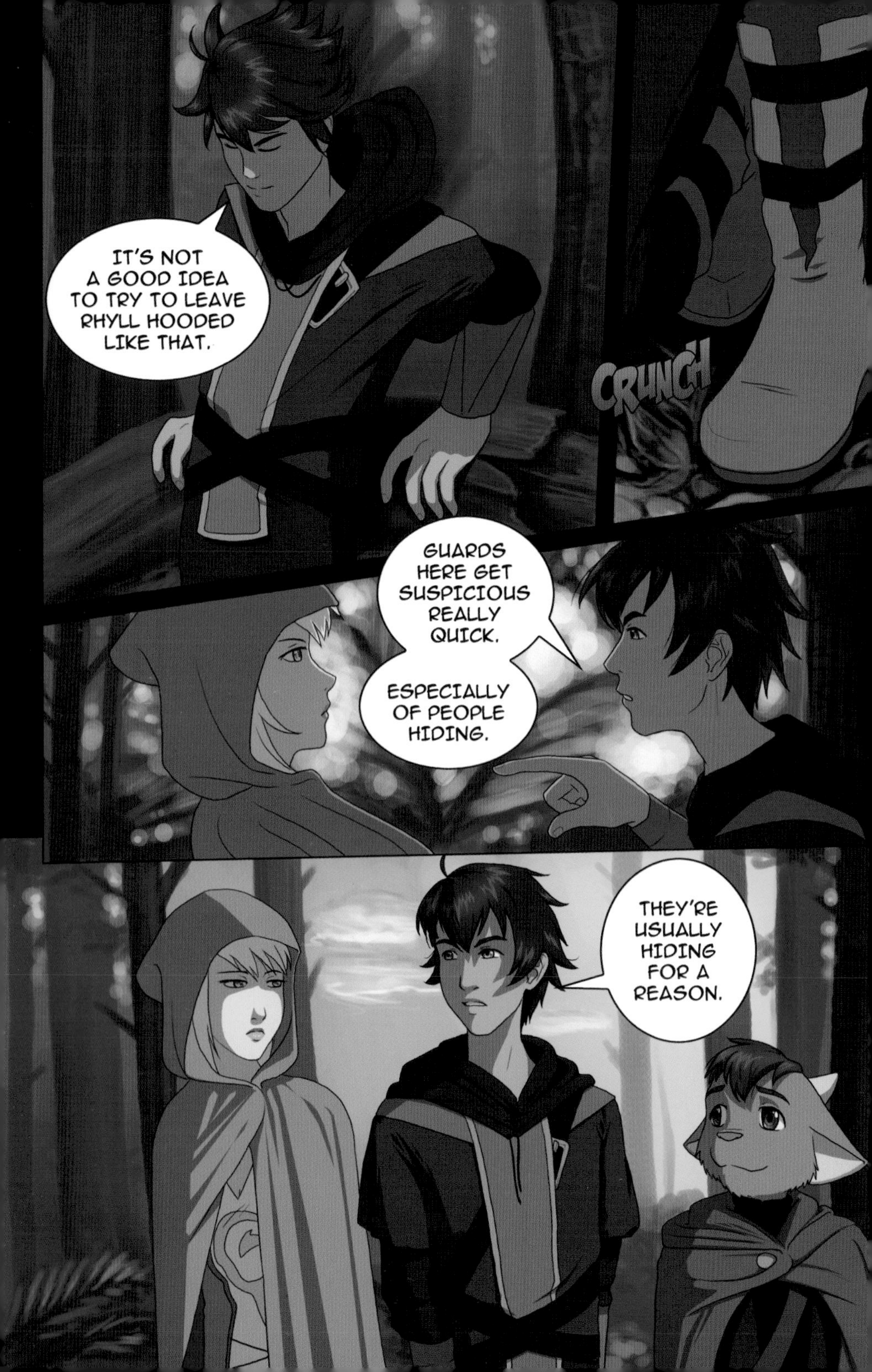
IT'S NOT A GOOD IDEA TO TRY TO LEAVE RHYLL HOODED LIKE THAT.
CRUNCH
GUARDS HERE GET SUSPICIOUS REALLY QUICK.
ESPECIALLY OF PEOPLE HIDING.
THEY'RE USUALLY HIDING FOR A REASON.

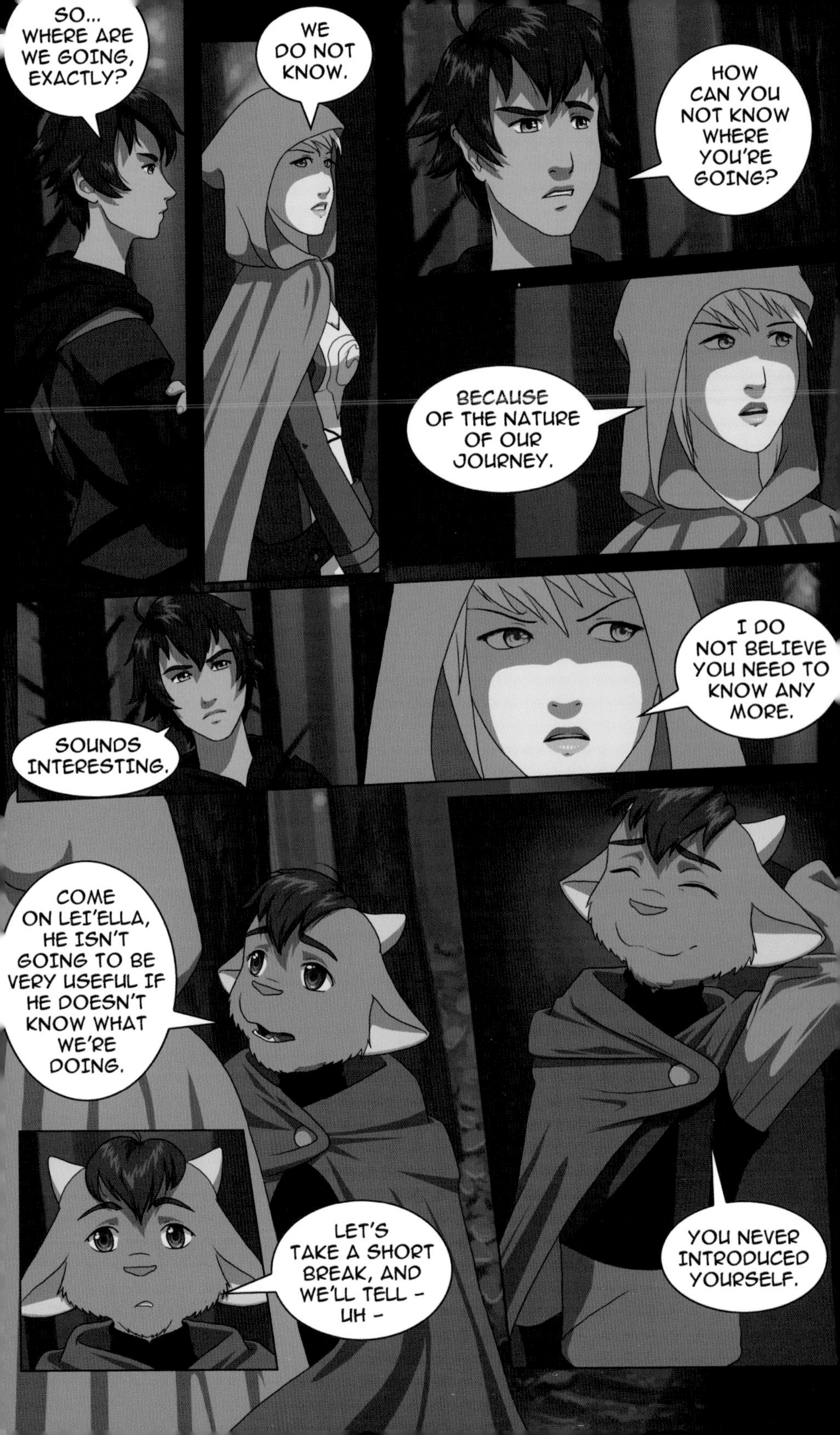
SO... WHERE ARE WE GOING, EXACTLY?
WE DO NOT KNOW.
HOW CAN YOU NOT KNOW WHERE YOU'RE GOING?
BECAUSE OF THE NATURE OF OUR JOURNEY.
SOUNDS INTERESTING.
I DO NOT BELIEVE YOU NEED TO KNOW ANY MORE.
COME ON LEI'ELLA, HE ISN'T GOING TO BE VERY USEFUL IF HE DOESN'T KNOW WHAT WE'RE DOING.
LET'S TAKE A SHORT BREAK, AND WE'LL TELL - UH -
YOU NEVER INTRODUCED YOURSELF.

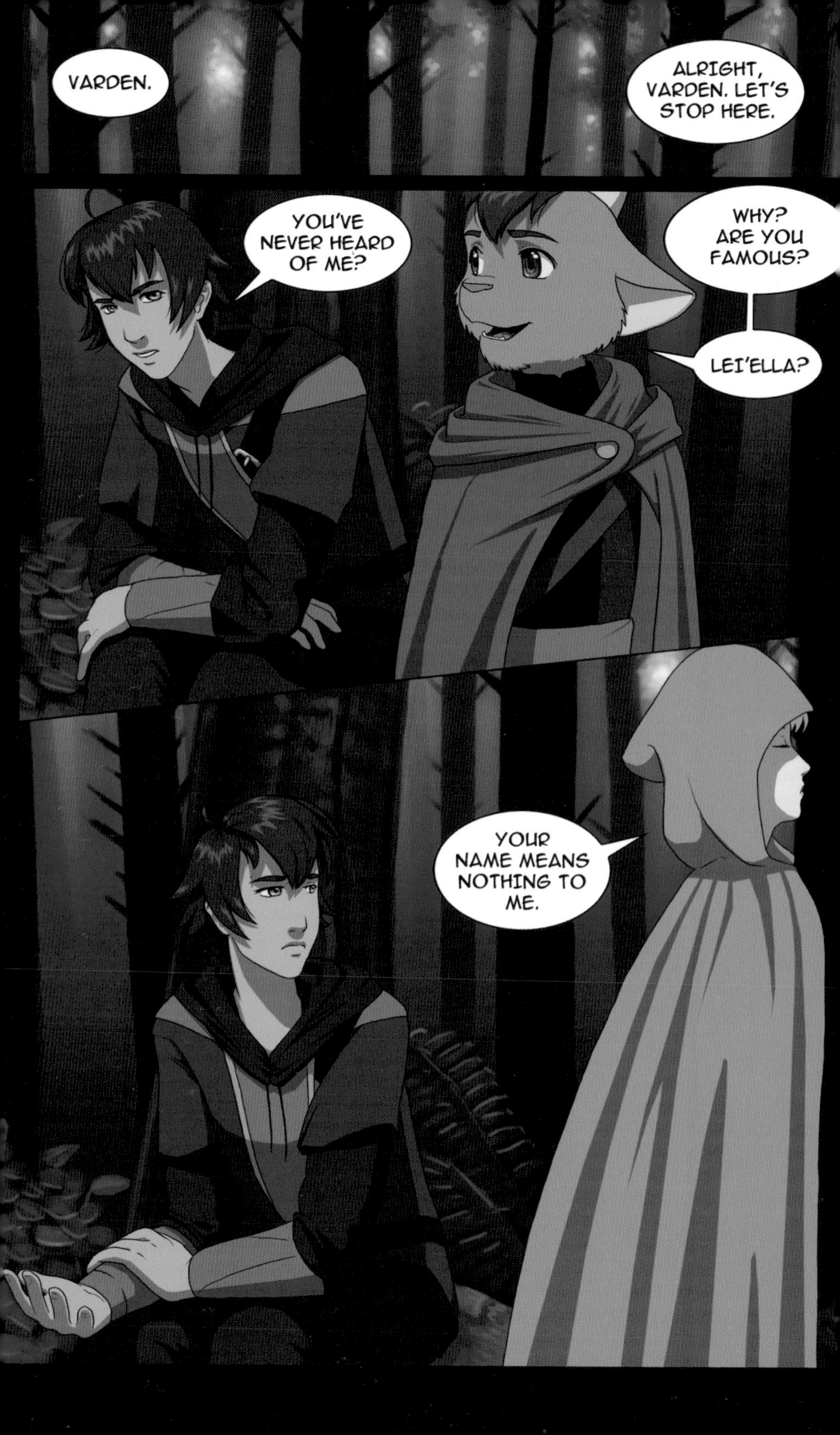
VARDEN.
ALRIGHT, VARDEN. LET'S STOP HERE.
YOU'VE NEVER HEARD OF ME?
WHY? ARE YOU FAMOUS?
LEI'ELLA?
YOUR NAME MEANS NOTHING TO ME.

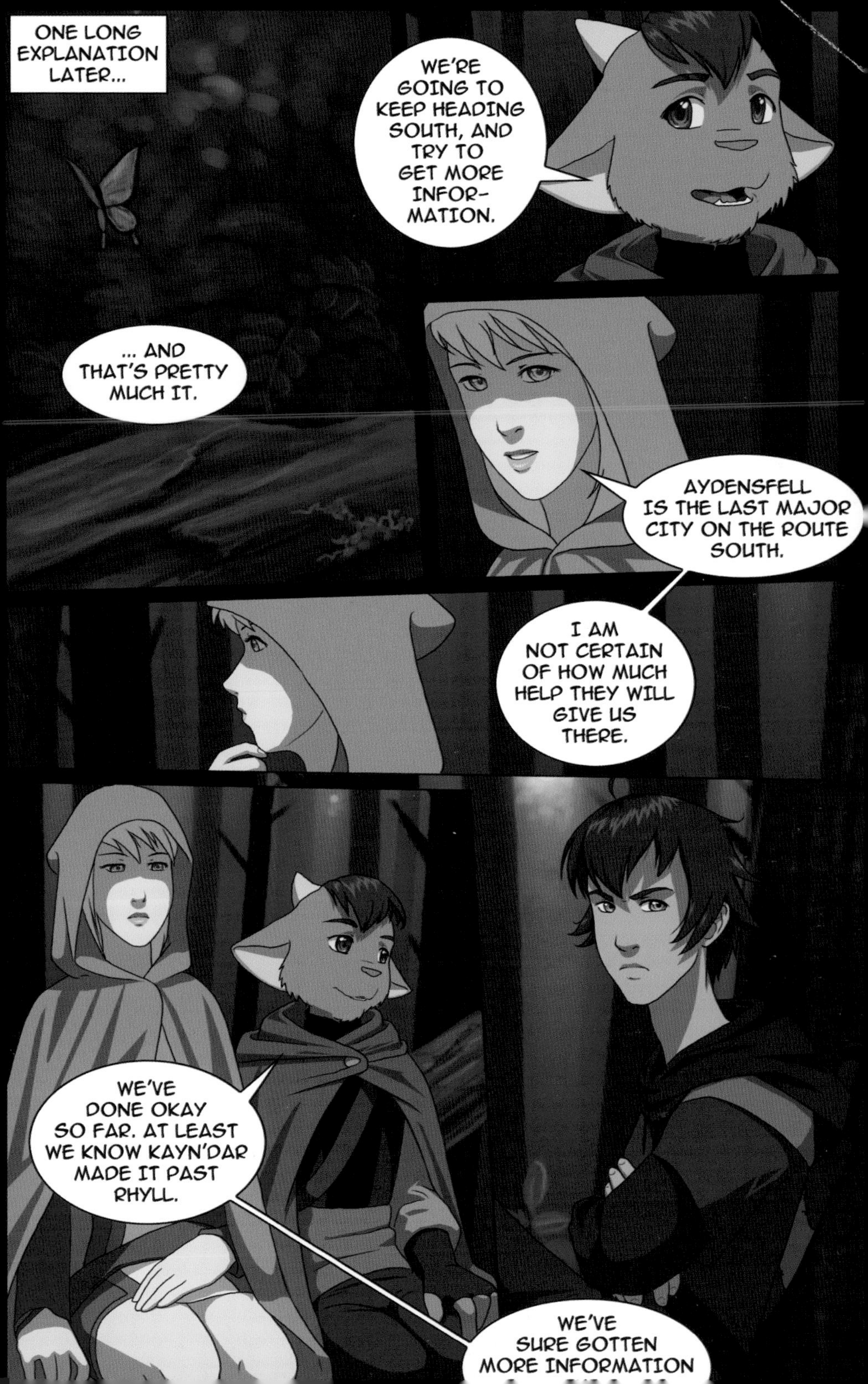
ONE LONG EXPLANATION LATER...
WE'RE GOING TO KEEP HEADING SOUTH, AND TRY TO GET MORE INFOR-MATION.
... AND THAT'S PRETTY MUCH IT.
AYDENSFELL IS THE LAST MAJOR CITY ON THE ROUTE SOUTH.
I AM NOT CERTAIN OF HOW MUCH HELP THEY WILL GIVE US THERE.
WE'VE DONE OKAY SO FAR. AT LEAST WE KNOW KAYN'DAR MADE IT PAST RHYLL.
WE'VE SURE GOTTEN MORE INFORMATION

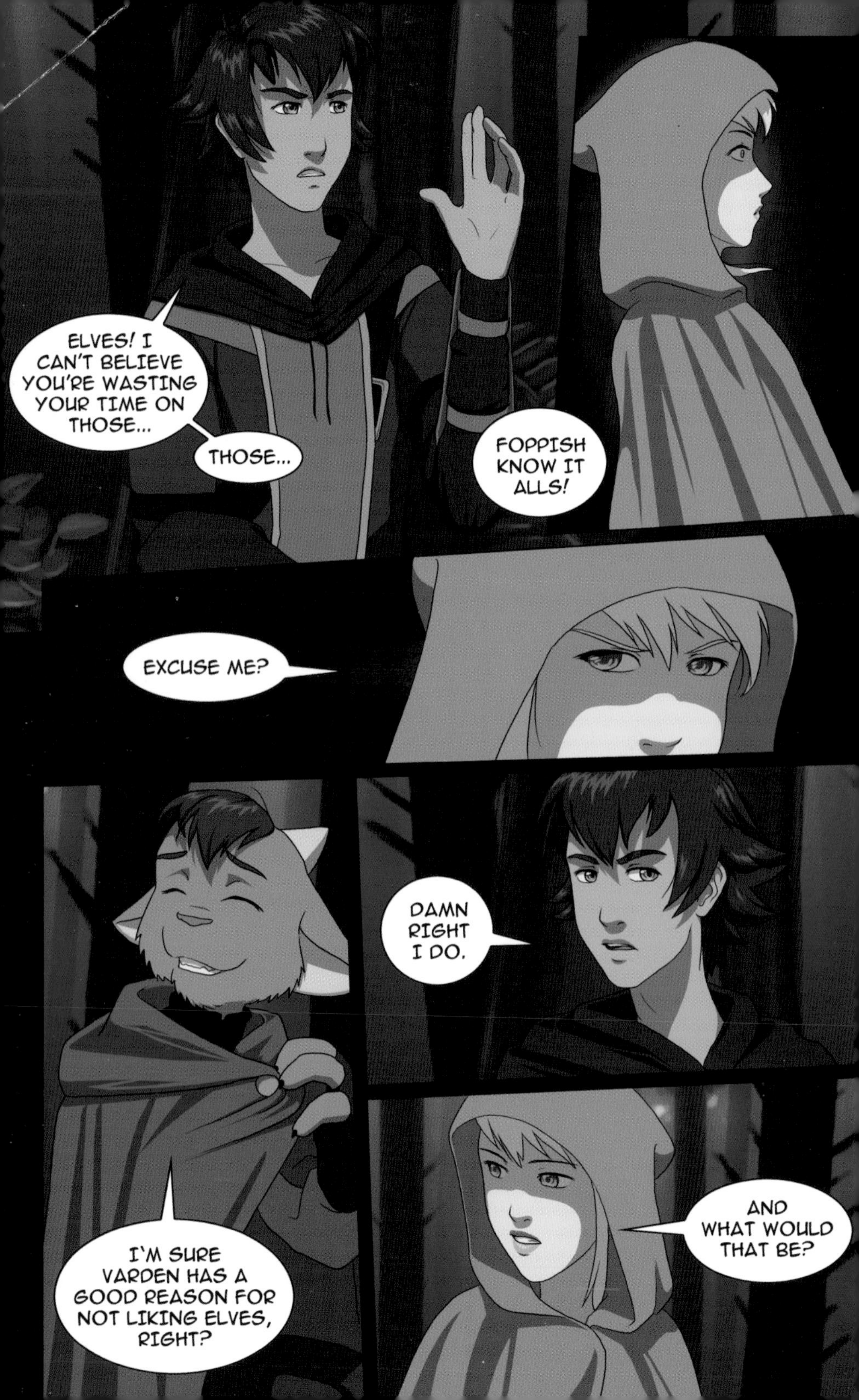
ELVES! I CAN'T BELIEVE YOU'RE WASTING YOUR TIME ON THOSE...
THOSE...
FOPPISH KNOW IT ALLS!
EXCUSE ME?
I'M SURE VARDEN HAS A GOOD REASON FOR NOT LIKING ELVES, RIGHT?
DAMN RIGHT I DO.
AND WHAT WOULD THAT BE?

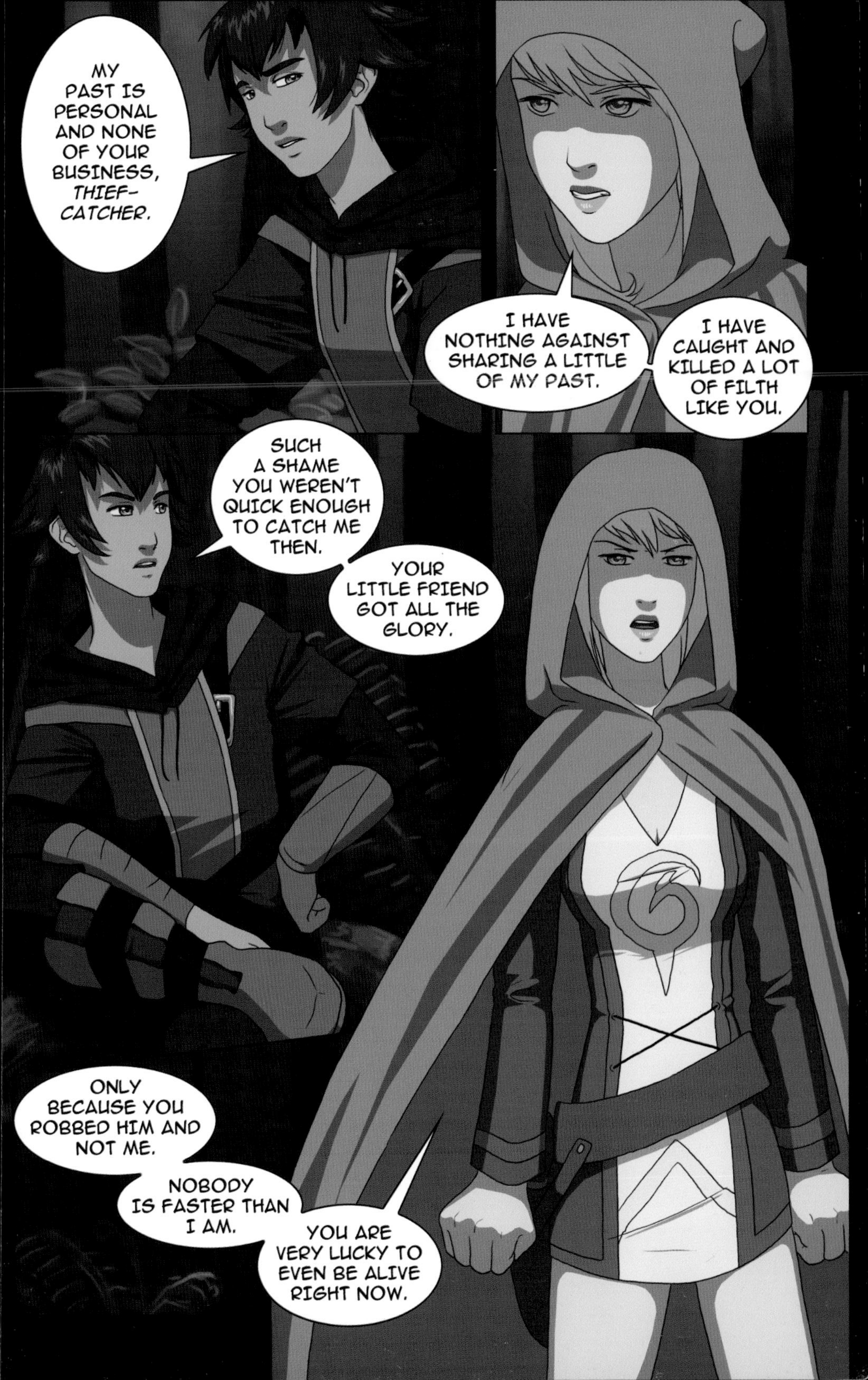
MY PAST IS PERSONAL AND NONE OF YOUR BUSINESS, THIEF-CATCHER.
I HAVE NOTHING AGAINST SHARING A LITTLE OF MY PAST.
I HAVE CAUGHT AND KILLED A LOT OF FILTH LIKE YOU.
SUCH A SHAME YOU WEREN'T QUICK ENOUGH TO CATCH ME THEN.
YOUR LITTLE FRIEND GOT ALL THE GLORY.
ONLY BECAUSE YOU ROBBED HIM AND NOT ME.
NOBODY IS FASTER THAN I AM.
YOU ARE VERY LUCKY TO EVEN BE ALIVE RIGHT NOW.

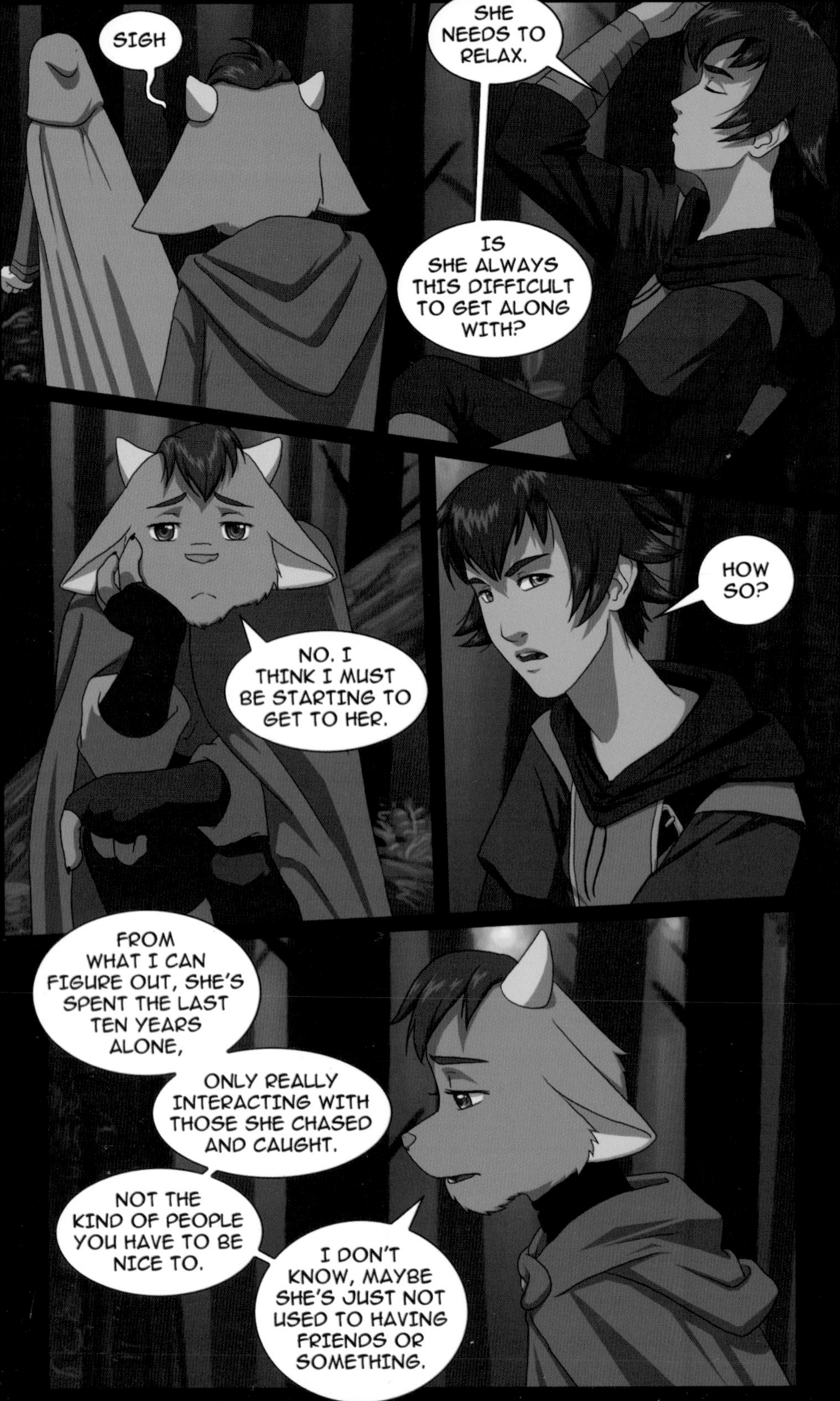
SIGH
SHE NEEDS TO RELAX.
IS SHE ALWAYS THIS DIFFICULT TO GET ALONG WITH?
NO. I THINK I MUST BE STARTING TO GET TO HER.
HOW SO?
FROM WHAT I CAN FIGURE OUT, SHE'S SPENT THE LAST TEN YEARS ALONE,
ONLY REALLY INTERACTING WITH THOSE SHE CHASED AND CAUGHT.
NOT THE KIND OF PEOPLE YOU HAVE TO BE NICE TO.
I DON'T KNOW, MAYBE SHE'S JUST NOT USED TO HAVING FRIENDS OR SOMETHING.

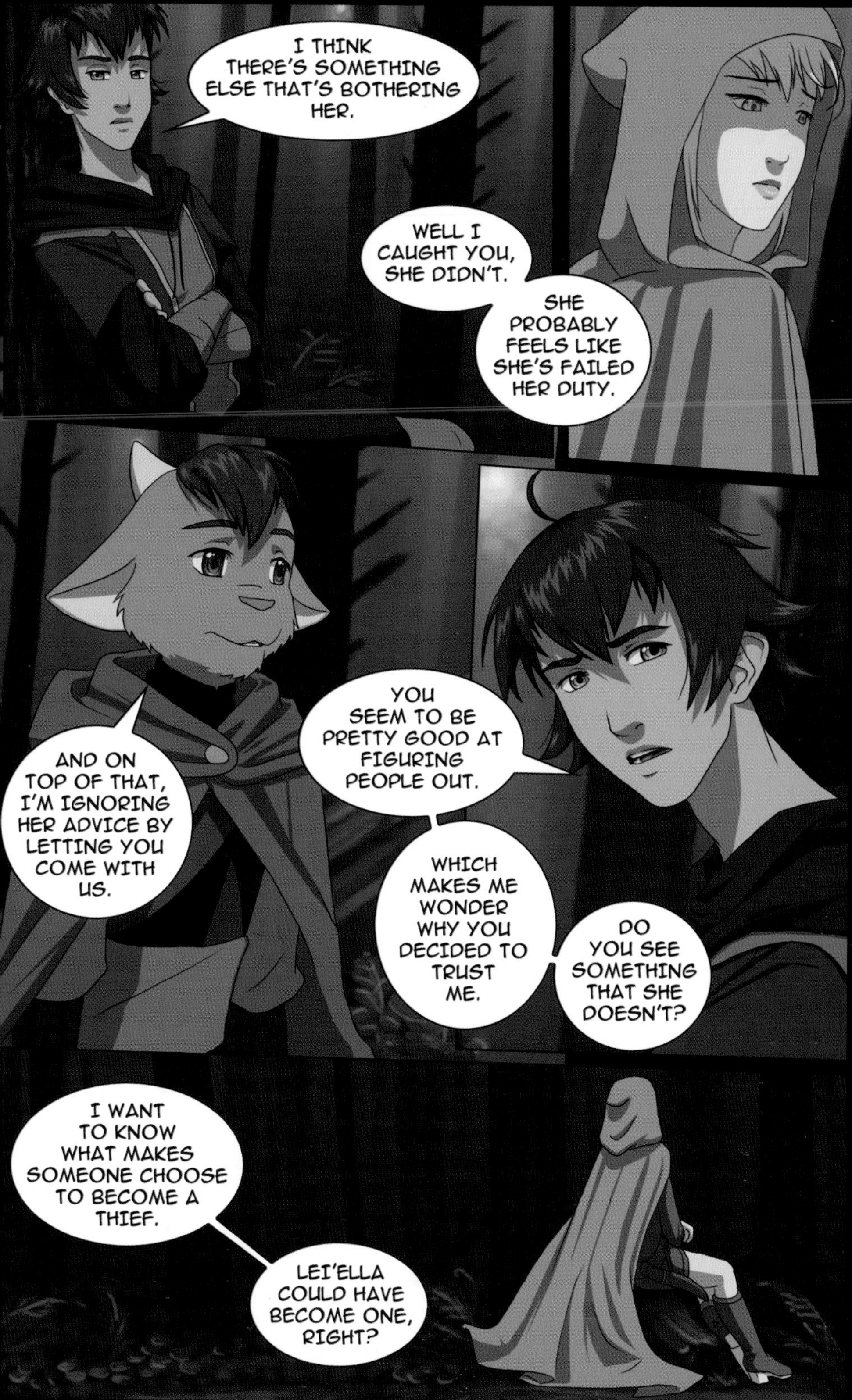
I THINK THERE'S SOMETHING ELSE THAT'S BOTHERING HER.
WELL I CAUGHT YOU, SHE DIDN'T.
SHE PROBABLY FEELS LIKE SHE'S FAILED HER DUTY.
AND ON TOP OF THAT, I'M IGNORING HER ADVICE BY LETTING YOU COME WITH US.
YOU SEEM TO BE PRETTY GOOD AT FIGURING PEOPLE OUT.
WHICH MAKES ME WONDER WHY YOU DECIDED TO TRUST ME.
DO YOU SEE SOMETHING THAT SHE DOESN'T?
I WANT TO KNOW WHAT MAKES SOMEONE CHOOSE TO BECOME A THIEF.
LEI'ELLA COULD HAVE BECOME ONE, RIGHT?

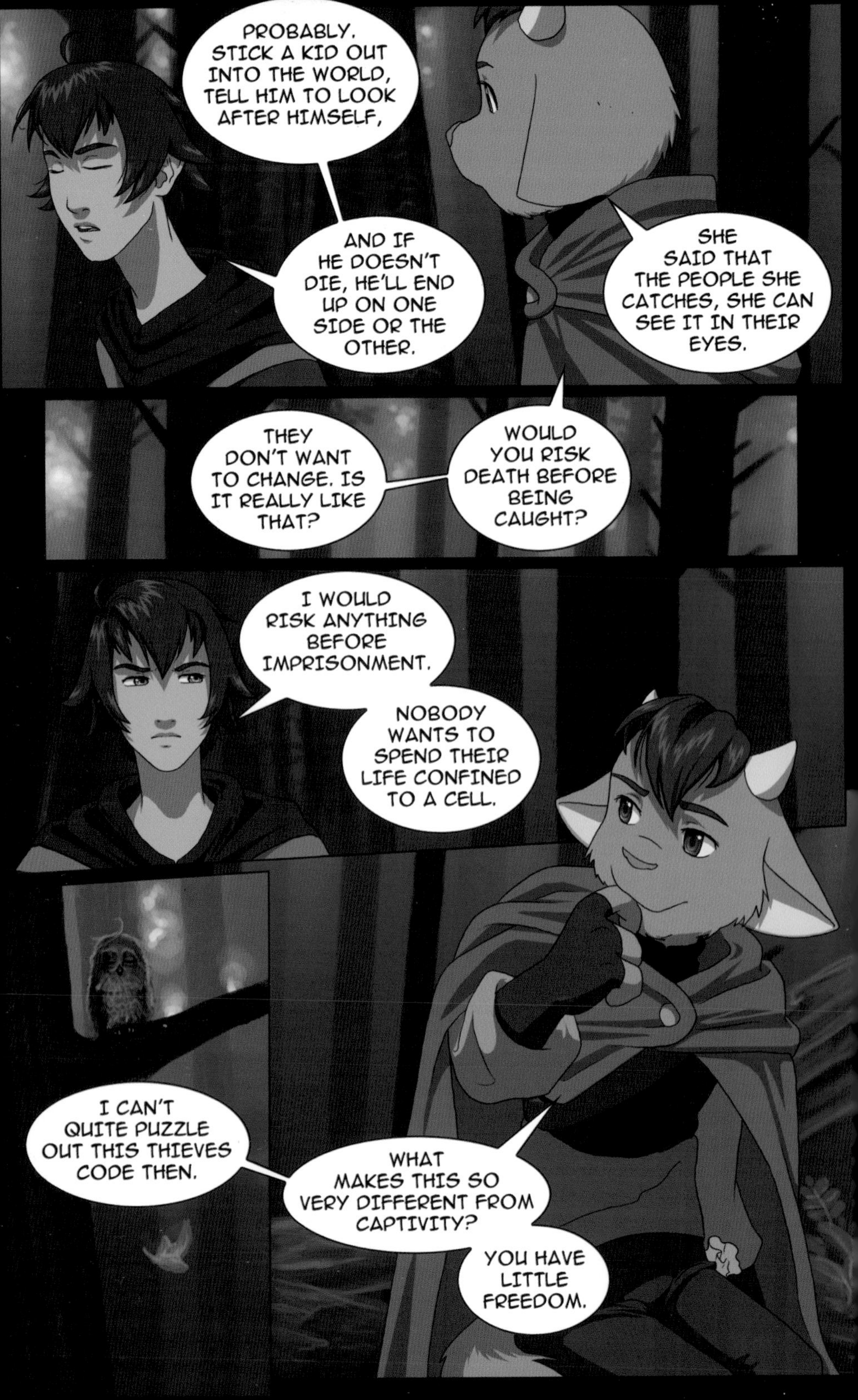
PROBABLY. STICK A KID OUT INTO THE WORLD, TELL HIM TO LOOK AFTER HIMSELF,
AND IF HE DOESN'T DIE, HE'LL END UP ON ONE SIDE OR THE OTHER.
SHE SAID THAT THE PEOPLE SHE CATCHES, SHE CAN SEE IT IN THEIR EYES.
THEY DON'T WANT TO CHANGE. IS IT REALLY LIKE THAT?
WOULD YOU RISK DEATH BEFORE BEING CAUGHT?
I WOULD RISK ANYTHING BEFORE IMPRISONMENT.
NOBODY WANTS TO SPEND THEIR LIFE CONFINED TO A CELL.
I CAN'T QUITE PUZZLE OUT THIS THIEVES CODE THEN.
WHAT MAKES THIS SO VERY DIFFERENT FROM CAPTIVITY?
YOU HAVE LITTLE FREEDOM.

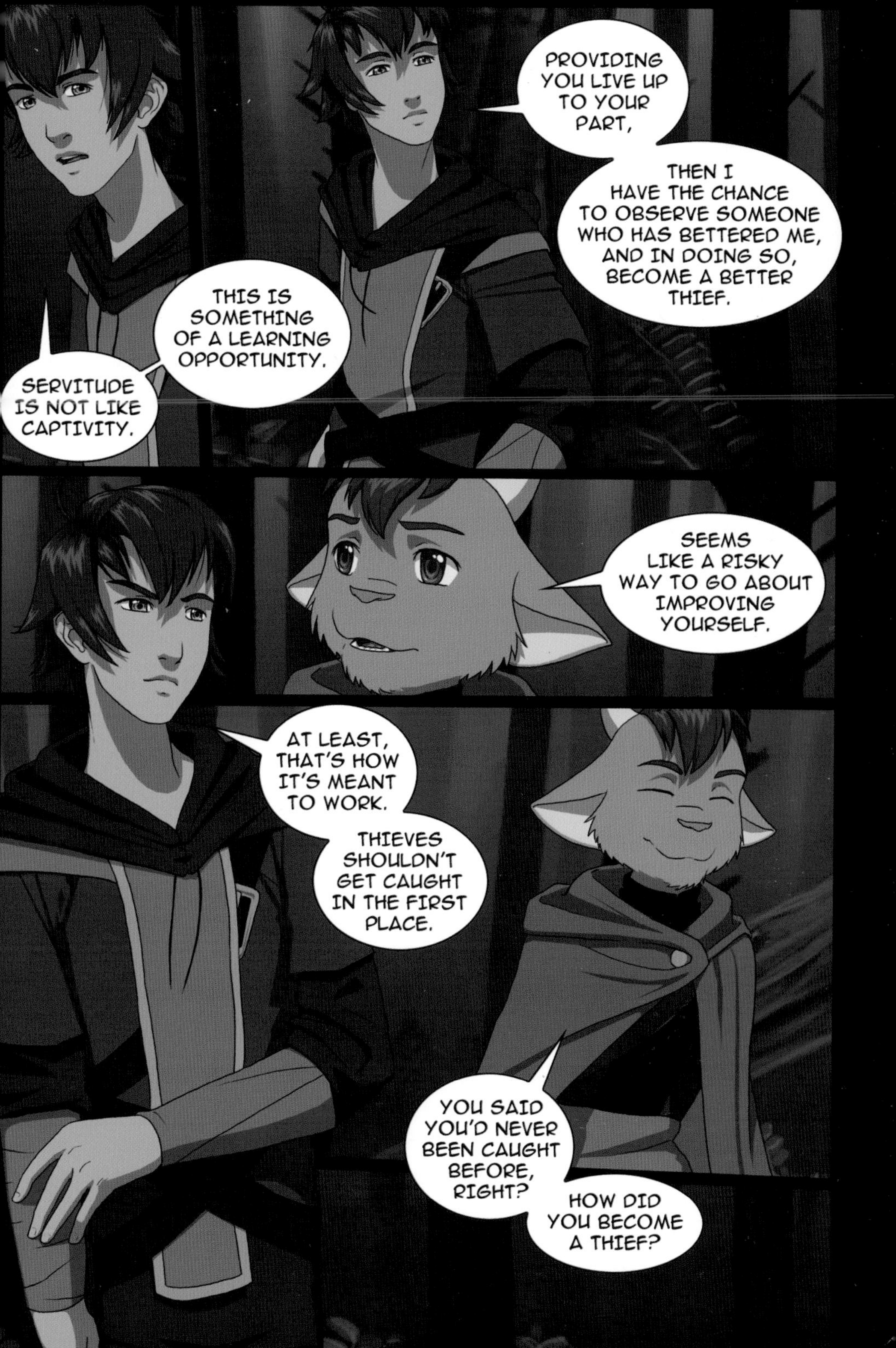
SERVITUDE IS NOT LIKE CAPTIVITY.
THIS IS SOMETHING OF A LEARNING OPPORTUNITY.
PROVIDING YOU LIVE UP TO YOUR PART,
THEN I HAVE THE CHANCE TO OBSERVE SOMEONE WHO HAS BETTERED ME, AND IN DOING SO, BECOME A BETTER THIEF.
SEEMS LIKE A RISKY WAY TO GO ABOUT IMPROVING YOURSELF.
AT LEAST, THAT'S HOW IT'S MEANT TO WORK.
THIEVES SHOULDN'T GET CAUGHT IN THE FIRST PLACE.
YOU SAID YOU'D NEVER BEEN CAUGHT BEFORE, RIGHT?
HOW DID YOU BECOME A THIEF?

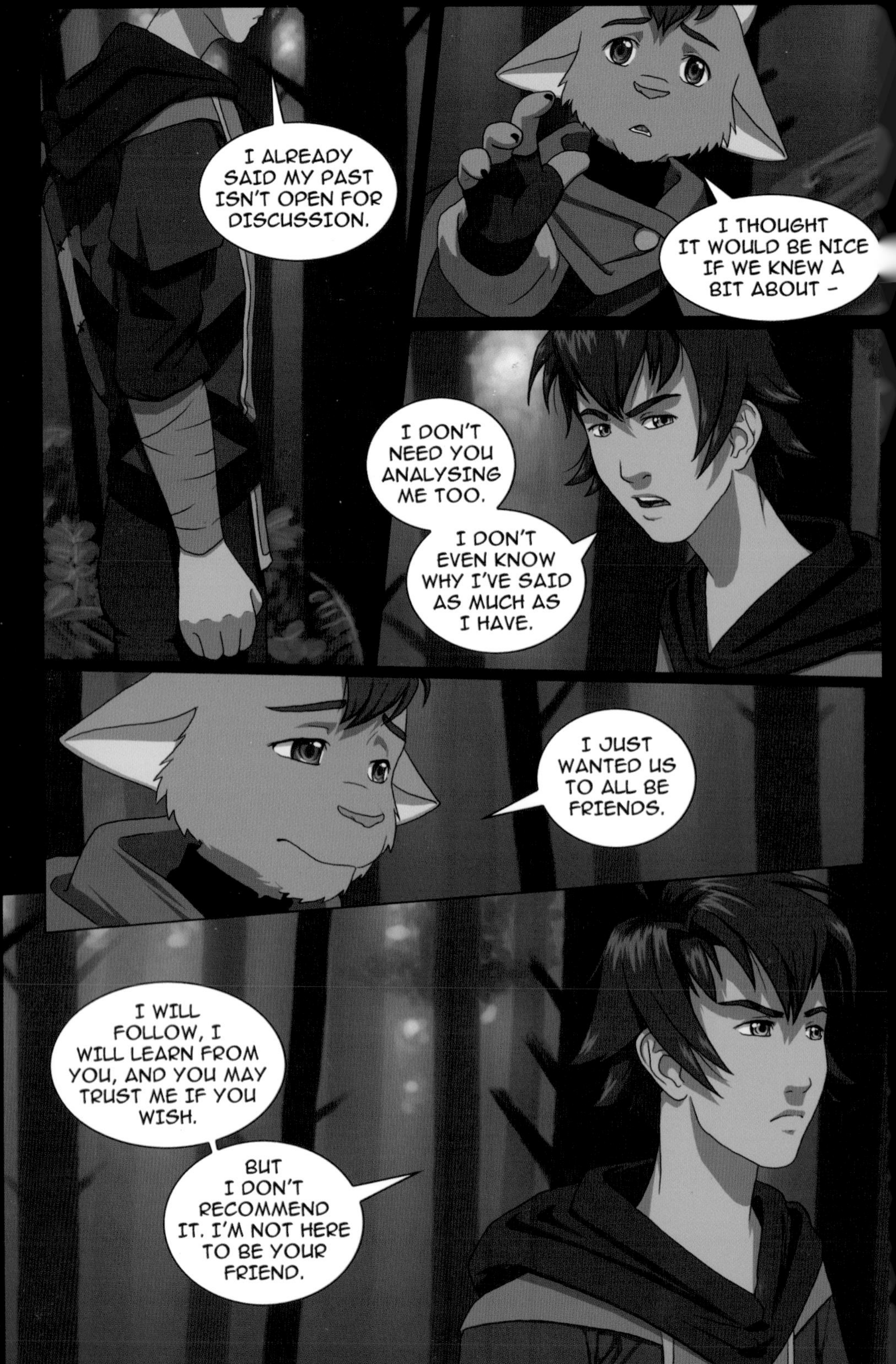
I ALREADY SAID MY PAST ISN'T OPEN FOR DISCUSSION.
I THOUGHT IT WOULD BE NICE IF WE KNEW A BIT ABOUT –
I DON'T NEED YOU ANALYSING ME TOO.
I DON'T EVEN KNOW WHY I'VE SAID AS MUCH AS I HAVE.
I JUST WANTED US TO ALL BE FRIENDS.
I WILL FOLLOW, I WILL LEARN FROM YOU, AND YOU MAY TRUST ME IF YOU WISH.
BUT I DON'T RECOMMEND IT. I'M NOT HERE TO BE YOUR FRIEND.

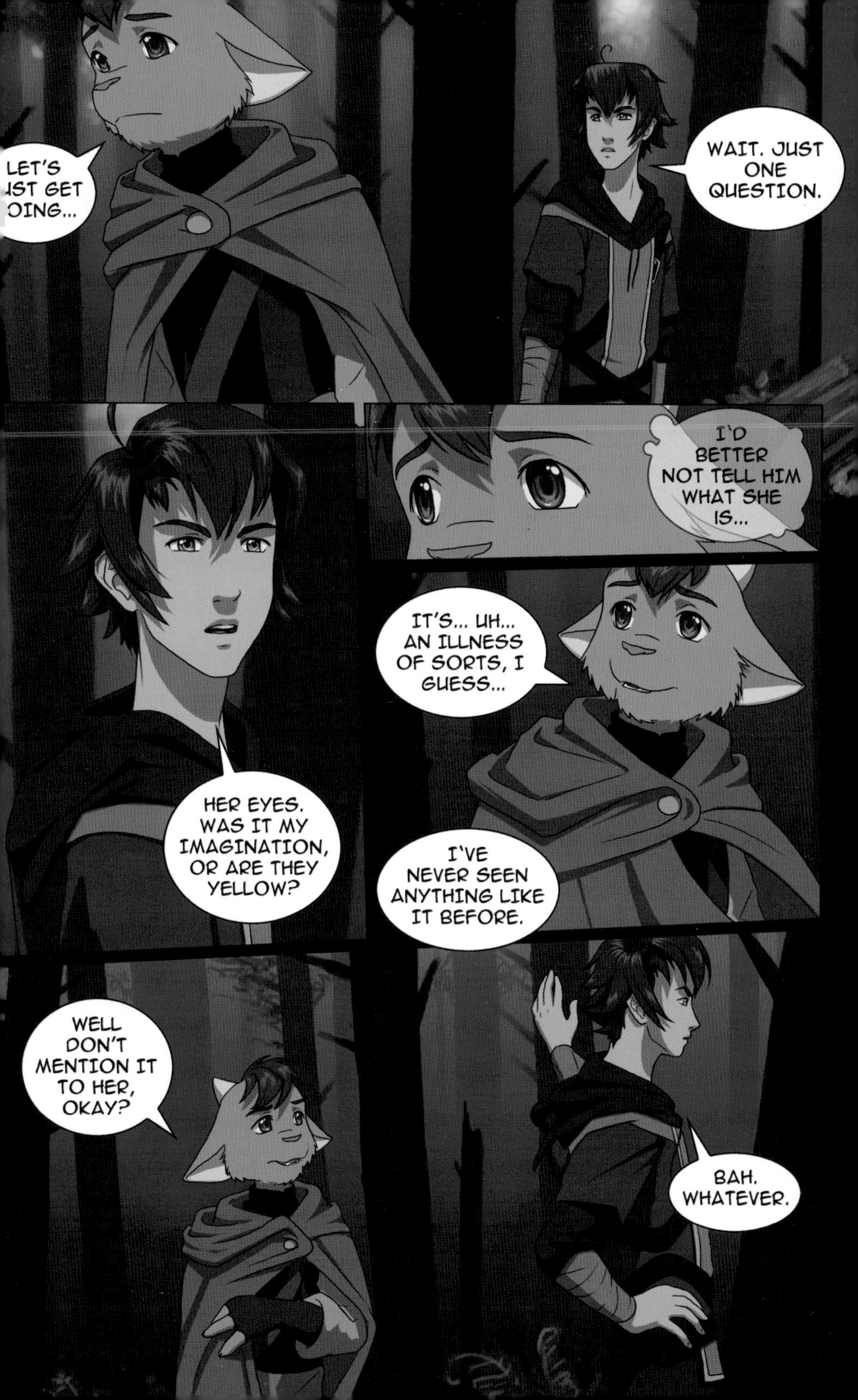
LET'S
IST GET
OING...
WAIT. JUST ONE QUESTION.
HER EYES. WAS IT MY IMAGINATION, OR ARE THEY YELLOW?
I'D BETTER NOT TELL HIM WHAT SHE IS...
IT'S... UH... AN ILLNESS OF SORTS, I GUESS...
I'VE NEVER SEEN ANYTHING LIKE IT BEFORE.
WELL DON'T MENTION IT TO HER, OKAY?
BAH. WHATEVER.

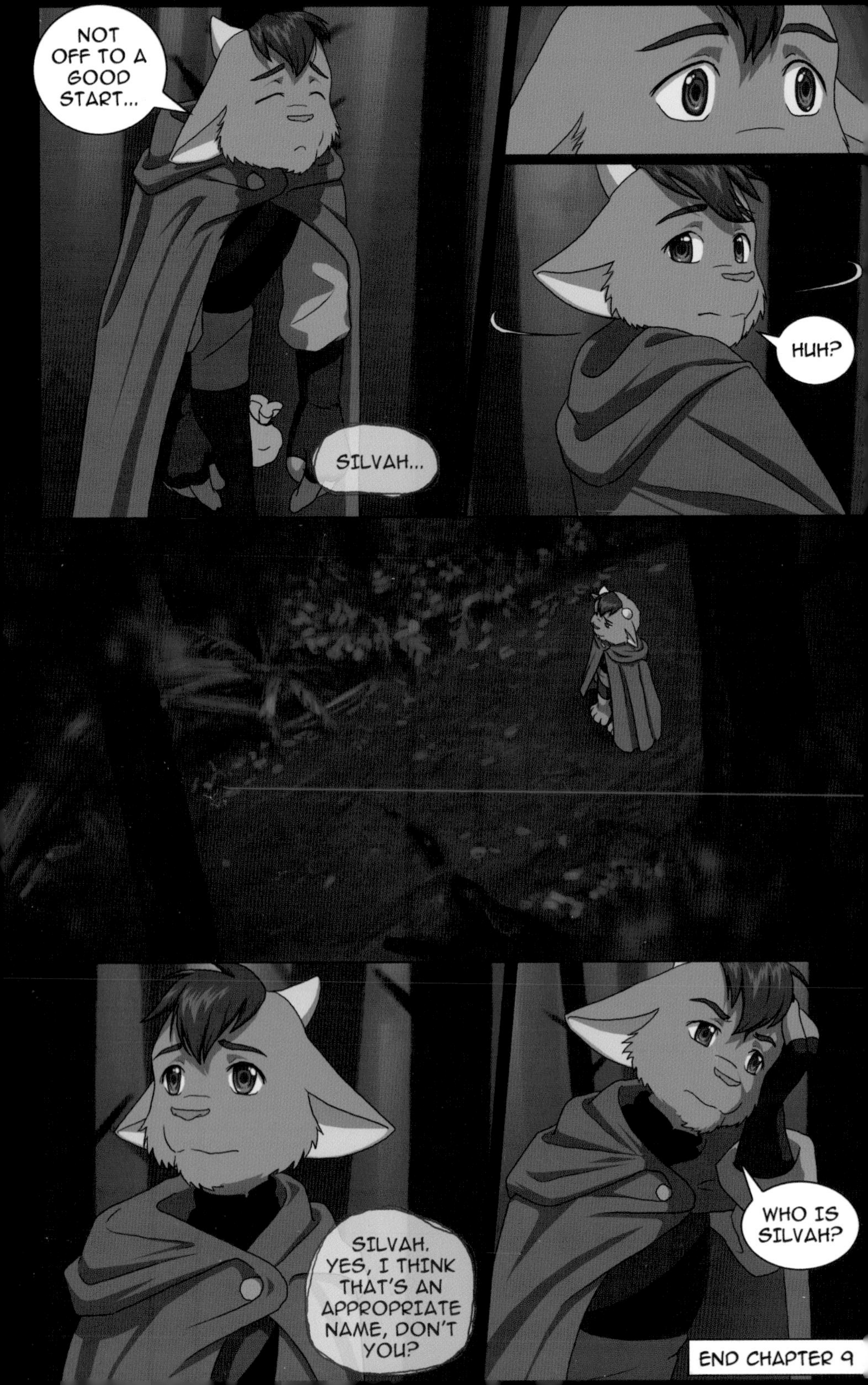
NOT OFF TO A GOOD START...
SILVAH...
HUH?
SILVAH. YES, I THINK THAT'S AN APPROPRIATE NAME, DON'T YOU?
WHO IS SILVAH?
END CHAPTER 9

CHAPTER 10 : ALIAS

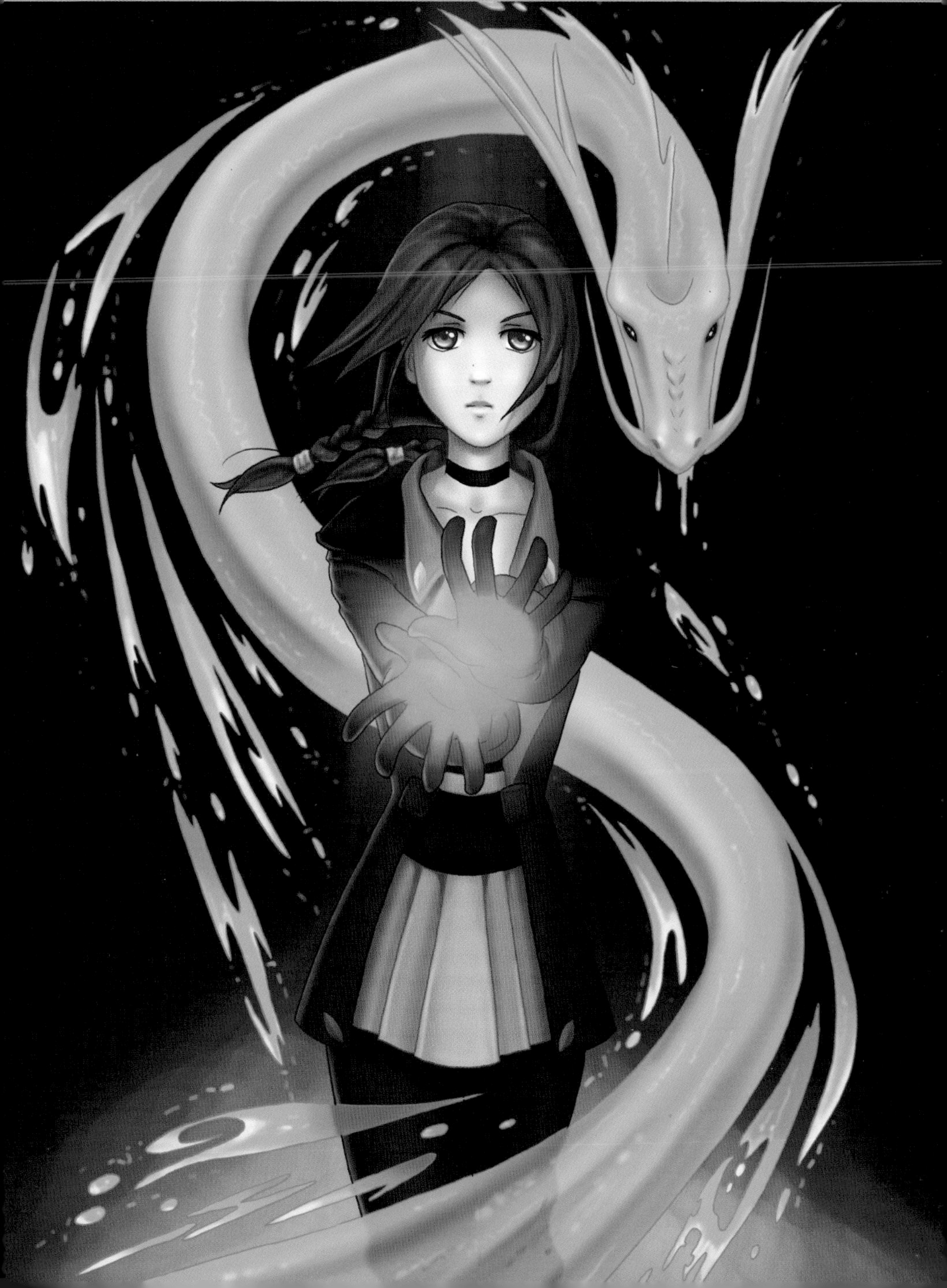

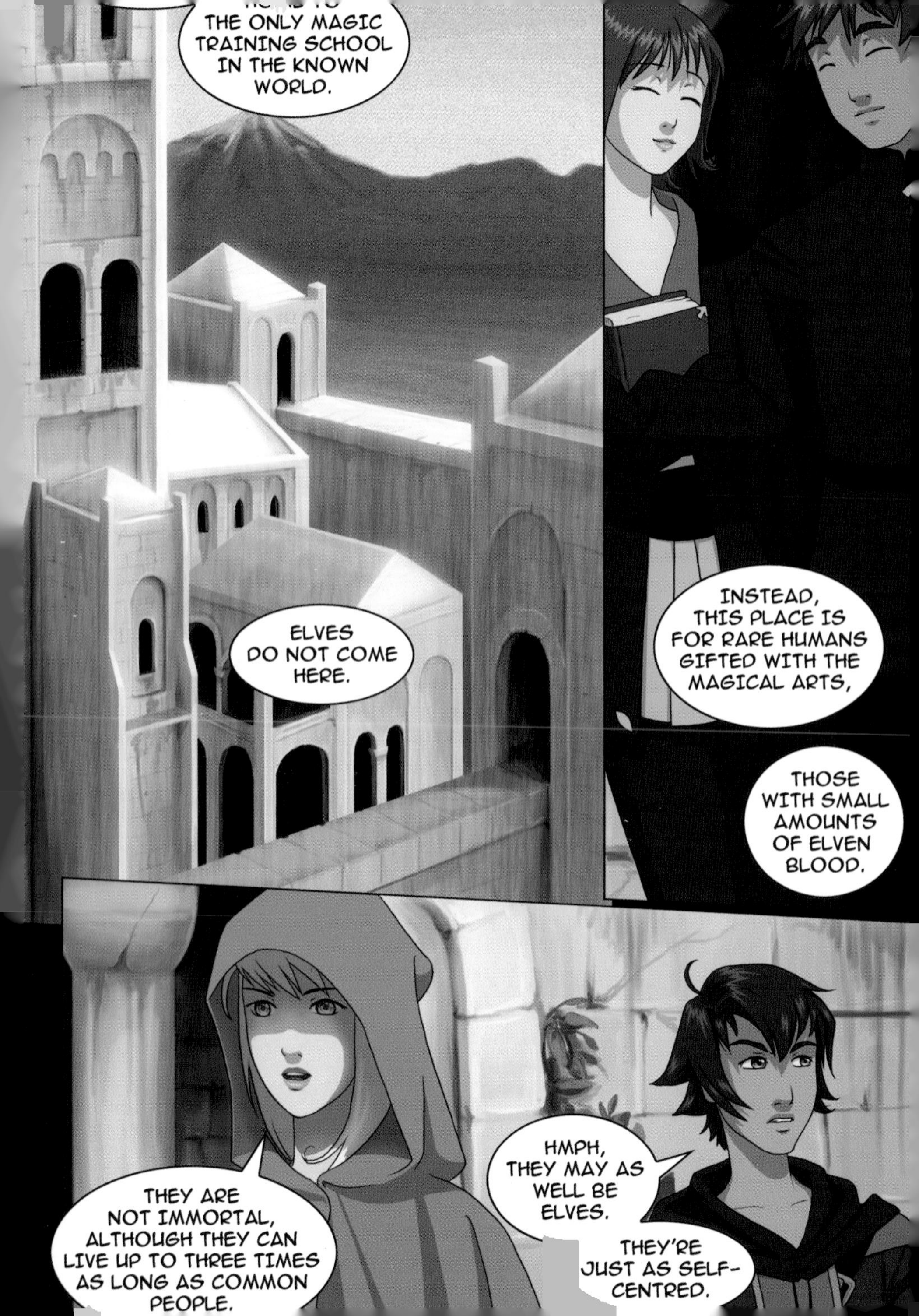
THE ONLY MAGIC TRAINING SCHOOL IN THE KNOWN WORLD.
ELVES DO NOT COME HERE.
INSTEAD, THIS PLACE IS FOR RARE HUMANS GIFTED WITH THE MAGICAL ARTS,
THOSE WITH SMALL AMOUNTS OF ELVEN BLOOD.
THEY ARE NOT IMMORTAL, ALTHOUGH THEY CAN LIVE UP TO THREE TIMES AS LONG AS COMMON PEOPLE.
HMPH, THEY MAY AS WELL BE ELVES.
THEY'RE JUST AS SELF-CENTRED.

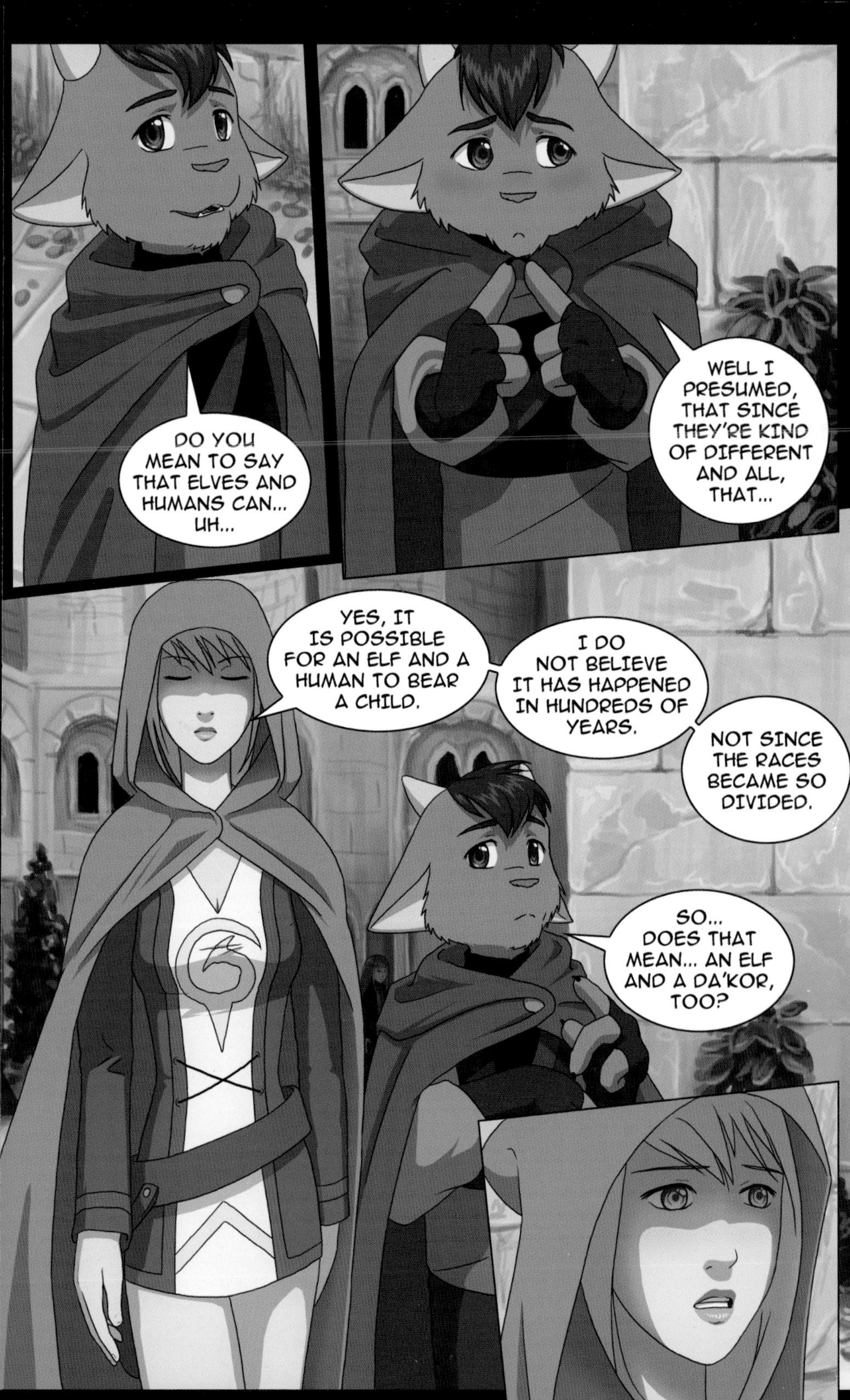
DO YOU MEAN TO SAY THAT ELVES AND HUMANS CAN... UH...
WELL I PRESUMED, THAT SINCE THEY'RE KIND OF DIFFERENT AND ALL, THAT...
YES, IT IS POSSIBLE FOR AN ELF AND A HUMAN TO BEAR A CHILD.
I DO NOT BELIEVE IT HAS HAPPENED IN HUNDREDS OF YEARS.
NOT SINCE THE RACES BECAME SO DIVIDED.
SO... DOES THAT MEAN... AN ELF AND A DA'KOR, TOO?

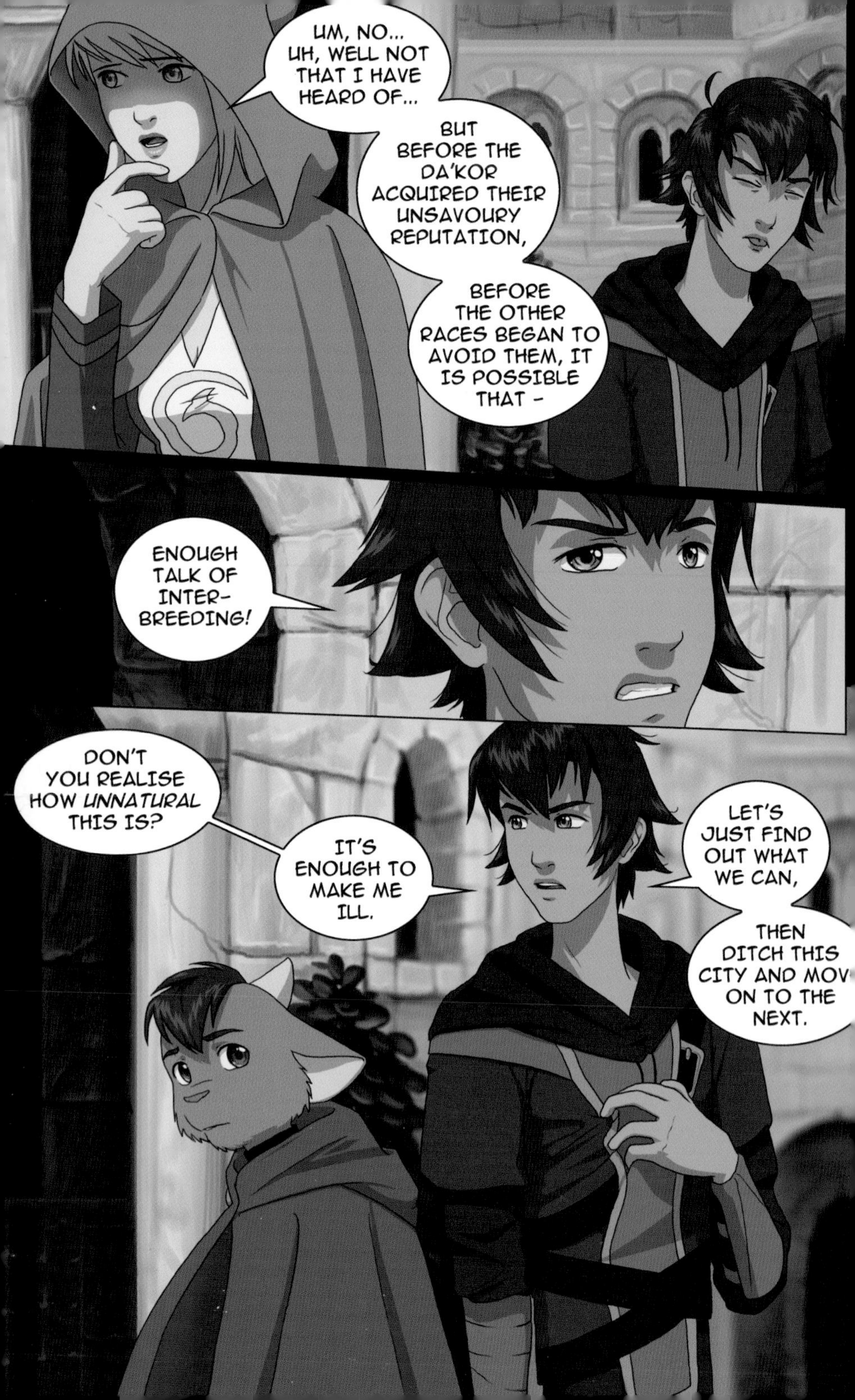
UM, NO... UH, WELL NOT THAT I HAVE HEARD OF...
BUT BEFORE THE DA'KOR ACQUIRED THEIR UNSAVOURY REPUTATION,
BEFORE THE OTHER RACES BEGAN TO AVOID THEM, IT IS POSSIBLE THAT –
ENOUGH TALK OF INTER-BREEDING!
DON'T YOU REALISE HOW *UNNATURAL* THIS IS?
IT'S ENOUGH TO MAKE ME ILL.
LET'S JUST FIND OUT WHAT WE CAN,
THEN DITCH THIS CITY AND MOV
ON TO THE NEXT.

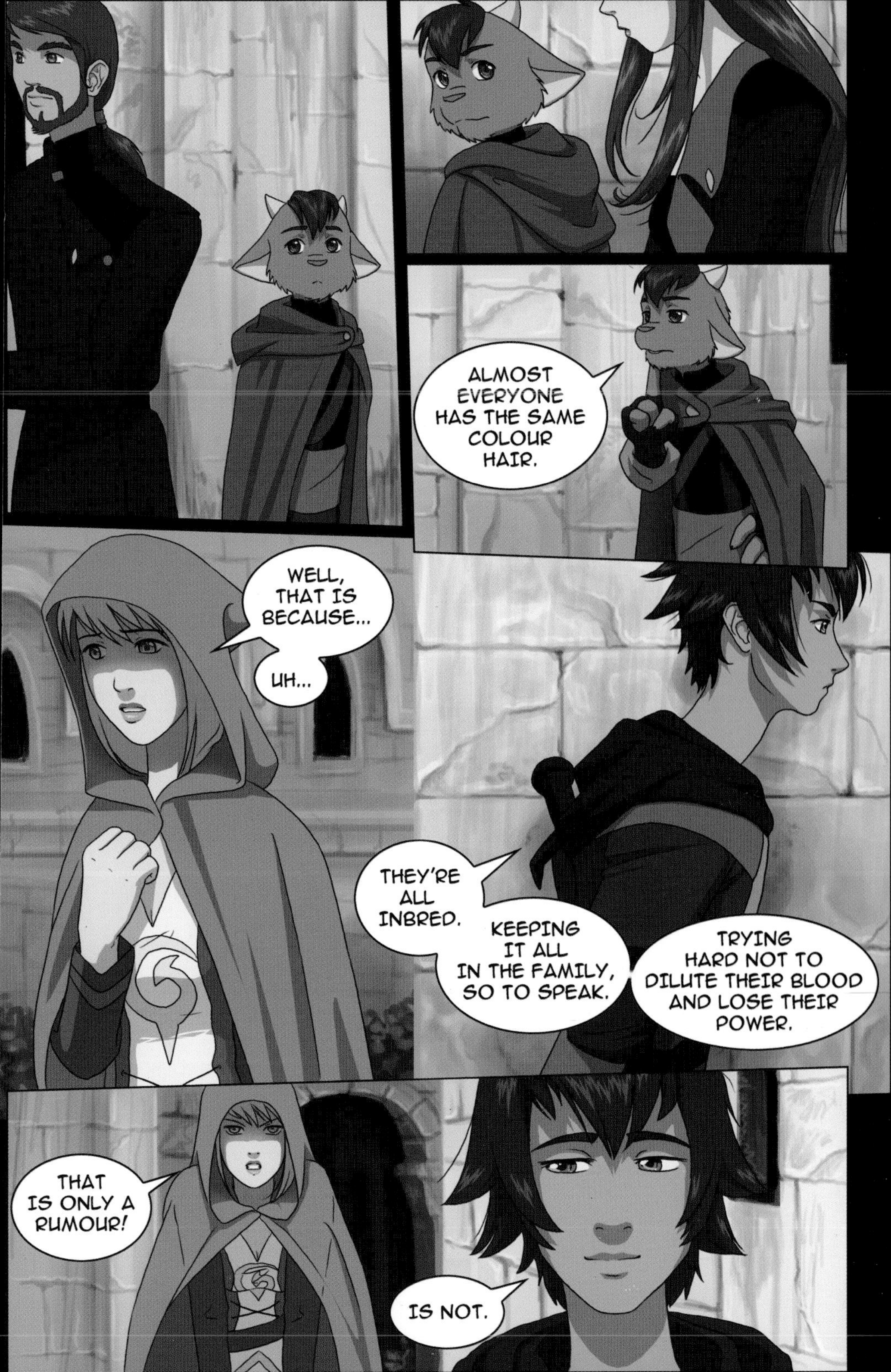

ALMOST EVERYONE HAS THE SAME COLOUR HAIR.
WELL, THAT IS BECAUSE...
UH...
THEY'RE ALL INBRED.
KEEPING IT ALL IN THE FAMILY, SO TO SPEAK.
TRYING HARD NOT TO DILUTE THEIR BLOOD AND LOSE THEIR POWER.
THAT IS ONLY A RUMOUR!
IS NOT.

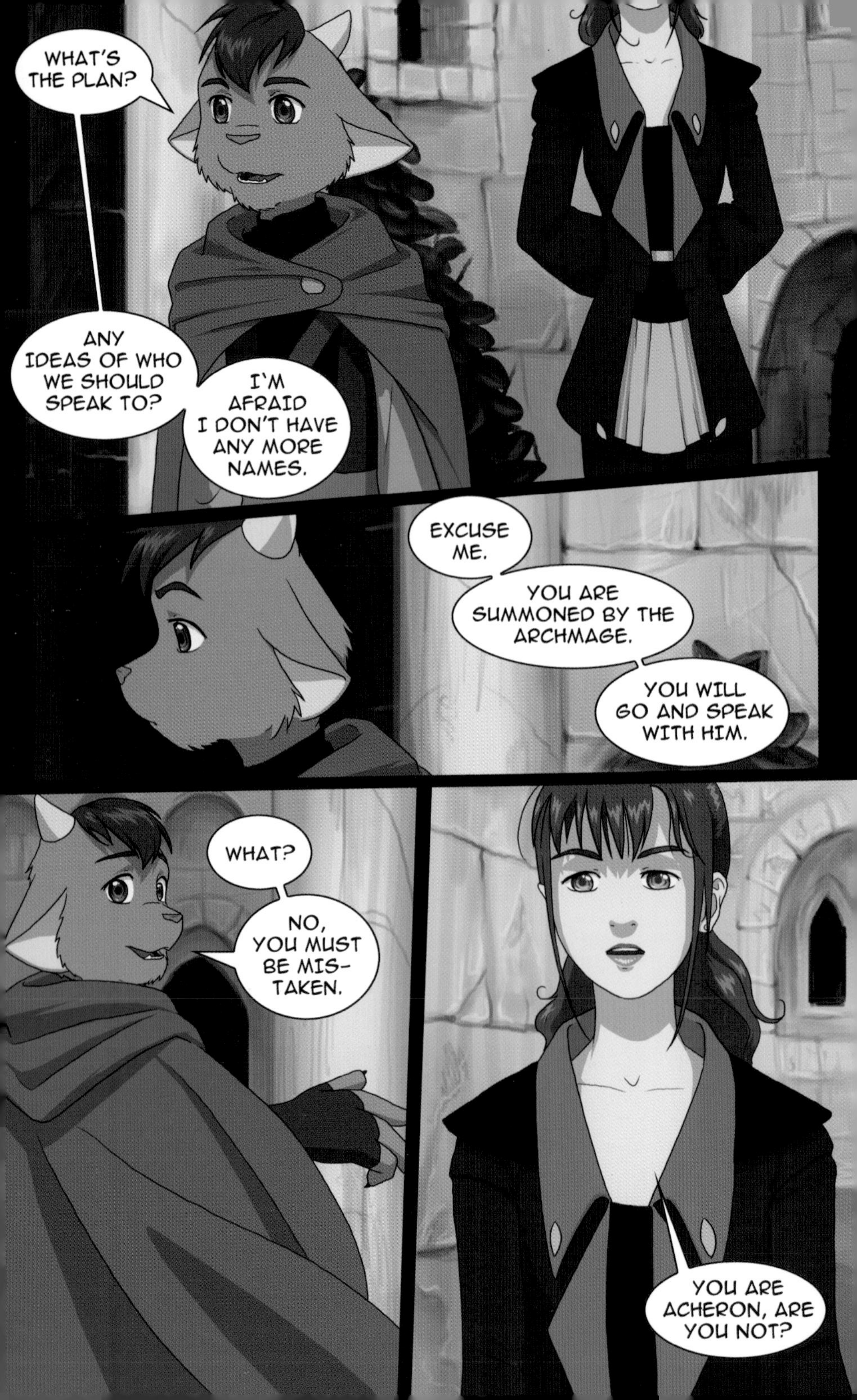
WHAT'S THE PLAN?
ANY IDEAS OF WHO WE SHOULD SPEAK TO?
I'M AFRAID I DON'T HAVE ANY MORE NAMES.
EXCUSE ME.
YOU ARE SUMMONED BY THE ARCHMAGE.
YOU WILL GO AND SPEAK WITH HIM.
WHAT?
NO, YOU MUST BE MIS-TAKEN.
YOU ARE ACHERON, ARE YOU NOT?

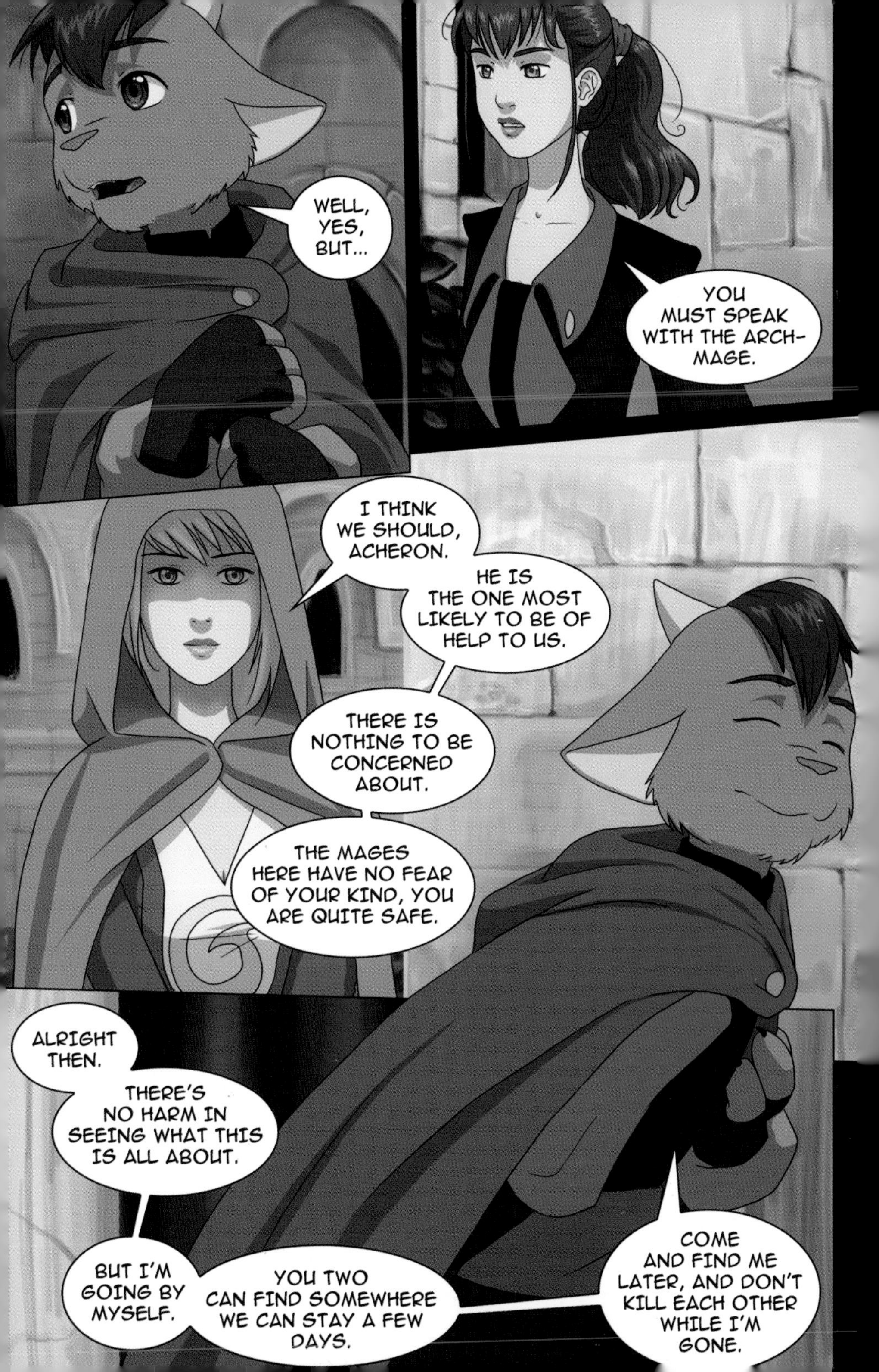
WELL, YES, BUT...
YOU MUST SPEAK WITH THE ARCH-MAGE.
I THINK WE SHOULD, ACHERON.
HE IS THE ONE MOST LIKELY TO BE OF HELP TO US.
THERE IS NOTHING TO BE CONCERNED ABOUT.
THE MAGES HERE HAVE NO FEAR OF YOUR KIND, YOU ARE QUITE SAFE.
ALRIGHT THEN.
THERE'S NO HARM IN SEEING WHAT THIS IS ALL ABOUT.
BUT I'M GOING BY MYSELF.
YOU TWO CAN FIND SOMEWHERE WE CAN STAY A FEW DAYS.
COME AND FIND ME LATER, AND DON'T KILL EACH OTHER WHILE I'M GONE.

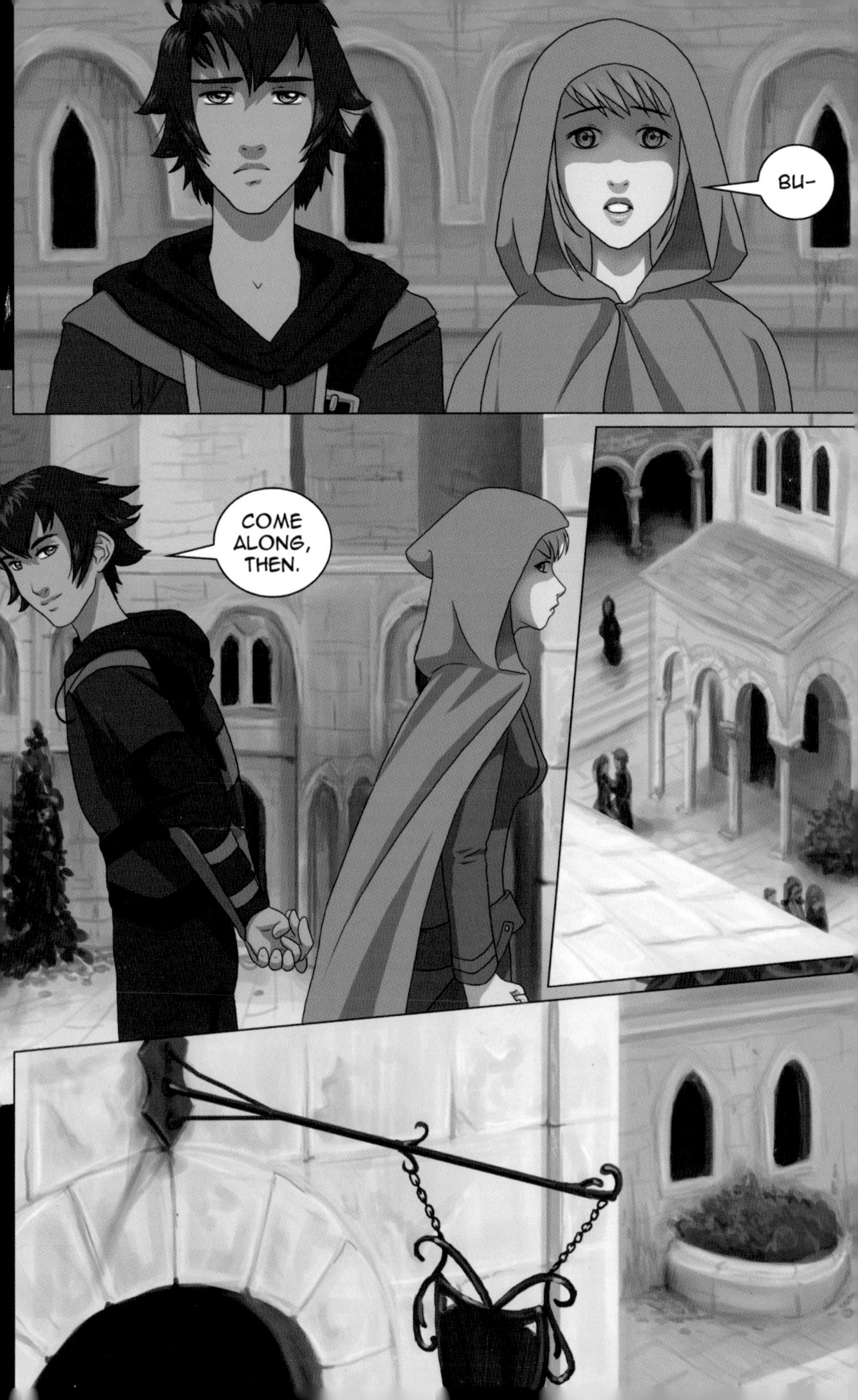
BU-
COME ALONG, THEN.

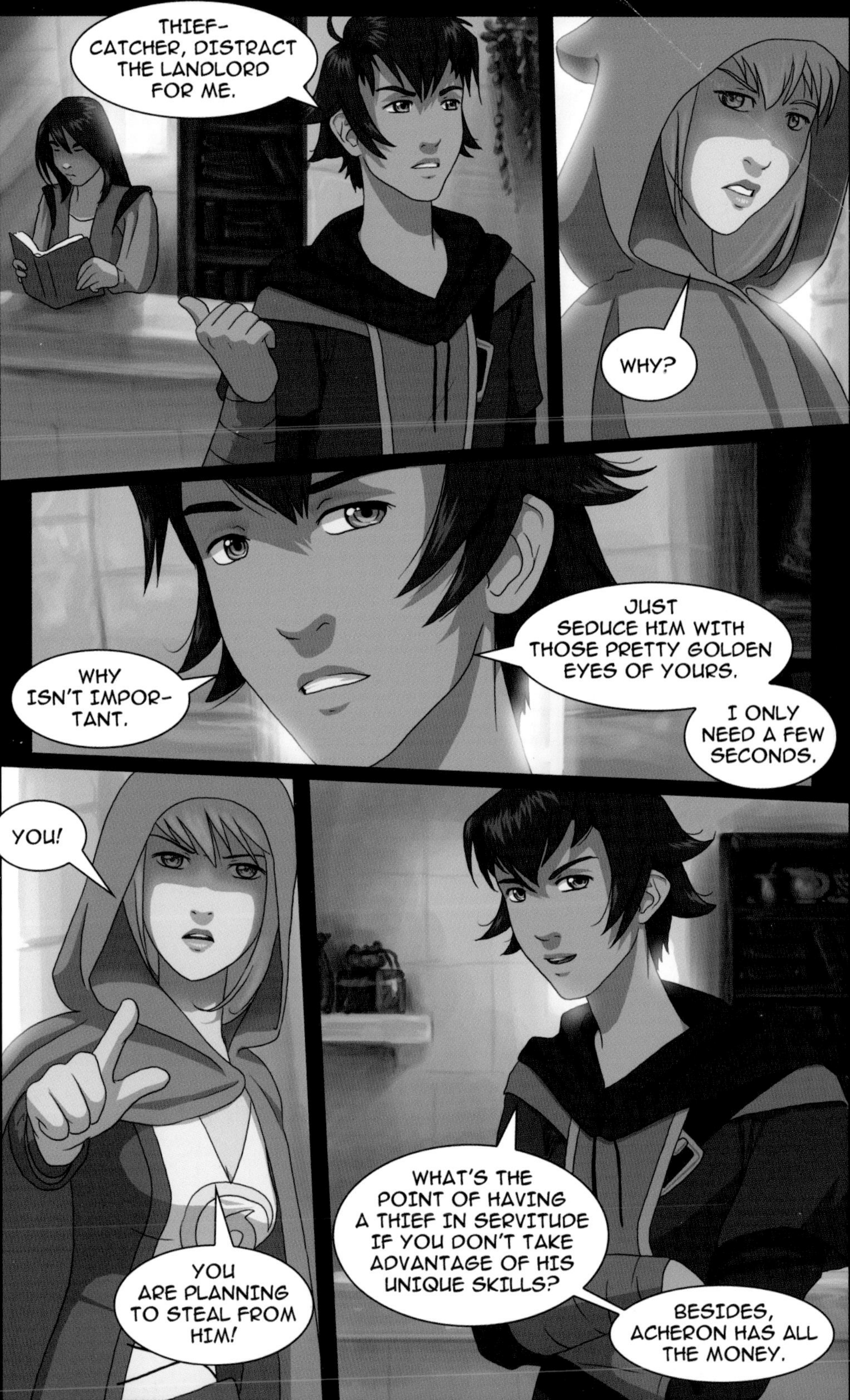
THIEF-CATCHER, DISTRACT THE LANDLORD FOR ME.
WHY?
WHY ISN'T IMPOR-TANT.
JUST SEDUCE HIM WITH THOSE PRETTY GOLDEN EYES OF YOURS.
I ONLY NEED A FEW SECONDS.
YOU!
YOU ARE PLANNING TO STEAL FROM HIM!
WHAT'S THE POINT OF HAVING A THIEF IN SERVITUDE IF YOU DON'T TAKE ADVANTAGE OF HIS UNIQUE SKILLS?
BESIDES, ACHERON HAS ALL THE MONEY.

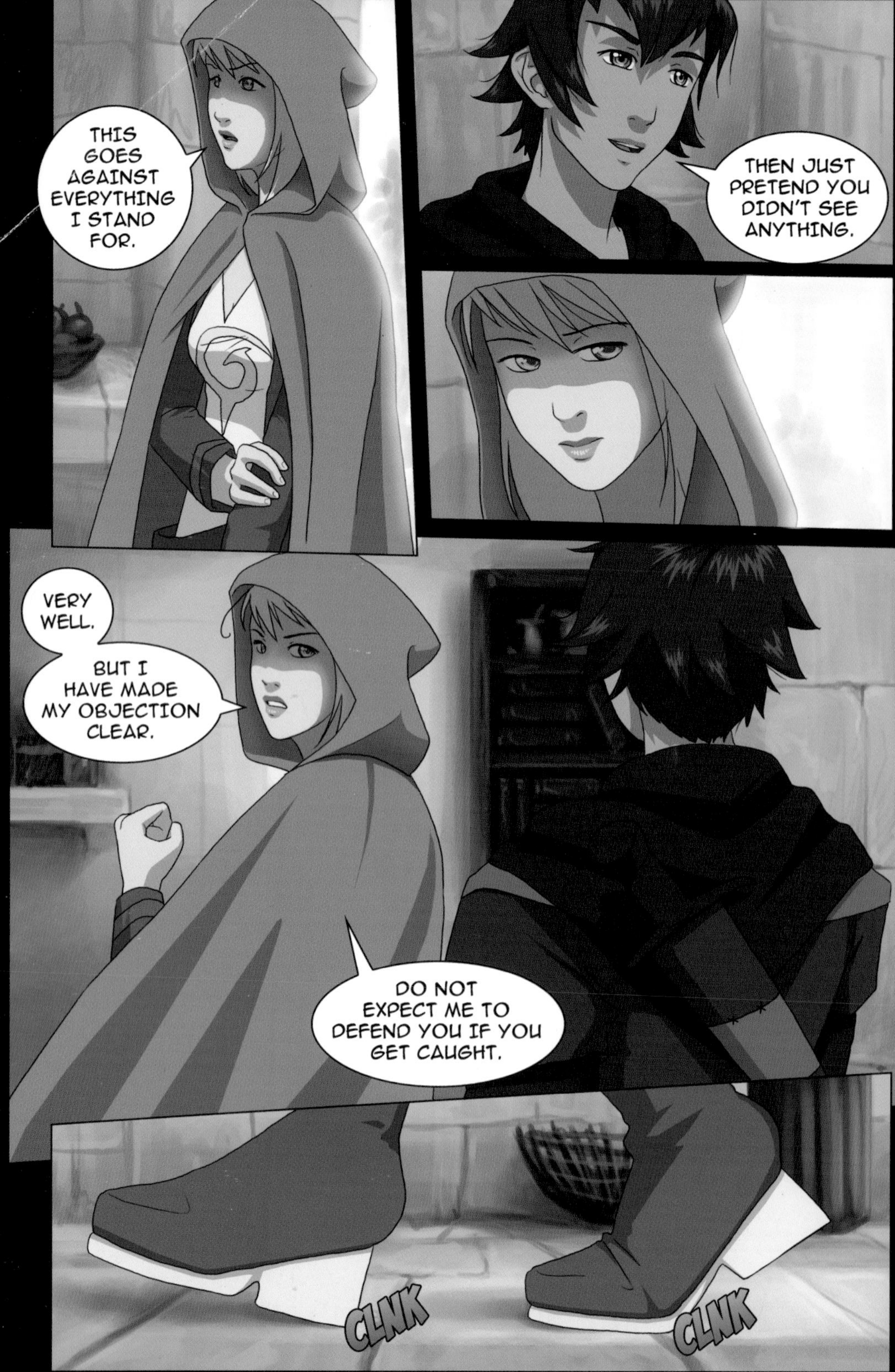
THIS GOES AGAINST EVERYTHING I STAND FOR.
THEN JUST PRETEND YOU DIDN'T SEE ANYTHING.
VERY WELL.
BUT I HAVE MADE MY OBJECTION CLEAR.
DO NOT EXPECT ME TO DEFEND YOU IF YOU GET CAUGHT.
CLNK
CLNK

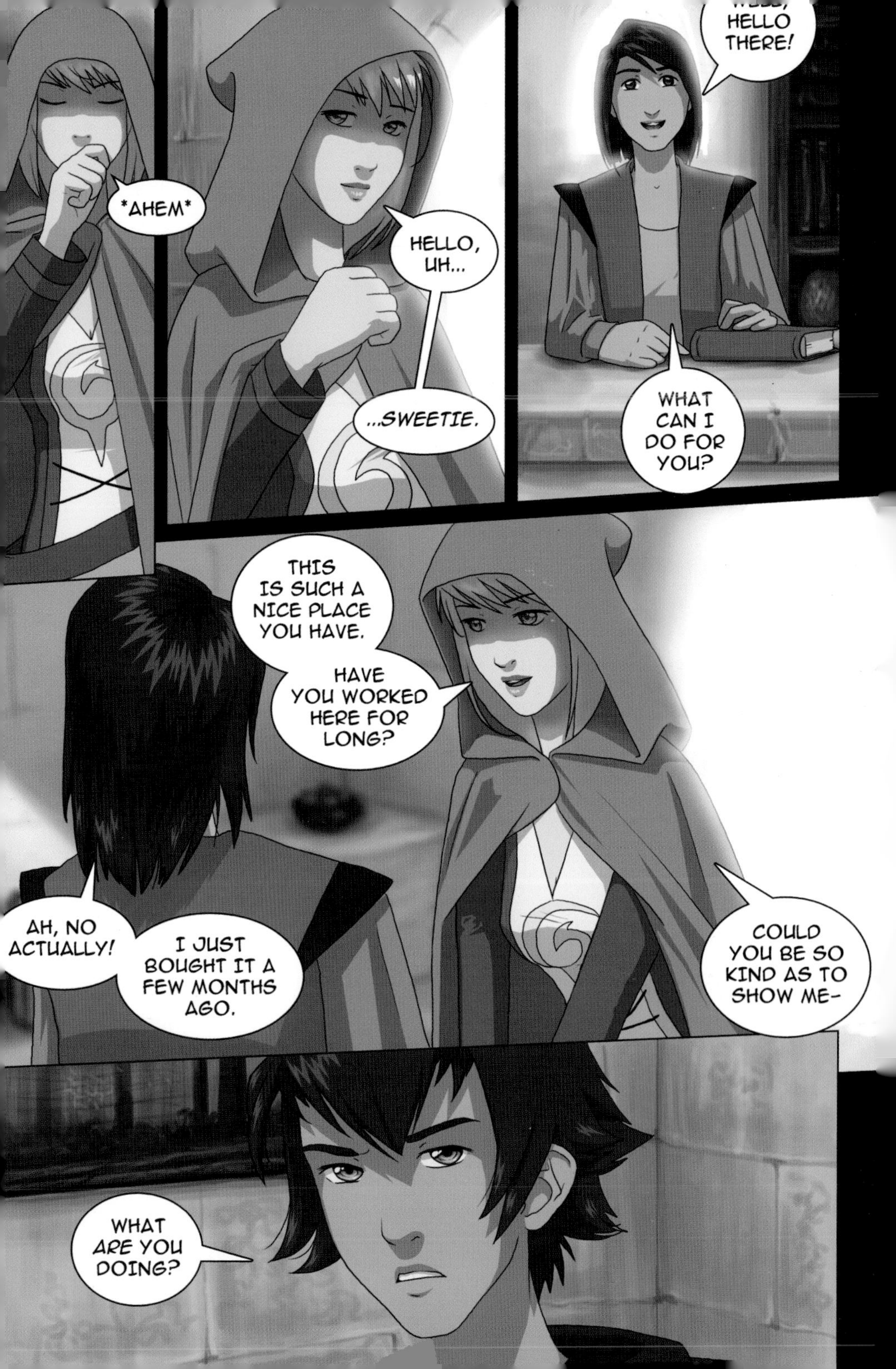
AHEM
HELLO, UH...
...SWEETIE.
HELLO THERE!
WHAT CAN I DO FOR YOU?
THIS IS SUCH A NICE PLACE YOU HAVE.
HAVE YOU WORKED HERE FOR LONG?
AH, NO ACTUALLY!
I JUST BOUGHT IT A FEW MONTHS AGO.
COULD YOU BE SO KIND AS TO SHOW ME-
WHAT ARE YOU DOING?

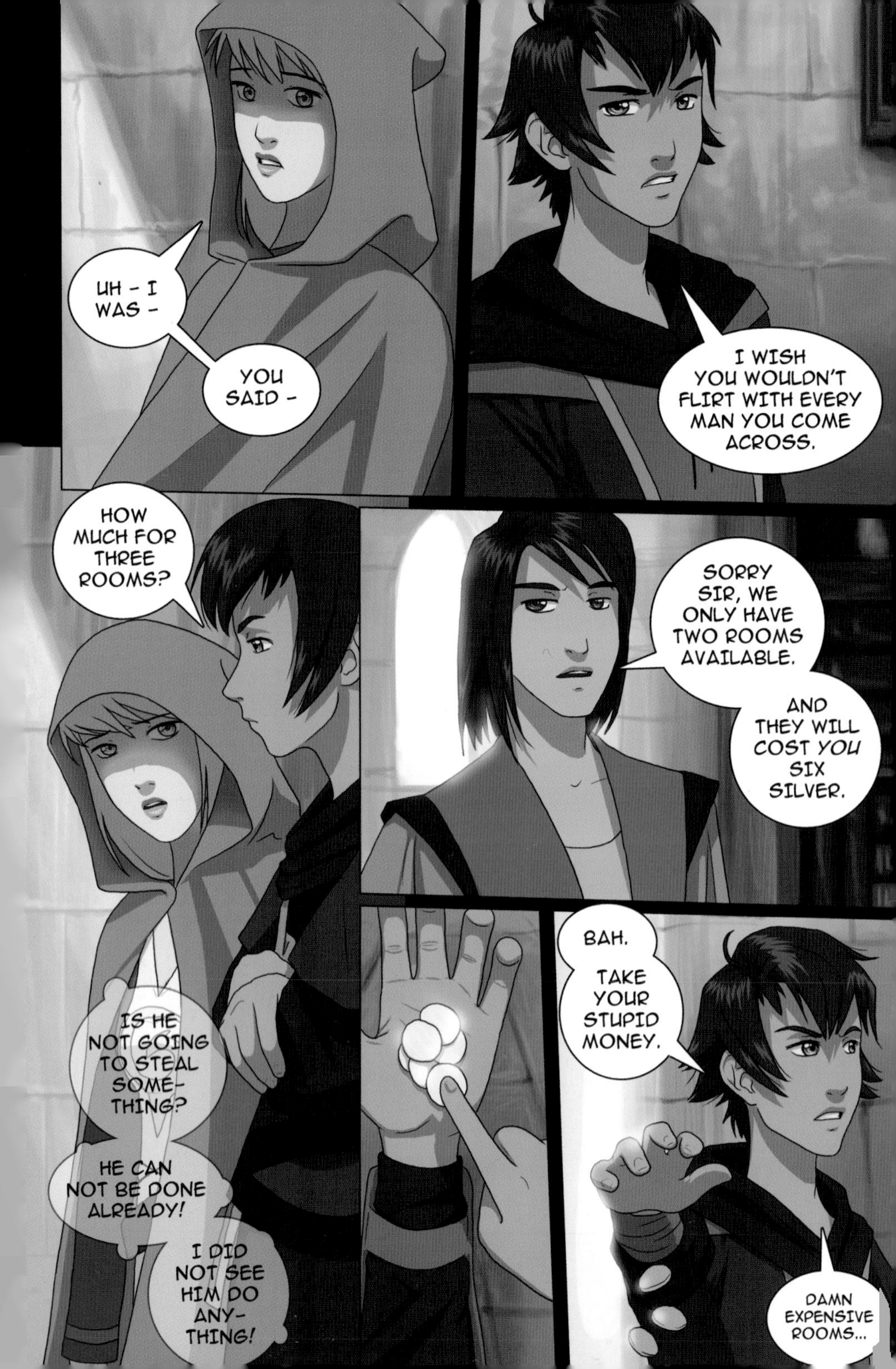
UH - I WAS -
YOU SAID -
I WISH YOU WOULDN'T FLIRT WITH EVERY MAN YOU COME ACROSS.
HOW MUCH FOR THREE ROOMS?
IS HE NOT GOING TO STEAL SOME-THING?
HE CAN NOT BE DONE ALREADY!
I DID NOT SEE HIM DO ANY-THING!
SORRY SIR, WE ONLY HAVE TWO ROOMS AVAILABLE.
AND THEY WILL COST *YOU* SIX SILVER.
BAH.
TAKE YOUR STUPID MONEY.
DAMN EXPENSIVE ROOMS...

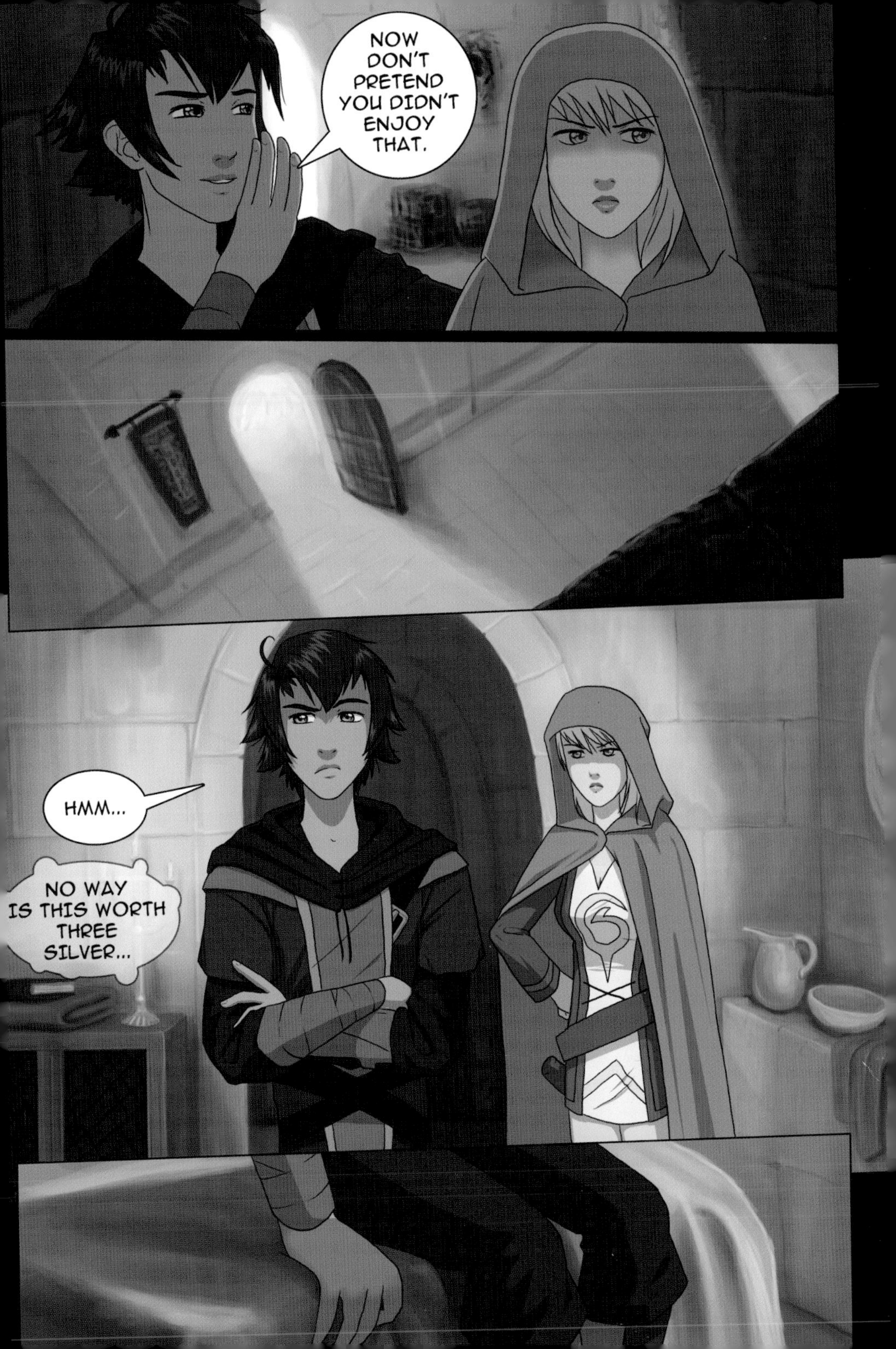
NOW DON'T PRETEND YOU DIDN'T ENJOY THAT.
HMM...
NO WAY IS THIS WORTH THREE SILVER...

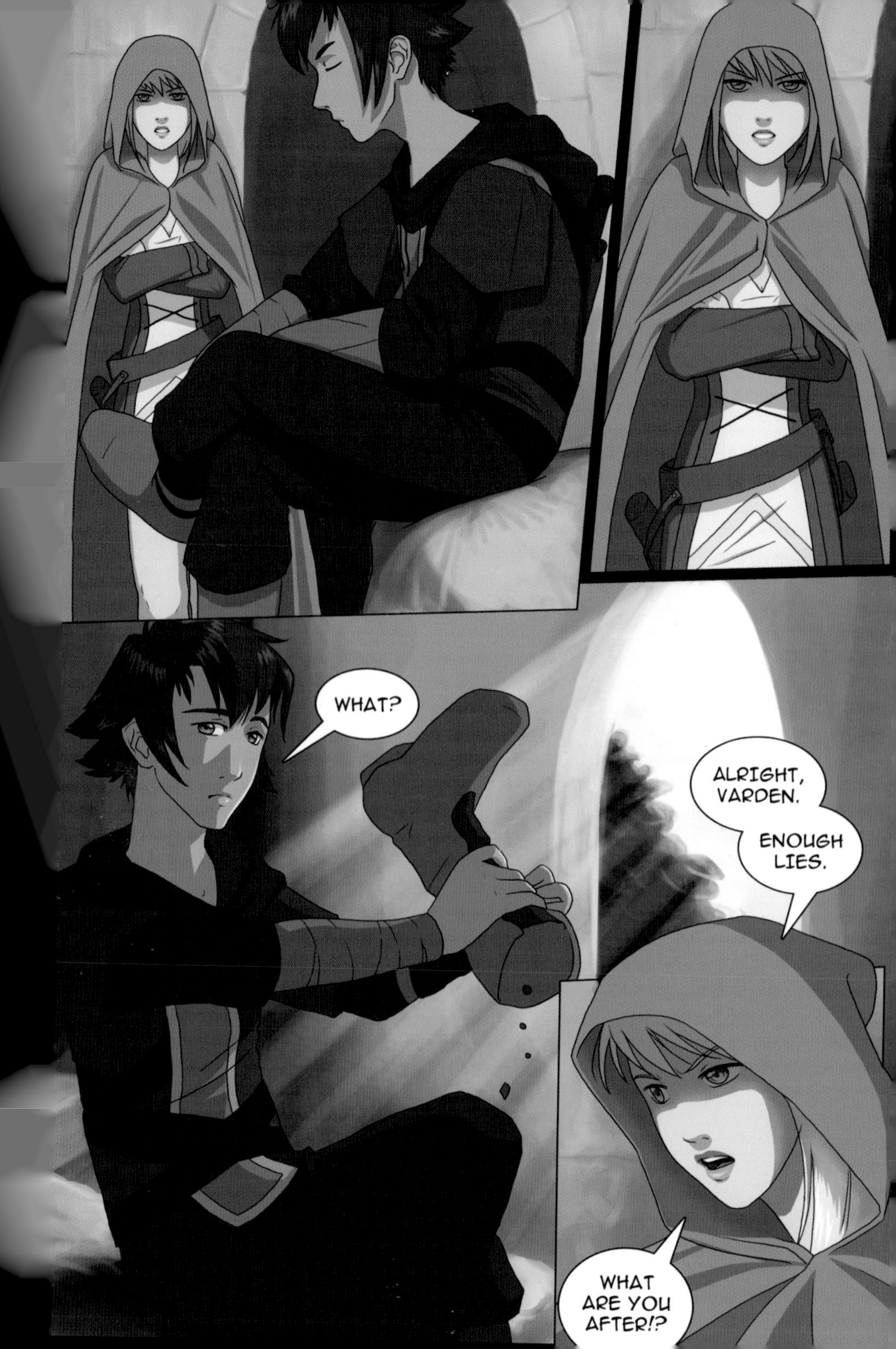
WHAT?
ALRIGHT, VARDEN.
ENOUGH LIES.
WHAT ARE YOU AFTER!?

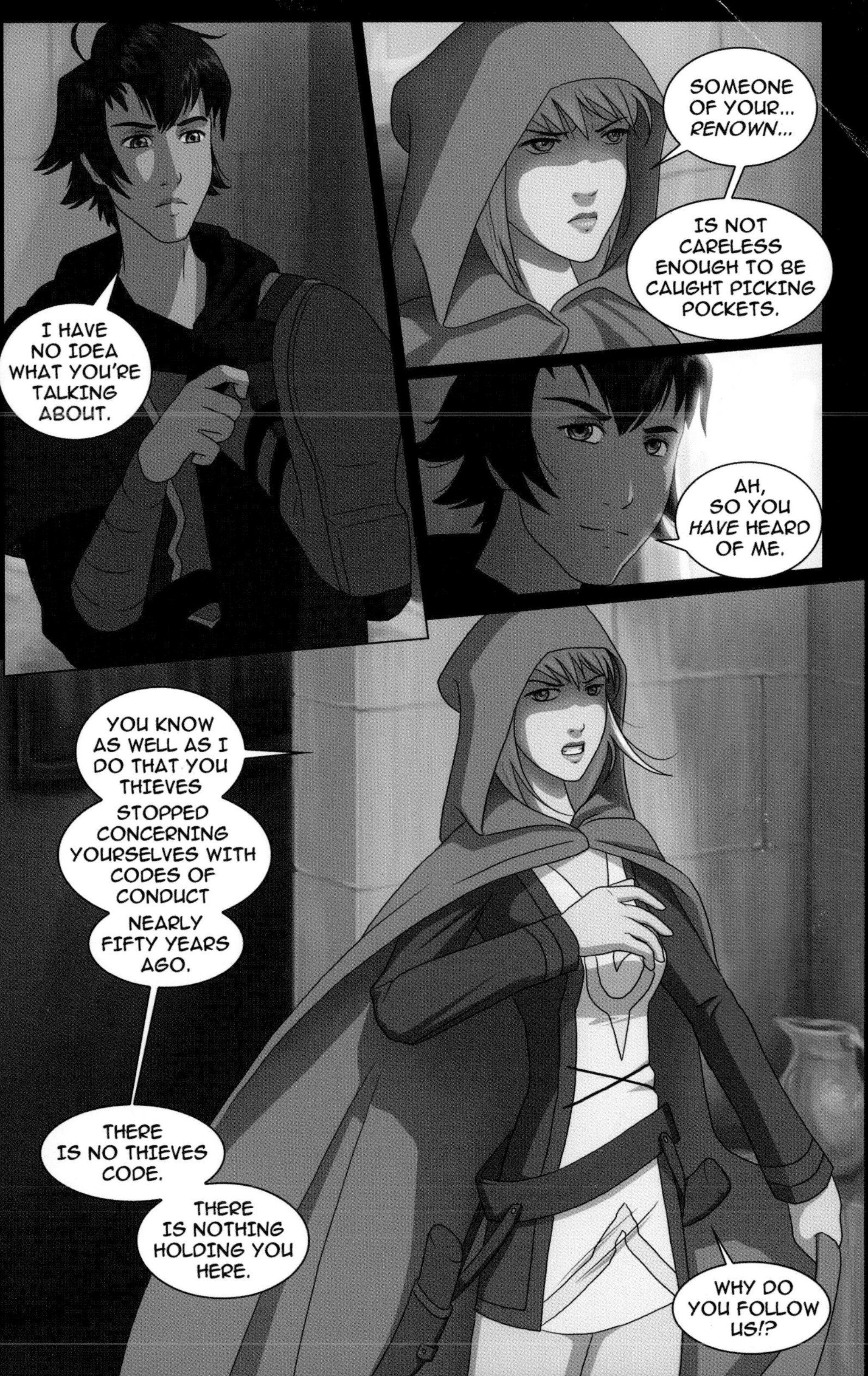
I HAVE NO IDEA WHAT YOU'RE TALKING ABOUT.
SOMEONE OF YOUR... *RENOWN*...
IS NOT CARELESS ENOUGH TO BE CAUGHT PICKING POCKETS.
AH, SO YOU *HAVE* HEARD OF ME.
YOU KNOW AS WELL AS I DO THAT YOU THIEVES
STOPPED CONCERNING YOURSELVES WITH CODES OF CONDUCT
NEARLY FIFTY YEARS AGO.
THERE IS NO THIEVES CODE.
THERE IS NOTHING HOLDING YOU HERE.
WHY DO YOU FOLLOW US!?

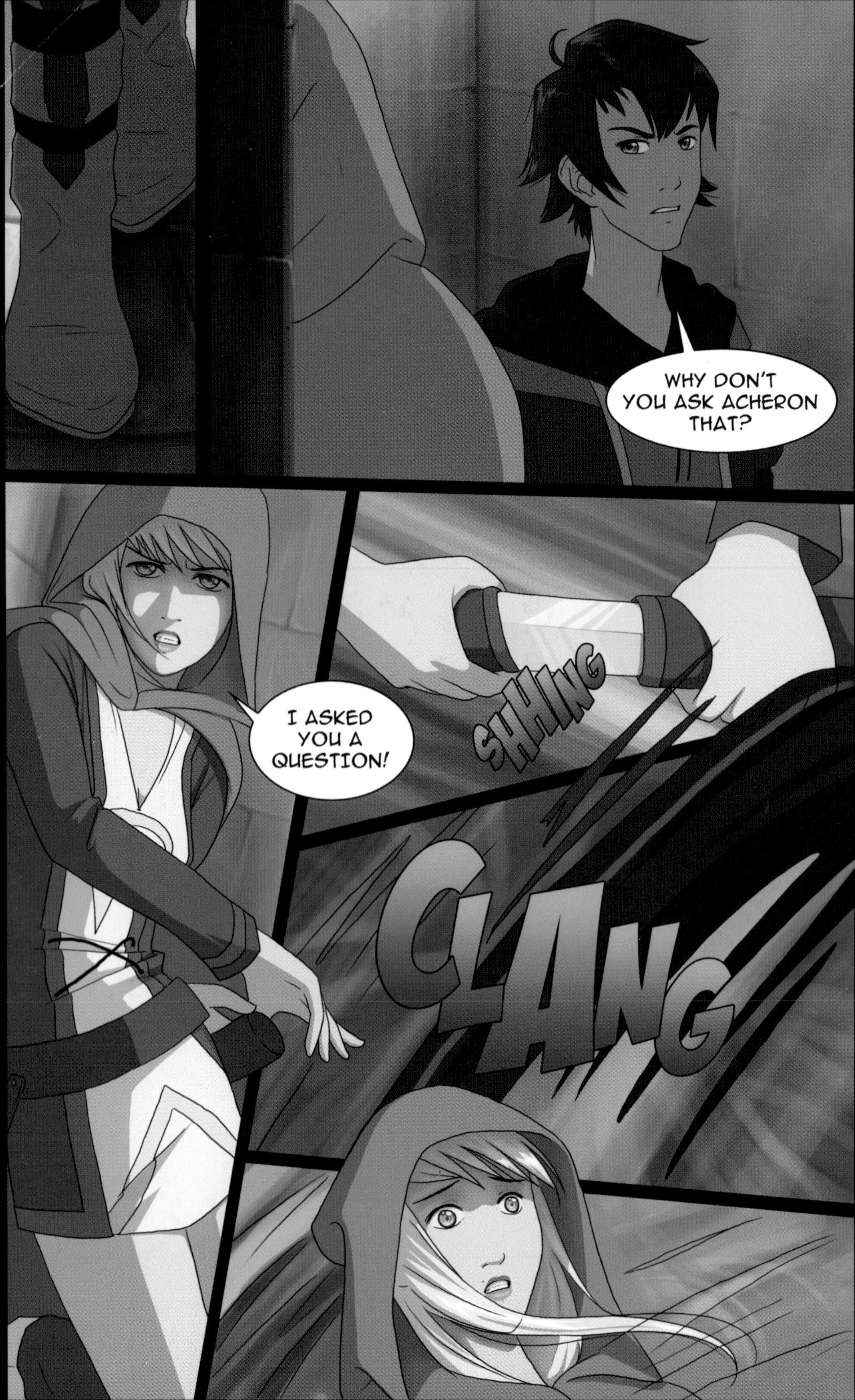
WHY DON'T YOU ASK ACHERON THAT?
I ASKED YOU A QUESTION!
SHHING
CLANG

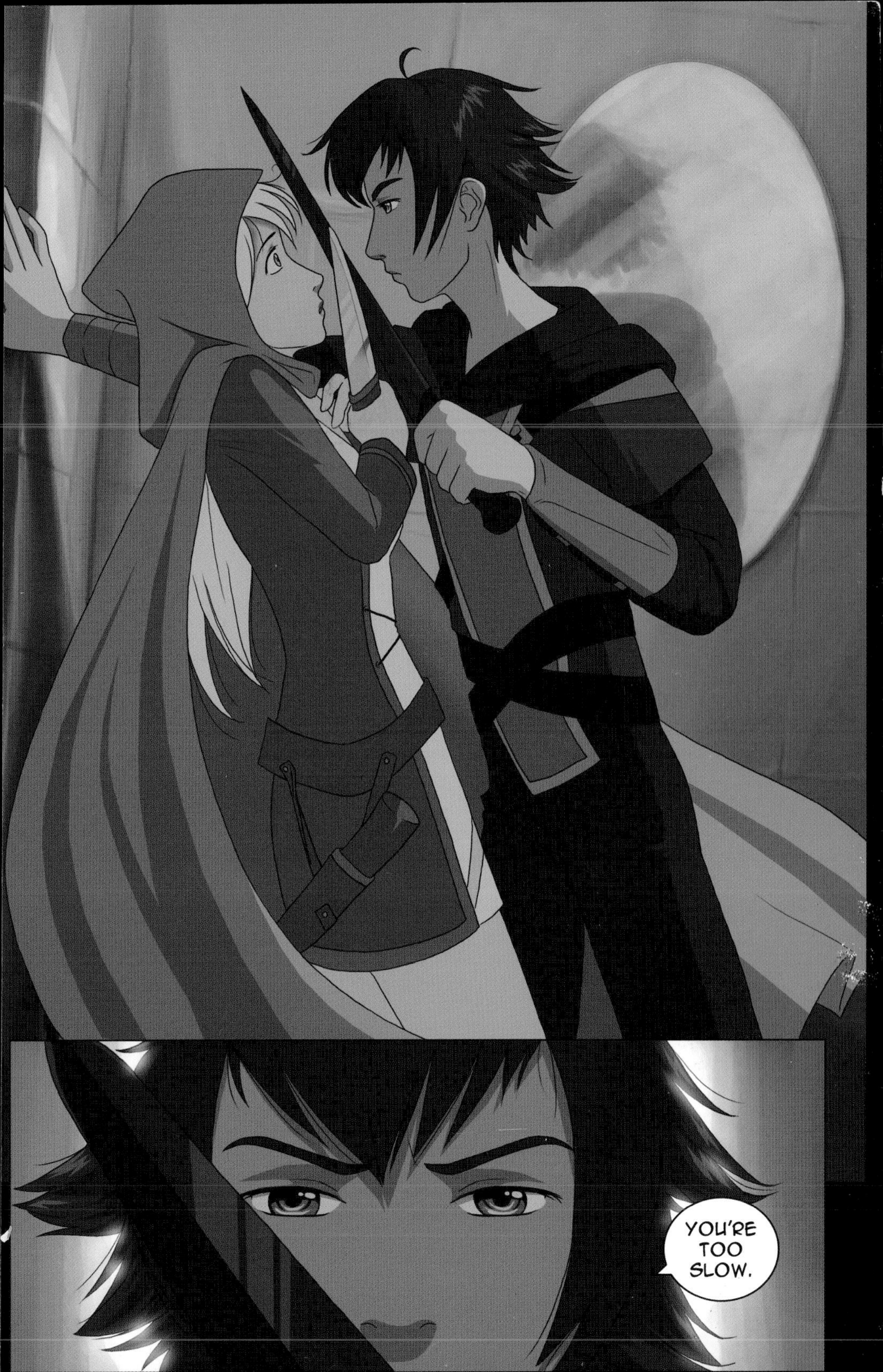
YOU'RE TOO SLOW.

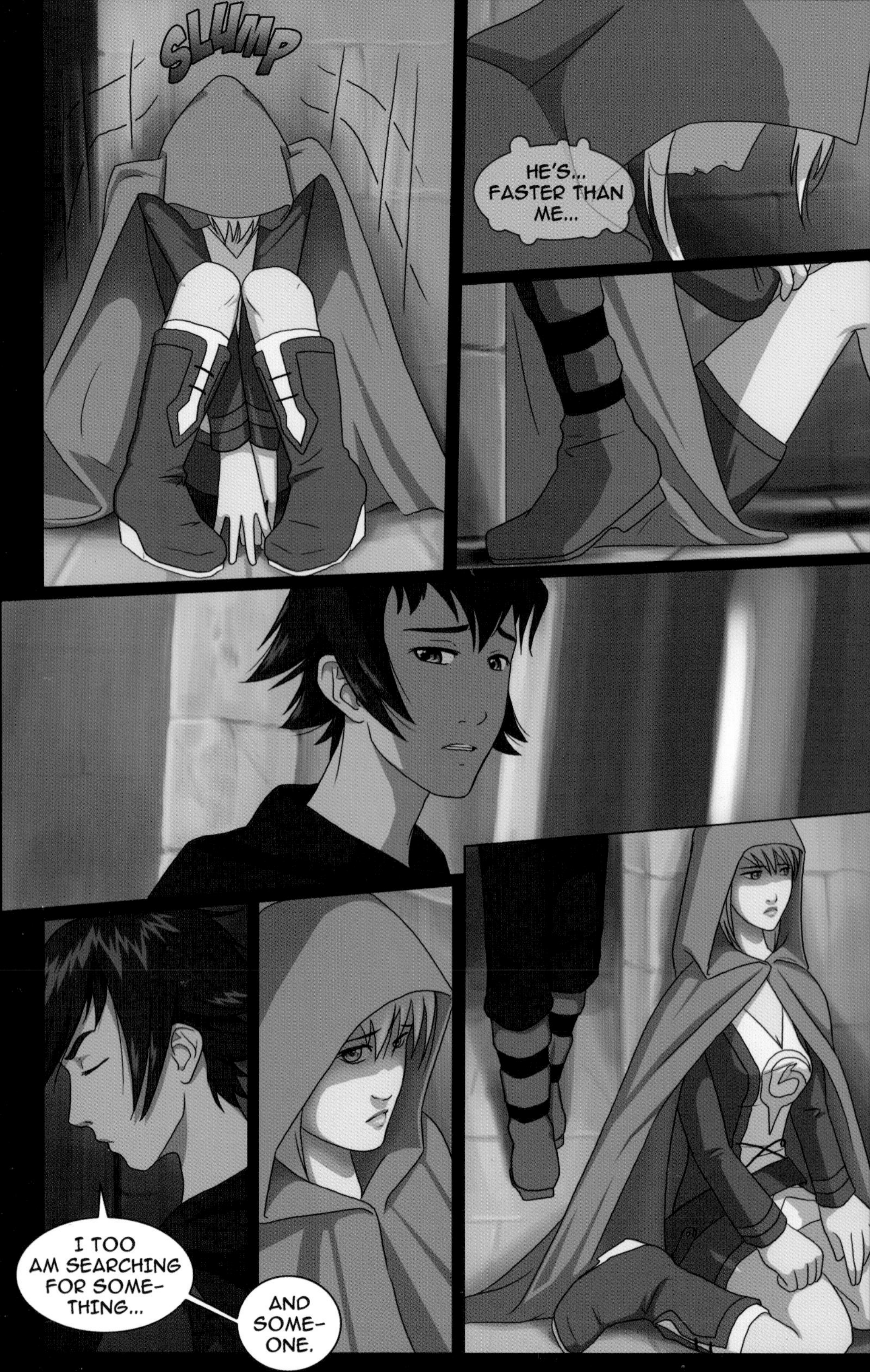
SLUMP
HE'S... FASTER THAN ME...
I TOO AM SEARCHING FOR SOME-THING...
AND SOME-ONE.

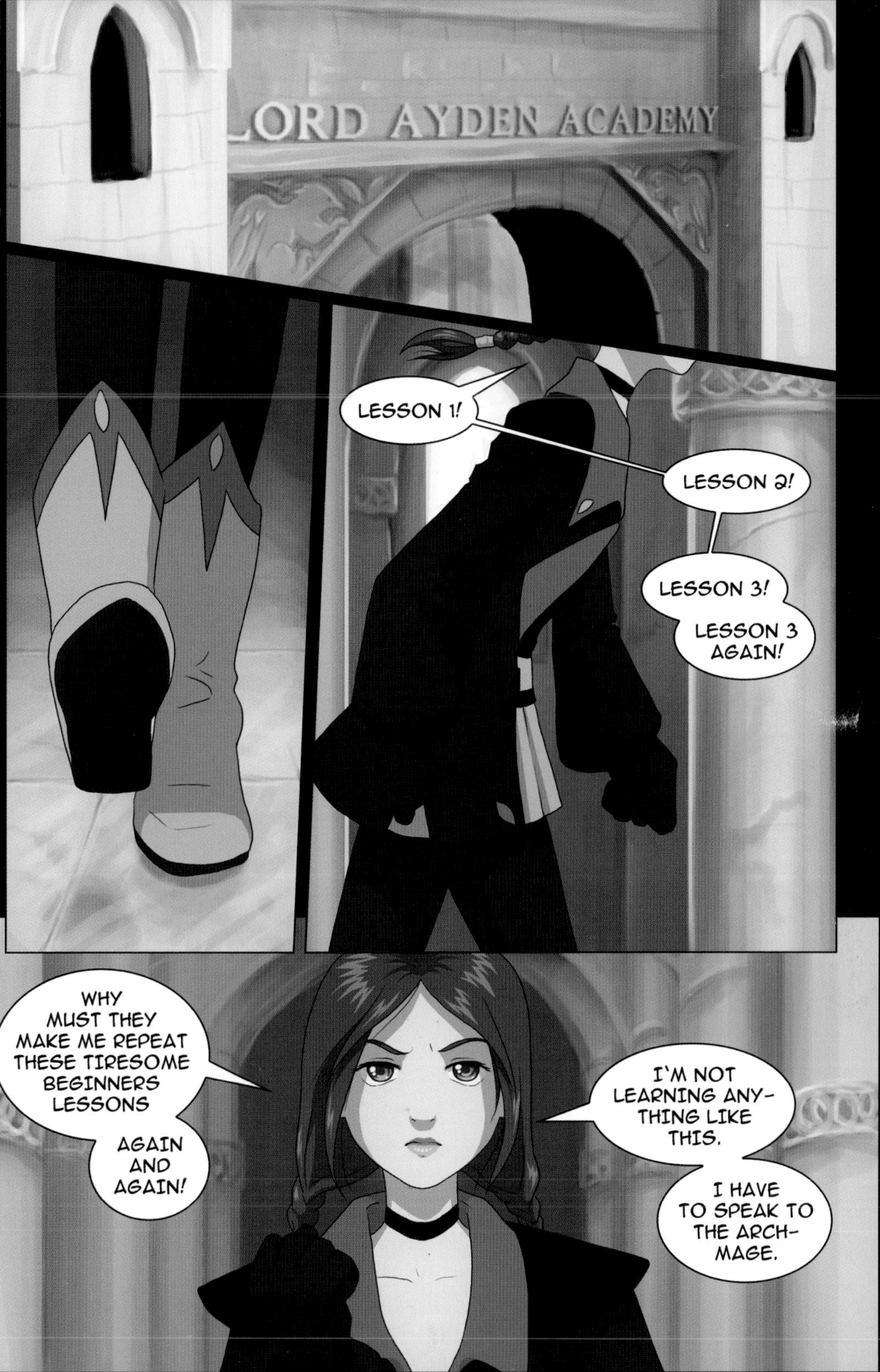
LORD AYDEN ACADEMY
LESSON 1!
LESSON 2!
LESSON 3!
LESSON 3 AGAIN!
WHY MUST THEY MAKE ME REPEAT THESE TIRESOME BEGINNERS LESSONS
AGAIN AND AGAIN!
I'M NOT LEARNING ANY-THING LIKE THIS.
I HAVE TO SPEAK TO THE ARCH-MAGE.

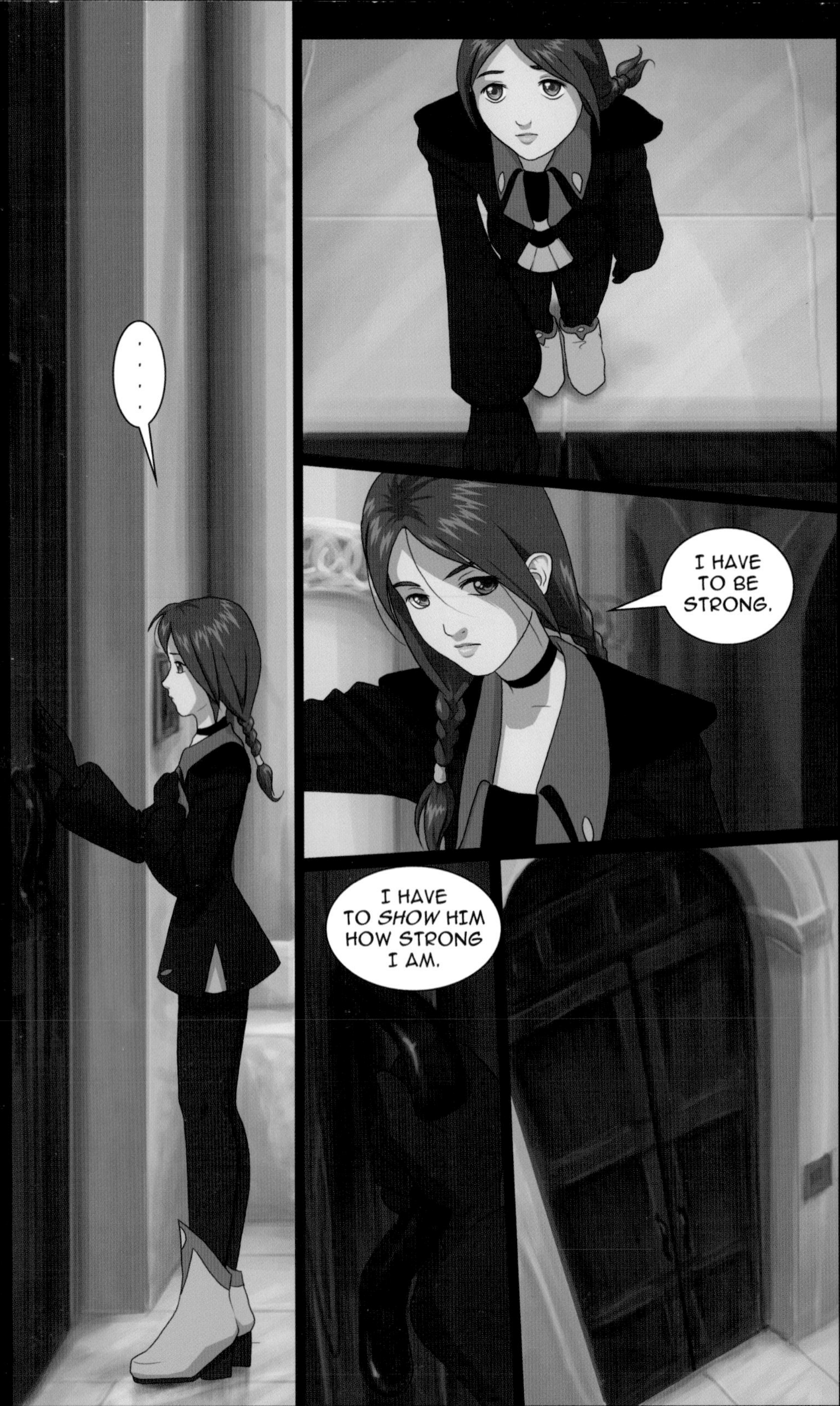
. . . .
I HAVE TO BE STRONG.
I HAVE TO *SHOW* HIM HOW STRONG I AM.

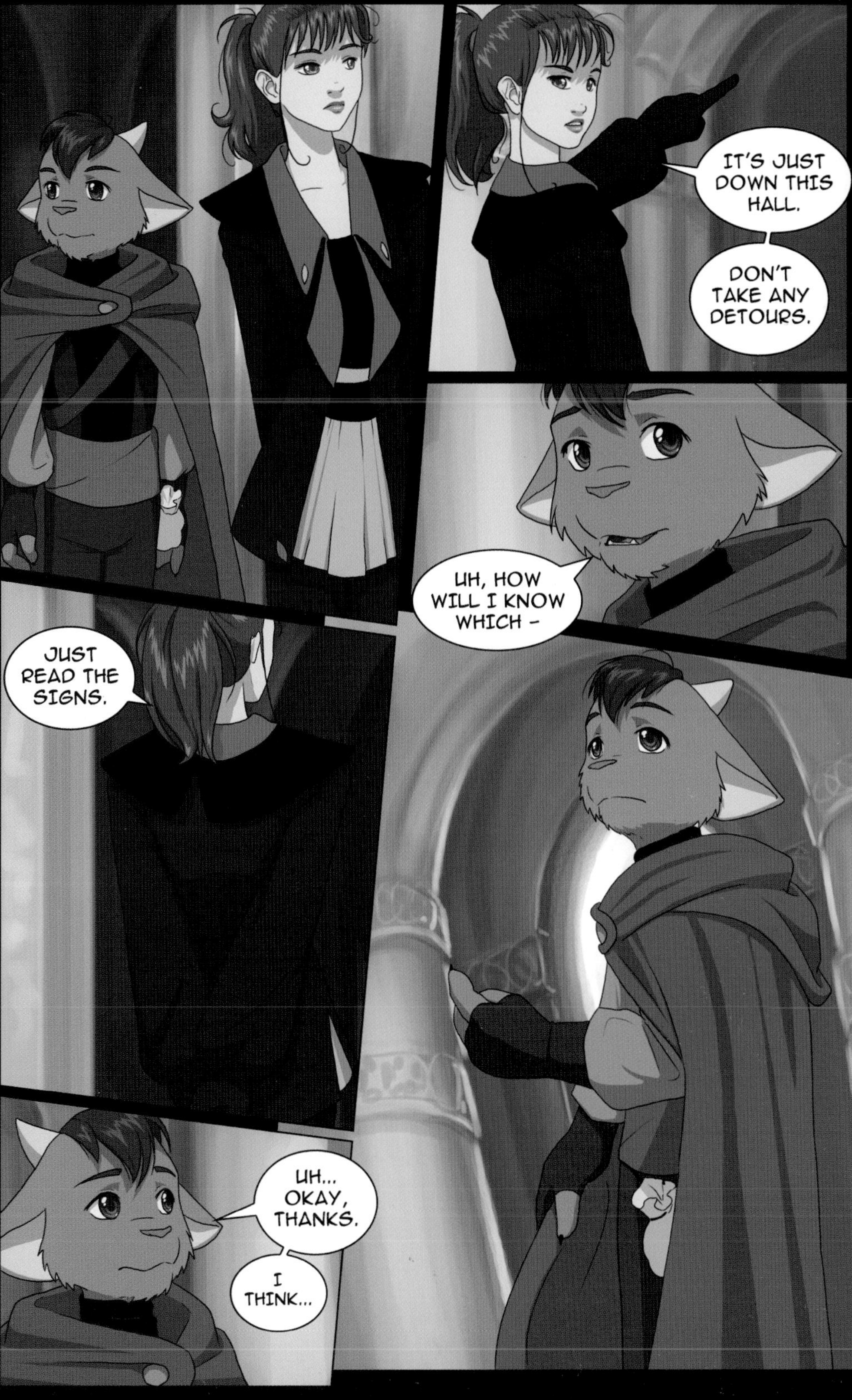
IT'S JUST DOWN THIS HALL.
DON'T TAKE ANY DETOURS.
UH, HOW WILL I KNOW WHICH –
JUST READ THE SIGNS.
UH... OKAY, THANKS.
I THINK...

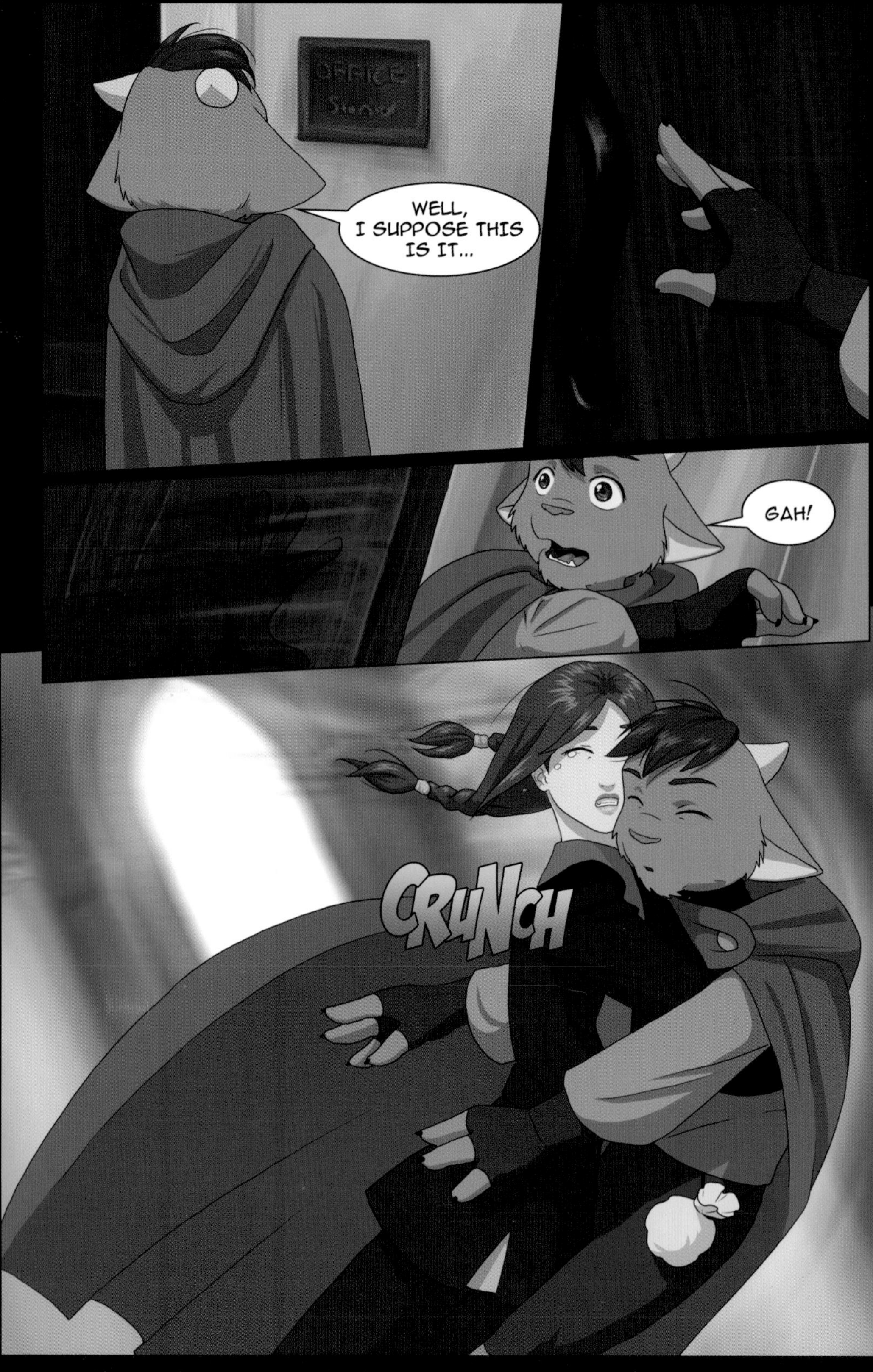
OFFICE
WELL, I SUPPOSE THIS IS IT...
GAH!
CRUNCH

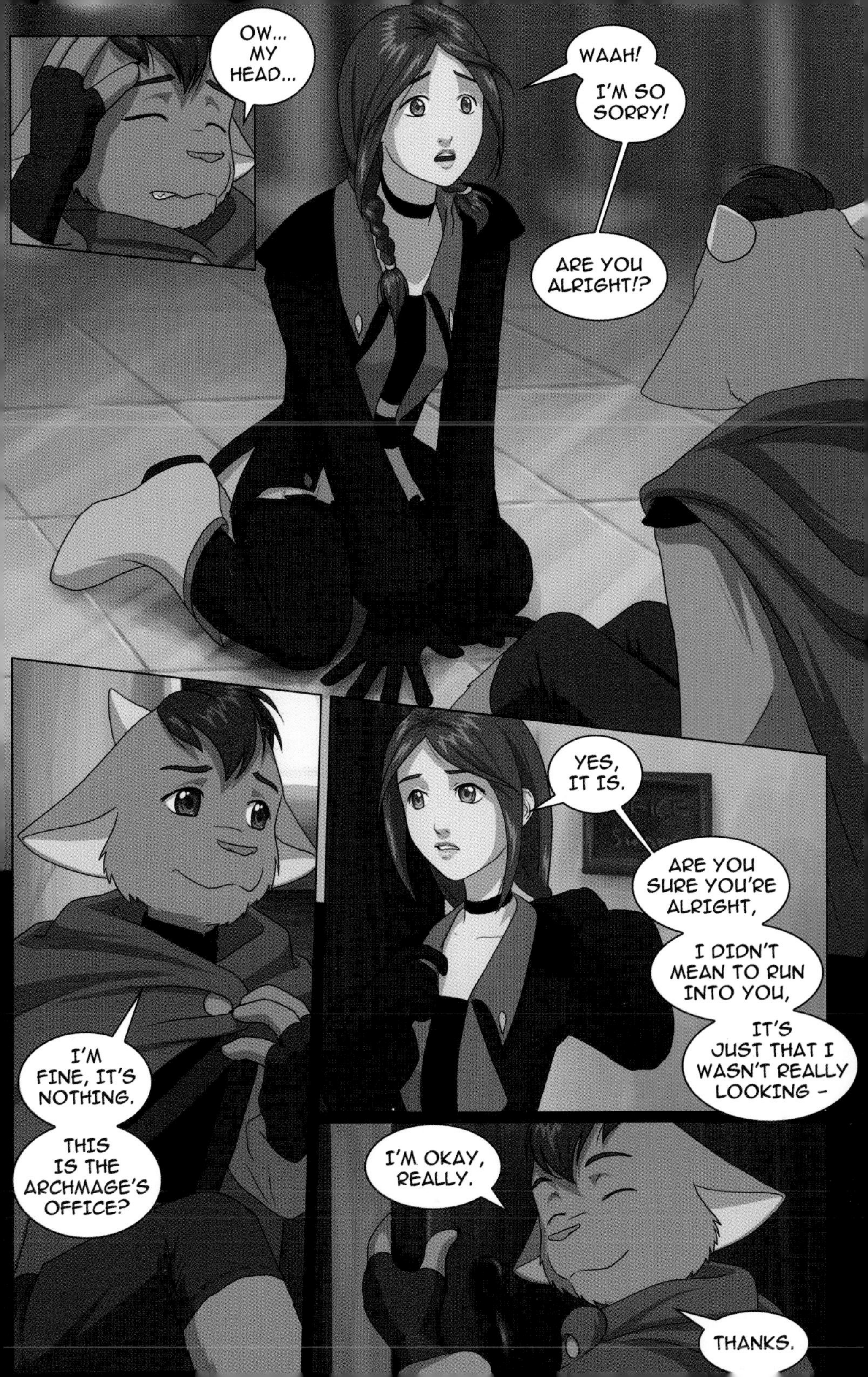
OW... MY HEAD...
WAAH!
I'M SO SORRY!
ARE YOU ALRIGHT!?
I'M FINE, IT'S NOTHING.
THIS IS THE ARCHMAGE'S OFFICE?
YES, IT IS.
ARE YOU SURE YOU'RE ALRIGHT,
I DIDN'T MEAN TO RUN INTO YOU,
IT'S JUST THAT I WASN'T REALLY LOOKING –
I'M OKAY, REALLY.
THANKS.

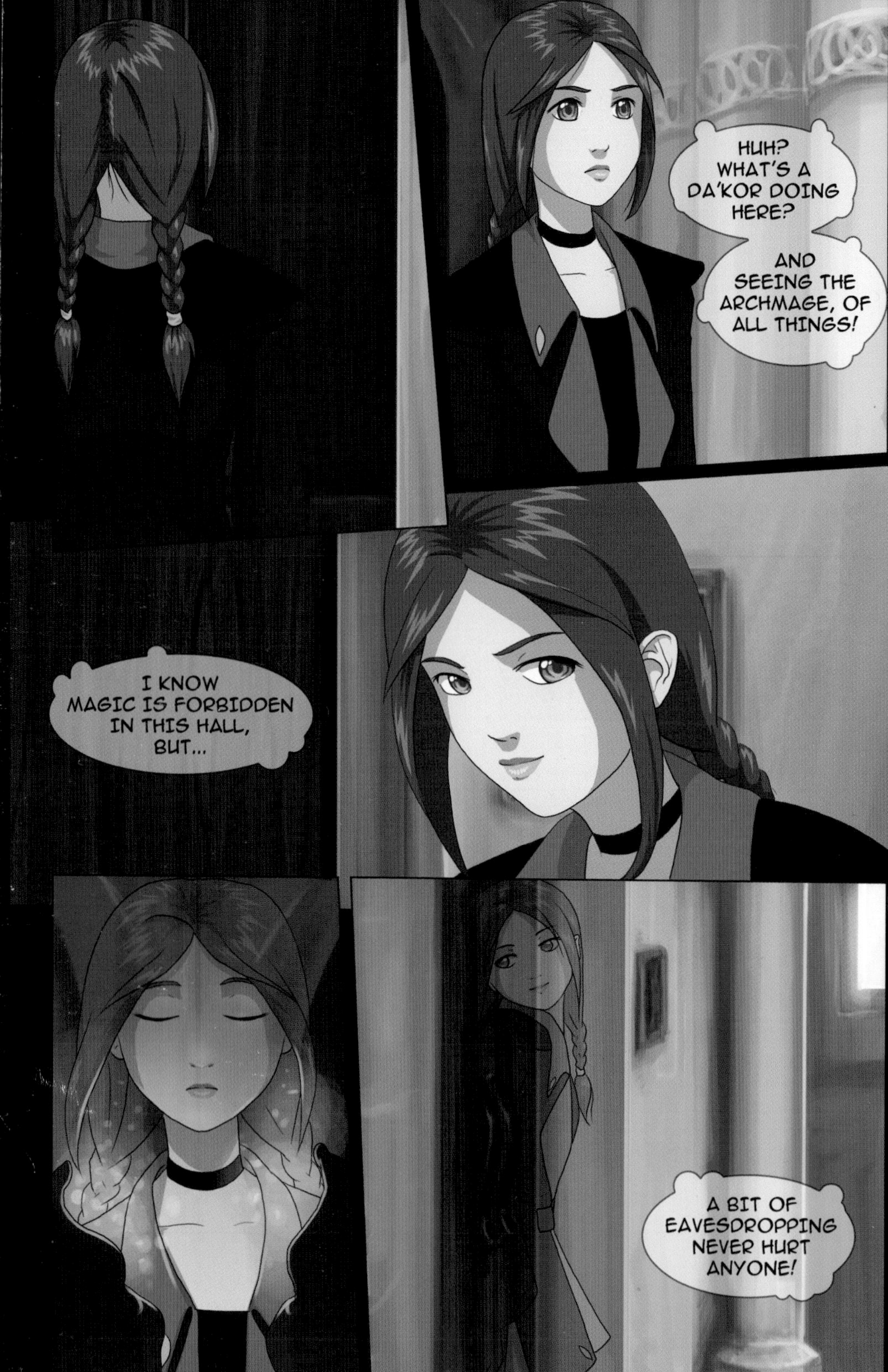
HUH? WHAT'S A DA'KOR DOING HERE?
AND SEEING THE ARCHMAGE, OF ALL THINGS!
I KNOW MAGIC IS FORBIDDEN IN THIS HALL, BUT...
A BIT OF EAVESDROPPING NEVER HURT ANYONE!

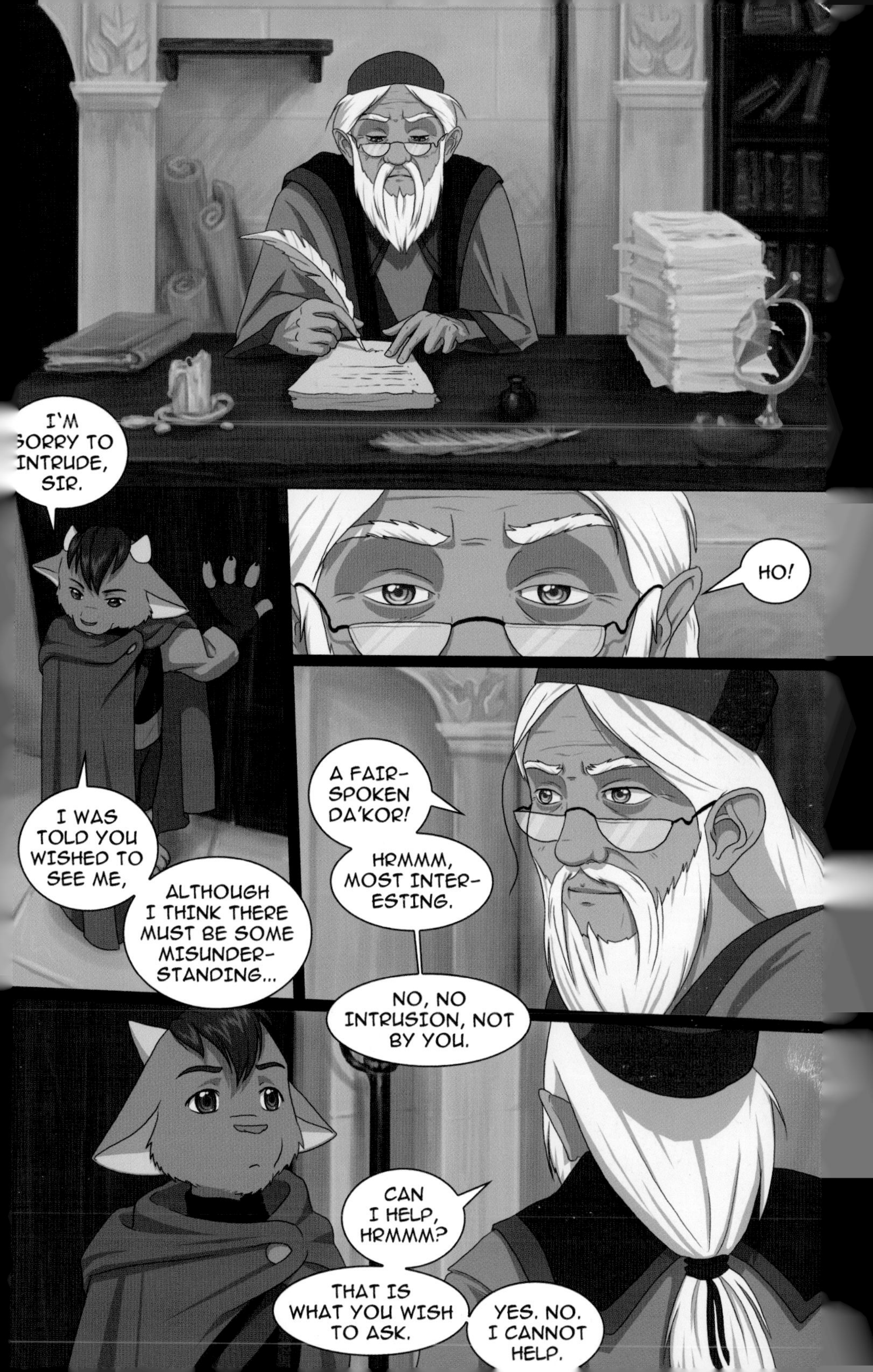
I'M SORRY TO INTRUDE, SIR.
HO!
I WAS TOLD YOU WISHED TO SEE ME,
ALTHOUGH I THINK THERE MUST BE SOME MISUNDERSTANDING...
A FAIR-SPOKEN DA'KOR!
HRMMM, MOST INTERESTING.
NO, NO INTRUSION, NOT BY YOU.
CAN I HELP, HRMMM?
THAT IS WHAT YOU WISH TO ASK.
YES. NO. I CANNOT HELP.

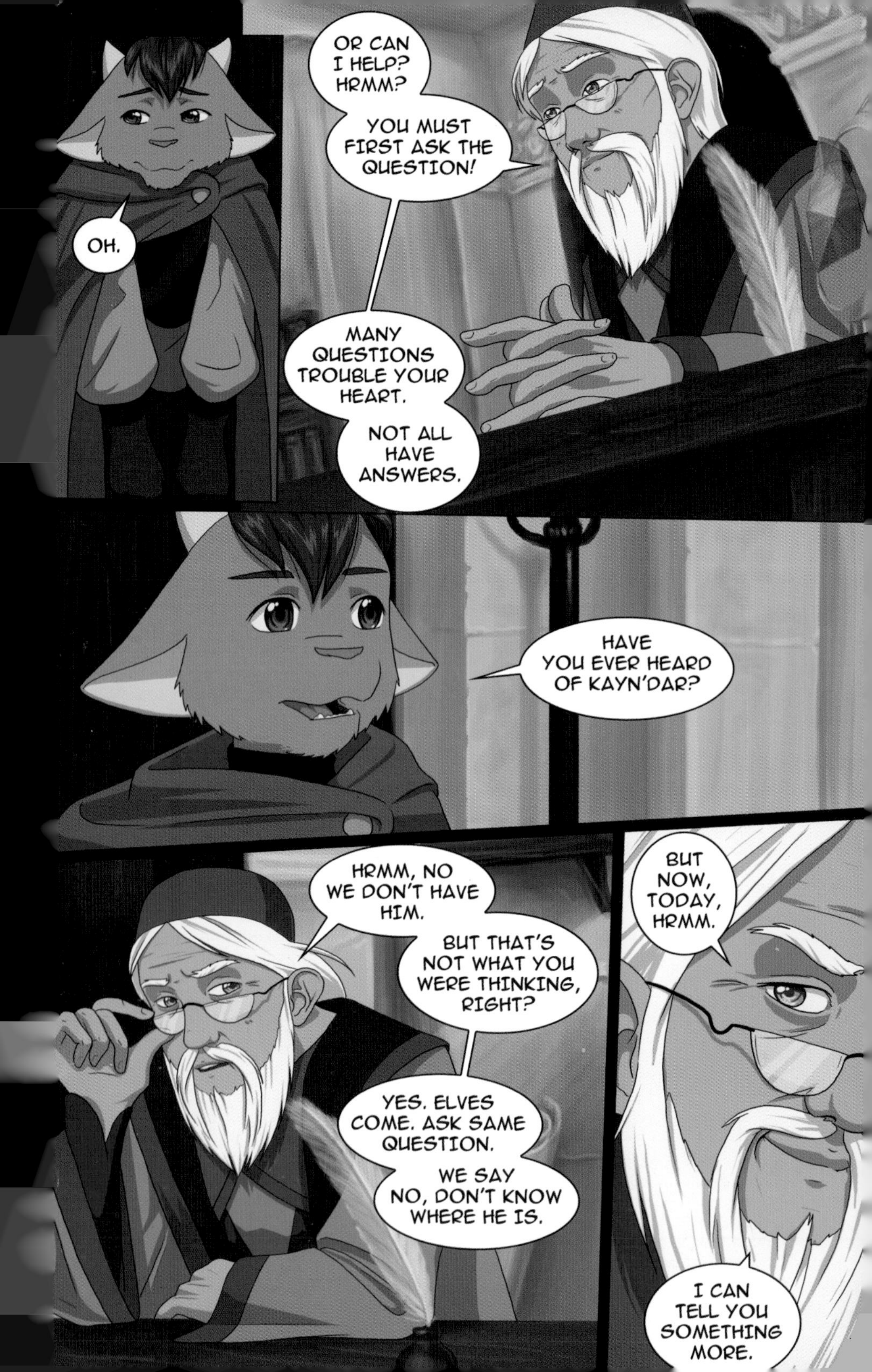
OH.
OR CAN I HELP? HRMM?
YOU MUST FIRST ASK THE QUESTION!
MANY QUESTIONS TROUBLE YOUR HEART.
NOT ALL HAVE ANSWERS.
HAVE YOU EVER HEARD OF KAYN'DAR?
HRMM, NO WE DON'T HAVE HIM.
BUT THAT'S NOT WHAT YOU WERE THINKING, RIGHT?
YES. ELVES COME. ASK SAME QUESTION.
WE SAY NO, DON'T KNOW WHERE HE IS.
BUT NOW, TODAY, HRMM.
I CAN TELL YOU SOMETHING MORE.

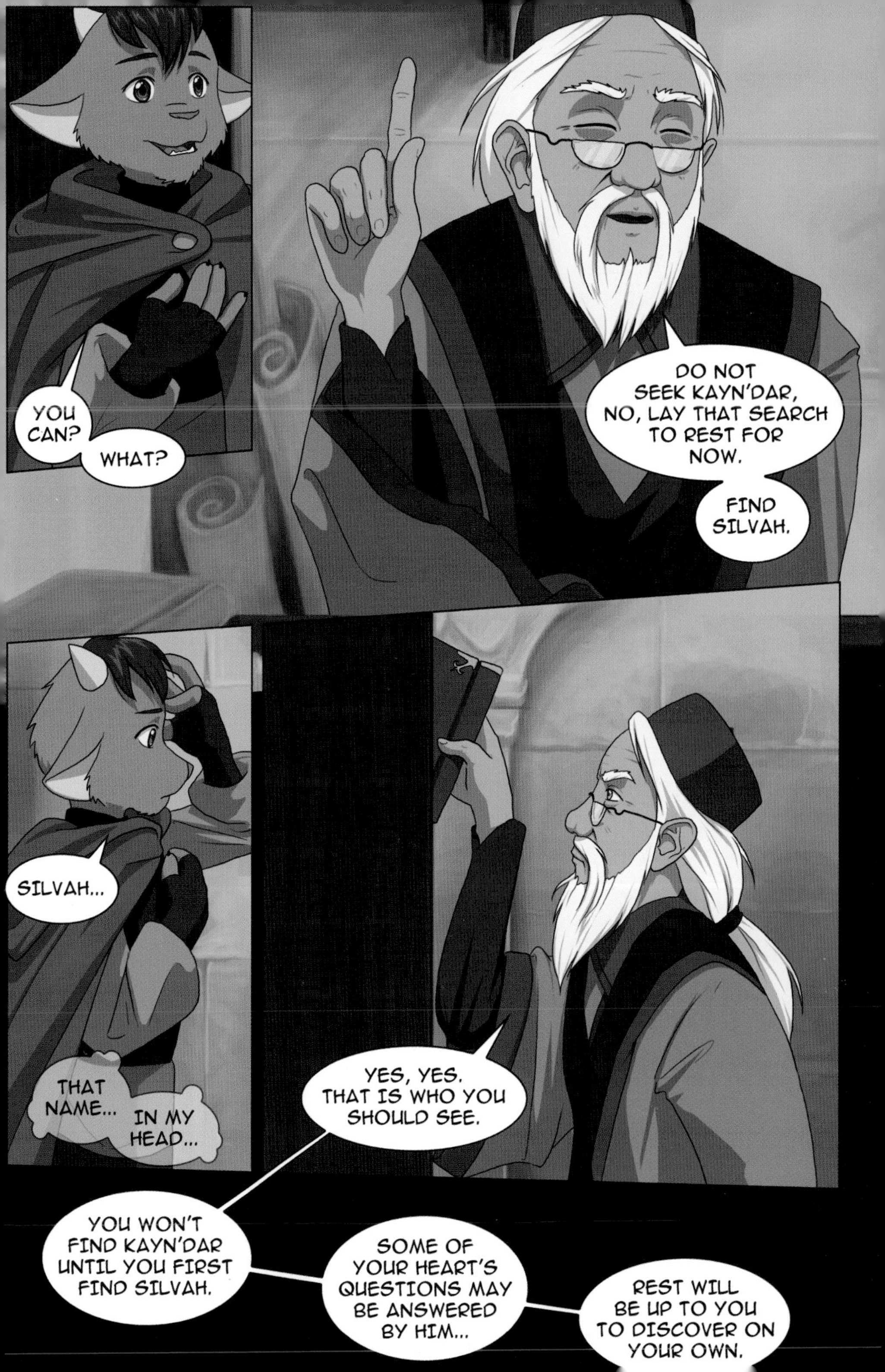
YOU CAN?
WHAT?
DO NOT SEEK KAYN'DAR, NO, LAY THAT SEARCH TO REST FOR NOW.
FIND SILVAH.
SILVAH...
THAT NAME...
IN MY HEAD...
YES, YES. THAT IS WHO YOU SHOULD SEE.
YOU WON'T FIND KAYN'DAR UNTIL YOU FIRST FIND SILVAH.
SOME OF YOUR HEART'S QUESTIONS MAY BE ANSWERED BY HIM...
REST WILL BE UP TO YOU TO DISCOVER ON YOUR OWN.

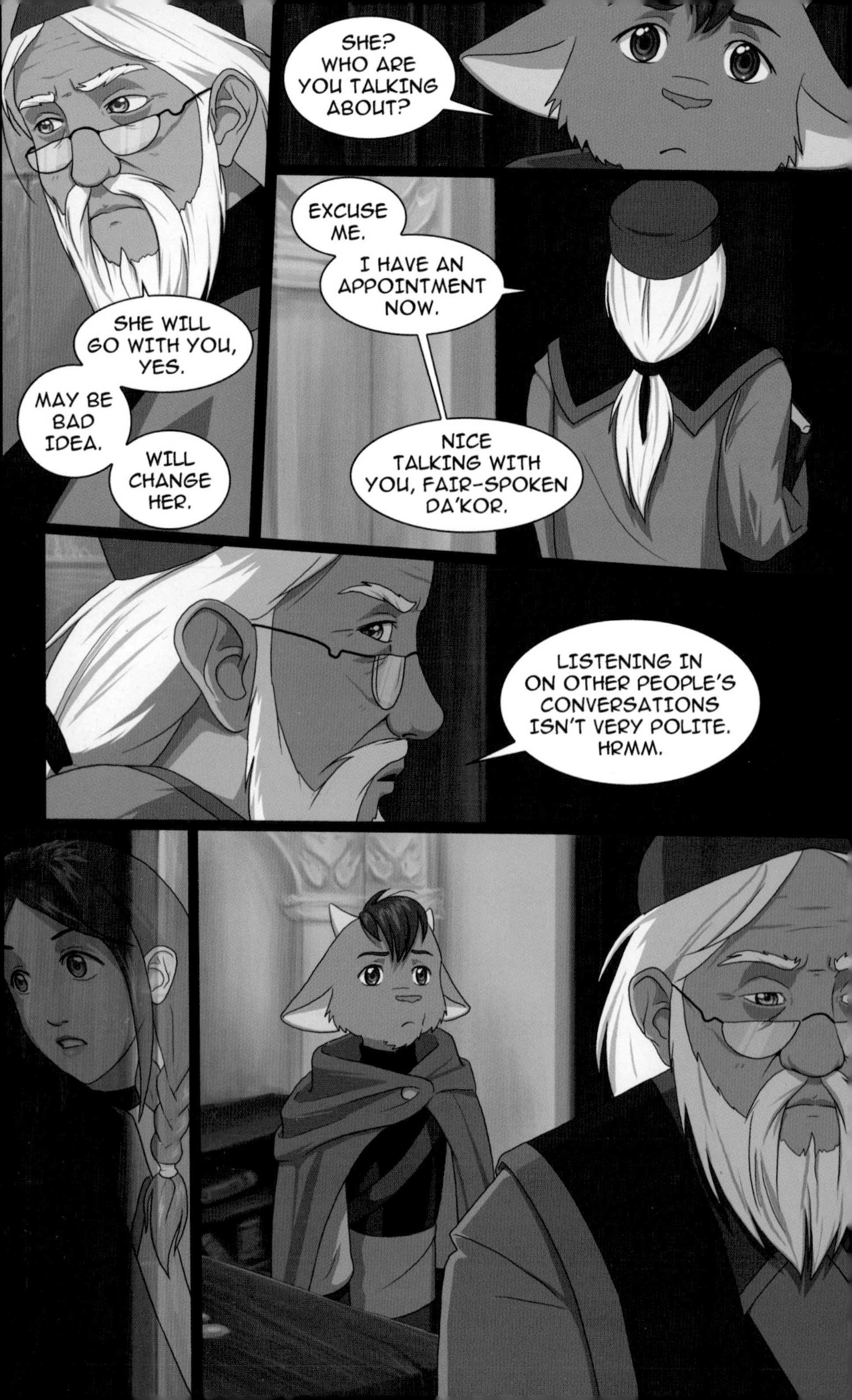
SHE? WHO ARE YOU TALKING ABOUT?
SHE WILL GO WITH YOU, YES.
MAY BE BAD IDEA.
WILL CHANGE HER.
EXCUSE ME.
I HAVE AN APPOINTMENT NOW.
NICE TALKING WITH YOU, FAIR-SPOKEN DA'KOR.
LISTENING IN ON OTHER PEOPLE'S CONVERSATIONS ISN'T VERY POLITE. HRMM.

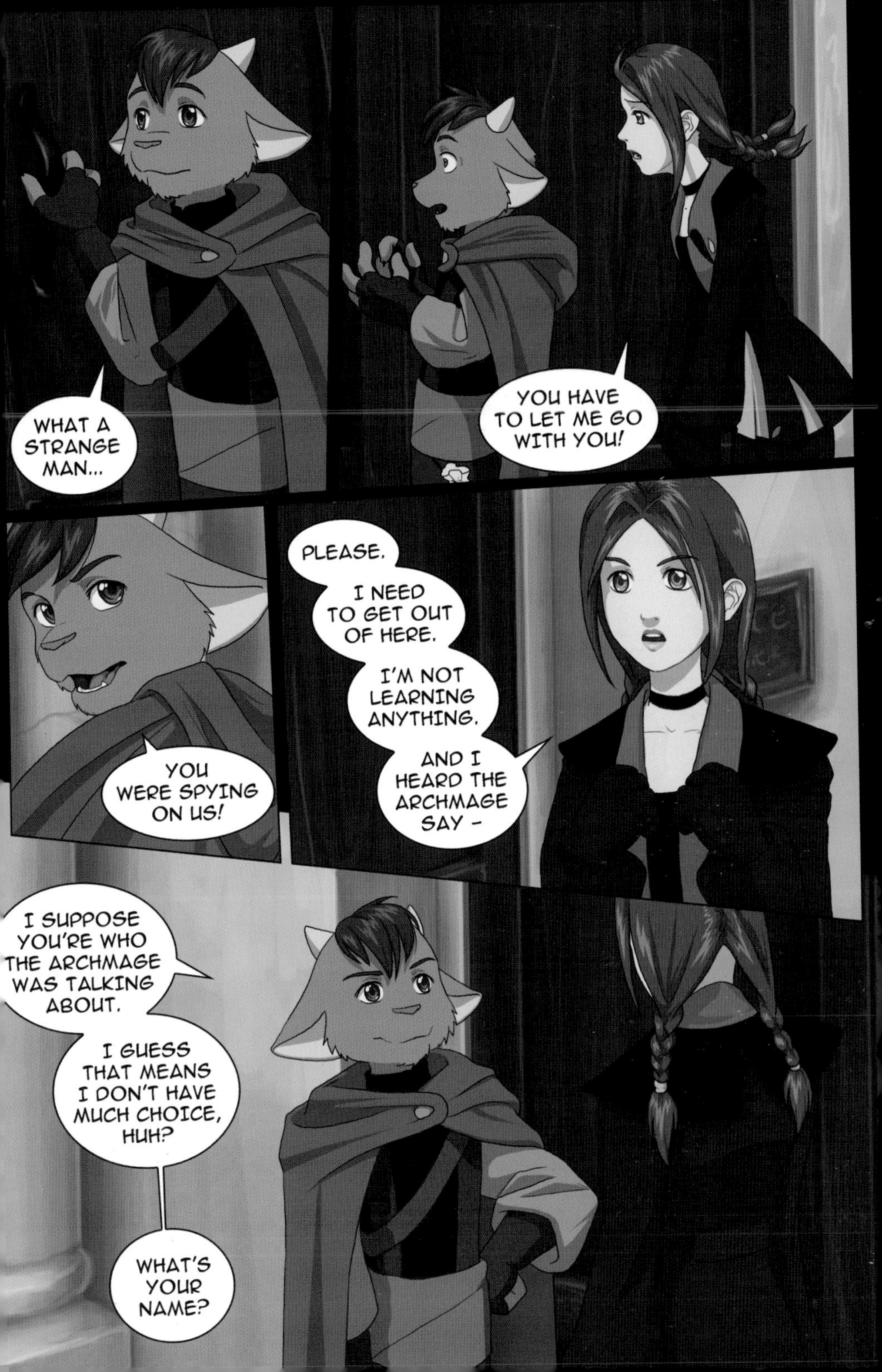
WHAT A STRANGE MAN...
YOU HAVE TO LET ME GO WITH YOU!
YOU WERE SPYING ON US!
PLEASE.
I NEED TO GET OUT OF HERE.
I'M NOT LEARNING ANYTHING.
AND I HEARD THE ARCHMAGE SAY -
I SUPPOSE YOU'RE WHO THE ARCHMAGE WAS TALKING ABOUT.
I GUESS THAT MEANS I DON'T HAVE MUCH CHOICE, HUH?
WHAT'S YOUR NAME?

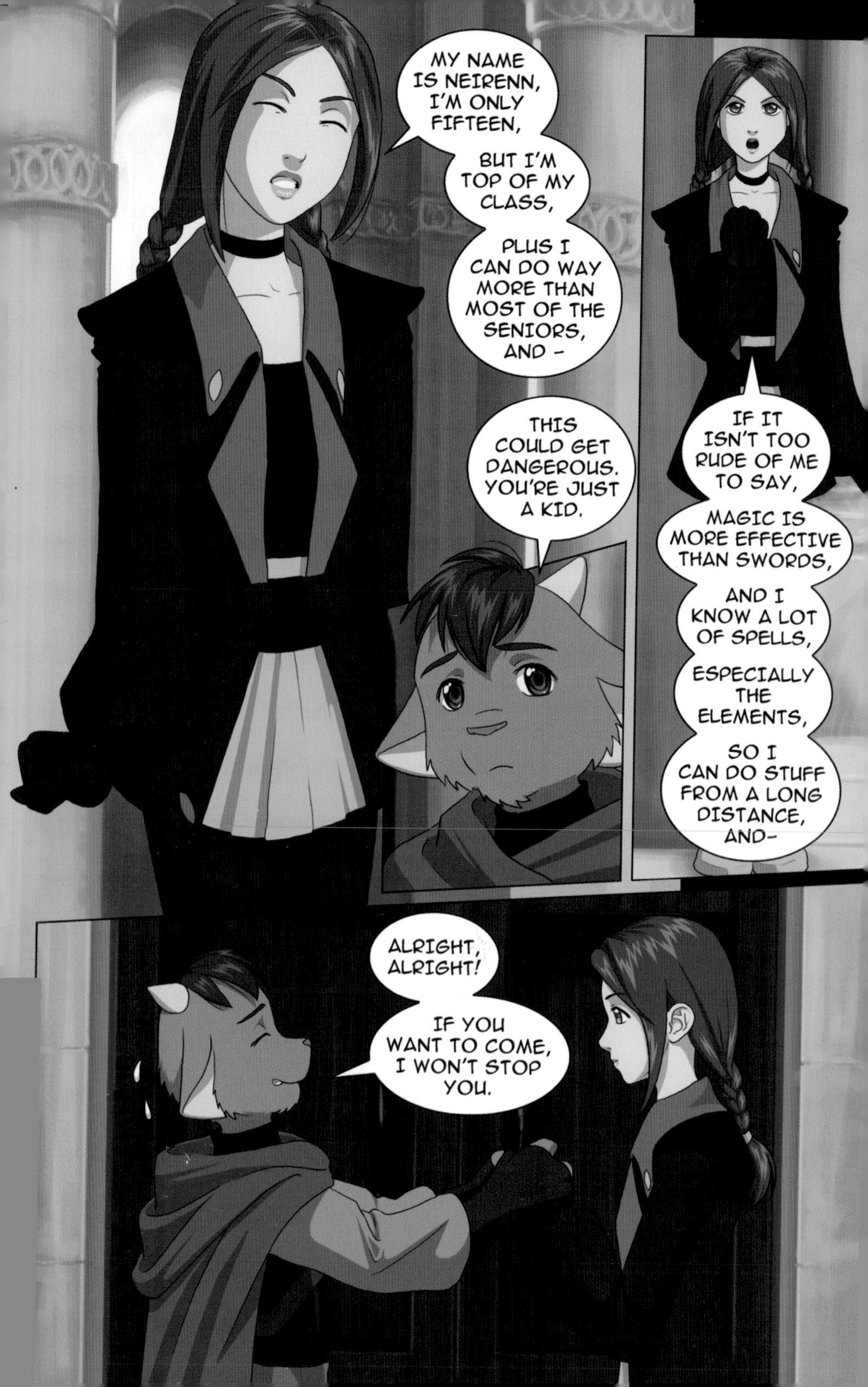
MY NAME IS NEIRENN, I'M ONLY FIFTEEN,
BUT I'M TOP OF MY CLASS,
PLUS I CAN DO WAY MORE THAN MOST OF THE SENIORS, AND -
THIS COULD GET DANGEROUS. YOU'RE JUST A KID.
IF IT ISN'T TOO RUDE OF ME TO SAY,
MAGIC IS MORE EFFECTIVE THAN SWORDS,
AND I KNOW A LOT OF SPELLS,
ESPECIALLY THE ELEMENTS,
SO I CAN DO STUFF FROM A LONG DISTANCE, AND-
ALRIGHT, ALRIGHT!
IF YOU WANT TO COME, I WON'T STOP YOU.

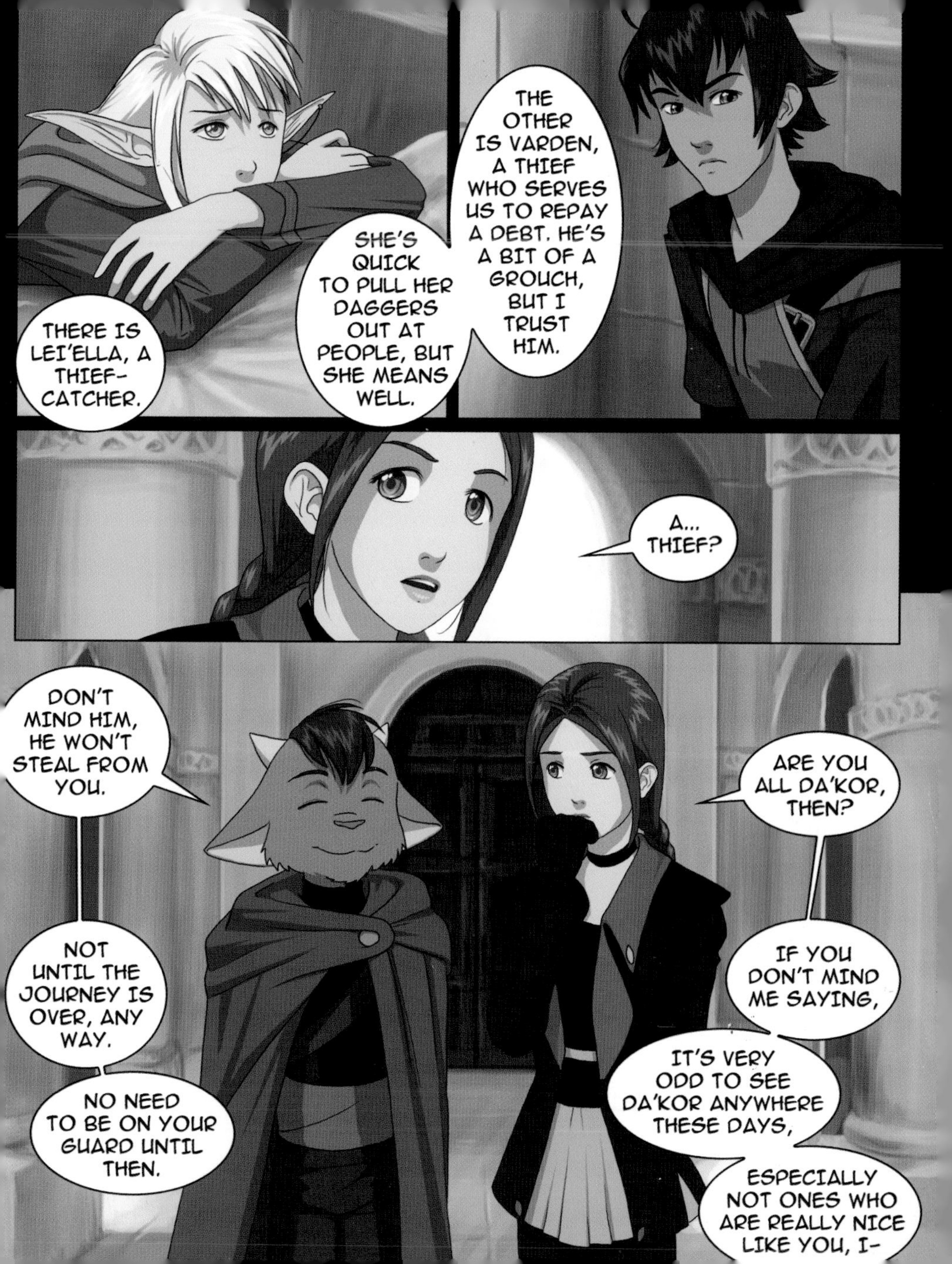
THERE IS LEI'ELLA, A THIEF-CATCHER.
SHE'S QUICK TO PULL HER DAGGERS OUT AT PEOPLE, BUT SHE MEANS WELL.
THE OTHER IS VARDEN, A THIEF WHO SERVES US TO REPAY A DEBT. HE'S A BIT OF A GROUCH, BUT I TRUST HIM.
A... THIEF?
DON'T MIND HIM, HE WON'T STEAL FROM YOU.
NOT UNTIL THE JOURNEY IS OVER, ANY WAY.
NO NEED TO BE ON YOUR GUARD UNTIL THEN.
ARE YOU ALL DA'KOR, THEN?
IF YOU DON'T MIND ME SAYING,
IT'S VERY ODD TO SEE DA'KOR ANYWHERE THESE DAYS,
ESPECIALLY NOT ONES WHO ARE REALLY NICE LIKE YOU, I-

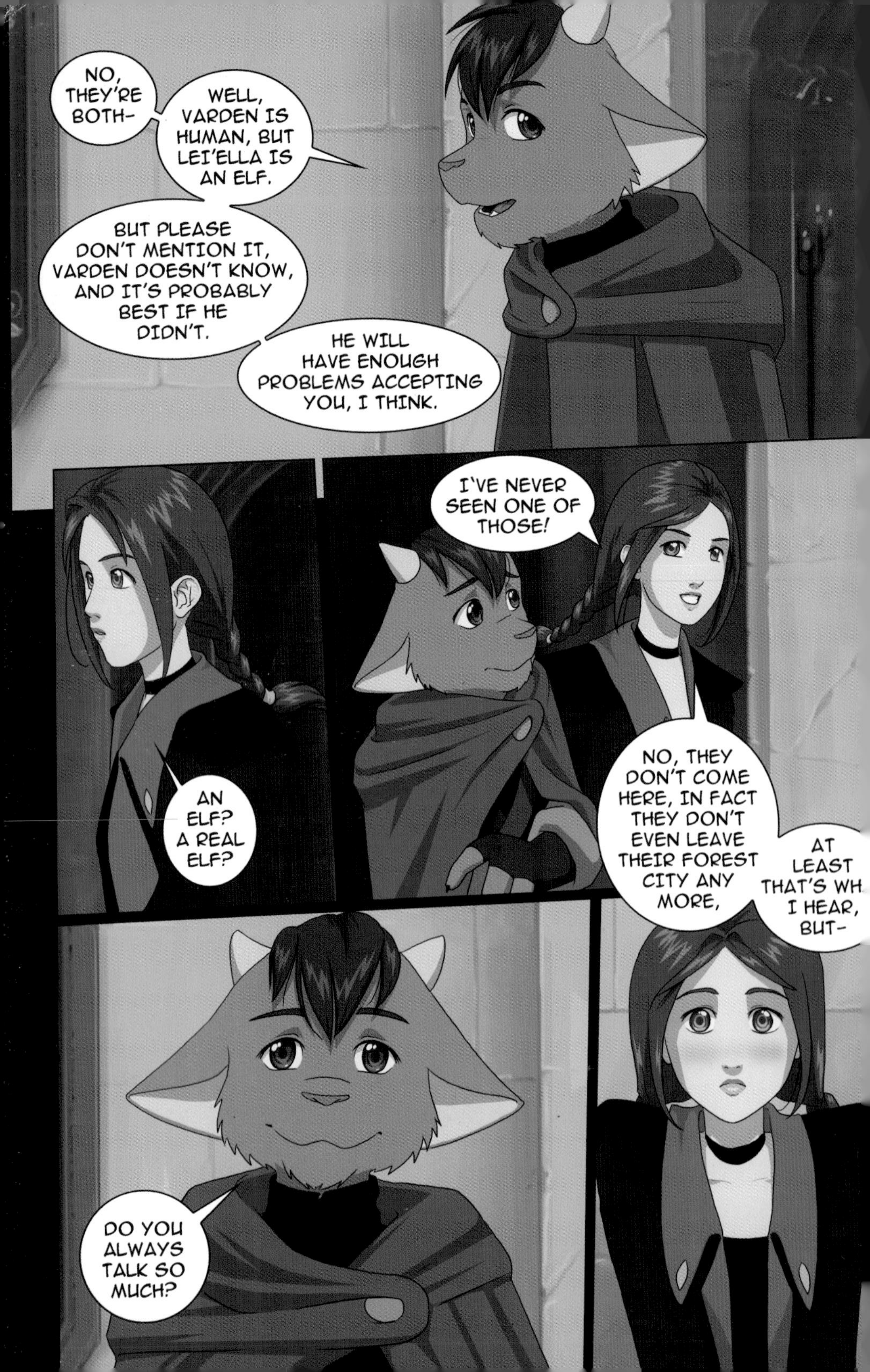
NO, THEY'RE BOTH-
WELL, VARDEN IS HUMAN, BUT LEI'ELLA IS AN ELF.
BUT PLEASE DON'T MENTION IT, VARDEN DOESN'T KNOW, AND IT'S PROBABLY BEST IF HE DIDN'T.
HE WILL HAVE ENOUGH PROBLEMS ACCEPTING YOU, I THINK.
AN ELF? A REAL ELF?
I'VE NEVER SEEN ONE OF THOSE!
NO, THEY DON'T COME HERE, IN FACT THEY DON'T EVEN LEAVE THEIR FOREST CITY ANY MORE,
AT LEAST THAT'S WH I HEAR, BUT-
DO YOU ALWAYS TALK SO MUCH?

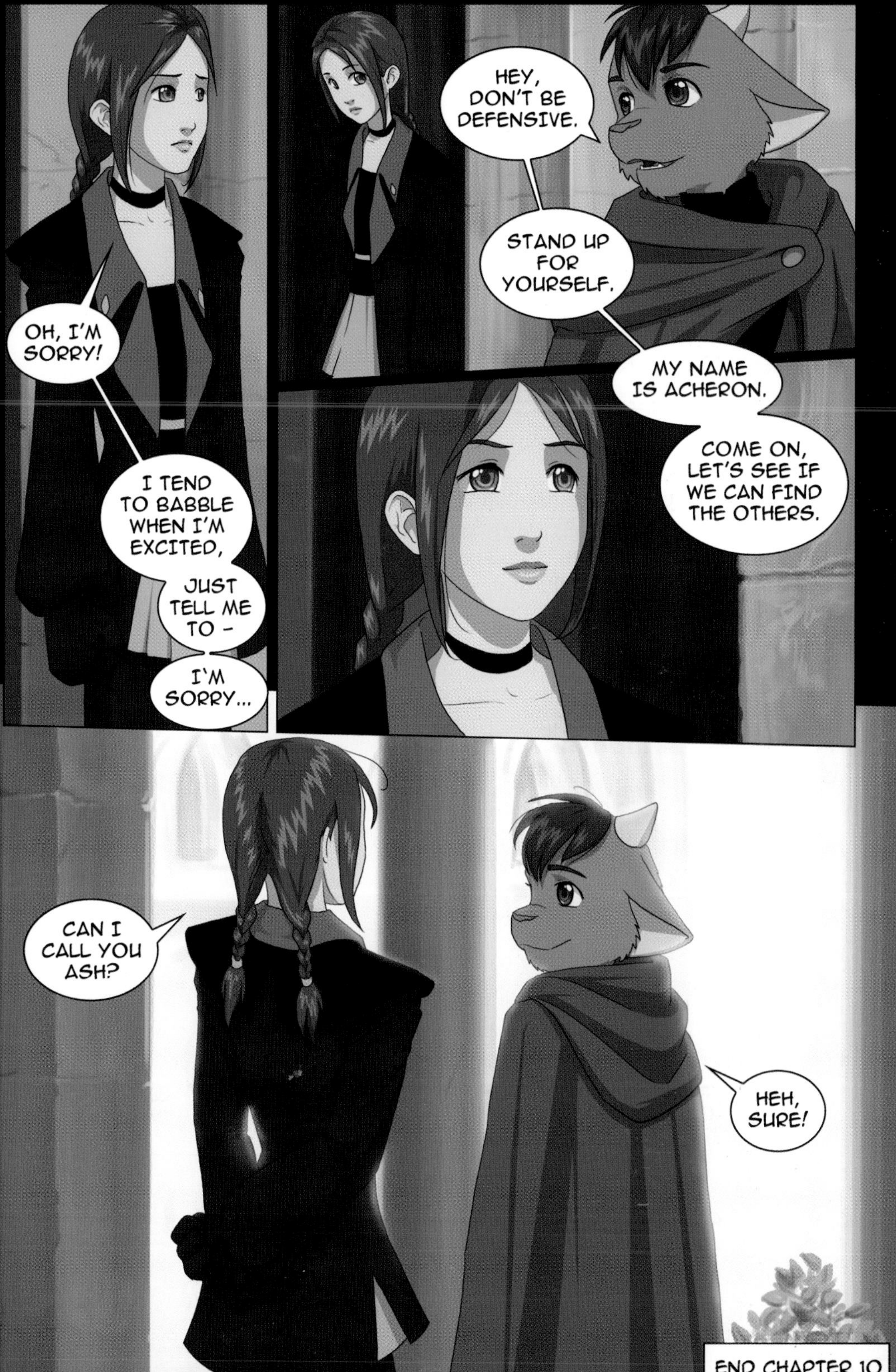
OH, I'M SORRY!
I TEND TO BABBLE WHEN I'M EXCITED,
JUST TELL ME TO -
I'M SORRY...
HEY, DON'T BE DEFENSIVE.
STAND UP FOR YOURSELF.
MY NAME IS ACHERON.
COME ON, LET'S SEE IF WE CAN FIND THE OTHERS.
CAN I CALL YOU ASH?
HEH, SURE!
END CHAPTER 10

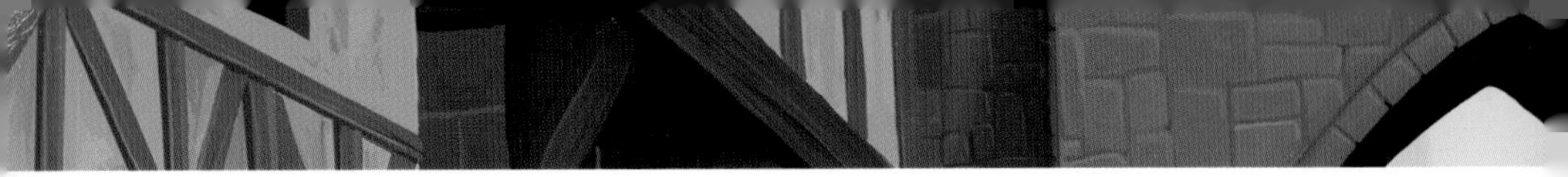

HUMANS

Humans are by far the most dominant race on the continent. They live in several large cities ruled by powerful lords, as well as numerous smaller settlements and farming communities. Their expansion into all areas of the known world have pushed out both the da'kor and the elves, leaving those races with only small pockets of land on which to live.

The majority of humans distrust and fear magic, and thus have not allowed it to be integrated into their lives, despite the improvements it would bring. In fact, many humans in the more isolated areas of the world have come to believe that neither magic, da'kor or elves even exist.

Because of stories passed down through generations, most humans have a fear of the da'kor, but individual attitudes and responses range from mild distrust to outright terror.

VARDEN

Varden is a skilled thief from Rhyll, who joins the party on somewhat dubious grounds. He's generally fairly relaxed and care-free, not bothering himself with the troubles of other people (unless, of course, it's profitable).

He carries with him the typical human trait of a dislike for both elves and magic, although for him, there seems to be a more personal reason for his opinions - and he's not willing to share the details.

This was the initial costume design for Varden, that was completely reworked by the time he appeared in the comic to make it more suitable for thievery.

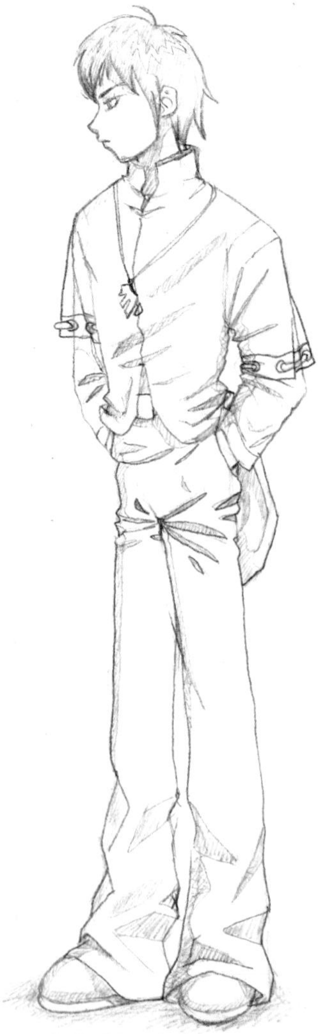

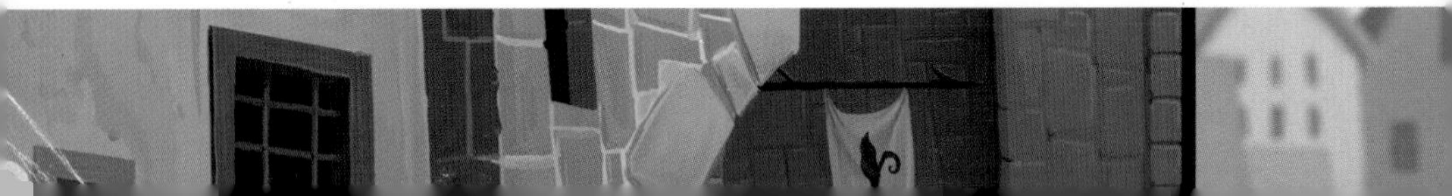

MAGES

Mages are not a distinct race on their own, but are in fact humans with minor amounts of elven heritage. This ancestry gives them the ability to use magic, which they study relentlessly in the mage-dominated city of Aydensfell. As the elves now keep to themselves, the mages are left to understand and experiment with magic on their own, and much knowledge is still unavailable to them.

Most mages have red hair and blue eyes, which is either an odd side effect of the mixing of races, or, as many humans whisper, is actually due to centuries of inbreeding in an attempt to keep the elven blood as highly concentrated as possible. It's something of an uncomfortable subject, and mages will either ignore or change the subject when asked about the peculiar colouring.

Because of their powers, mages have no fear of da'kor, humans, or elves. They are generally more interested in scholarly matters than the troubles of the other races.

NEIRENN

Neirenn is a young and talented mage from the academy in Aydensfell. Feeling as though she's not being taught to her skill level, she befriends Acheron and leaves with the party in the hopes of gaining some practical experience.

She has little respect for authority, and has an erratic personality, which lands her in trouble more often than not.

◀ Neirenn's costume was simplified slightly for easier drawing in the comic, but otherwise remains unchanged from its initial concept.

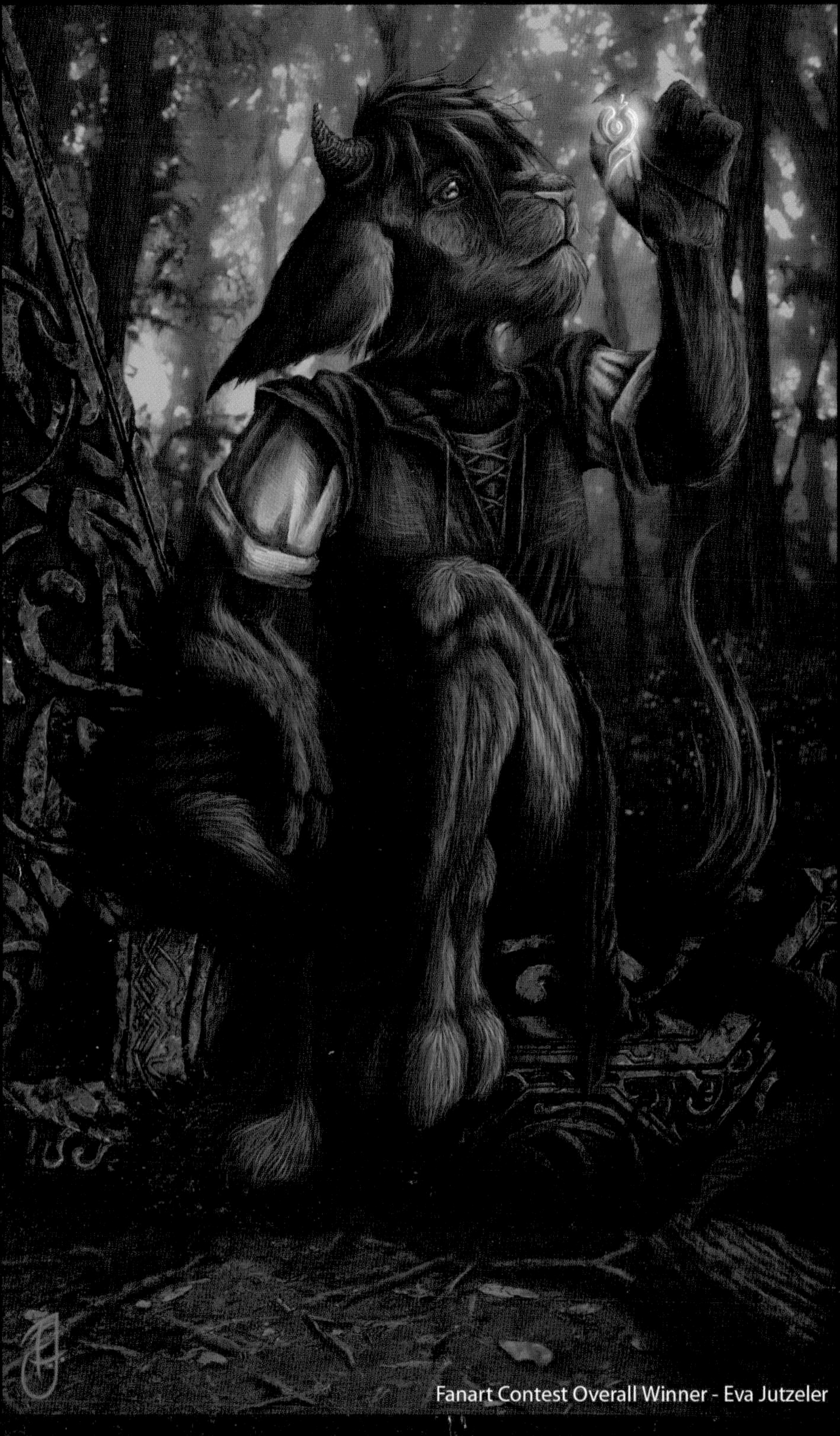

Fanart Contest Overall Winner - Eva Jutzeler

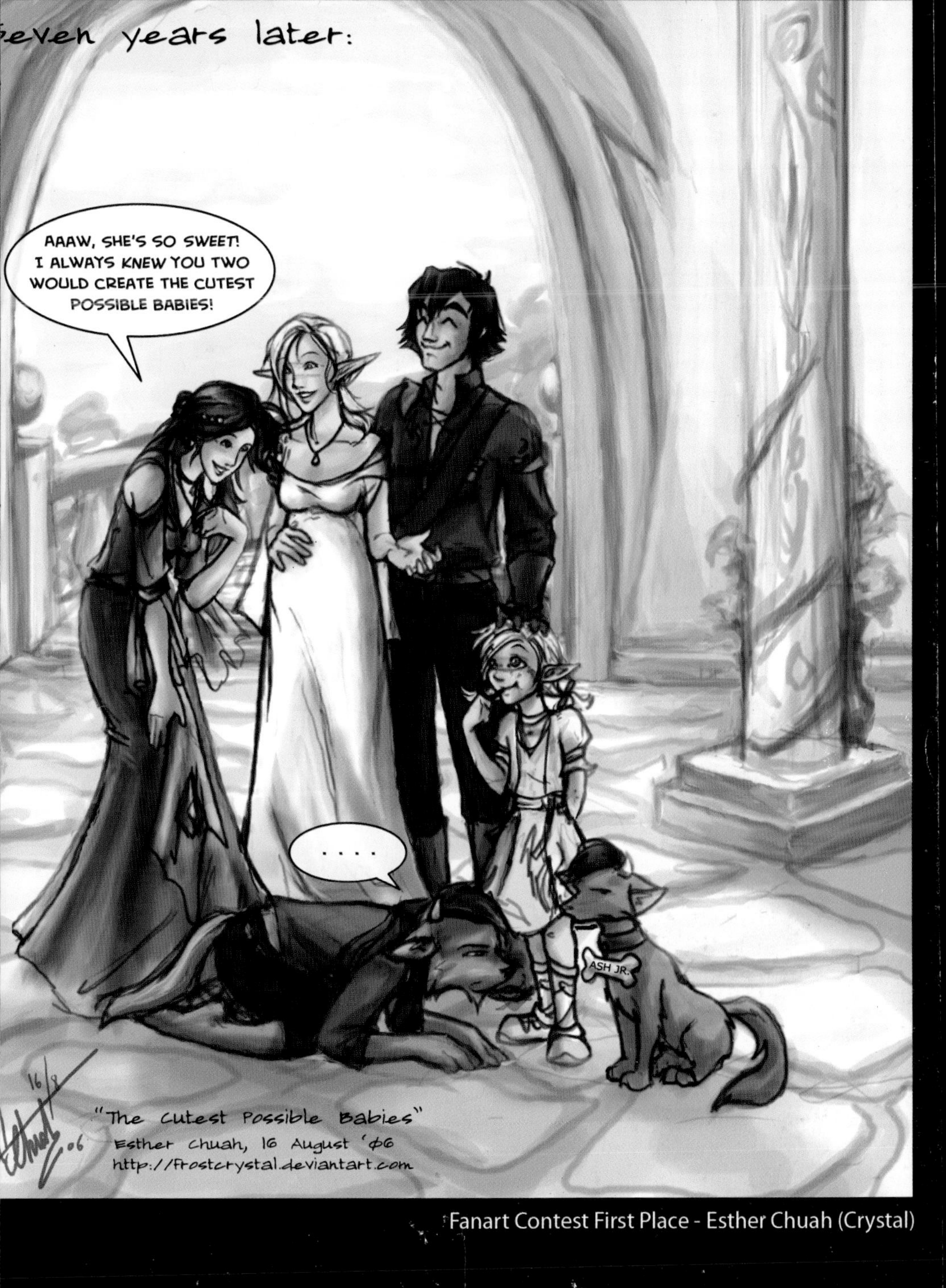
even years later:
AAAW, SHE'S SO SWEET! I ALWAYS KNEW YOU TWO WOULD CREATE THE CUTEST POSSIBLE BABIES!
. . . . .
ASH JR.
16/8 '06
"The Cutest Possible Babies"
Esther Chuah, 16 August '06
http://frostcrystal.deviantart.com

Fanart Contest First Place - Esther Chuah (Crystal)

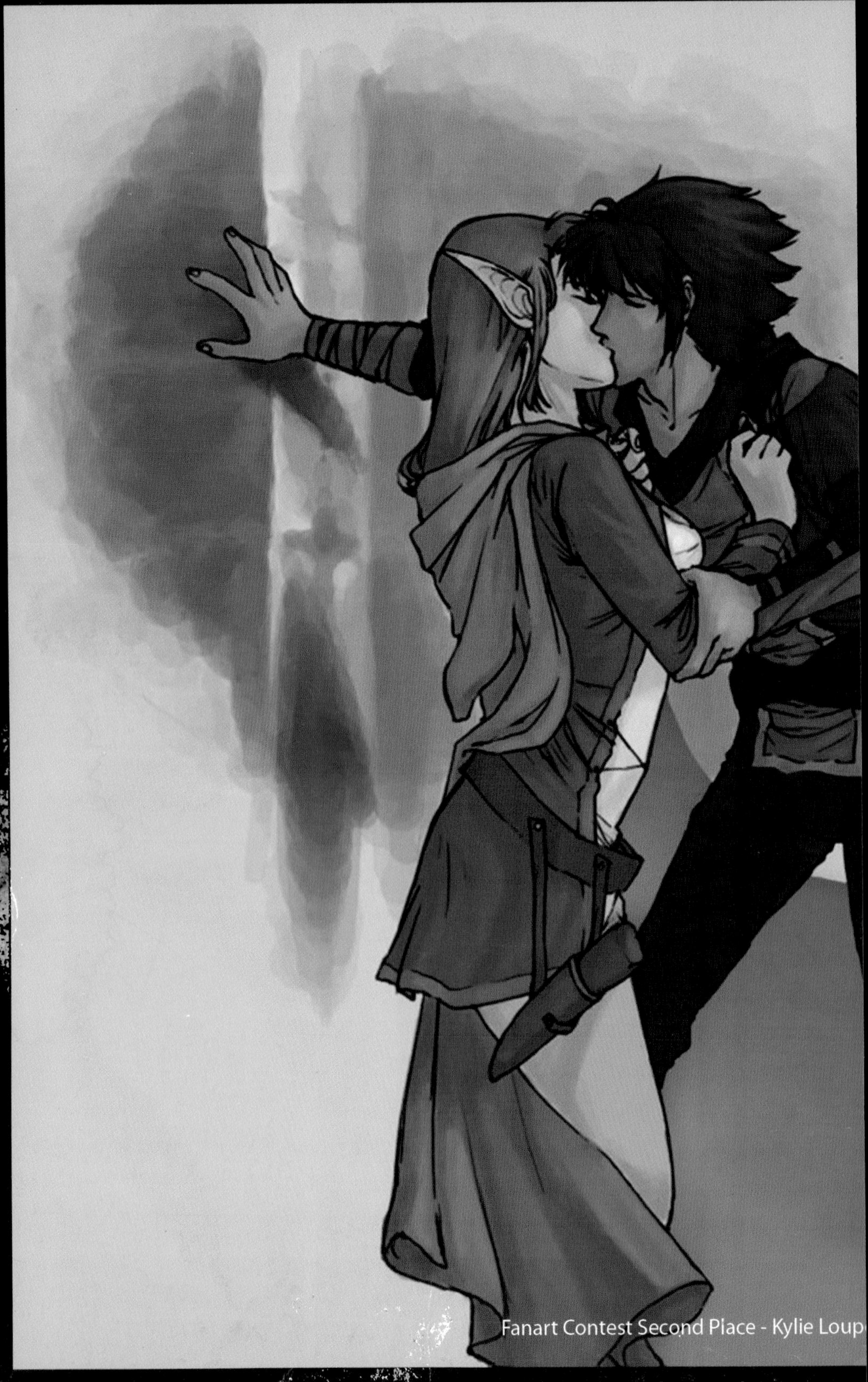
Fanart Contest Second Place - Kylie Loup

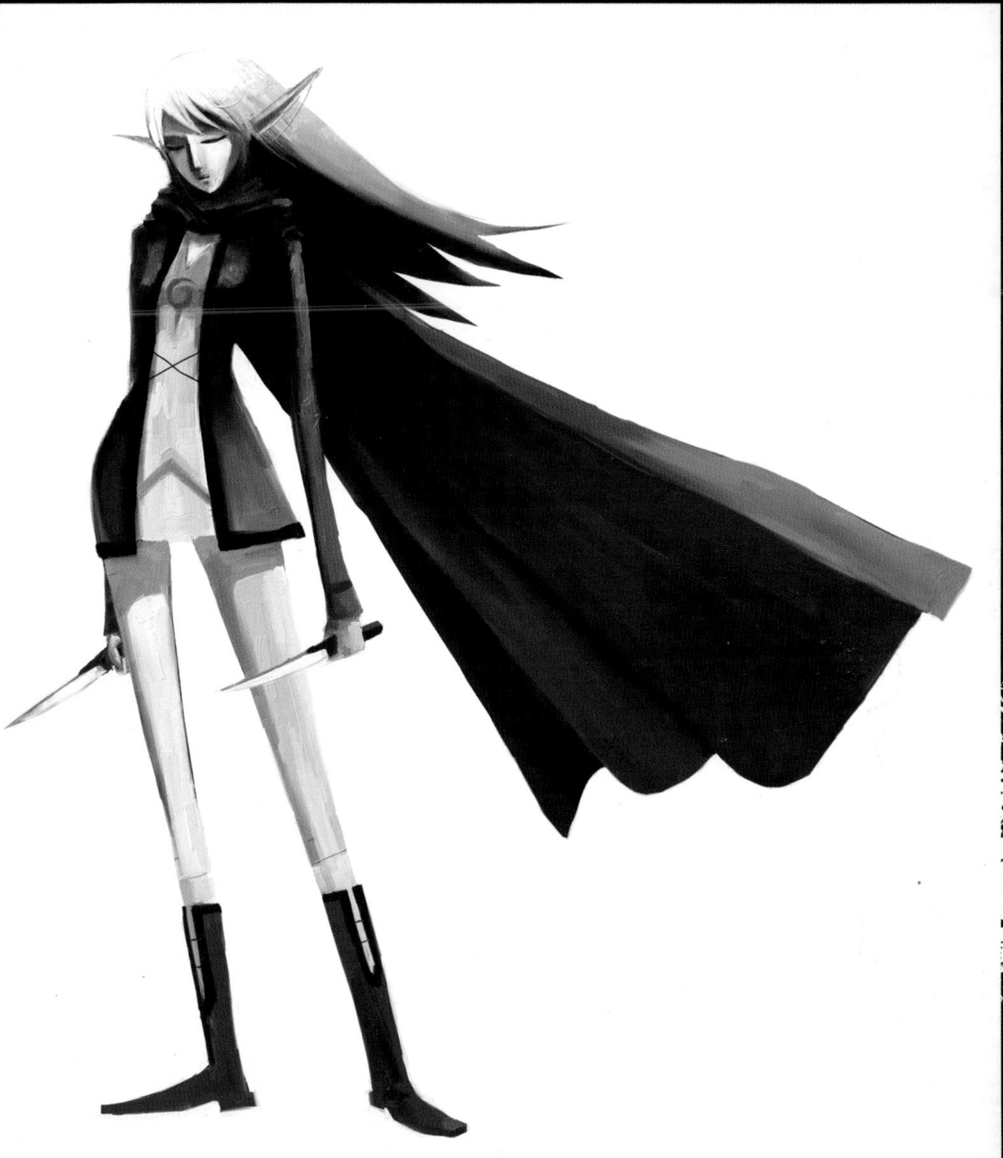

Fanart Contest Third Place - Andrew Tan

Coming in VOLUME 3...

Following the Archmage's strange advice (and with a little help from some magic), Acheron and his friends journey west to find the mysterious Silvah and see what he knows about Kayn'dar's disappearance.

But the world proves to be a more dangerous place than Acheron ever expected, and he soon discovers what fate befalls any da'kor foolish enough to venture so far from home.

Read it online now at www.seraph-inn.com!

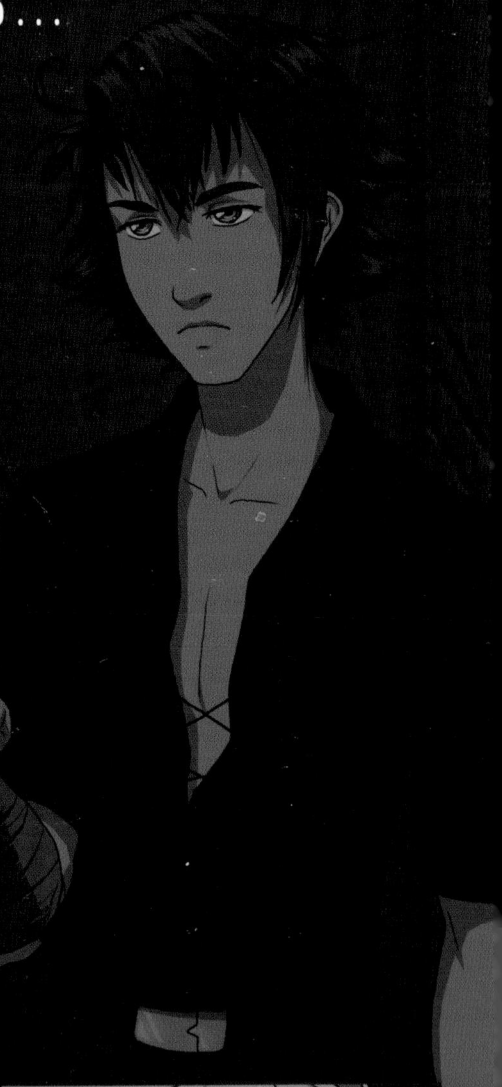

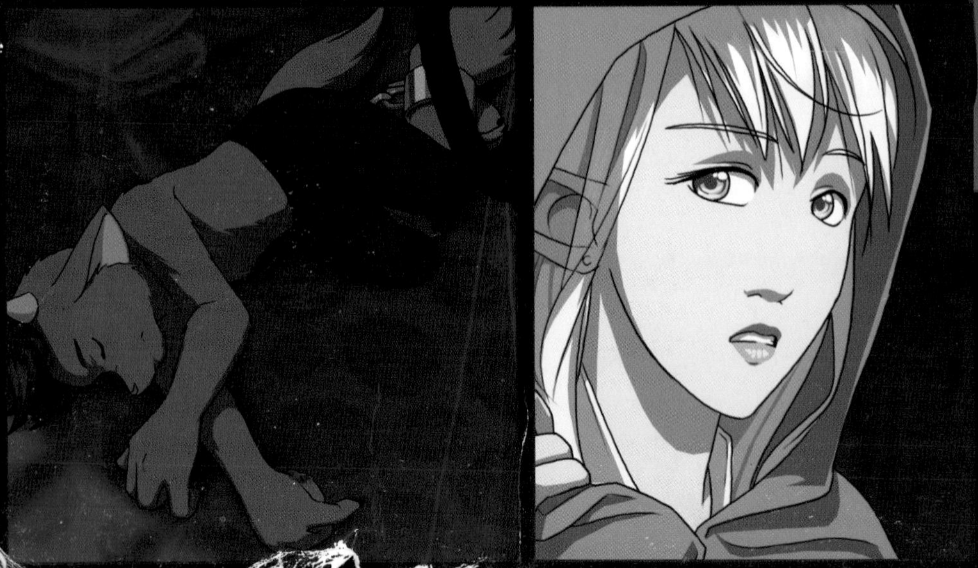